Books for You

A Booklist for Senior High Students

New Edition

Donald R. Gallo, Chair,

and the Committee on the Senior High School Booklist
of the National Council of Teachers of English

LIBRARY
BRYAN COLLEGE
DAYTON, TN 37321

National Council of Teachers of English
1111 Kenyon Road, Urbana, Illinois 61801

90680

Committee on the Senior High School Booklist

Donald R. Gallo, Chair, Central Connecticut State University, New Britain, Connecticut

Patricia A. Aubin, Watertown Public Schools, Watertown, Massachusetts

Marion D. Bradley, North Branford High School, North Branford, Connecticut

Kathleen Custer, Merrimack High School, Merrimack, New Hampshire

Catherine Dorsey-Gaines, Kean College, Union, New Jersey

Kristina Elias, Conard High School, West Hartford, Connecticut

Thomas P. Fitzgerald, State Education Department, Albany, New York

Sharron Freeman, Kidlit, West Hartford, Connecticut

Audrey Friedman, Attleboro High School, Attleboro, Massachusetts

Esther Fusco, Shoreham-Wading River Public Schools, Shoreham, New York

Ann O. Gebhard, State University College, Cortland, New York

Marsha Gibilisco, Bristol Central High School, Bristol, Connecticut

Barbara Grey, Conard High School, West Hartford, Connecticut

Christina Jagger, New Readers Press, Division of Laubach Literacy International, Syracuse, New York

Judith Mitchell, Rhode Island College, Providence, Rhode Island

Brian Monahan, Gorton High School, Yonkers, New York

Janet Pagano, West Hartford Public Library, West Hartford, Connecticut

Ronald Savage, Castleton State College, Castleton, Vermont

Gwendolyn Alexander, Executive Committee Liaison

Paul O'Dea, NCTE Staff Liaison

LIBRARY
BRYAN COLLEGE
DAYTON, TN 37321

Books for You

NCTE Editorial Board: Candy Carter, Julie M. Jensen, Delores Lipscomb, John S. Mayher, Thomas Newkirk, John C. Maxwell, *ex officio*, Paul O'Dea, *ex officio*

Staff Editors: Jane M. Curran and Rona S. Smith

Book Design: Tom Kovacs for TGK Design

NCTE Stock Number 03634

© 1985 by the National Council of Teachers of English. All rights reserved. Printed in the United States of America.

It is the policy of NCTE in its journals and other publications to provide a forum for the open discussion of ideas concerning the content and the teaching of English and the language arts. Publicity accorded to any particular point of view does not imply endorsement by the Executive Committee, the Board of Directors, or the membership at large, except in announcements of policy, where such endorsement is clearly specified.

Library of Congress Cataloging in Publication Data

Gallo, Donald R.
    Books for you.

    Rev. ed. of: Books for you/Robert C. Small, chair, and the Committee on the Senior High School Booklist of the National Council of Teachers of English. New ed. © 1982.
    Includes indexes.
    1. Young adult literature—Bibliography.
2. Children's literature—Bibliography. 3. High school libraries—Book lists. 4. Bibliography—Best books— Young Adult Literature. 5. Bibliography—Best books— Children's literature. I. Small, Robert C. Books for you. II. National Council of Teachers of English. Committee on the Senior High Booklist. III. Title.
Z1037.G217   1985   [PN1009.A1]   028'.9   85-21666
ISBN 0-8141-0363-4

Contents

Acknowledgments   vii

Introduction to the Student   ix

Adventure and Survival   1

Animals and Pets   12

Archaeology and Anthropology   21

Art and Architecture   24

Biography and Autobiography   27

Careers and Jobs   43

Cars, Motorcycles, and Racing   51

Classics—Old and Modern   53

Computers and Microprocessors   60

Death and Suicide   65

Drama and Theater   71

Drugs and Alcohol   75

Easy Reading   78

Education, Language, and Self-Improvement   83

Essays   90

Ethnic Experiences   95

Family Conflicts   100

Fantasy   121

Handicaps—Physical and Emotional   133

Health and Physical Fitness   140

Historical Fiction   145

History   153

Hobbies and Crafts   161

Holocaust   164

Horror, Witchcraft, and the Occult   167

Human Rights   173

Humor and Satire   179

Inspiration   182

Music and Dance   185

Mysteries, Spies, and Crime   189

Myths, Legends, and Folklore   205

Outdoor Life and Travel   210

Poetry   213

Politics and Law   217

Recreation   221

Religion and Cults   225

Romance   227

Science   240

Science Fiction   252

Sexuality   268

Short Stories   271

Social Situations   281

Sociology   296

Space and Space Exploration   299

Sports   303

Television, Movies, and Entertainment   319

War   322

The West   326

Women   331

Directory of Publishers   335

Author Index   340

Title Index   350

Acknowledgments

A collection of this sort is never possible without the combined talents and cooperation of a number of people and organizations. As chair of the Committee to Revise *Books for You,* I appreciate the opportunity to hereby recognize and thank all of the following:

The numerous publishers, through their directors of publicity or marketing, who sent us copies of their books to consider. We should rejoice in the mutual benefits we provide each other.

The individual members of the committee who—often under pressures from greatly strained personal lives—diligently read, selected, and annotated the best of hundreds of new books produced during the past three years. The insights, talents, and extensive time commitment of each member were necessary for the completion of this project.

The schools and libraries which employ members of our committee, for their cooperation and assistance with duplicating and mailing, and especially Central Connecticut State University for providing graduate assistants' support.

Christine Nybakken and Mary Ann Walters for their tireless recording, categorizing, filing, and mailing of books.

Gordon Korstange, Dawn Starr, Peggy Thomas, and Patricia Trumbull for filling in at the end.

Bob Small, committee chair of the previous edition of this book, for his initial guidance, insightful advice, and continuous sympathetic encouragement.

Paul O'Dea, Director of Publications at NCTE, for his unfailing support, encouragement, and trust.

Donald R. Gallo

Introduction to the Student

Except for school assignments, most of the reading you do is likely to be for enjoyment. Fiction accounts for the largest proportion of the reading which students (as well as adults) do on their own. But you also sometimes read for information—to get an expert's advice on taking better photographs, for example; to learn how to repair a racing bike; to answer your questions about caring for a pet; or perhaps to learn more about a specific event in history. But even that kind of reading can give you pleasure when you find answers to your questions or gain new insights into areas you were previously unaware of.

Reading for pleasure was what we tried to keep foremost in our minds as we compiled this collection. We hope that the books described here will, more than anything else, provide enjoyment. Reading should not be a chore. Because there are so many books to choose from, if you start to read one and find it too difficult, too abstract, or even too simple, then there are usually others you can try.

How This Book Is Arranged

Because many students prefer to read certain kinds of books, we have organized this collection by categories and have arranged them in alphabetical order. Within each category, the books are listed in alphabetical order by the author's or editor's last name, followed by the title in **bold** print. So, if you are interested in locating an exciting science fiction novel or a juicy romance, turn to that section of the book and see which authors and titles capture your attention; then read the brief comments that follow. If you already have a favorite author in mind, turn to the back of the collection where you will find an **Author Index.** You will also find, at the back of the book, a **Title Index** which you can use if you have a particular title in mind and wish to see if that book is included here.

How Books Were Selected

Don't be surprised if you can't find all of your favorite books listed in this collection. Most of the books listed here were published during the years 1982 through 1984. (If you want to locate a book published prior to 1982, look in the previous editions of *Books for You.*) We have also included several books which were originally published prior to 1982 but which were reprinted between 1982 and 1984. For example, *Ransom*—an adventure story about the kidnapping of five teenagers on a school bus—was originally published in 1966. It was reprinted several years later under the title *Five Were Missing.* The paperback publisher recently reissued it under its original title, and we have included it in this collection. We have also included a few classics that, while not new, continue to be of interest to high school readers.

Unfortunately, not all recent books are included in this edition. We were, for the most part, limited in our choices by the books that publishers sent to us. At the start of this project, we asked over one hundred publishing companies to send us copies of books that might be of interest and value to high school students. Some publishers mailed us boxes and boxes of their latest books; others sent us only a couple. In a few instances, we were able to request specific titles from some publishing companies by scanning their catalogs.

A few publishers never sent us any books. In some cases, members of our committee had heard about books that sounded as if they were worth reading and including in this collection but that the publishers did not submit to us. We sought these books out to read and evaluate, and the best of them are also included here. But we know that there are many more good books out there somewhere that we have not had access to and so were unable to include in this edition.

In order to make it possible to locate books by topic, we first established categories of books that high school students seem most interested in. We knew it was essential to include the categories of Mysteries, Spies, and Crime; Sports; Romance; Science Fiction; Horror, Witchcraft, and the Occult; Fantasy; and Computers and Microprocessors. We also thought it was important to include books about politics, health, archaeology, careers, women, and ethnic experiences, along with books about cars and motorcycles, art and architecture, history, religion, and science. In addition, we included the traditional genres of biographies, essays, short stories, poetry, and drama.

Knowing the large number of recent books written about teenagers' lives and problems, we chose not to group all such books into one category. Instead, we subdivided those books into several categories: Family Conflicts, Drugs and Alcohol, Social Situations, Death and Suicide, Sexuality, and Handicaps—Physical and Emotional.

After the categories were agreed upon, we each examined all the books in our assigned categories. Collectively we examined over twenty-five hundred new and reprinted books, looking for those that were most likely to appeal to high school students in terms of reading level and interest. Then we read those books more carefully before finally selecting the best ones to summarize.

That does not mean that all the books included here will appeal to every reader. Because high school students have such varied interests and abilities, we have tried to include a variety in both quality and complexity. Some of the selections listed here are award-winning books; others will never win a prize for the quality of their writing, but they are nevertheless interesting to some readers. A few of the books are very sophisticated and not easily read by the average student; several other books are written quite simply (in fact, we have even included a category called Easy Reading). By offering such variety, we hoped to include something for every level of reader and every kind of taste.

In a few instances, you may find books whose subject matter or language may offend you, since some of the books we list contain unhappy endings, violence, sex, death, or obscenities. If such things offend you, then choose another book from among the hundreds listed. Our purpose is not to offend; on the other hand, we did not wish to exclude good books from this collection just because some individuals might find parts of them controversial or distasteful.

Because all books do not fit easily into specific categories, and we did not want to have a category called Misfits, we had to force a few books into categories that might not seem appropriate at first glance. But we made certain choices and will have to live with them. On the other hand, many books are not about only one topic, and so you will find quite a few books listed under two or more categories. For example, a book about a veterinarian might appear under Animals as well as under Careers, or a book about a sports figure might appear under Biography and Autobiography as well as under Sports.

Choosing Books

The best way to find a good book—if you don't have a particular author or title in mind—is to scan through the categories to find one you are interested in. Then read through several of the annotations which describe the books in that category. One is bound to attract your attention, and we hope your local library or bookstore carries that book. If not, ask your librarian or bookseller if he or she might be able to order it for you. In the meantime, find another book of interest, and sit down and enjoy it. After all, these are *Books for You.*

Adventure and Survival

Benchley, Peter. **The Girl of the Sea of Cortez.** Doubleday, 1982.

Sixteen-year-old Paloma loves the sea. This love, a legacy from her father, is tested one day when she is diving and is frightened by something in the blackness of the deep, mysterious water. Paloma discovers a mythical creature and decides she must be the one to uncover its secret. Fiction.

Bennett, Jack. **The Voyage of the Lucky Dragon.** Prentice-Hall, 1982.

Planes and war are a natural part of fourteen-year-old Quan's life in Vietnam, and his life doesn't improve any when the war ends. Quan's family is forced to flee Vietnam because they are considered capitalists. They escape on the fishing boat *Lucky Dragon* and sail toward a new home in Australia. The novel recounts their hardships there, along with many of the historical facts of the time, and the author's political perspective is woven throughout the adventure. Fiction.

Binchy, Maeve. **Light a Penny Candle.** Viking Press, 1983.

In 1940, when Elizabeth White is ten years old, she is evacuated from London—her school is closing because of bombings. Elizabeth's mother arranges for Elizabeth to go and stay with an old school friend, Eileen O'Connor, who has a ten-year-old daughter, Aisling. From the moment the two girls meet, they are at ease. This book is the tale of their friendship and survival. Fiction.

Bosse, Malcolm J. **The Barracuda Gang.** Lodestar Books, 1982.

Twelve essay-contest finalists from high schools across America come together for a week at a Caribbean resort. They start out as strangers and become friends through the daily games and nightly fun. Then the Barracuda Gang—Ava, Justin, and Parker—become trapped overnight in an underwater cave and discover strength through the high stakes of competition and survival. Fiction.

Bunting, Eve. **Someone Is Hiding on Alcatraz Island.** Clarion Books, 1984.

Danny stops a mugging, and the Outlaws, a tough high school gang, want revenge because Danny's act of courage has put a gang member's brother in jail. Trying to avoid the gang, Danny jumps on an excursion boat heading for Alcatraz Island. There he meets Biddy, a young woman ranger. Together they face the Outlaws—who are determined not to let them leave the island alive. Fiction.

Calvert, Patricia. **The Hour of the Wolf.** Charles Scribner's Sons, 1983.

Jake Matthieson's father sends his "loner" son from their home in Minnesota to live with friends in Alaska with the hope that the wayward boy will become someone the whole family can be proud of. When Jake and his friend Danny Yumart, a native Alaskan, join a thirteen-hundred-mile dogsled race from Anchorage to Nome, Jake has an adventure that does, indeed, change him forever. Fiction.

Calvert, Patricia. **The Snowbird.** Signet Vista Books, 1982.

Thirteen-year-old Willie Bannerman and her brother TJ are orphaned by a suspicious fire in 1883. Sent to the Dakota Territory to live on a poor farm with an unknown aunt and uncle, Willie and TJ arrive just in time for the birth of a foal—the Snowbird. Aunt Belle and Uncle Randall see the birth as a good omen and give the foal to Willie, a gift which enables her to begin her life again. Willie's interactions with Aunt Belle, the Snowbird, and the many other characters create an unusual story. Fiction.

Chester, William L. **Kioga of the Wilderness.** DAW Books, 1976.

Kioga, first published in 1936, is an old-fashioned adventure story steeped in the tradition of heroic fiction. It is the tale of Kioga, or Snow Hawk, who rises to war chieftain in the wild newfound region beyond the Arctic north of Siberia. Fiction.

Cleaver, Vera, and Bill Cleaver. **A Little Destiny.** Bantam Books, 1982.

Lucy is grief stricken by her father's death. While she can't bring him back, she can satisfy part of her pain by seeking revenge. Along with her brother Lyman, she plots her reprisal. Her plan takes the two of them on a wild struggle through the Georgia hills and to a moment in which they overcome evil. Fiction.

Clements, Bruce. **I Tell a Lie Every So Often.** Farrar, Straus and Giroux, 1984.

> Fourteen-year-old Henry occasionally tells a lie but rarely gets in trouble for it. This time, however, the lie gets out of hand, and Henry ends up traveling five hundred miles through the nineteenth-century Missouri Territory. There he and his seventeen-year-old brother Clayton go in search of their cousin Hanna, hoping to rescue her from captivity. Fiction.

Conford, Ellen. **To All My Fans, with Love, from Sylvie.** Archway Paperbacks, 1983.

> Fifteen-year-old Sylvie runs away from her third foster home and sets out for Hollywood. She hopes to find fame and fortune, but the way isn't paved with gold and adventure. Rather, she continues to face a cruel, difficult, and abusive world. Although the story takes place in the 1950s, it contains a very current message on sexual abuse. Fiction.

Davidson, Robyn. **Tracks.** Pantheon Books, 1983.

> Robyn Davidson recounts—in vivid detail and sometimes strong language—the events of her seventeen-hundred-mile trip across the Australian outback. In this mature book, the reader will be intrigued by the author's "lunatic idea" to train camels and walk in and about the central desert area of Australia. During her amazing journey, Davidson faces many ordeals and finally concludes that you are as powerful and strong as you allow yourself to be, and that things do not begin or end but merely change form. Nonfiction.

Doig, Ivan. **The Sea Runners.** Penguin Books, 1983.

> The promise of freedom is the key that keeps the men of this adventure moving. This is the story of four indentured servants in Russia in 1853 who battle a hostile environment, starvation, and each other as they escape from the Czar's empire, traveling twelve hundred miles of treacherous coast in a canoe. Fiction.

Duncan, Lois. **Ransom.** Laurel-Leaf Library, 1984.

> On their way home from high school, Bruce and his brother Glenn and their friends Dexter, Marianne, and Jesse are the last five on a school bus that is hijacked. The inner emotions of each of the characters are revealed as they try first to understand the reasons

for their kidnapping and then to escape from their captors. Previously published as *Five Were Missing*. Fiction.

Fortune, J. J. **Evil in Paradise.** Laurel-Leaf Library, 1984.

In another of the Race against Time series, Stephen and his Uncle Richard launch their latest venture in the Pacific islands of Hawaii. From sharks to a gun-wielding pilot, intense danger once again threatens Stephen. The two days he spends on the islands are action filled if not quite believable. Fiction.

Fortune, J. J. **Revenge in the Silent Tomb.** Laurel-Leaf Library, 1984.

Stephen suspects that there is something strange about his Uncle Richard. He never dreams, however, that Uncle Richard is a special agent who will suddenly whisk him off to a desert in North Africa. Stephen's escapade there is similar to a James Bond movie with all its tricks and hazards. The easy-to-read style propels the exciting adventure to a rapid conclusion. This story is the first in the Race against Time series. Fiction.

French, Michael. **Pursuit.** Laurel-Leaf Library, 1983.

After Gordy's brother Martin falls to his death on a hiking trip, Gordy must set out alone in the Sierras to get help. But Gordy is pursued all the way by Roger, the person Gordy has accused of causing Martin's death. Fiction.

Fuller, Elizabeth. **Nima: A Sherpa in Connecticut.** Dodd, Mead, 1984.

In 1980, Nima Dorje, an eighteen-year-old Sherpa, guided the Fullers on a forty-day expedition through the Himalayas. A bond grew between them during the days they spent together, and when the Fullers discovered Nima had tuberculosis, they arranged to have him treated in the United States. This story recounts his visit to the U.S. and allows the author to relive her mountain adventure. Nonfiction.

Garden, Nancy. **Watersmeet.** Farrar, Straus and Giroux, 1983.

Something strange occurs in Fours Crossing, a small town in New Hampshire, when fourteen-year-old friends Melissa and Jed encounter a mad hermit and are held captive. After their rescue, Melissa thinks that much of the bad weather they're experiencing may have a connection to the hermit. This simply written adventure story reveals the characters wrestling with the mysterious, the unknown, and the truth. Fiction.

Gauch, Patricia Lee. **Morelli's Game.** Archway Paperbacks, 1982.

> Jerry Sebastian wonders what Morelli's game is. Why is he sending two student teams on a two-hundred-mile bicycle trip to Washington, D.C.? What does Morelli, a Lockwood Academy English teacher, hope to prove? Jerry feels certain that he can make the trip, if he goes it alone. But he feels trapped into helping the other students, whom he perceives to be losers. Fiction.

George, Jean Craighead. **The Talking Earth.** Harper and Row, 1983.

> The Florida Everglades is the setting of this adventure novel in which Billie Wind, a plucky young Seminole, survives on her own in an unfriendly environment. As in her book *Julie of the Wolves,* the author writes here of an Indian girl whose courage finds a link between an ancient and a modern culture. Fiction.

Hamilton, Virginia. **A Little Love.** Philomel Books, 1984.

> Sheba's mother is dead, and her father disappeared when she was a baby. Although she has been raised by loving grandparents, she still has a need to find her father; his absence gnaws at her. *A Little Love* is the sensitive story of Sheba's journey in search of her father and of the characters who support and nurture her along the way. Fiction.

Hammer, Charles. **Me, the Beef, and the Bum.** Farrar, Straus and Giroux, 1984.

> George is Rosie Matlock's silky, long-haired white charolois steer. Rather than have George sold for beef summer sausage, Rosie walks him right out of the livestock show in Kansas City. She's determined to stay out of sight, and does so until she meets up with a bum, George "Matt" Halsey. Together they head for his farm, where Rosie finally has to decide whom and what she is running away from. Fiction.

Hayes, Billy (with William Hoffer). **Midnight Express.** Warner Books, 1984.

> This is Billy Hayes's story of survival. Billy is arrested at Yesilkoy International Airport in Turkey as he is about to make a return flight to the United States. Placed in prison for drug possession, Billy describes the terror and suspense of his five-year ordeal. The reader will see the effects of Billy's mistake on the lives of his family and friends, and will sigh in relief when the story ends. Nonfiction.

Healey, Larry. **Angry Mountain.** Dodd, Mead, 1983.

Sixteen-year-old Doug Morley is sent by his wealthy father to live in Alaska. His father feels that Doug's chances of surviving near a volcano are better than his chances in Connecticut, where Doug is constantly in trouble with the law. Doug agrees to go merely because he does not want to be cut off from his father's fortune. But his new home turns out to be far more dangerous than the one he left behind. On the volcanic island, Doug needs both courage and strength to deal with the terror that awaits him. Fiction.

Herbert, Marie. **Winter of the White Seal.** Signet Books, 1983.

Angry with his parents, Jonathan Horn slips away one night from his home in Liverpool. He signs aboard a whaler by mistake, and for a short period becomes involved with the slaughter of seals. On one seal beaching, he is accidentally knocked unconscious and left behind. Thus begins his life on an uninhabited island. Fiction.

Heyerdahl, Thor. **The Tigris Expedition: In Search of Our Beginnings.** Plume Books, 1982.

Thor Heyerdahl, well-known anthropologist and explorer, describes his third ocean voyage. This time Heyerdahl has taken his international crew on board a reed ship designed from the drawings of ancient Sumerian ships. Their purpose is to prove that the ancient peoples who lived in the region of Mesopotamia actually communicated with each other. They use scientific knowledge, determination, and an adventurous spirit to get themselves through the dangerous four-thousand-mile journey. Nonfiction.

Houston, James. **Black Diamonds: A Search for Arctic Treasure.** Illus. by author. Margaret K. McElderry Books, 1982.

This fast-paced continuation of *Frozen Fire* takes place on the rugged Baffin Island where Matthew Morgan and his friend Kayak are desperately searching for Matt's father. While these fifteen-year-olds are making their search, they come across gold nuggets in a frozen stream and later, amazingly, find oil. The boys race against the odds because they must leave the island before winter comes, or they will die. Fiction.

Hughes, Monica. **Hunter in the Dark.** Flare Books, 1984.

Mike Rankin, star basketball player, battles leukemia and overprotective parents as he tries to understand his illness. His close friend,

Doug, helps him escape into the Canadian wilderness to stalk the elusive white-tailed deer. The unforgiving wilderness and a trophy-sized buck help Mike recognize that death is not necessarily an enemy. Fiction.

Kennedy, William. **Ironweed.** Penguin Books, 1984.

Francis Phelan, a professional baseball player turned alcoholic hobo, returns to Albany, the city of his birth. Like the weed that gives the novel its name, Francis is tough—he has killed two men. But he is also compassionate toward others who are down and out. Interweaving fantasy and reality in telling the story of Francis's past and present life, the novel is rich with interesting events and vivid characters. Fiction.

Kotzwinkle, William. **Superman III.** Warner Books, 1983.

Clark Kent returns to his hometown to attend his high school reunion and write a story about it, and to receive an award for a rescue mission. The novel pits Superman against a computer with no sense of right or wrong that has been programmed to put one man in charge of the world. Based on the screenplay by David Newman and Leslie Newman. Fiction.

Magill, Kathleen. **Megan.** Dodd, Mead, 1983.

An independent, courageous, and uncompromising woman struggling for freedom and self-realization, Megan flees from her father's farm to a boomtown in Idaho, where she discovers the truth about herself and her passions. A marvelous cast of realistic characters helps to capture the period and to show Megan's perseverance in a rough and tough town. Fiction.

Matthee, Dalene. **Circles in a Forest.** Alfred A. Knopf, 1984.

Saul Barnard was born and raised in the forests of South Africa. During a flashback, the reader has the opportunity to review Saul's youth and separation from his father. Then the reader follows Saul through another struggle in the present as he searches for "Old Foot," the most cunning and revered elephant in the forest. A story of a man and his interaction with his environment. Fiction.

Matthews, Greg. **The Further Adventures of Huckleberry Finn.** Crown, 1983.

They're at it again. Huck Finn and Jim continue their adventures—this time set during the period of the Gold Rush of 1849. Taking

up where Mark Twain left them, these delightful characters leave
Missouri and head west for California. The book is rich in char-
acterization and packed with suspense and thrills, as Huck continues to keep the reader informed of their antics, struggles, and
mischief. Huck says, "We're on a quest, Jim, and it's a prideful
thing." Fiction.

Mazer, Harry. **The Island Keeper.** Laurel-Leaf Library, 1983.

Disappear completely—that's sixteen-year-old Cleo's plan for coping with family pressures and her sister's tragic death. Cleo chooses
a deserted island where she struggles to survive the hardships of a
Canadian winter and the inadequacy she feels. This is an absorbing
story which realistically allows the heroine to prove herself again
and again. Fiction.

Mowat, Farley. **Lost in the Barrens.** Illus. Charles Geer. Bantam Books,
1984.

Jamie and Awasin's mountain adventure suddenly places them in
a dangerous position. When their canoe is destroyed, they are
forced to manage alone in the Canadian wilderness. With only a
few tools and their ingenuity, they must deal with their precarious
situation—fighting a grizzly bear, killing a caribou for food and
clothing, taming wild huskies—and also discover a way home.
Fiction.

Myers, Walter Dean. **The Nicholas Factor.** Viking Press, 1983.

College freshman Gerald McQuillen thinks the Crusade Society is
just a bunch of "do-gooders." The U.S. Government, however,
suspects them of having right-wing extremist tendencies and so
recruits Gerald to infiltrate this elitist international student group.
In this action-packed thriller, Gerald's survival depends on his
ability to rely on his own judgment. Fiction.

Paulsen, Gary. **Popcorn Days and Buttermilk Nights.** Lodestar Books,
1983.

There is something mean in Carley. He is sent to his Uncle David's
Minnesota farm so that he can come face to face with his inner
spirit. Carley initially believes that needing someone is a sign of
weakness, but after the summer with his uncle, Carley knows that
it means something altogether different. Fiction.

Petersen, P. J. **The Boll Weevil Express.** Laurel-Leaf Library, 1984.

Lars is depressed and tired of his strict father and of the isolation he feels in school. Things begin to change for him when Doug, a ward from the local youth home, arrives. Together they decide to run away to Idaho. But they don't get away unnoticed. They are followed by Cindy, Doug's younger sister. Reluctantly, the boys agree to take her along, and thus the three of them embark on an adventure that leads them to themselves. Fiction.

Petersen, P. J. **Nobody Else Can Walk It for You.** Delacorte Press, 1982.

Laura's confidence is shaken but never shattered in this wilderness adventure. While it is only her first time as a leader on a backpacking trip, she has prepared for every detail. Unfortunately, she has not anticipated the arrival of a motorcycle trio who decide to terrorize her group. Fiction.

Roberts, David. **Great Exploration Hoaxes.** Sierra Club Books, 1982.

Roberts, himself a mountain explorer, examines the once-accepted accomplishments of ten famous explorers and reveals all but one of them as deliberate hoaxes. The author skillfully describes the qualities and achievements of each explorer, from Sebastian Cabot (1508) to Donald Crowhurst (1968), and concludes with an examination of their psychological makeups, which might have contributed to their need to fake their accomplishments. Included among the explorations are Dr. Frederick Cook's ascent of Mount McKinley, Robert Peary's trek to the North Pole, and Admiral Richard Byrd's flight over the North Pole. Nonfiction.

Roberts, Rachel Sherwood. **Crisis at Pemberton Dike.** Herald Press, 1984.

The sudden melting of a heavy winter snow causes flooding and the evacuation of thousands of families. Fifteen-year-old Carol Norton manages to deal with the flood, family problems, and even a meeting with the president of the United States that makes her an instant celebrity. Fiction.

Roth, Arthur. **The Castaway.** Illus. R. M. Laso. Scholastic Book Services, 1983.

Based on a true event, this is Daniel Ross's story of raw courage and inner strength. Eighteen-year-old Daniel signs on the ship *Catherine* after an argument with his brother. But the *Catherine* sinks in the South Pacific, and Daniel is the lone survivor. He is cast on a rocky reef where he lives in isolation for five years. Fiction.

Salassi, Otto R. **And Nobody Knew They Were There.** Greenwillow Books, 1984.

A squad of Marines is missing. Nobody knows where they are except for two thirteen-year-old cousins who have been thrown together for the summer. In this adventure, Jakey and Hogan discover more than the Marines. They realize that they are friends and that they can deal with the challenges of life. Fiction.

Saperstein, Alan. **Camp.** Ticknor and Fields, 1982.

Camp Freedom is an unusual camp. The children are innocently sent there to enjoy themselves, but once there, they encounter Dr. Stone, a stern, almost evil man. Strange, scary, and suspenseful moments masterfully bring the story to a powerful but sad ending. Fiction.

Scortia, Thomas N., and Frank M. Robinson. **The Gold Crew.** Warner Books, 1981.

What starts out to be a simple drill on a nuclear submarine turns into an unexpected crisis. Will the submarine crew follow their official orders and, by doing so, start World War III? Fiction.

Southhall, Ivan. **The Long Night Watch.** Farrar, Straus and Giroux, 1984.

Sixteen-year-old Jon Griffiths is among the one hundred passengers who leave Melbourne, Australia, in 1941. They are members of the Society for World Order under Divine Rule, or S.W.O.R.D. Their destination is Tangu, where they hope to be safe from Hitler and the Japanese. This adventure recounts Jon's lonely months, his dreams, and his struggle to survive. Fiction.

Sullivan, Mary Ann. **Child of War.** Holiday House, 1984.

Life in Northern Ireland changes for Maeve after her little brother Brendan is killed. Caught up in her feelings of guilt and horror about his death, Maeve becomes despondent. She tries to join the other neighborhood children in their fight against the IRA, but only falls deeper and deeper into an unreal world. Fiction.

Thompson, Julian F. **The Grounding of Group Six.** Flare Books, 1983.

Arriving at what they believe is an exclusive school, five sixteen-year-olds are unaware that they have been sent there to be exterminated and that their teacher is a murderer for hire. Fiction.

Townsend, Peter. **The Girl in the White Ship.** Holt, Rinehart and Winston, 1983.

How did the youth in Vietnam survive? This is a powerful documentation of a Chinese family who for generations had lived in Vietnam. In September of 1978, under the Communist Vietnamese, they were forced to flee the country. This is not only a historical overview of Vietnam but also the incredible story of Tran Hue Hue, a thirteen-year-old girl who battles to survive and escape. Nonfiction.

Turner, Ann. **The Way Home.** Crown, 1982.

During the spring of 1349, Anne, a teenager, is forced to flee her beloved English village. Lord Thomas's men are searching for her, claiming she is a witch who has caused Lord Thomas's death and created the great plague. For months, Anne is forced to live in the great marsh, waiting for the summer to end so she can return home. Fiction.

Watson, James. **Talking in Whispers.** Alfred A. Knopf, 1984.

Sixteen-year-old Andres Larreta has continued the resistance activities of his father, who was taken away by the security forces of the military government of Chile. Now Andres, too, is a wanted man. But with the help of his friends, he is able to stand up to the members of the Junta and expose them as the assassins they are. Fiction.

Young, Herbert V. **Water by the Inch: Adventures of a Pioneer Family on an Arizona Desert Homestead.** Northland Press, 1983.

The author, with the aid of his family, recounts the experiences of his pioneer father's existence over two decades on a hot dusty ranch in Arizona. Nonfiction.

Animals and Pets

Brenner, Barbara. **The Gorilla Signs Love.** Lothrop, Lee and Shepard Books, 1984.

Life changes very quickly for Maggie after she wins a prize for a science project on gorilla communication. She is sent to Africa to work with Charlotte Wingate, a leading authority on the western lowland gorilla. There she meets Naomi and discovers that gorillas can communicate. But her discovery and their friendship put Naomi's life in jeopardy. Maggie's search and her confrontations with society shape a sensitive and vivid struggle for survival. Fiction.

Burton, Philip. **Vanishing Eagles.** Illus. Trevor Boyer. Dodd, Mead, 1983.

Traditionally eagles have been regarded as regal birds. Their appearance, mannerisms, and visual impact as they soar through the air have contributed to this image. The author and illustrator have remarkably captured the beauty and grace of this vanishing species, leaving the reader with the desire to protect this magnificent bird. Nonfiction.

Calvert, Patricia. **The Money Creek Mare.** Signet Vista Books, 1983.

Ella Rae's life changes dramatically on the first day of the summer when her mother leaves Money Creek, Missouri, for the glamour and excitement of Hollywood. At fifteen, Ella Rae becomes responsible for Buster and Chloe, her younger siblings, for the family diner, and for her father's dream of owning a champion horse. By getting a job at Fairfield Farms, she manages to win the affection of the wealthy and childless Puckett-Smythes and to secretly mate the stallion Dark Victory with her father's red mare. All this leads Ella Rae to some important decisions about her life. Fiction.

Calvert, Patricia. **The Snowbird.** Signet Vista Books, 1982.

Thirteen-year-old Willie Bannerman and her brother TJ are

orphaned by a suspicious fire in 1883. Sent to the Dakota Territory to live on a poor farm with an unknown aunt and uncle, Willie and TJ arrive just in time for the birth of a foal—the Snowbird. Aunt Belle and Uncle Randall see the birth as a good omen and give the foal to Willie, a gift which enables her to begin her life again. Willie's interactions with Aunt Belle, the Snowbird, and the many other characters create an unusual story. Fiction.

Cavanna, Betty. **Wanted: A Girl for the Horses.** William Morrow, 1984.

At sixteen, Charlotte is expelled from boarding school. Returning to live with her mother and stepfather is out of the question, so she is delighted to obtain a position as a groom at the Exeside Manor in Devonshire, England. For Charlotte it is an opportunity to learn to experience the adventures of life. Fiction.

Corbett, W. J. **The Song of Pentecost.** Illus. Martin Ursell. E. P. Dutton, 1983.

After the sudden death of his father, Snake's life changes dramatically. He is forced out of his home at the Oily Green Pool by another snake who claims to be his cousin. Miserable and alone, Snake searches for answers to his problems. Along the way, he meets Pentecost, a mouse from the Pentecost farm. The two animals form a partnership, and thus their saga begins. Fiction.

Curtis, Patricia. **Animal Partners: Training Animals to Help People.** Lodestar Books, 1982.

Using animals to help the handicapped is a stimulating and relatively new occupation; scientists are still investigating this field of human-and-animal bonding. The belief is that animals used as helpers or companions will add dimension to the lives of the human and the animal, as long as the animal is not pushed beyond its limit. Thus, the role of the animal trainer is significant. The training and requirements for the occupation are presented here, along with examples of people like Alexandria, a horse trainer; Steve, a farm animal trainer; and Bob, an apprentice guide-dog trainer. Nonfiction.

Curtis, Patricia. **The Animal Shelter.** Photographs by David Cupp. Lodestar Books, 1984.

What happens to stray, unwanted, lost, and abused animals? *The Animal Shelter* carefully answers this question and then outlines the history and function of the SPCA and other humane societies.

This book is part of a series designed to educate those concerned with the care and treatment of animals. Nonfiction.

Fossey, Dian. **Gorillas in the Mist.** Houghton Mifflin, 1983.

When Dian Fossey follows her dream and goes off into the African rain forest to study the mountain gorillas, she ends up spending fifteen years observing four gorilla families. This book is a fascinating account of the familial organization and behavioral patterns of these engaging animals. Nonfiction.

Freedman, Russell. **Can Bears Predict Earthquakes? Unsolved Mysteries of Animal Behavior.** Prentice-Hall, 1982.

Many fascinating mysteries about animals and their behaviors are explored in this book. Scientists hope that by investigating these behaviors we may be able to answer questions about our own lives. There are stimulating ideas to ponder throughout the entire book, such as, can people hibernate? Nonfiction.

Gardner, Robert. **The Whale Watchers' Guide.** Illus. Don Sineti. Julian Messner, 1984.

Whale watching is becoming a very popular pastime on both American coasts. While it may present some difficulty for the whales, it is providing an abundance of data for the scientists and developing a network of concerned, excited watchers. This guide contains enough information to allow you to identify twenty-six different species of whales. Nonfiction.

Goodall, Jane. **In the Shadow of Man.** Photographs by Hugo van Lawick. Houghton Mifflin, 1983.

In a unique close-range study of animal behavior—the chimp in its natural setting—Goodall and her staff systematically recorded all phases of their experiences. Thus, the reader feels a real acquaintance with the chimps and the adventures described in the study, which was first reported in 1971. Upon completion of the book, one recognizes the amazing relationship between these creatures and humans. Nonfiction.

Griffiths, Helen. **The Dog at the Window.** Holiday House, 1984.

Alison feels quite alone. She rarely explains much to her mother, since they usually have exactly the opposite feelings. One day she notices a German shepherd staring out of a window. With his black nose pressed against the window pane, he seems as isolated as Alison. Eventually she gets up the courage to find out about this lonely creature, and thus begins her struggle to save him and to establish a relationship with her mother. Fiction.

Haas, Jessie. **Working Trot.** Greenwillow Books, 1983.

Instead of going to college, James decides—against his parents' wishes—to go to his uncle's Vermont horse farm to study dressage. There he is given Ghozal, part Lippizaner, part Polish Arab, as his project. Through his responsibilities of schooling, training, and competition, James learns a great deal about people, animals, and even life itself. Fiction.

Hanby, Jeannette. **Lions Share: The Story of a Serengeti Pride.** Illus. David Bygott. Houghton Mifflin, 1982.

This book presents a wealth of information about the lions of Serengeti, their social structure, their behavior, and the beautiful but hostile plains they roam. The author and illustrator capture the essence of these animals, as they describe how lions survive along with many other species in a wild environment. There is a foreword by Jane Goodall, the well-known animal behaviorist. Nonfiction.

Hansen, Skylar. **Roaming Free: Wild Horses of the American West.** Photographs by author. Northland Press, 1983.

Brilliant photography and fascinating text capture the magnificent spirit of untamed horses in today's West. Hansen chronicles the four-hundred-year history of wild horses in North America and explains their dominant qualities, nature, and habits, including their communication process and daily rituals. Nonfiction.

Koebner, Linda. **Forgotten Animals: The Rehabilitation of Laboratory Primates.** Lodestar Books, 1984.

Millions of animals are used by laboratory scientists, and some of them are kept under inhumane conditions or treated cruelly. While the animals may serve to assist medical research, should they be treated in this manner? What happens to these animals when they are no longer needed? The author uses chimpanzees, now an endangered species, to discuss her concern. Koebner also suggests some alternatives to using live animals in scientific research. Nonfiction.

Kohl, Judith, and Herbert Kohl. **Pack, Band, and Colony: The World of Social Animals.** Illus. Margaret La Farge. Farrar, Straus and Giroux, 1983.

Wolves, lemurs, and termites are used as examples of social animals and how we may observe them in their natural settings. While the book contains many interesting facts about animals, its real value lies in the notion that we can learn more about ourselves and develop a respectful attitude toward life when we study and observe other creatures. Nonfiction.

Kritsick, Stephen, and Patti Goldstein. **Creature Comforts: The Adventures of a City Vet.** Coward-McCann, 1983.

Dealing with the pain and suffering of animals is the business of a veterinarian. But the life of a vet goes much beyond that. Here Dr. Stephen Kritsick successfully relates his personal experiences in a city animal hospital, as he tells about the problems that vets encounter, the decisions they must make, and the necessity for them to be mature and sensitive. Nonfiction.

Lawrence, R. D. **The Ghost Walker.** Holt, Rinehart and Winston, 1983.

Here Lawrence describes his ten-month exploration in the Selkirk Mountains of British Columbia, where he built himself a cabin and then tracked and studied the North American cat in its natural habitat. His skill and familiarity with primitive environments allowed him to survive and to develop a special relationship with a puma. Nonfiction.

Leslie, Robert Franklin. **Ringo, the Robber Raccoon: The True Story of a Northwoods Rogue.** Illus. Leigh Grant. Dodd, Mead, 1984.

Robert Franklin Leslie sets out in the wilderness of Manning Provincial Park in southern British Columbia to locate and study Bigfoot colonies. While looking for clues that could lead him to the Sasquatch, he meets Ringo, a wild raccoon. This is the story of their friendship. Nonfiction.

McCoy, J. J. **The Complete Book of Cat Health and Care.** Photographs by Joseph F. Morsello. Perigee Books, 1982.

Cats, cats, cats . . . all you've ever wanted to know about these individualistic animals. This book is ideal for feline lovers or prospective owners and contains an interesting section on the evaluation and history of the cat. Nonfiction.

Milne, Lorus, and Margery Milne. **A Time to Be Born: An Almanac of Animal Courtship and Parenting.** Illus. Sarah Landry. Sierra Club Books, 1982.

The behavior of mammals is biologically regulated by a master clock and influenced by seasonal and environmental changes. The authors consider these factors as they review the courtship and parenting of over one hundred species of mammals on six continents. The wealth of fascinating details and illustrations helps us understand how these animals have survived by adapting over the centuries. Nonfiction.

Morpurgo, Michael. **War Horse.** Greenwillow Books, 1982.

Joey the horse tells the story of his life: his separation from his mother, his service as a cavalry horse in World War I, and his eventual reunion with his beloved master. Fiction.

Mowat, Farley. **The Dog Who Wouldn't Be.** Illus. Paul Galdone. Bantam Books, 1982.

This is the story of Mutt, a highly unusual dog, and his boy. Their experiences growing up on the Canadian prairies during the 1930s create a humorous series of escapades. Fiction.

Patient Care Publications. **Your Dog: An Owner's Manual.** Patient Care Publications, 1981.

Choosing a dog is an exciting experience, yet caring for it can sometimes be a problem. This manual contains easy-to-read flow charts that illustrate effective procedures for choosing, training, and caring for a dog. The section on health problems and emergency care is helpful to all dog owners. Nonfiction.

Pinkwater, Jill. **Cloud Horse.** Illus. Irene Brady. Lothrop, Lee and Shepard Books, 1983.

Arnora, a Viking who lived many centuries ago, and Kate, a modern American, are two young girls whose lives are woven together by their love of the free-spirited horses of Iceland. Their beautiful story of adventure, love, and discovery will captivate the reader. Fiction.

Prabhu, Barbara Williams. **. . . And Still in the Running: A Horse Called Port Conway Lane.** Julian Messner, 1984.

Port Conway Lane is a living legend. At a time when most of his peers have been retired or have died, he continues to win races.

. . . *And Still in the Running* traces the career of this fourteen-year-old gelding who has won fifty-two races. Nonfiction.

Rabkin, Richard, and Jacob Rabkin. **Nature in the West: A Handbook of Habitats.** Holt, Rinehart and Winston, 1982.

This book gives the reader an opportunity to become immersed in the sights and sounds of eight Western environments and to understand the ecosystems found in each. Colorful illustrations of the life-forms in each zone are included. Nonfiction.

Rowland-Entwistle, Theodore. **Illustrated Facts and Records Book of Animals.** Arco, 1983.

A fascinating collection of information about the animal kingdom, this book contains easy-to-understand language, clear illustrations, and brilliant photographs. While this is an excellent resource for science students and instructors, it will also be enjoyable to individuals who truly enjoy reading about unusual animals. Nonfiction.

Rubins, Harriett. **Guinea Pigs: An Owner's Guide to Choosing, Raising, Breeding, and Showing.** Illus. Pamela Carroll. Lothrop, Lee and Shepard Books, 1982.

This comprehensive, simply written book describes the characteristics of guinea pigs and gives advice on how to select, care for, and breed them. Readers can learn how to predict the genetically determined outward appearance of the offspring of six breeds of these cuddly animals. Nonfiction.

Sattler, Helen Roney. **Fish Facts and Bird Brains: Animal Intelligence.** Illus. Giulio Maestro. Lodestar Books, 1984.

Many people do not consider animals to be intelligent. Scientists now believe, however, that animals do have some kind of intelligence. Helen Roney Sattler discusses how animals' intelligence can be measured and how this knowledge will help us better understand human intelligence. Nonfiction.

Sterling Editors. **Horse Identifier.** Sterling, 1982.

In this pictorial guide to the horse breeds of the world, the reader is able to discover a multitude of facts related to horses, including their origin and evolution. The excellent pictures concisely illustrate the physical structure of each breed of horse. Nonfiction.

Terhune, Albert Payson. **Lad of Sunnybank.** Signet Books, 1980.

This is a captivating story about the adventures of a champion collie who readily protects his owners and his home. The author successfully captures the remarkable nature of this thoroughbred as he interacts with various wildlife and visitors at Sunnybank. Dog lovers will especially enjoy the chapters describing Lad's involvement with Rameses the raccoon, Mrs. Lejeune, and four-year-old Bobby. Originally published in 1929. Fiction.

True, Dan. **Flying Free.** Dodd, Mead, 1984.

Dan True produces a wildlife program for television. While studying an eagle family for his show, he sees a female golden eagle shot from an airplane. Thus he begins his parenting of Lucy, a newborn baby eagle. The struggle he faces to help Lucy grow and be able to fly free demonstrates the bond that can develop between humans and other animals. Nonfiction.

Twelveponies, Mary. **There Are No Problem Horses—Only Problem Riders.** Houghton Mifflin, 1982.

Mary Twelveponies offers solutions for safe riding based on her knowledge of both the physical capability of the horse and the way the horse thinks. She says that rider-horse communication is essential. Safe for beginners, her advice covers the problems of negative behavior (runaways, biting, kicking, shying, etc.) as well as problems of handling (trainer loading, leading, and tying). The author includes many colorful incidents from her varied experiences, described in a comfortable conversational style. Nonfiction.

Varner, John Grier, and Jeannette Johnson Varner. **Dogs of the Conquest.** University of Oklahoma Press, 1983.

Dogs of the Conquest is an unusual book written to acknowledge the role dogs played in the Spanish conquest of Latin America. The authors illustrate how dogs were used as food, as guards, and as hunters. All too often during this period, however, they were used to terrorize the Indians or to perform sadistic acts against other people. In the end, though, dogs served as a natural adjunct to humans and performed with equal bravery and heroism during this time of conquest. Nonfiction.

Vine, Louis L. **Common Sense Book of Complete Cat Care.** Warner Books, 1983.

While it may seem strange to compare this book with Benjamin Spock's book on child rearing, the analogy is appropriate. Vine, a practicing veterinarian, has written an extremely thorough guide to cat care. This book will help the pet owner to raise a healthy, happy, and well-adjusted cat, and to learn to recognize the behaviors and symptoms that signal problems. Nonfiction.

Vine, Louis L. **The Total Dog Book.** Warner Books, 1984.

Problems in raising a dog are unnecessary. A dog owner who deals with the dog in a responsible manner will raise a caring, understanding pet. Using this theme, the author attempts to answer all questions that may arise during a dog's life cycle. Nonfiction.

Wayne, Kyra Petrovskaya. **Max, the Dog That Refused to Die.** Illus. Becky Bristow. Bantam Books, 1983.

Three-year-old Max, a champion Doberman pinscher, is lost in the High Sierras during a camping trip. A sudden accidental fall separates him from the Waynes, who frantically search the woods for their lost pet. Max courageously faces a difficult ordeal and overcomes many obstacles as he struggles to survive. Nonfiction.

Wood, Gerald L. **The Guinness Book of Animal Facts and Feats.** 3d ed. Guinness Superlatives, 1983.

Which is the largest marine mammal? The longest-lived insect? Answers to these and other questions about the extremes of the animal world are presented in this collection of fascinating facts and feats. Nonfiction.

Young, John Richard. **The Schooling of the Horse.** Rev. ed. University of Oklahoma Press, 1982.

In this revised edition, the author writes about training riding horses using an approach that is determined by the circumstances and by the particular horse. Nonfiction.

Archaeology and Anthropology

Allen, T. D. **Navahos Have Five Fingers.** Photographs by Arthur Dodd. University of Oklahoma Press, 1982.

T. D. Allen is the pen name of a couple who have written several books together. In the mid-1950s they substituted for a nurse at a health center on a large Navaho reservation; this book is an account of their experiences. It gives an insight into this tribe and their many problems, several of which have been caused by whites. The title comes from a Navaho expression which means that Navahos are people too. This is a new printing of a volume in the Civilization of the American Indian series. Nonfiction.

Braymer, Marjorie. **Atlantis: The Biography of a Legend.** Margaret K. McElderry Books, 1983.

Braymer tells two stories in this book. The first is the history of the lost city of Atlantis and the legends that follow the city, first written about by Plato. The second story describes the recent archaeological excavations at Thera, in the Aegean Sea, where thirty buildings—destroyed by a volcanic eruption—have been unearthed since 1967. Could Thera prove to be the legendary Atlantis? Nonfiction.

Duffy, Kevin. **Children of the Forest.** Photographs by author. Dodd, Mead, 1984.

This book tells of the author's experiences living with a tribe of Mbuti Pygmies in Zaire. He spent time with both net-hunting and spear-hunting Pygmies, and gives a great deal of insight into these people's way of life. Adding to the book's interest are several pages of photographs by the author, who has spent over twenty years studying aboriginal peoples from the Arctic to the equator and has produced award-winning films of his travels. Nonfiction.

Ewers, John C. **Blackfeet: Raiders on the Northwestern Plains.** University of Oklahoma Press, 1982.

First published in 1958, this two-hundred-year history of one of the strongest and fiercest tribes on the Western plains relies not just on historical facts but also on firsthand accounts which give the presentation an honesty and liveliness that make it highly readable. The text is accompanied by several informative drawings and photographs and followed by an extensive bibliography. A volume in the Civilization of the American Indian series. Nonfiction.

Ford, Barbara, and David C. Switzer. **Underwater Dig: The Excavation of a Revolutionary War Privateer.** William Morrow, 1982.

This account of the archaeological excavation of the Revolutionary War privateer *Defence,* which was sunk in Penobscot Bay, Maine, in 1779, provides a clear look at the new science of nautical archaeology. The six-year-long scientific undertaking shed new light on an often overlooked defeat in American naval history. Illustrated with photographs and diagrams. Nonfiction.

Freilich, Morris, editor. **The Pleasures of Anthropology.** Mentor Books, 1983.

This collection of twenty-seven essays written by persons in anthropology or closely related fields is divided into eight sections dealing with such topics as fieldwork, reconstructing the past, sex and sex roles, culture, religion, politics, law, and war. The selections vary from popular to scholarly in style, and the book is of value either as a reference tool or for general reading. Nonfiction.

Gowlett, John. **Ascent to Civilization: The Archaeology of Early Man.** Alfred A. Knopf, 1984.

Lavishly and beautifully illustrated, this oversized volume traces the development of the human race from the earliest ages to civilization as we know it. The index, glossary, and appendices make this book a useful research tool, but it is also engaging reading for anyone interested in archaeology and prehistory. Nonfiction.

Marriott, Alice. **The Ten Grandmothers.** University of Oklahoma Press, 1983.

The Ten Grandmothers relates the saga of the Kiowa Indians from 1847 to 1940 in a complete, very readable, and moving fashion. Readers using this book for research purposes will find the series of four calendars, the map, and the bibliography very helpful. Originally printed in the 1940s, this book is part of the Civilization of the American Indian series. Nonfiction.

Olesky, Walter. **Treasures of the Deep: Adventures of Undersea Exploration.** Julian Messner, 1984.

Sunken treasure and the secrets of past civilizations are the object of countless underwater expeditions carried out by archaeologists, scientists, and fortune hunters. Black-and-white photographs of artifacts are included here, as well as suggestions for additional reading. Nonfiction.

Reader's Digest Editors. **Atlas of the Bible: An Illustrated Guide to the Holy Land.** Reader's Digest Association, 1981.

Maps, up-to-date archaeological finds, artifacts, and clear color photographs contribute to a fascinating look at the life and times of the people of the Bible. Nonfiction.

Art and Architecture

Arnosky, Jim. **Drawing from Nature.** Illus. by author. Lothrop, Lee and Shepard Books, 1982.

Do you want to be able to draw the changing shapes of water droplets as they fall from a tap to the pail? Or buds opening? Or birds or bats or babies? In the four parts of this book, Jim Arnosky provides many drawings and gives clear advice about how to capture the character of the almost infinite variations of water, landscapes, plants, and animals. More than simply an instructional guide, this book reflects the artist's wonder and enjoyment of nature. Nonfiction.

Conner, Patrick. **People at Home.** Margaret K. McElderry Books, 1982.

This collection of paintings shows people from a variety of cultures and times engaged in activities associated with the home—giving birth, getting married, and dying; working and playing; being happy and unhappy; being alone and interacting with others. Readers who follow Conner's perceptive explanations of the individual paintings and his comparisons of them are bound to enjoy these works from a new perspective. A volume in the Looking at Art series. Nonfiction.

Conner, Patrick. **People at Work.** Margaret K. McElderry Books, 1982.

Conner has carefully selected pairs of paintings which represent often contasting views of similar jobs. He includes men, women, and children, both past and present, involved in their work, whether it be building the ark, laboring on a farm or in a factory, or attending school. As he examines each picture, Conner gives the reader insights into not only what these particular artists were trying to do, but also how artists, as masters of imagination, communicate. Part of the Looking at Art series. Nonfiction.

Cumming, Robert. **Just Imagine: Ideas in Painting.** Charles Scribner's Sons, 1982.

By examining paintings from various centuries, Cumming illustrates that knowledge of the elements commonly used by artists can significantly increase people's appreciation of art. Included in his discussion are symbols, patterns, texture, color, and the importance of both artists' and viewers' imaginations. Nonfiction.

Macaulay, David. **Pyramid.** Illus. by author. Houghton Mifflin, 1975.

Macaulay acquired international attention in 1973 when he published *Cathedral,* an insightful and graphic examination of how those massive and awesome structures are constructed, stone by stone. Here he uses the same kind of line drawings and clearly stated text to illustrate the step-by-step construction of a giant pyramid with nothing but hand tools and ingenious planning. Nonfiction.

Macaulay, David. **Underground.** Illus. by author. Houghton Mifflin, 1976.

If you've ever wondered what's under the streets of our major cities and how it got there, David Macaulay's intricate drawings and illuminating text provide the answers. Building supports, gas lines, electrical wires, sewers, subways, storm drains, and all sorts of tubes and tunnels are revealed in a most enlightening manner. Nonfiction.

Plotz, Helen, compiler. **Eye's Delight: Poems of Art and Architecture.** Greenwillow Books, 1983.

An offbeat collection of poems inspired by the forms of art and architecture, *Eye's Delight* contains over one hundred poems through which artists celebrate the different faces of creativity while themselves creating structures with words.

Ventura, Piero. **Great Painters.** G. P. Putnam's Sons, 1984.

Ever wonder how or why the great painters came to paint what they did? The author of this book not only shows you the works of these masters but tells the unique stories behind them through both words and creative illustrations. Clearly and quickly, this book brings paintings from Giotto to Picasso into perspective. Also included are biographical sketches of each painter. Nonfiction.

Wade, Edwin, Carol Haralson, and Rennard Strickland. **As in a Vision: Masterworks of American Indian Art.** University of Oklahoma Press and Philbrook Art Center, 1983.

Although the names of the men and women who created many Native American pieces of art are lost to history, their work

remains and provides us with a picture of the cultures that produced them. This book, with its many fine photographs, is a fascinating study of the wide variety of style, composition, and
symbolic content found in Native American art. And by including
the texts of many poems, songs, and prayers, the authors increase
our understanding and appreciation of these cultures. Nonfiction.

Waldron, Ann. **True or False? Amazing Art Forgeries.** Hastings House,
1983.

This entertaining and informative book tells the stories behind
some of the most famous art forgeries in history. The forgeries
range from the creation of an entire Stone Age culture to church
wall paintings depicting turkeys supposedly painted three hundred
years before those birds appeared in Europe. The reader learns
why these forgeries were created and how investigators uncovered
them. More than one-hundred illustrations accompany these fascinating stories. Nonfiction.

Waterfield, Giles. **Faces.** Margaret K. McElderry Books, 1982.

Faces interest artists and museum-goers alike, for they tell us not
only about the outer person but the inner character as well. Waterfield gives the reader a real feeling for the fascinating variety of
faces artists have created through the ages by including in his book
works ranging from ancient masks to modern art. And his clear
explanations of the qualities the artists have captured give the
reader deeper understanding of and appreciation for these works
of art. Nonfiction.

Weitzman, David. **Windmills, Bridges, and Old Machines: Discovering
Our Industrial Past.** Charles Scribner's Sons, 1982.

David Weitzman speaks directly to readers, inviting us to journey
with him into our country's past and, through industrial archeology,
to trace how we came to be what we are today. On the coast-to-
coast journey we visit many sites, both urban and rural, and meet
the people who worked on these industrial wonders. Along the
way, we are exposed to how the machines worked, and we cannot
help but gain an appreciation for their quality, beauty, and inno-
vativeness. Nonfiction.

Biography and Autobiography

Alsop, Joseph. **FDR: A Centenary Remembrance, 1882–1945.** Washington Square Press, 1982.

Alsop begins his biography by characterizing the Roosevelt family at the time of FDR's birth in 1882; however, the thrust of the work is the political and personal life of the adult FDR. The author attempts to present the man, not the legend—the man who suffered the agony of polio; the man who jeopardized his marriage with a love affair; the man who brought this country through the Great Depression and World War II. Nonfiction.

Ashe, Arthur (with Neil Amdur). **Off the Court.** Signet Books, 1982.

How does a world-class athlete face the fact that at age thirty-seven he must undergo quadruple bypass surgery? This is the problem Arthur Ashe must face after suffering a heart attack. Here, he also shares with his readers the experiences that shaped his earlier life. Growing up in the segregated South was not always easy for young Arthur and his widowed father. Glimpses of his early tennis career and of those who influenced him complement Ashe's story of his rise to fame as a professional athlete. Nonfiction.

Baker, Russell. **Growing Up.** Plume Books, 1983.

"When I was your age. . . ." (Where have you heard that before?) Here Russell Baker presents a sensitive, sometimes humorous account of his childhood in rural Virginia, his youth in a small New Jersey town, and his early manhood in Baltimore. While this is Baker's story, we also learn much about the strong women in his life: his grandmother, the family matriarch; his mother, who struggled to raise her family during the depression; his sister Doris; and his wife, Mimi. Nonfiction.

Baldwin, Neil. **To All Gentleness: William Carlos Williams, the Doctor-Poet.** Atheneum, 1984.

William Carlos Williams, a gentle man who lived a simple life in the small New Jersey town of Rutherford, was known through most of his life as a country doctor. The only difference between him and other doctors most of us know is that Williams spent his spare hours writing poetry. Through Williams's poetry, which was born out of his love of nature and his sympathetic understanding of those around him, we learn what he was really like. Nonfiction.

Bober, Natalie S. **Breaking Tradition: The Story of Louise Nevelson.** Atheneum, 1984.

Born in turn-of-the-century Russia, Louise Nevelson was five when her family emigrated to the United States. Louise's earliest memories, both of life in Russia and of her new home in Rockland, Maine, were of color and of art. At age nine she knew she wanted to be an artist. Bober traces the trials and struggles of a young woman who chooses to compete in the art world and succeeds because of her willingness to sacrifice and break with tradition. Nonfiction.

Bruce, Preston. **From the Door of the White House.** Lothrop, Lee and Shepard Books, 1984.

As doorman for five presidents, Preston Bruce had the opportunity to view and sometimes participate in some of the most important events in recent American history. Here he provides an insider's perspective on the personal and professional lives of Presidents Dwight D. Eisenhower, John F. Kennedy, Lyndon Johnson, Richard Nixon, and Gerald Ford, and tells of his role in such momentous events as the funeral of President Kennedy and the resignation of Richard Nixon. Nonfiction.

Busoni, Rafaello. **The Man Who Was Don Quixote: The Story of Miguel de Cervantes.** Illus. by author. Prentice-Hall, 1982.

Miguel de Cervantes, famous Spanish novelist and playwright, is best known for creating *Don Quixote*. This biography, along with giving a good picture of Cervantes the man, also gives an interesting view of Spain and southern Europe during the sixteenth and early seventeenth centuries. Clever pen-and-ink sketches on almost every page add a great deal. Nonfiction.

Caesar, Sid (with Bill Davidson). **Where Have I Been?** Signet Books, 1983.

Sid Caesar is a living legend in the world of comedy. His television success on *Your Show of Shows* and *Caesar's Hour*, when he worked with the likes of Mel Brooks and Carl Reiner, is oftentimes referred to as "the glory years" of television comedy. While his autobiography does capture many funny moments, the focus of this story is on his life-and-death battle to overcome a pill and alcohol addiction that nearly destroyed him, his career, and his loved ones. Nonfiction.

Capote, Truman. **One Christmas.** Random House, 1983.

As a child, Capote lived with his mother's family in Alabama and counted as his best friend an elderly cousin named Sook Faulk. Knowing how much he would miss Sook, young Truman was both terrified and furious when he found out that his father wanted Truman to spend Christmas with him in New Orleans. Years later, Capote shares his memories of that one brief visit. Nonfiction.

Ching, Lucy. **One of the Lucky Ones.** Doubleday, 1982.

This inspiring autobiography tells of a blind Chinese girl's fight for an education and a future. When Lucy Ching was born in the 1930s, a blind girl in China was an outcast with no future other than begging or prostitution. Her family did not throw her out or sell her, but they did ignore her. It was her *amah* (nanny), Ah Wor, who helped Lucy find a productive life that resulted in her helping many other blind Chinese. Nonfiction.

Cook, Don. **Charles de Gaulle: A Biography.** G. P. Putnam's Sons, 1983.

Born in 1890, de Gaulle became one of the most powerful political figures in the twentieth century. Cook draws the portrait of a man who from his youth aspired to and prepared for power. A general, a politician, and a statesman, de Gaulle was the force that brought France to the status of a world power. He dealt with Hitler, Roosevelt, Stalin, and Kennedy. The author recounts these meetings and offers an American perspective on this man who was destined for greatness. Nonfiction.

Debo, Angie. **Geronimo: The Man, His Time, His Place.** University of Oklahoma Press, 1982.

Who was the real Geronimo? Debo responds with a thoroughly researched and definitive account that separates the reality from the myth of this great Apache leader. While most of this biography is devoted to Geronimo's youth in New Mexico, his years of leadership, and the Apache wars, Debo also deals with the end of an era for the Apache people and the governmental policies toward Indians. Nonfiction.

de Mille, Agnes. **Reprieve: A Memoir.** Signet Books, 1982.

In May of 1975, when Agnes de Mille was preparing for a dance concert, she suddenly discovered that half of her body no longer responded to her commands. She had sustained a cerebral hemorrhage (a stroke). *Reprieve* is de Mille's first-person account of her long road to recovery. Hers is a story of courage, of perseverance, and of a family reunited in love in the face of adversity. Nonfiction.

Easwaran, Eknath. **Gandhi the Man.** 2d ed. Nilgiri Press, 1983.

Gandhi's own words and an array of photographs accompany this chronicle of the life of one of the most imposing figures of our time. A string of academic and professional failures led the young Gandhi to a job in South Africa, where he found that the secret to success in life is service to others. It was this love of others that led to the development of Gandhi's doctrine of nonviolent revolution, first in South Africa and later in India. Nonfiction.

Esquire Press. **Fifty Who Made the Difference.** Esquire Press, 1984.

Esquire magazine presents fifty concise portraits that celebrate those men and women whose lives and work have helped to shape this country during the last fifty years. Trailblazers Jonas Salk and Jackie Robinson, legends John F. Kennedy and Elvis Presley, and visionaries such as Martin Luther King are among the people profiled. Ken Kesey, William Styron, Norman Mailer, and Arthur Miller are only a few of the notable writers who have contributed to this collection. Nonfiction.

Faber, Doris. **Love and Rivalry: Three Exceptional Pairs of Sisters.** Viking Press, 1983.

The subject of sisterhood is as much a subject of *Love and Rivalry* as are the three sets of sisters whose lives are explored by Faber. Poet Emily Dickinson, novelist Harriet Beecher Stowe, and actress Charlotte Cushman each had a sister whose affection supported her art and with whom she shared a rivalry that was an important force in her artistic growth. Nonfiction.

Gadney, Reg. **Kennedy.** Holt, Rinehart and Winston, 1983.

Based on the television film *Kennedy,* Gadney's book begins and ends by remembering November 22, 1963, when the country mourned the loss of John F. Kennedy, thirty-fifth president of the United States. The rest of Gadney's picture-laden text covers the victories and defeats of Kennedy's presidency. Nonfiction.

Gilbert, Martin. **Winston Churchill: The Wilderness Years.** Houghton Mifflin, 1982.

The Wilderness Years represents only ten years in the life of Winston Churchill, but they were ten difficult years when he found himself at odds with his colleagues, his Conservative Party was defeated, and his personal life was invaded by financial problems. Churchill never gave up, though, and this account chronicles his fight to regain power and to warn the British people of the dangers of Hitler. Nonfiction.

Goodchild, Peter. **J. Robert Oppenheimer: Shatterer of Worlds.** Houghton Mifflin, 1981.

Shatterer of Worlds is the story of J. Robert Oppenheimer, brilliant young scientist and teacher, father of the atomic bomb—and eventually a national security risk. Along with Oppenheimer's life story, the author traces the development of the bomb and focuses on the anticommunist movement which was so strong in the decade following the war. Here we learn the injustices suffered by Oppenheimer under the scrutiny of the Atomic Energy Commission and the House Un-American Activities Committee. Nonfiction.

Guthrie, Woody. **Bound for Glory.** Illus. by author. Plume Books, 1983.

Here Woody Guthrie tells his own story, painting vivid pictures of the people he met and the experiences he shared with them. Guthrie was born in Okemah, Oklahoma, in 1912, and grew up in poverty in the midst of the Oklahoma dust bowl. He did not have an easy time, but his difficulties never dimmed his love of life and of this country. In Guthrie's recollections of his boxcar travels, we hear the music of one of America's best-loved folk poets. The foreword is by Pete Seeger. First published in 1943. Nonfiction.

Hamill, Dorothy (with Elva Clairmont). **Dorothy Hamill: On and off the Ice.** Alfred A. Knopf, 1983.

In 1976 at Innsbruck, Dorothy Hamill caught the attention of the world when she became the Olympic gold medalist in women's figure skating. Her autobiography takes us from her first pair of skates to international acclaim and her current professional success with the Ice Capades. Nonfiction.

Haskins, James. **I'm Gonna Make You Love Me: The Story of Diana Ross.** Laurel-Leaf Library, 1982.

From her birth in 1944 in a Detroit ghetto to her superstar status of today, the story of Diana Ross reveals her tenacity in her climb to the top. Haskins traces Ross's musical beginnings with the Primettes to her move to Motown with the Supremes to movie stardom. Although professional success does not always ensure personal satisfaction for Ross, her personal life is enriched by family love, friends, and understanding. Nonfiction.

Haskins, James. **Sugar Ray Leonard.** Lothrop, Lee and Shepard Books, 1982.

Sugar Ray Leonard began his boxing career at age fourteen when he went to the Palmer Park Recreation Center and met Dave Jacobs, a volunteer coach there. Biographer James Haskins follows the personal and professional life of Ray Charles Leonard from his beginnings in Wilmington, South Carolina, to his introduction to boxing, to the 1976 Montreal Olympics, and to his turning pro. Coverage of two world championship bouts and a look at the ringside action add to the story of this champion fighter. Nonfiction.

Holiday, Billie (with William Dufty). **Lady Sings the Blues.** Penguin Books, 1984.

The daughter of a thirteen-year-old mother and a fifteen-year-old father, Billie Holiday did not have a happy childhood, and life became more difficult as she tried to make it on her own. Poverty and prostitution marked her teen years until she got a job doing what had always given her pleasure—singing. Holiday tells her own story of life in New York during the 1920s and 1930s when she became Lady Day, singing in jazz clubs with some of the greats of American music. Along with the joys, Holiday shares the heartaches when she describes the prejudice she found during her tours through the South and her ongoing battle with heroin addiction. Nonfiction.

Hollander, Phyllis, and Zander Hollander, editor. **Dan Fouts, Ken Anderson, Joe Theismann and Other All-Time Great Quarterbacks.** Zander Hollander Sports Books, 1983.

The Hollanders present portraits of Theismann, Staubach, Namath, Bradshaw, and six other famous American quarterbacks. The sketches include highlights from the career accomplishments of these great athletes, as well as stories of their childhood experiences and their college days. Nonfiction.

Hopkins, Jerry, and Danny Sugerman. **No One Here Gets Out Alive.** Warner Books, 1981.

> Jim Morrison earned early fame and notoriety from his music and from his singing group, The Doors, and there is still interest in the myths surrounding his death in Paris in 1971. This biography is full of stories that relate his early rise to fame and fortune to his crashing demise. The authors investigate Morrison's early childhood and family background and find that even then there were signs of an ill-fated life. Nonfiction.

Jackson, Reggie (with Mike Lupica). **Reggie: The Autobiography.** Villard Books, 1984.

> Reggie Jackson shares his private life and gives us an insider's view of professional baseball. We meet such sports personalities as Charles O. Finley, George Steinbrenner, and Billy Martin as they struggle with the often controversial Jackson. But the most revealing part of the autobiography comes in the early chapters when Jackson tells of his growing-up years in Philadelphia. Nonfiction.

Johnson, Earvin "Magic," and Richard Levin. **Magic.** Viking Press, 1983.

> Capturing the excitement of professional basketball without neglecting the personal story of Johnson's rise to stardom, the authors present alternating chapters of past and present. Here we watch "Magic" develop from a schoolboy athlete in Lansing, Michigan, into a multimillionaire superstar with the Los Angeles Lakers. Nonfiction.

Kerr, M. E. **Me Me Me Me Me: Not a Novel.** Signet Vista Books, 1984.

> M. E. Kerr, best known to teenagers as the author of *Dinky Hocker Shoots Smack!* and *Gentlehands,* offers hilarious glimpses into her own rebellious teenage years in this lively autobiography. By doing so, she introduces the reader to some of the real-life people who provided the models for characters in *Is That You, Miss Blue?; The Son of Someone Famous; If I Love You, Am I Trapped Forever?;* and her other novels for young adults. Nonfiction.

Kresh, Paul. **Isaac Bashevis Singer: The Story of a Storyteller.** Illus. Penrod Scofield. Lodestar Books, 1984.

> The life of this notable Jewish author begins in the ghettos of Poland at the turn of the century. As early as age eight, Isaac loved to hear and tell stories. His imagination was vivid and wild. Thus, the seeds were planted early for the storyteller who was to earn

the Nobel Prize for literature in 1978. The author follows Singer's adult years, many of which were spent living in the shadow of his older brother, writer I. J. Singer. It was the elder Singer who brought Isaac to the United States, where he was to build a new life, find fame, and meet his beloved wife, Alma. A book in the Jewish Biography series. Nonfiction.

Lindsey, Robert. **The Falcon and the Snowman.** Pocket Books, 1985.

Christopher Boyce and Daulton Lee came from upper-middle-class, stable homes. Growing up in the turbulent sixties, they turned to drugs and to values different from those of their parents. This turning away eventually led them to become spies for the Soviet Union and to turn over valuable secrets about satellites and other space programs. This book—which provided the basis for the film of the same name—covers the young men's lives, including their spy activities, eventual capture, and trial. Nonfiction.

Lockhart, Robin Bruce. **Reilly: Ace of Spies.** Penguin Books, 1984.

Sigmund Rosenblum, alias Sidney Reilly, was considered by many to be one of the most brilliant spies of this century. Active in the period prior to World War I through the mid-1920s, Reilly performed incredible feats of espionage. This book relates what is known of his colorful personal life as well as his undercover activities, and formed the basis for a series on public television. Nonfiction.

Mack, John E., and Holly Hickler. **Vivienne: The Life and Suicide of an Adolescent Girl.** Mentor Books, 1982.

Bright and attractive, fourteen-year-old Vivienne Loomis committed suicide. Using her letters and diary entries, the authors (a clinician and a teacher) write about Vivienne's life and death. In the second half of the text, they offer their views on teenage suicide. Nonfiction.

Madden, John (with Dave Anderson). **Hey, Wait a Minute, I Wrote a Book!** Villard Books, 1984.

Perhaps best known as a coach of the Oakland Raiders, John Madden is familiar to television viewers today for his work as a sports commentator and a celebrity in beer commercials. Always quick with a quip, Madden transfers that same wit to his book as he takes us behind the scenes of college and professional football. More a collection of anecdotes than an autobiography, Madden's book parades one football personality after another in front of us. Nonfiction.

McTaggart, Lynne. **Kathleen Kennedy: Her Life and Times.** Dial Press, 1983.

Kathleen "Kick" Kennedy was the fourth child born to Rose and Joe Kennedy. Loved and admired by all who met her, she took London by storm when her father was the American Ambassador there. Kathleen fit easily into England's social set before and during World War II, but earned the disapproval of her parents when she married a Protestant aristocrat, William Hartington, Marquess of Hartington. This biography covers only ten years in Kathleen Kennedy's life, but tells much about her family and the friends who surrounded her during these years. Nonfiction.

Mebane, Mary E. **Mary.** Fawcett Juniper Books, 1982.

Growing up in poverty in rural North Carolina was not easy for Mary, for she was no ordinary little girl: she had a dream of making something of herself. Her story takes us through her childhood, describing her family, the difficulties she faced with a disapproving mother, and her introduction to Aunt Jo, the first person to believe in her. Later, Mary pursued her dream of a college education and dealt with many problems, not the least of which was racism on the part of those who should have been the most anxious to help her. Nonfiction.

Mebane, Mary E. **Mary, Wayfarer.** Viking Press, 1983.

In *Mary, Wayfarer,* Mary Mebane continues her life story that she began telling in *Mary.* Her strength, independence, and endurance carry her through as she fights to fulfill her life's ambitions in the South during the 1950s and 1960s. Being black and gifted, Mary holds various teaching jobs and studies to earn her Ph.D. while she witnesses the growth of black pride and power. Through her we meet James Baldwin and Malcolm X; but more importantly, we meet Mary herself, a woman who fights prejudice from both blacks and whites and wins. Nonfiction.

Mellow, James R. **Nathaniel Hawthorne in His Times.** Houghton Mifflin, 1982.

While presenting the life of Hawthorne, Mellow includes an exposé of mid-nineteenth-century New England and the literary masters of that time. This portrait of Hawthorne is a most complete and scholarly account of one of the geniuses of American literature. Nonfiction.

Miller, Jonathan. **Darwin for Beginners.** Illus. Borin Van Loon. Pantheon Books, 1982.

This biography is probably unlike any you have ever read. The combination of humor, fact, and sophistication make this a must not only for the Darwin enthusiast but for anyone else as well. The illustrations are clever and fascinating, and the content is informative and enjoyable. Nonfiction.

Neimark, Anne E. **A Deaf Child Listened: Thomas Gallaudet, Pioneer in American Education.** William Morrow, 1983.

The beginning of the nineteenth century was a difficult time for a deaf child. Not until the summer of 1814, when Thomas Gallaudet met a nine-year-old deaf child named Alice Cogswell, was there any hope of education for the deaf. Sickly himself, Gallaudet had tried many occupations prior to his fateful meeting with Alice. When he was able to reach her with hand signs, he found his calling. Anne Neimark shows the reader how Gallaudet's life was shaped by the educational and emotional needs of the deaf. Nonfiction.

Nixon, Richard. **Leaders.** Warner Books, 1983.

In this collection of short biographies, former President Nixon provides personal insights into the character and behavior of influential statesmen he met during his long political career. Included here are accounts of the lives of Winston Churchill, Charles de Gaulle, Douglas MacArthur, Shigeru Yoshidida, Nikita Khrushchev, Zhou Enlai, and others. Reflecting de Gaulle's remark, "Nothing great is done without great men," these biographies offer an interesting commentary on the ways of greatness as perceived and reported by a controversial president. Nonfiction.

Oates, Stephen B. **Let the Trumpet Sound: The Life of Martin Luther King, Jr.** Plume Books, 1983.

This biography of Martin Luther King, Jr., begins on a Sunday in the spring of 1934 when five-year-old "ML" joins the church. Oates traces the religious, educational, political, and intellectual development of his subject, making it possible for the reader to understand the driving forces that directed the public life of Martin

Luther King. Oates discloses the heart of this man who fought social injustice and racial discrimination and who gave his life trying to achieve his dream of social change through nonviolent means. Nonfiction.

Parmet, Herbert S. **Jack: The Struggles of John F. Kennedy.** Dial Press, 1980.

Covering the years 1917 to 1960, this book tells of John F. Kennedy's early childhood, his schooling, and his entry and growth in the political arena. Always in the shadow of his older brother, young Jack found himself thrust into the spotlight after Joe's death during World War II. In pain much of the time and later afflicted with Addison's disease, Jack Kennedy struggled to live up to his father's image of what he could become. Beyond a well documented account of these Kennedy years, Parmet paints vivid pictures of politicians and political life during four decades. Nonfiction.

Peavy, Linda, and Ursula Smith. **Women Who Changed Things.** Charles Scribner's Sons, 1983.

Described as "nine lives that made a difference," this collection of biographies researches the lives of nine women who made an impact on our social history. They lived in turn-of-the-century America, and together they made significant changes in the fields of medicine, religion, politics, business, the arts, education, athletics, and social action. They opened doors to new opportunities for generations of women to come. Nonfiction.

Prugh, Jeff. **Herschel Walker: From the Georgia Backwoods and the Heisman Trophy to the Pros.** Zander Hollander Sports Books, 1983.

Herschel Junior Walker was the fifth child born to Willis and Christine Walker, tenant farmers in rural Georgia. It was here in the rural South that Herschel grew up, went to school, ran foot races with his sister Veronica, and started to play football for the Johnson County Trojans. This book traces Walker's success in football and concludes with his controversial decision to leave college for a career in the newly formed United States Football League. Nonfiction.

Robinson, Phyllis C. **Willa: The Life of Willa Cather.** Owl Books, 1984.

Willa Cather died at age seventy-three in 1947, having spent the last forty years of her life in New York working as a novelist and short story writer. Beginning with Cather's birth in Virginia, this biography looks at the Nebraska years, which provided Cather with the spirit and materials for her classic novels of the American frontier, and then covers in detail Cather's years of creative genius in New York. Nonfiction.

Rodriguez, Richard. **Hunger of Memory: The Education of Richard Rodriguez.** Bantam Books, 1983.

This collection of autobiographical essays covers a myriad of themes as Richard Rodriguez describes his growth from a little boy who enters school barely able to speak English to a man who achieves academic success with his work at the British Museum. Throughout the essays Rodriguez discusses the importance of language and the ways in which his assimilation into an English-speaking world has altered his life. His views on bilingual education in America are controversial and thought-provoking. Nonfiction.

Rogers, Betty. **Will Rogers: His Wife's Story.** University of Oklahoma Press, 1981.

When Betty Rogers first heard the name of her future husband, Will Rogers, it was the fall of 1900 and she was visiting relatives in Oologah, Oklahoma. The story of their first meeting, their courtship, and their long married life together provide the framework for this personal account of a great American humorist and performer. A cowboy, a Wild West performer, a vaudevillian, and a radio and movie star, Rogers is perhaps best remembered for his homespun wit whose appeal was worldwide. Betty's story is enriched with Will's own comments on the human condition. Nonfiction.

Rollin, Betty. **Am I Getting Paid for This?** Plume Books, 1984.

Starting with her graduation from Sarah Lawrence College in 1957, Betty Rollin takes us through three phases of her professional life with honesty, candor, and humor. An actress in off-Broadway and touring productions and later an accomplished writer for *Vogue* and *Look* magazines, Rollin faced the problems of a career woman in the 1960s and 1970s. She dealt with the conflicts of career and marriage and moved into the competitive world of the TV correspondent, then earned fame and praise for her book *First, You Cry,* which details her bout with cancer. Her autobiography concludes with hope as we see in Betty Rollin a woman who, through struggle, is secure in both her personal and professional life. Nonfiction.

Roosevelt, Elliott. **Eleanor Roosevelt, with Love: A Centenary Remembrance.** Lodestar Books, 1984.

Written to honor the centennial of Eleanor Roosevelt's birth, Elliott Roosevelt's biography of his mother gives a complete and personal view of the life of one of America's best-known and best-loved first ladies. Born in 1884, Eleanor was orphaned at age ten and raised by her maternal grandmother. She was educated in Europe, and when she returned home, she was expected "to come out" and assume her place in New York society. It was during this social whirl that Eleanor met the man who would shape the rest of her life, Franklin Delano Roosevelt. Elliott Roosevelt fills his biography with family anecdotes and personal remembrances of his mother's private and public life. Nonfiction.

Rosa, Joseph G. **They Called Him Wild Bill: The Life and Adventures of James Butler Hickok.** 2d ed. University of Oklahoma Press, 1982.

Wild Bill Hickok is a legendary figure of the Old West. However, this biography moves beyond the legend and introduces us to James Butler Hickok the man. Born in 1837, Hickok led a colorful life, working as a United States marshall, as a scout for the U.S. Army during the Civil War, and as a performer in a Wild West show. General George Custer, Buffalo Bill Cody, and Calamity Jane are only a few of the characters included in Wild Bill's life story. Nonfiction.

Samuels, Peggy, and Harold Samuels. **Frederic Remington: A Biography.** Doubleday, 1982.

Frederic Remington used his art to immortalize the American West. Born in 1861, Remington was raised in upstate New York and educated at Yale. But it is his work as a chronicler of the West for which he is best remembered. His illustrations, paintings, and pieces of sculpture bring to life the cowboy, the Indian, and the cavalry soldier of the Old West. Nonfiction.

Schaap, Dick. **Steinbrenner!** G. P. Putnam's Sons, 1982.

We all know George Steinbrenner as the controversial owner of the New York Yankees. Here, through the author's personal observations as well as interviews with Steinbrenner's friends and foes, we get a balanced view of both the public and private life of one of the most famous men in sports. In his analysis of Steinbrenner's childhood and early family relationships, the author examines forces that may have motivated and shaped George Steinbrenner. Nonfiction.

Schreiber, Flora Rheta. **Sybil.** Warner Books, 1974.

Sybil tells the true story of a woman who lived with sixteen separate personalities. The story is based on accounts from Sybil herself, as well as from the doctor who worked with her for over ten years to uncover the horrors of a childhood that led to the development of her multiple personalities. Nonfiction.

Shirley, Glenn. **Belle Starr and Her Times: The Literature, the Facts, and the Legends.** University of Oklahoma Press, 1982.

Just about everybody has heard of Belle Starr, famous outlaw of the Old West. This biography traces Starr from her birth in Missouri in 1848 to her travels throughout the West after the Civil War. Belle lived among renegade Indians, married, had children, and, although never convicted of a major crime, spent most of her life outside of the law. The author presents both myth and reality, fact and fiction in this portrait of an Old West figure. Nonfiction.

Siegal, Aranka. **Upon the Head of the Goat: A Childhood in Hungary, 1939–1944.** Signet Vista Books, 1983.

Piri Davidowitz is nine at the start of this autobiography and fourteen when she and her family leave the ghetto bound for the Nazi death camp Auschwitz in 1944. In between are her vivid memories of growing up in the countryside and cities of Hungary, as well as surviving in the ghetto in the weeks before deportation. This Newbery Honor Book is a gripping, inspiring story. Nonfiction.

Sullivan, Tom, and Derek Gill. **If You Could See What I Hear.** Signet Books, 1976.

Blinded shortly after birth, Sullivan struggled to achieve a normal boyhood. With the help of Derek Gill, Sullivan relates here the story of his efforts and successes in school, in sports, and in the entertainment business. Told with both humor and pathos, his is a story of one man's courage and persistence to compete in a sighted world. Nonfiction.

Thomas, Lewis. **The Youngest Science: Notes of a Medicine-Watcher.** Viking Press, 1983.

Lewis Thomas, author of *The Lives of a Cell*, presents here a history of medicine as much as the story of his professional life. Beginning with his childhood memories of his father's medical practice during the 1920s, Thomas describes the early medical practitioner who made house calls and established a personal relationship with the patient. When Thomas entered medical school, medicine moved from art to science. Using his personal experiences, he chronicles the changes in the medical profession with the advent of technology and its promises for research and practice. Nonfiction.

Wheeler, Robert W. **Jim Thorpe: World's Greatest Athlete.** University of Oklahoma Press, 1983.

Jim Thorpe is probably best known as the Olympic athlete who won the decathlon and pentathlon in 1912, only to be disqualified later for having already given up his amateur status. This biography traces Thorpe's life from his birth in 1888 to his death in 1953 and the restoration of his Olympic medals in 1982. While Jim's early life on a reservation, his studies at Indian schools, his football triumphs, and his Olympic feats make for interesting reading, what distinguishes this work is its use of firsthand information. The best source is Jim's own scrapbook, which was given to the author by Thorpe's daughter. Nonfiction.

Wideman, John Edgar. **Brothers and Keepers.** Holt, Rinehart and Winston, 1984.

Two brothers are raised in the same environment. What makes one pursue an education and become a college professor and a published writer while the other commits petty crimes, one of which ends in a man's death, sending that brother to prison for life? John Wideman tries to determine the answer in this poignant account of his conversations and letters with his jailed brother Rob. Nonfiction.

Wiener, Jon. **Come Together: John Lennon in His Time.** Random House, 1984.

This biography of John Lennon focuses on the revolutionary spirit of the 1960s and the ways in which the music Lennon wrote as one of the Beatles served as a response to political and social issues.

Wiener covers the period from the mid-1960s when Lennon made his first public statements against the Vietnam War up to the final interview granted by Lennon just six hours before his death in December 1980. Nonfiction.

Wilkins, Roy (with Tom Mathews). **Standing Fast: The Autobiography of Roy Wilkins.** Viking Press, 1982.

Standing Fast is not only the autobiography of Roy Wilkins, it is the story of the civil rights movement in this century as seen by one who was in the front lines. This very readable book offers insights into the role of the NAACP and other black groups in obtaining civil rights. A complete index makes this book a valuable research tool. Nonfiction.

Careers and Jobs

Anderson, Scott, and James Byrne. **Mega Tips: How to Get and Keep Any Restaurant Job.** Illus. Grace Marie Sheehan and Bo Zaunders. Dodd, Mead, 1984.

Why would anyone be interested in working in a restaurant? The authors explore the answer to that question as they look at both the positive and negative aspects of working in this customer-service career and humorously recount on-the-job anecdotes from waiters, bartenders, managers, and other restaurant personnel. Readers not considering this career may still find the book of value in selecting a restaurant when dining out. Nonfiction.

Bolles, Richard N., and Victoria B. Zenoff. **The Beginning Quick Job-Hunting Map: A Fast Way to Help.** Ten Speed Press, 1979.

This guide presents the two major methods for finding a job: the want-ad-and-employment-agency method and the authors' procedure, which uses their own job-hunting map. Bolles and Zenoff show the advantages of their approach and tell job hunters how they can learn to assess their individual skills, identify jobs of interest, and get hired. Nonfiction.

Catalyst Editors. **Upward Mobility.** Warner Books, 1983.

In order to reach the top of a stimulating career, an individual must assess his or her own strengths and weaknesses and actively plan strategies that will develop into constructive steps forward. This book contains guidelines and worksheets that will help with this self-analysis so that one can create a solid plan for future success. Although the book was written by an organization dedicated to expanding the careers of women, the suggestions are excellent for everyone. Nonfiction.

Chancellor, John, and Walter R. Mears. **The News Business.** Mentor Books, 1984.

The whole news cycle is reported in this easy-to-read primer for young journalists, which contains a blend of concrete examples, anecdotes, and how-to strategies. The chapters on leads and analysis are especially effective, and readers can get many clues on how to successfully enter this profession. Nonfiction.

Clemens, Virginia Phelps. **Behind the Filmmaking Scene.** Westminster Press, 1982.

The author of this book went to the people who work behind the scenes in filmmaking and asked them to describe their jobs. This guide is the result. It covers familiar behind-the-scenes jobs such as director and stunt person, as well as some not-so-familiar ones such as sound mixer, editor, and cinematographer. In each case, the education, experience, and personality needed are described. Nonfiction.

Curtis, Patricia. **Animal Partners: Training Animals to Help People.** Lodestar Books, 1982.

Using animals to help the handicapped is a stimulating and relatively new occupation, and scientists are still investigating this field of human-and-animal bonding. The belief is that animals used as helpers or companions will add dimension to the lives of the human and the animal, as long as the animal is not pushed beyond its limit. Thus, the role of the animal trainer is significant. The requirements for the occupation are presented here, along with examples of people like Alexandria, a horse trainer; Steve, a farm animal trainer; and Bob, an apprentice guide-dog trainer. Nonfiction.

Douglas, Martha C. **Go for It! How to Get Your First Good Job: A Career-Planning Guide for Young Adults.** Ten Speed Press, 1983.

Deciding on a career can be both difficult and confusing. The aim of this book is to give readers a system that will enable them to see the options open to them, set goals for success, mesh their skills and values, and find careers to suit their personality types. The author uses many students' experiences to demonstrate how to work through the process. Nonfiction.

Froman, Katherine. **The Chance to Grow.** Everest House, 1983.

This book can be many things to many people, but most of all, it offers hope to the parents of handicapped children. Through the use of case studies, it offers insights into the many common types of handicaps resulting from genetic defects, birth or other injury, and/or prenatal problems. In addition, the book explains what a physical therapist does, and contains valuable appendices that list sources for additional information. Nonfiction.

Gillers, Stephen, editor. **Looking at Law School: A Student Guide from the Society of American Law Teachers.** Rev. ed. Meridian Books, 1984.

Anyone considering a legal career will find this book a useful overview of law school and the life of a lawyer. The information is well presented, with each chapter written by an eminent professor from a leading law school in the United States. The risks and the commitment that a legal education requires are intelligently reported. Nonfiction.

Gordon, Suzanne. **Off Balance: The Real World of Ballet.** Photographs by Earl Dotter. Pantheon Books, 1983.

As with any artistic or athletic activity, the good performers make ballet look easy. But behind the beauty and grace of ballet are painful realities seldom seen or even heard about by the general public. Here Suzanne Gordon exposes "the real world of ballet"— life in the ballet schools, the daily strain of being part of a dance company, the constant struggle to remain thin, the injuries that must be endured, and the physical and psychological strain of competition. Nonfiction.

Greenberg, Jan W. **Theater Careers: A Comprehensive Guide to Non-Acting Careers in the Theater.** Holt, Rinehart and Winston, 1983.

This book provides a comprehensive description of backstage careers through a series of interviews and profiles of established professionals working in commercial, university, and amateur theaters. The careers discussed include those of general and company manager, managing director, director of audience development, vocal arranger, costume designer, lighting designer, and many more. Nonfiction.

Hallstead, William F. **Broadcasting Careers for You.** Lodestar Books, 1983.

An enormous variety of jobs is available in the complex profession of broadcasting. For example, one could have an on-camera assignment, be a member of a studio crew or production team, or work as a control-room engineer or a programming and promotion specialist. This book assists the reader in discerning the qualities and skills required for employment in broadcasting and explores the many job categories that the field offers, their requirements, and the educational route to follow. Nonfiction.

Harragan, Betty Lehan. **Knowing the Score: Play-by-Play Directions for Women on the Job.** Signet Books, 1984.

Knowing the Score is derived from Betty Lehan Harragan's columns in *Savvy* and *Working Woman.* Designed to give women information on how to analyze a job situation, the book presents specific strategies for dealing with career advancement. In the section on the basic rules of the working game, for example, Harragan explains how to understand the madness that often prevails on the job and the unwritten rules implied in the system. Nonfiction.

Hawes, Gene R. **Hawes on Getting into College.** Plume Books, 1983.

This book offers helpful advice on how to get into college, including valuable information on admission practices, financial aid, and SAT preparation. The chapters called "Gauging Your Chances of Admission at the Top Colleges" and "Putting Yourself Across in Your Applications" are extremely useful for college-bound students and their parents. Nonfiction.

Henry, Fran Worden. **Toughing It Out at Harvard: The Making of a Woman MBA.** G. P. Putnam's Sons, 1983.

Henry's book reaffirms that the work involved in being educated at a school like Harvard is worth going through. The author's astute personal analysis descriptively presents the struggles as well as the opportunities available at this famous business school. Nonfiction.

Kingstone, Brett. **The Student Entrepreneur's Guide: How to Start and Run Your Own Part Time Small Business.** Ten Speed Press, 1981.

If you have ever considered starting and operating your own business, then this can be your guide. A variety of interesting business ventures are outlined in a very readable style so that you can learn from other people's successes and failures. Nonfiction.

Krefetz, Gerald, and Philip Gittelman. **The Book of Incomes.** Holt, Rinehart and Winston, 1982.

If income is a consideration for you in selecting a career, then you will find this book a must to read. It contains information about pay scales and earning data for all professions, presented in a clear and interesting manner, as well as stories about the richest people in the world and how they developed their fortunes. Nonfiction.

Kritsick, Stephen, and Patti Goldstein. **Creature Comforts: The Adventures of a City Vet.** Coward-McCann, 1983.

Dealing with the pain and suffering of animals is the business of a veterinarian. But the life of a vet goes much beyond that. Here Dr. Stephen Kritsick successfully relates his personal experiences in a city animal hospital as he tells about the problems that vets encounter, the decisions they must make, and the necessity for them to be mature and sensitive. Nonfiction.

LaBastille, Anne. **Women and Wilderness.** Sierra Club Books, 1984.

Excitement, adventure, and commitment mark the lives and careers of the fifteen women naturalists profiled in this book. From white-water rafting to Olympic monitoring and Alaskan home-steading, the ways these vital modern women embrace the outdoors are vastly different from the roles women have historically played in the wilderness. These former roles are detailed in brief case studies of pioneer women on the American frontier, and, as a contrast, the book also explores the opening of new and varied career options for women interested in outdoor occupations. Nonfiction.

Lerner, Elaine (with C. B. Abbott). **The Way to Go: A Woman's Guide to Careers in Travel.** Warner Books, 1982.

If you want a quickly growing, never repetitious, always challenging profession, the travel and leisure business may be for you. This book is designed to give direction and encouragement to people interested in the field. Although written for women, many of the suggestions are also appropriate for men. The chapters on breaking into the business, how to be a travel agent, and opening your own agency are particularly insightful. Nonfiction.

Martin, Toni. **How to Survive Medical School.** Holt, Rinehart and Winston, 1983.

Dr. Martin's medical experience serves as the source for this very readable book in which she sensitively portrays the rigor, loneliness, and stress of medical school. As she covers the data related to applications, internships, and residency, the reader realizes that a tremendous effort is necessary to complete such a program. Yet her success attests that it can be done. Nonfiction.

Mitchell, Joyce Slayton. **Your Job in the Computer Age: The Complete Guide to the Computer Skills You Need to Get the Job You Want.** Charles Scribner's Sons, 1984.

Almost every job in today's job market, according to Mitchell, requires some level of computer knowledge. In this guide, the prospective applicant is able to learn which computer skills are needed for which occupation. The chapter "Computer-Age Talk: A New Language" is written to strengthen the reader's understanding of computer language and is beneficial to anyone interested in catching up with all the new terminology. Nonfiction.

Muller, Peter. **The Fast Track to the Top Jobs in Computer Careers.** Perigee Books, 1983.

This book can make it easier for you to select a career in the rapidly growing and diverse field of computers. It describes the range of employment opportunities and suggests guidelines for developing appropriate educational and other credentials for these jobs. One section forecasts the "hot fields" and speculates on what the job market will be like in ten years. Nonfiction.

Muller, Peter. **The Fast Track to the Top Jobs in Engineering Careers.** Perigee Books, 1983.

Enjoying an engineering career depends upon getting the right training, landing an exciting job, and advancing to the most profitable levels within a company. The commitment and the technical background required to achieve this are explained in this guide. Useful suggestions for educational preparation, including accelerated degrees and job options, are also presented. The reader learns that engineers are in a unique position in the job market, for they make up the largest force of degreed professionals in the country. Nonfiction.

Saunders, Rubie. **Baby-Sitting for Fun and Profit.** Illus. Tomie de Paola. Archway Paperbacks, 1984.

Baby-sitting is often called the youngest profession. This easy-to-read, well-illustrated book helps young professionals perform their services more appropriately and clearly defines the advantages of this money-making position. The Baby-Sitters' Checklist is an excellent reference to review before every baby-sitting job, and many of the skills discussed may even make the work pleasurable. Nonfiction.

Seide, Diane. **Careers in Health Services.** Lodestar Books, 1982.

This book describes over fifty different careers in the field of medicine, such as nursing, cytotechnology, respiratory technology, optometry, and others. The author indicates the educational requirements and financial opportunities for each field, and has included the names of organizations and agencies that will provide further information. Nonfiction.

Seuling, Barbara. **How to Write a Children's Book and Get It Published.** Charles Scribner's Sons, 1984.

Have you ever wanted to write for children? This book clearly describes the step-by-step process of becoming a published children's author. Seuling's observations and insights will help you turn flat characters into flesh and blood. Her questions and format will guide you through this creative process, from conception of the idea through marketing. While her approach is excellent for writing, it can also be used as a template for many other endeavors. Nonfiction.

Shanahan, William F. **College—Yes or No.** Arco, 1983.

With an emphasis on vocational education and the armed services, this guide informs readers of career opportunities open to high school graduates. The chapter on choosing a career contains self-help worksheets designed to target jobs that are suited to an individual's interests and talents. Other chapters include helpful tips on writing letters and résumés and on preparing for job interviews. Nonfiction.

Shook, Robert L. **Why Didn't I Think of That!** Signet Books, 1983.

How does one promote a unique product, service, or special business? What does it take to have an idea succeed? This book is a tribute to the ingenuity and persistence of ten people who followed their dreams and became successes. Read their stories and learn of the qualities and circumstances that allow an entrepreneur to develop. Nonfiction.

Switzer, Ellen. **Dancers! Horizons in American Dance.** Photographs by Costas. Atheneum, 1982.

Switzer begins by noting that in the early 1980s more people attended dance performances than went to baseball games. For those who enjoy dance performances of all kinds, especially ballet, Switzer provides a brief history and a glimpse into the makeup and philosophy of today's important dance companies, such as the New York City Ballet, the Alvin Ailey Company, and the Dance Theatre of Harlem. She includes personal comments from young dancers as well as from star performers such as Mikhail Baryshnikov and Natalia Makarova. Nonfiction.

Cars, Motorcycles, and Racing

Burness, Tad. **The Auto Album.** Illus. by author. Houghton Mifflin, 1983.

A fascinating and informative look at vintage autos and trucks from the 1900s to the 1970s. Pen-and-ink drawings include details of tire size, original price, speed, body and frame construction, engines, and special features. Stories on the vehicles and notes about their eras make *The Auto Album* great browsing material. Nonfiction.

Coombs, Charles. **BMX: A Guide to Bicycle Motocross.** William Morrow, 1983.

Interested in BMX biking? Here, Charles Coombs tells you how to choose and care for this special bicycle. Pages filled with pictures and a plain, readable style make it easy for you to learn how to perform stunts that are an important part of this sport. A glossary explains various terms, and a bibliography gives suggestions for further reading. Nonfiction.

Hoffman, Jeffrey. **Corvette: America's Supercar.** JEM Books, 1984.

The Corvette was born in 1952, a dream car come true. This slim and well-illustrated volume traces the development of the 'Vette to the present day. A 'Vette—who wouldn't love one? Nonfiction.

Jenkinson, Denis. **Porsche Past and Present.** Arco, 1983.

Everybody knows the difference between an ordinary Volkswagon Beetle and a sophisticated Porsche. But few people know that Dr. Ferdinand Porsche developed his car as a result of his work on the VW in Hitler's Germany. This history of the Porsche is filled with photographs and stories from the author's own half-million miles of driving in this respected foreign car. Nonfiction.

King, Stephen. **Christine.** Viking Press, 1983.

Arnie Cunningham, Leigh Cabot, and Dennis Guilder, three high school students from Pittsburgh, become involved with a supernatural car named Christine, whose dark forces slowly begin to come alive and take over their lives. Dennis and Leigh then face death as they try to break Christine's terrifying hold on Arnie. The use of street language is realistic. Fiction.

Murphy, Jim. **The Indy 500.** Clarion Books, 1983.

Action photos accent this thoroughly enjoyable book about one of the most important car races in the world. Here you'll find out about the long hours of testing and practice that go into qualifying cars and drivers, as well as the dangers that are involved in the Indy 500. Nonfiction.

Olney, Ross R. **Super Champions of Auto Racing.** Clarion Books, 1984.

What type of personality does it take to be a champion race car driver? Read these six profiles of racing champions and find out what it takes to succeed at the various types of professional racing such as championship, NASCAR, sprint, and drag racing. Many photos accompany the brief biographies. Nonfiction.

Ready, Kirk L. **Custom Cars.** Lerner, 1982.

Are you bored with the sameness of cars off the assembly line? Then this look into the world of custom cars will interest you. A car can be altered to make the engine more efficient or the body unique, and changes are limited only by an owner's imagination. This is a good introduction to the different aspects of building and showing cars in competition. Nonfiction.

Stambler, Irwin. **Off-Roading: Racing and Riding.** G. P. Putnam's Sons, 1984.

If you're interested in off-road racing, you'll like this introduction to jeeps, vans, pickup trucks, dune buggies, and other four-wheel-drive vehicles. Here you'll read about development of the vehicles, and get practical tips on driving on beaches, deserts, and specially constructed dirt tracks. Photos are provided at the end of the book, along with a list of off-road clubs and associations. Nonfiction.

Classics—Old and Modern

Alcott, Louisa May. **Little Women.** Signet Classics, 1983.

A small New England village in the 1800s provides the background for this story of the March family. Meg, Jo, Beth, and Amy are the March girls, whose lives and loves are the basis for this sentimental romance. But this is Jo's story, and it is she who introduces us to her sisters and to Marmee, Aunt March, and their neighbor, Laurie. Fiction.

Austen, Jane. **Pride and Prejudice.** Signet Modern Classics, 1980.

A comedy of manners set in nineteenth-century rural England, *Pride and Prejudice* tells of the lives and loves of the Bennet family. Five daughters mean a busy household, but it is on the proud Elizabeth Bennet and her suitor Darcy that the story concentrates. Fiction.

Bellow, Saul. **Henderson the Rain King.** Penguin Books, 1983.

Weary of suburbia, bored with his pig farm and his wife, eccentric millionaire E. H. Henderson journeys to Africa in search of adventure. His wanderings lead him to a remote village where he becomes enmeshed in bizarre and often comic tribal rites with animals and natives that force him to face his deepest fears as he fights for his life. Fiction.

Bellow, Saul. **Mr. Sammler's Planet.** Penguin Books, 1984.

Artur Sammler is a survivor. He has lived through World War II and the ordeal of a Nazi death camp, and has lost his sight in one eye, his wife, his homeland, and all his possessions. But can this frail, elderly man now survive the turbulent, violent society of Manhattan? Mr. Sammler wages a quiet, private struggle to preserve decency and compassion in a bewildering world. Fiction.

Brontë, Charlotte. **Jane Eyre.** Signet Classics, 1982.

Orphaned and abused, Jane Eyre spends her early years at the Lowood School. Later, she leaves to become the governess at

Edward Rochester's estate, Thornfield. It is there that she finds herself in the midst of mysterious happenings: unexplained fires, maniacal laughter at midnight, and the eerie Grace Poole. When Jane falls in love with Mr. Rochester, she doubts that her love will ever be returned. But he does love the gentle Jane, and it isn't until their wedding day that the truth about the secrets of Thornfield is revealed. Fiction.

Brontë, Emily. **Wuthering Heights.** Signet Classics, 1973.

The windswept moors of England during the late eighteenth and early nineteenth centuries provide the backdrop for this tale of passion and violence. Through Mr. Lockwood and Nelly Dean, the narrators, we learn the story of Heathcliff, an orphan taken in by the Earnshaw family, and his great love for Catherine, the daughter in the household. Thwarted in his quest for Catherine, Heathcliff spends his life wreaking havoc on the lives of others. Only the love of the next generation can bring peace. Fiction.

Collins, Wilkie. **The Moonstone.** Signet Classics, 1984.

The moonstone in the title of this mystery novel is a rare yellow diamond complete with a curse and three Indian guardians who are sworn to protect it. The gem, stolen from a shrine in India, and its ill-fated owners produce a story told from several viewpoints. Originally published in 1868. Fiction.

Cooper, James Fenimore. **The Deerslayer; or, The First Warpath.** Signet Classics, 1980.

The Deerslayer, considered to be the first of Cooper's Leather-Stocking Tales, introduces us to the youthful Natty Bumpo and his adventures, conflicts, and romance as he enters manhood. Together with frontier scout Hurry Harry, his Indian friend Chingachgook, and the Hutter family, the Deerslayer travels through the frontier of New York state during the 1740s. Fiction.

Cooper, James Fenimore. **The Last of the Mohicans: A Narrative of 1757.** Signet Modern Classics, 1980.

Another of Cooper's Leather-Stocking Tales, this historical romance captures the excitement and adventure of the Indian wars of the 1750s. Cooper's story is filled with Indian lore and the further adventures of Natty Bumpo and his loyal Indian friend, Chingachgook. Fiction.

Crane, Stephen. **The Red Badge of Courage: An Episode of the American Civil War.** Avon Books, 1983.

Henry Fleming is only a boy when he says goodbye to his mother, leaves his farm, and goes off to fight in the Civil War. He is filled with dreams of the glories of battle, but what he finds instead are the realities of war, the horrors, and the high price a man must pay to receive his red badge of courage. Fiction.

Dana, Richard Henry, Jr. **Two Years before the Mast: A Personal Narrative.** Signet Classics, 1964.

Originally published in 1841, *Two Years before the Mast* is Richard Dana's travel record of the years 1834–1836, when he served as a sailor aboard the brig *Pilgrim*. Less an adventure than a realistic account, this work depicts the harsh life and injustices often faced by the American sailor in the nineteenth century. Nonfiction.

Darwin, Charles. **The Origin of Species.** Mentor Books, 1958.

Originally published in 1859, Charles Darwin's *Origin of Species* is still a magnificent testament to the importance of persistent observation and careful hypothesis. This classic recounts Darwin's revolutionary investigation into the science of evolution and reveals his genius, acute perception, and inspired vision of where humanity has been and where it is going. Nonfiction.

Defoe, Daniel. **Robinson Crusoe.** Signet Classics, 1980.

For years Robinson Crusoe longed for the sea and all of its excitement. However, one of his adventures has left him shipwrecked on what appears to be an uninhabited island off the coast of South America. We share his daily routine on the island until finally, after years of solitude, he meets his friend Friday. This is the story of their adventures, which take place in the late 1600s. Fiction.

Dickens, Charles. **The Life and Adventures of Nicholas Nickleby.** Signet Classics, 1982.

After his father's death, Nicholas Nickleby, his sister Kate, and his mother travel to London, where they hope to find comfort and assistance from Nicholas's Uncle Ralph. A series of adventures involves Nicholas in the plight of the unfortunate Smike; the heartless schoolmaster, Wackford Squeers; and the loyal helpmate, Newman Noggs. Together Smike, Nicholas, and Kate meet a cast of marvelous characters in this sentimental romance set in the early nineteenth century. Fiction.

Dickens, Charles. **A Tale of Two Cities.** Signet Classics, 1980.

Set in the midst of the French Revolution, *A Tale of Two Cities* introduces such memorable characters as Madame Defarge, Lucie Manette, and Sydney Carton. Dickens captures the terror and tumult of the times and, in addition, weaves a love story in which a man is willing to give up his life to ensure the happiness of a woman who loves another man. Fiction.

Doyle, Sir Arthur Conan. **The Adventures of the Speckled Band and Other Stories of Sherlock Holmes.** Signet Classics, 1965.

"The Adventures of the Speckled Band" is the first of twelve stories highlighting the shrewd detective Sherlock Holmes. Characterized by his cool analytical skills, his keen powers of observation, and his brilliant inductive reasoning, Holmes solves the seemingly unsolvable. In one story after another, the reader is invited to walk along with Holmes and his faithful companion Dr. Watson as the two discuss the clues of a case. Fiction.

Hardy, Thomas. **Tess of the D'Urbervilles: A Pure Woman.** Signet Classics, 1980.

In the hopes of helping her family by making a good marriage, Tess Durbeyfield is sent to meet her famous relatives, the D'Urbervilles. But instead of finding marriage, she is seduced and abandoned by Alec D'Urberville. Alone after her baby dies, Tess makes a new life for herself as a dairymaid. Eventually she marries Angel Clare who, after finding out about her past, also leaves her. A series of fateful incidents leads to her meeting Alec and later Angel for a final time. Hardy's novel, set in the nineteenth century, questions the part fate plays in the lives of his characters. Fiction.

Hugo, Victor. **The Hunchback of Notre Dame.** Signet Classics, 1964.

Quasimodo, the hunchback bell ringer of Notre Dame; Esmeralda, a beautiful gypsy; and Frollo, the evil archdeacon of Notre Dame; are the main characters in this historical romance set in fifteenth-century France. Grotesque because of his extreme physical ugliness, Quasimodo faces betrayal from Frollo but remembers a kindness once paid him by Esmeralda. As Frollo gives in to temptation, it falls to Quasimodo to protect Esmeralda from Frollo's evil. Fiction.

James, Henry. *The Turn of the Screw* **and Other Short Novels.** Signet Classics, 1980.

It doesn't take long for the new governess of the country estate at Bly to find out that strange happenings occur around her charges, ten-year-old Miles and eight-year-old Flora. Set in mid-nineteenth-century England, *The Turn of the Screw* revolves around the children and the ghosts with whom they communicate. Five other short novels equally as intriguing complete this collection. Fiction.

Lee, Harper. **To Kill a Mockingbird.** Warner Books, 1982.

Jem and Scout are raised by their father, Atticus Finch, in a dusty little town in the pre–civil rights South. Atticus's defense of a black man, Tom Robinson, in an alleged rape case creates a stir and teaches the children and the adults of the town a lesson in justice and common decency. Originally published in 1960. Fiction.

London, Jack. *The Call of the Wild* **and Selected Stories.** Signet Classics, 1971.

In *The Call of the Wild,* the wolflike Buck is stolen from his home in California, and then finds himself facing the harsh life of an Alaskan sled dog in the 1890s. From there he battles with Spitz, his mortal enemy, to become the lead dog and meets Joe Thornton, who turns out to be his friend for life. Several other adventure stories complete the collection. Fiction.

Orczy, Baroness. **The Scarlet Pimpernel.** Signet Classics, 1982.

In 1792, during France's Reign of Terror, aristocrats face certain death at the guillotine. Only one man is brave enough and clever enough to mastermind their escape and elude capture himself: the Scarlet Pimpernel. Interwoven amidst the mystery, adventure, and intrigue is the romantic tale of Sir Percy Blakeney and his love, Lady Marguerite. Fiction.

Orwell, George. **1984.** Signet Classics, 1983.

First published in 1949, *1984* is George Orwell's satire of a totalitarian society. Winston Smith, caught in the midst of mind control with Big Brother watching, works at the Ministry of Truth. Although love is forbidden in Oceania, he falls in love with Julia. In a world where "freedom is slavery" and "war is peace," Winston and Julia must face the consequences of forbidden intimacy. Fiction.

Poe, Edgar Allan. **The Fall of the House of Usher and Other Tales.** Signet Classics, 1980.

Fourteen gothic tales of terror are presented in this Poe collection. In "The Fall of the House of Usher," the narrator leads us to the family estate of Roderick Usher, where he meets Roderick's sister Madeline and senses the death and decay of the Usher family. What follows, as the morbid figure of Usher unfolds, is an eerie story of cataleptic seizures, premature entombment, and death. Fiction.

Porter, Jane (edited by Kate Douglas Wiggin and Nora A. Smith). **The Scottish Chiefs.** Illus. N. C. Wyeth. Charles Scribner's Sons, 1956.

It's the time of Scotland's defeat under King Edward of England, a time of bravery and love for God, country, and truth. Sir William Wallace, King Edward, and Ladies Marion, Helen, and Mary are some of the characters who bring excitement to these tales of love and adventure. Based on a true story. Fiction.

Shakespeare, William. **Four Great Comedies.** Signet Classics, 1982.

This collection of Shakespearean comedies includes *The Taming of the Shrew, A Midsummer Night's Dream, Twelfth Night,* and *The Tempest.* Readers will find the introduction very useful because it discusses the nature of Elizabethan comedy and includes brief analyses of the plays. Notes accompany each play, which make the unfamiliar Elizabethan language of the texts more accessible to the modern reader.

Shakespeare, William. **Four Great Tragedies: *Hamlet, Othello, King Lear, Macbeth*.** Signet Classics, 1982.

As in *Four Great Comedies,* this volume includes a brief analysis of each play and textual notes that clarify elements of the Elizabethan language.

Shelley, Mary; Bram Stoker; Robert Louis Stevenson. *Frankenstein; Dracula; Dr. Jekyll and Mr. Hyde.* Signet Classics, 1978.

The first novel in this collection of classic horror stories introduced by Stephen King is Mary Shelley's eighteenth-century gothic romance, *Frankenstein.* Here, Victor Frankenstein discovers the secret of creating life and fashions a creature out of materials collected from butchers and dissection labs. When the creature later turns into a monster, Victor must spend his final days in pursuit. *Dracula* is the nineteenth-century tale of a vampire who survives on the blood of his victims as he is hunted throughout dreary castles and open graves. The third novel, *Dr. Jekyll and Mr. Hyde,* is about a good man, Dr. Henry Jekyll, who is turned evil by a potent drug. When the evil Mr. Hyde's personality becomes stronger, Dr. Jekyll must find a way to destroy him. Fiction.

Spark, Muriel. **The Prime of Miss Jean Brodie.** Plume Books, 1984.

The setting is Scotland in the 1930s at the staid Marcia Blaine School for Girls. The colorful teacher, Jean Brodie, dominates this story of a woman "in her prime" and the influence she exerts on a group of young girls, each in her own way devoted to Miss Brodie. Before the story ends, Jean Brodie teaches her charges much about life, love, and passion. Yet one of them will betray her and cause her downfall. Fiction.

Stevenson, Robert Louis. *Kidnapped* **and** *Treasure Island.* Signet Classics, 1981.

In *Kidnapped,* Ebenezer Balfour, coveting his nephew David's inheritance, tricks the young man into boarding the ship *Covenant* where he becomes a prisoner bound for a life of slavery. But David escapes and, with a new friend, sets out on a series of adventures that take him across Scotland and finally home to assume his rightful place as heir to the Balfour fortune. *Treasure Island* is set in the eighteenth century on the high seas. Young Jim Hawkins signs on as a cabin boy aboard the *Hispaniola* and finds himself in the midst of a treasure hunt and a mutiny. When Jim fights the mutineers to protect his friends, he is wounded; but his life is saved by one of the book's most interesting characters, Long John Silver. Fiction.

Thoreau, Henry David. *Walden; or, Life in the Woods* **and** *On the Duty of Civil Disobedience.* Signet Classics, 1980.

Henry David Thoreau went to Walden Pond in the 1840s to live his life more fully. *Walden* is his naturalistic description of daily activities at the pond, of the animals there, and of his reflections on life. It is followed by "On the Duty of Civil Disobedience," Thoreau's essay on the need for a more effective government, in which he claims that principles are more important than the power of the majority, and that indeed, a person who is right constitutes a majority of one. Thoreau calls out to the people to follow their principles, even if they must face the possibility of going to jail— as he did. Some of Thoreau's poems are also included in this volume. Nonfiction.

Computers and Microprocessors

Babbie, Earl. **Apple Logo for Teachers.** Wadsworth, 1984.

Although this text was intended for teachers, it can serve as a valuable guide for anyone who wishes to learn the Logo programming language. With its easy-to-use spiral format and many illustrations and examples, the book can help even a beginner to create simple programs. Although the book was written specifically for Apple Logo, an appendix provides a comparison with other versions of the language. Nonfiction.

Berger, Phil. **The State-of-the-Art Robot Catalog.** Dodd, Mead, 1984.

Illustrated with photographs, this introductory guide is written in nontechnical language and covers all types of robots, from those that are little more than toys to those costing several hundred thousand dollars. The guide also traces the historical, mythological, literary, and engineering roots of robotics. It is especially valuable to those with more than an academic interest in this area, since it includes names, addresses, and phone numbers of manufacturers, as well as prices. Nonfiction.

Cassell, Dana K. **Making Money with Your Home Computer.** Dodd, Mead, 1984.

If you are thinking about using your home computer as part of a business venture, you'll be interested in the specific ideas Cassell has to offer. While the book does not provide computer programs, it does suggest possible money-making areas. Among the topics covered are word processing, contract programming, researching, and record keeping. Nonfiction.

Consumer Guide Editors, and Forest M. Mims III. **Easy-to-Understand Guide to Home Computers.** Signet Books, 1982.

This reference book explains what computers are, how they work, and the ways in which they can be useful. It includes a section on elementary programming in BASIC and a comparison of several of the more popular microcomputers on the market. Nonfiction.

Crichton, Michael. **Electronic Life: How to Think about Computers.** Alfred A. Knopf, 1983.

This book by a well-known novelist places computers in their proper place in society and in our lives. It explains in clear, simple English the things that those who want to understand computers without having to take them apart need to know. Nonfiction.

Curran, Susan, and Ray Curnow. **Overcoming Computer Illiteracy: A Friendly Introduction to Computers.** Penguin Books, 1984.

If you want to understand how a computer works and the role that it plays in modern society, you will find this book to be a comprehensive—though at times technical—introduction. The book makes use of extensive charts, drawings, and tables to illustrate key ideas and goes into more detail than do most introductory manuals. Nonfiction.

D'Ignazio, Fred. **Working Robots.** Lodestar Books, 1982.

Robots have come a long way from the mechanical creatures found in science fiction movies. This book examines the "brains" of the modern robots—actually computers—as well as the sensors that allow the machines to interact with the outside world. The author also discusses the future of the machines and provides insights for those who wish to consider entering the fascinating field of robotics. Nonfiction.

Dock, V. Thomas. **Structured COBOL: American National Standard.** 2d ed. West, 1984.

After a brief introduction to computers in general, this text describes the techniques for programming in COBOL, the most widely used computer language for business applications. Each chapter includes illustrations of COBOL syntax, questions for study, and sample programs. The principles of structured, top-down programming are stressed throughout the text, and flow charts are used frequently to illustrate program logic. Nonfiction.

Gilbert, Harry M., and Arthur I. Larky. **Practical Pascal.** South-Western, 1984.

Although Pascal is a relatively standardized programming language, there are some syntactic differences as one moves from one computer to another, and the text offers some suggestions on how to deal with those differences. Each chapter contains helpful examples and numerous Pascal programs. Though the text is designed for beginners, those with no previous experience may find some sections difficult. Nonfiction.

Goldstein, Larry Joel. **IBM PCjr: Introduction, BASIC Programming and Applications.** Robert J. Brady, 1984.

This introduction to one of the most popular personal computers, the IBM PCjr, covers everything a user will need to know to get the machine started and to begin writing programs in BASIC. Each point that the author makes is amply illustrated with sample programs. Questions to test the reader's understanding of the material appear at frequent intervals throughout the text. Nonfiction.

Goldstein, Larry Joel, and Martin Goldstein. **IBM PC: An Introduction to the Operating System, BASIC Programming and Applications.** Rev. ed. Brady Communications, 1984.

For first-time users of the IBM PC, this book can serve to replace or supplement the manual offered by the manufacturer. The text is written in a nontechnical, easy-to-read style, and the sections on BASIC programming include sample programs and questions to test the reader's understanding. The final chapters cover the use of the computer for file processing and producing graphics and sound. Nonfiction.

Herbert, Frank (with Max Barnard). **Without Me You're Nothing: The Essential Guide to Home Computers.** Pocket Books, 1981.

Now that small computers have become affordable and easy to use, you may be thinking of buying one. This book will take you through the process of buying and getting to know a home computer. The unique feature of the book is the "programap," which redesigns the traditional flowchart into a two-dimensional diagram using the common road map as a guide. Nonfiction.

Knight, David C. **Robotics: Past, Present, and Future.** William Morrow, 1983.

Robots are nothing new—they can be found in fiction dating back thousands of years. This book reviews the history of robots, discusses their place in society today, and makes some predictions about their future. Numerous black-and-white illustrations are provided. Nonfiction.

Krasnoff, Barbara. **Robots: Reel to Real.** Arco, 1982.

Once existing only in science fiction stories and movies, robots are now here for real. They can be found in industry, in space, and soon, perhaps, even in the home. This text provides descriptions and numerous pictures of all types of robots. The final chapter offers some thoughts on what robots will be doing in the future. Nonfiction.

Lien, David A. **Learning IBM BASIC.** CompuSoft, 1982.

A comprehensive introduction to programming the IBM Personal Computer, this book includes many examples to illustrate the programming techniques which the author covers. Lien writes in a humorous, informal style that makes the book easy and fun to read. Nonfiction.

Math, Irwin. **Bits and Pieces: Understanding and Building Computing Devices.** Charles Scribner's Sons, 1984.

This book is designed for those who have some experience in using computers and now want to know how they work. Through the use of clearly presented diagrams and illustrations, the author traces the development of analog and digital computers. He goes on to demonstrate how to build computer devices that actually work. Nonfiction.

Muller, Peter. **The Fast Track to the Top Jobs in Computer Careers.** Perigee Books, 1983.

This book can make it easier for you to select a career in the rapidly growing and diverse field of computers. It describes the range of employment opportunities and suggests guidelines for developing appropriate educational and other credentials for these jobs. One section forecasts the "hot fields" and speculates on what the job market will be like in ten years. Nonfiction.

Norton, Peter. **Inside the IBM PC: Access to Advanced Features and Programming.** Robert J. Brady, 1983.

For people who are already masters of the BASIC programming language and the operating system of the IBM PC, this book offers the opportunity to explore features and capabilities of the machine that are ignored by most introductory texts. The reading level and the level of computer knowledge needed to master this book are both quite high. Nonfiction.

Porter, Kent. **The New American Computer Dictionary.** Signet Books, 1983.

Those who have become interested in computers and wish to expand their reading to include computer books and journal articles will often come across terms that are unfamiliar. That is where this dictionary will come in handy; it is comprehensive and up-to-date and includes over two thousand terms, many with illustrations. Nonfiction.

Shane, June Grant. **Programming for Microcomputers: Apple II BASIC.** Houghton Mifflin, 1983.

This text, in an easy-to-use spiral format, is designed for those with no computer experience. It begins with an introduction to the Apple computer and covers programming in BASIC up to and including the use of two-dimensional arrays. Numerous examples and exercises are provided. Throughout the book, emphasis is placed on training the reader to plan carefully when developing programs. This text is appropriate only for those with access to an Apple computer. Nonfiction.

Wulforst, Harry. **Breakthrough to the Computer Age.** Charles Scribner's Sons, 1982.

Although today's computers are built by large corporations, that has not always been the case. The history of electronic computing includes the work of scientists, many working independently, who developed the concepts that led to the building of these remarkable machines. Today's modern computers would not exist if it had not been for the work of these little-known individuals. Nonfiction.

Death and Suicide

Asher, Sandy. **Missing Pieces.** Delacorte Press, 1984.

When Heather Connelly's father dies unexpectedly, Heather and her mother are left alone. As they search for the missing pieces in their lives, Mrs. Connelly begins a new job and Heather finds her first romance with Nicky Simpson. Through Nicky and his overwhelming family problems, Heather discovers new strength in herself and in her relationship with her mother. Fiction.

Bach, Alice. **Waiting for Johnny Miracle.** Bantam Books, 1982.

When seventeen-year-old Becky Maitland learns she has bone cancer, she experiences shock, then fear and denial. Her subsequent depression gives way to determination to fight against the inevitable. But she also has to deal with her healthy twin sister, her unaccepting boyfriend, and a mother who suffers in her own way. Fiction.

Biebel, David B. **Jonathan: You Left Too Soon.** Signet Books, 1982.

A father who loved his son more than life itself is forced to face the many emotions brought on by the boy's untimely death. Here David Biebel shares the inner turmoil and overpowering grief he experienced as Jonathan's condition worsened. In the end, the author demonstrates how one man overcame near self-destruction. Nonfiction.

Blume, Judy. **Tiger Eyes.** Laurel-Leaf Library, 1983.

Davey Wexler is stunned when her father is killed in a holdup. After her family moves to New Mexico to live with relatives, Davey watches her mother's emotional struggle and her little brother Jason's adjustment to a different life. Davey's feelings of anger, grief, and fear confuse her until she meets Wolf, a young man also facing a tragedy. Fiction.

Bond, Nancy. **A Place to Come Back To.** Margaret K. McElderry Books, 1984.

In the small New England town of Concord, Charlotte and her friend Oliver seem to live in two different worlds. Oliver lives with and cares for his eighty-two-year-old uncle, whose sudden death shatters Oliver's world. As Oliver tries to redirect himself, he struggles with his feelings for Charlotte, who shares with him the tender and difficult process of moving through adolescence and trying to understand life. Fiction.

Brancato, Robin F. **Facing Up.** Alfred A. Knopf, 1984.

Charming and popular Jep and his conservative best friend Dave do everything together. But Jep's gorgeous girlfriend soon has eyes for Dave. Dave measures his friendship with Jep and makes a decision—but he is too late. Fiction.

Branfield, John. **The Fox in Winter.** Margaret K. McElderry Books, 1982.

Fran finds herself becoming more and more involved in the life of ninety-year-old Tom Treloar. Soon they are tape-recording his memories as he explores the loss of his wife and the hardships of sickness and old age. When Tom passes away, Fran learns what losing someone you love is really all about. Fiction.

Calvert, Patricia. **The Stone Pony.** Charles Scribner's Sons, 1982.

Pretty and popular Ashley Cunningham's death brings mixed emotions to her younger sister, JoBeth. As JoBeth continues to research a stone pony bought by her father's museum, she tries to overcome her grief and guilt. But it is the time she spends with Ashley's horse and a young stable hand that helps JoBeth accept life's challenges. Fiction.

Cormier, Robert. **The Bumblebee Flies Anyway.** Pantheon Books, 1983.

Barney Snow lives in the Complex, an experimental hospital for terminally ill people. As he discovers the secret of the "bumblebee," his journey in and out of reality begins to make sense. Along with his hospital friends, Billy and Mazzo, sixteen-year-old Barney battles to take the final ride of his life. Fiction.

Girion, Barbara. **A Tangle of Roots.** Laurel-Leaf Library, 1981.

Called out of class, Beth Frankle learns of her mother's sudden death. As Beth tries to make sense of this loss, she also has to deal with her father's loneliness, her grandmother's Jewish customs, and her boyfriend's inability to understand the changes in her life. Fiction.

Hughes, Monica. **Hunter in the Dark.** Flare Books, 1984.

Mike Rankin, star basketball player, battles leukemia and overprotective parents as he tries to understand his illness. His close friend, Doug, helps him escape into the Canadian wilderness to stalk the elusive white-tailed deer. The unforgiving wilderness and a trophy-sized buck help Mike recognize that death is not necessarily an enemy. Fiction.

Klagsbrun, Francine. **Too Young to Die: Youth and Suicide.** Pocket Books, 1984.

With the suicide rate among teenagers continuing to rise, the information Klagsbrun presents is particularly useful for both teenagers and their parents. Divided into three parts, the book examines the realities of suicide (myths, motives, and methods), suggests ways to identify the signs that indicate someone is thinking about suicide, and looks at what individuals as well as society in general might do to prevent premature deaths. Nonfiction.

Mack, John E., and Holly Hickler. **Vivienne: The Life and Suicide of an Adolescent Girl.** Mentor Books, 1982.

Vivienne Loomis, a bright, attractive, fourteen-year-old girl, committed suicide. Using Vivienne's letters and diary entries, the authors write about her life and death. In the second half of the text, they offer the views of a clinician and a teacher on teenage suicide. Nonfiction.

Manes, Stephen. **I'll Live.** Flare Books, 1982.

Dylan Donaldson's father is the most courageous man Dylan has ever known. When it is announced that Mr. Donaldson may have only six months to live, Dylan is devastated. The only things that keep his hopes alive are his girlfriend Barbara and a special red-and-yellow hang glider—neither of which can save his father's life. Fiction.

Miklowitz, Gloria D. **Close to the Edge.** Laurel-Leaf Library, 1984.

Smart and popular in high school, Jennifer Hartley seems to have everything in the world—except inner strength. Her indifferent family, a suicidal friend, and her volunteer work with senior citizens begin to make Jennifer aware of the most precious gift one can possess. Jenny's struggles help her to understand the purpose of life. Fiction.

Oneal, Zibby. **A Formal Feeling.** Viking Press, 1982.

Sixteen-year-old Anne Cameron has isolated herself ever since her mother's death a year before. But when she leaves her life of seclusion at prep school to spend Christmas break at home, she must deal with her father's remarriage and with her brother, who thinks everything is fine. Anne sees her new world through a frosty pane of glass which never seems to clear—until she finally confronts her own feelings for herself and for her mother. Fiction.

Peck, Richard. **Close Enough to Touch.** Delacorte Press, 1983.

The sudden death of his sweetheart Dory leaves Matt Moran desolate, unable to cope with life at school or at home. To escape his pain, Matt tries alcohol and then long-distance running, but nothing helps much until he meets Margaret Chasen. Older than Matt, strong-willed Margaret puzzles and intrigues him. Eventually Matt must make a decision that reflects a sensitive young man's attitude toward the loss and renewal of love. Fiction.

Pfeffer, Susan Beth. **About David.** Dell, 1982.

When David kills his adoptive parents and then takes his own life, he leaves behind a lot of unanswered questions. His friend Lynn, through her journal and through the journal David left behind, tries to answer those questions. She thereby brings to light not only the feelings of a bright young man overcome with unrelenting pressures but also the resulting pain which the survivors experience in wondering what they could have done differently. Fiction.

Rinaldi, Ann. **Term Paper.** Bantam Books, 1983.

Six months after her father's death, Nicki is still guilt-ridden even though her father never really loved her and could not have cared less about her welfare. Nicki's brother Tony not only raised her, but now he is her English teacher. In class Tony gives Nicki the toughest assignment of all: she must write a term paper about her father's death. Fiction.

Smith, Robert Kimmel. **Jane's House.** Pocket Books, 1984.

After the death of their mother, seventeen-year-old Hilary and her younger brother Bobby cannot continue living their own lives because they are imprisoned by memories. Their troubles continue when their father brings his new wife into their home. Fiction.

Strasser, Todd. **Friends till the End.** Laurel-Leaf Library, 1982.

Senior David Gilbert has it all: he's a star soccer player, he's a member of the "in" crowd, and he's headed for college. But his life is changed when he befriends newcomer Howie Jamison, a victim of leukemia. In trying to deal with the ups and downs of Howie's illness, David must also handle his family's and girlfriend's questioning of his new goals and the new direction he sets for himself. Fiction.

Stretton, Barbara. **You Never Lose.** Alfred A. Knopf, 1982.

As Jim Halpert begins his senior year in high school, he learns that his father, who is also his football coach and hero, is dying of cancer. Jim's adjustments to his friends, who idolize his father, and to his girlfriend Mimi begin to confuse him. Then along comes new student, Agnes "Gus" Palmer, who helps Jim understand that "you never lose. But sometimes the clock runs out on you." Fiction.

Voigt, Cynthia. **Tell Me If the Lovers Are Losers.** Fawcett Juniper Books, 1983.

In this award-winning novel, sensible Ann, brash Niki, and serene Hildy enter their first year of college. The three roommates clash instantly, but eventually they work out their differences on the volleyball court and become friends. Then a sudden accident changes everything about school, sports, and their very lives. Fiction.

Wright, L. R. **The Favorite.** Pocket Books, 1983.

In this family story about love, death, and guilt, Margaret Kennedy, an aspiring actress, falls in love with and marries Ted Griffin, a young English professor. Marriage brings many changes in Margaret's life, but none is more significant than the birth of her daughter Sarah. For seventeen years Sarah is absolutely sure that she is her father's favorite, but when she herself falls in love, her father's affection seems to turn to resentment. Then the family learns that Ted is dying of cancer. Fiction.

Yolen, Jane. **The Stone Silenus.** Philomel Books, 1984.

Sixteen-year-old Melissa Standhold cannot recover from her poet-father's drowning death the year before. Her father's works dealt with fauns and satyrs, and when Melissa meets a strange boy who is faunlike in appearance and who resembles her father, she thinks her father may have returned. Fiction.

Drama and Theater

Anderson, Mary. **You Can't Get There from Here.** Atheneum, 1982.

Regina Whitehall, a senior from upper-middle-class Larchmont, runs away from her family problems—a recent divorce, a mother who has pursued a mid-life career, and an older brother far away at college. She joins the Studio, a live-in theater workshop, where the Stanislavski method is carried one step too far by the resident playwright and teacher, Adam Bentley. The glitter and glamour of New York theater life seem to be a haven from personal problems and confronting one's identity. But Regina soon finds out that she can't bury herself behind a stage persona and that her drama teacher is less than honest. Fiction.

Brown, John Russell. **Shakespeare and His Theatre.** Illus. David Gentleman. Lothrop, Lee and Shepard Books, 1982.

Based on scholarly research, *Shakespeare and His Theatre* is a lively, readable description of the English theater during Shakespeare's time. It covers the history of the Globe Theatre, its design, the actors who walked its stage, and the dramatic style of the plays that were featured there. Although the book focuses primarily on the Globe, some attention is also given to theaters at Whitehall and Blackfriars. Interesting and helpful illustrations are found on every page. Nonfiction.

Davis, Ossie. **Langston: A Play.** Delacorte Press, 1982.

This play about author Langston Hughes begins in a prologue where Hughes is asked just why writers write. The rest of the play unfolds in a series of discussions that explore the sources of a writer's inspiration. Dramatic tension created by means of flashbacks to incidents in Hughes's life prompts discussions of his development as a writer.

Fugard, Athol. **"Master Harold"** . . . **and the Boys.** Penguin Books, 1984.

Set in South Africa, *"Master Harold"* . . . *and the Boys* explores the experiences of a young white man who has been lovingly raised

71

by black servants. At the play's end, he finds that he must choose between accepting the societal demands of apartheid, which would require him to assert his superiority over his black friends and advisors, or to continue to live as an equal with the people who have given him both love and dignity.

Geiogamah, Hanay. **New Native American Drama: Three Plays.** University of Oklahoma Press, 1980.

The three plays in this volume are the first ever published by a Native American. In them Geiogamah attempts to portray the condition of Indians in contemporary America without the stereotyping that many writers have resorted to: *Foghorn* is about the prejudice that Native Americans suffer; *Body Indian* is about their mistreatment of one another; and *49* is a call for self-understanding and solidarity.

Greenberg, Jan W. **Theater Careers: A Comprehensive Guide to Non-Acting Careers in the Theater.** Holt, Rinehart and Winston, 1983.

This book provides a comprehensive description of backstage careers through a series of interviews and profiles of established professionals working in commercial, university, and amateur theaters. The careers discussed include those of general and company manager, managing director, director of audience development, vocal arranger, costume designer, lighting designer, and many more. Nonfiction.

Judy, Susan, and Stephen Judy. **Putting on a Play: A Guide to Writing and Producing Neighborhood Drama.** Charles Scribner's Sons, 1982.

Putting on a Play is an ideal resource book for teenagers who need or want to develop drama out of their own experiences and imaginations. Especially helpful chapters are "Plays without Scripts," "Creating Your Own Play," and "Reader's Theatre." Many outlines for improvisations are also included. Nonfiction.

Kamerman, Sylvia E., editor. **Space and Science Fiction Plays for Young People.** Plays, Inc., 1983.

This collection of easy-to-produce, one-act, royalty-free plays focuses on young people caught up in adventures that are filled with astronauts, extraterrestrials, robots, and outer-space travel. Each play includes production notes on sets, costumes, lighting, sound effects, and properties.

McCallum, Andrew. **Fun with Stagecraft.** Illus. E. J. O'Toole. Enslow, 1982.

A handy resource for students who want basic instruction in play production, these clearly written chapters offer easy-to-understand explanations of the elements of stagecraft including stage lighting, sound effects, makeup, costuming, and set design and construction. There are plenty of helpful photographs and illustrations. Nonfiction.

Miller, Jason. **That Championship Season.** Penguin Books, 1983.

Every year for twenty years, four of the starting five of a small-town Pennsylvania high school championship basketball team re-unite to praise their ailing coach and to remember old times. Under this gala and memory-ridden surface lie the tattered lives of the present: an inept mayor deluding himself about reelection, a construction worker who makes his fortune from corruption, a fatalistic drunkard, and a high school principal who disdains teachers. This adult drama forces the reader to accept the fact that old glory is worthless and going home again is a pitiful deception.

Murray, John. **Modern Monologues for Young People.** Plays, Inc., 1982.

This collection of twenty-four short, humorous, royalty-free dramatic monologues covers a range of subjects, from home computers and family squabbles to hospital visits. Each monologue includes a character sketch of the speaker and stage directions.

Nemiroff, Robert, editor. **Lorraine Hansberry: The Collected Last Plays.** Plume Books, 1983.

The last three plays written by Lorraine Hansberry, the author of *A Raisin in the Sun,* deal with group pride, frustrated ambition, and everyone's desire for freedom and control over his or her own life. *Les Blancs,* set in Africa, questions whether or not the liberation of oppressed peoples can ever be accomplished by anything other than a violent upheaval. *The Drinking Gourd* speaks of slavery, which dehumanizes and demoralizes both master and slave. And *What Use Are Flowers?* is a fantasy that questions the meaning of American civilization.

Nolan, Paul T. **Folk Tale Plays round the World.** Plays, Inc., 1982.

This collection presents a look into the folklore of both the Eastern and the Western world in short play format. The plays offer an understanding of basic customs and discuss themes which peoples of all lands have in common, such as clan rivalry and the need for goals and dreams.

O'Neal, Regina. **And Then the Harvest: Three Television Plays.** Broadside Press, 1974.

Each of these three television plays—*Walk a Tight Rope, And Then the Harvest,* and *Night Watch*—explores the impact of racial prejudice on black characters as they struggle to succeed in America during the turbulent period of the 1960s. Included is a short but handy chapter which explains screenwriting terms used throughout the teleplays, such as *covershot, dubbing,* and *stock shot.*

Shaffer, Peter. **Equus.** Penguin Books, 1984.

Alan Strang, a psychologically disturbed teenager, has blinded six horses with a spike, and Martin Dysart, a psychiatrist with his own problems, is determined to find the cause. Leading Alan along a meandering path through his troubled mind, Dysart reconstructs the boy's experiences and feelings that lead up to the horrifying climax.

Shakespeare, William. **Four Great Comedies.** Signet Classics, 1982.

This collection of Shakespearean comedies includes *The Taming of the Shrew, A Midsummer Night's Dream, Twelfth Night,* and *The Tempest.* Readers will find the introduction very useful because it discusses the nature of Elizabethan comedy and includes brief analyses of the plays. Notes accompany each play, which make the unfamiliar Elizabethan language of the texts more accessible to the modern reader.

Shakespeare, William. **Four Great Tragedies: *Hamlet, Othello, King Lear, Macbeth*.** Signet Classics, 1982.

As in *Four Great Comedies,* this volume includes a brief analysis of each play and textual notes that clarify elements of the Elizabethan language.

Stolzenberg, Mark. **Exploring Mime.** Photographs by Jim Moore. Sterling, 1983.

Step-by-step instructions in Stolzenberg's lively text will start you working in mime immediately. The book includes warm-up exercises, routines, makeup tips, and information on creating your own shows. Nonfiction.

Drugs and Alcohol

Califano, Joseph A., Jr. **The 1982 Report on Drug Abuse and Alcoholism.** Warner Books, 1982.

This comprehensive report to the governor of New York on the problems of drug abuse and alcoholism in America explains the nature of addiction to alcohol and heroin and notes present and past attitudes toward the problem, including changes that have occurred in governmental policies. The report further describes current services available to addicts and recommends a plan of action to stop the "senseless destruction of lives." Nonfiction.

Culin, Charlotte. **Cages of Glass, Flowers of Time.** Laurel-Leaf Library, 1983.

Deserted by her artist-father at thirteen, Clair is forced to live with her alcoholic and abusive mother. Clair is hungry, often bruised black and blue, and finds little solace in life. In spite of her loner attitude, two new friends try to help her deal with her problems. But Clair avoids telling them the truth about her situation, fearing her mother will send her off to an even worse fate—her abusive grandmother. Fiction.

Due, Linnea A. **High and Outside.** Bantam Books, 1982.

Seventeen-year-old Nikki is a fantastic student and the star of her high school softball team. She's such a "good" kid that no one questions her integrity or her actions. Even her parents excuse her "light social drinking" as normal for a modern teenager. But Nikki soon progresses from innocent tasting to drinking fifths of gin, which causes blackouts and serious impairment to her physical and intellectual abilities. The book explores Nikki's losses, depression, hysteria, and ultimate decision to help herself. Fiction.

Major, Kevin. **Far from Shore.** Laurel-Leaf Library, 1983.

Dependent on alcohol and afraid to admit it, fifteen-year-old Chris Slade manages to find trouble in his life at every turn. His home life is in a shambles; he has just failed his sophomore year; and summer work seems impossible to find. He starts to hang out with the wrong crowd until, when in a drunken, blacked-out state, he is accused of a crime he can't remember committing. Fiction.

Miner, Jane Claypool. **Alcohol and Teens.** Photographs by Maureen McNichols. JEM Books, 1984.

In sixty-three short pages, this book deals in a simple way with teenage use of alcohol—deciding whether or not to drink, coping with the pressure of family and friends, and, most importantly, recognizing the dangers of alcoholism, a problem which affects not only adults but also teenagers. Above all, the book helps readers to decide whether or not they or someone they know has a problem with alcohol, and it tells them where they can go for help. Nonfiction.

Neff, Pauline. **Tough Love: How Parents Can Deal with Drug Abuse.** Abingdon Press, 1982.

Tough Love describes a twelve-step program which directs parents and young people to responsible self-discipline and belief in a higher power as methods to deal with drug abuse. Seven families discuss in great depth how their children became involved in the Palmer Drug Abuse Program (PDAP) to beat their drug dependencies. Nonfiction.

Roth, Arthur. **The Caretaker.** Fawcett Juniper Books, 1981.

Because seventeen-year-old Mark Cooper and his family are in charge of the off-season maintenance of sumptuous summer cottages in the Hamptons, Mark has responsibilities for house "checkups" after school. But because of his father's drinking problem, Mark must assume his maintenance duties as well. Then, unexpectedly, Pam Sheehy, a sixteen-year-old runaway, is discovered hiding in one of the cottages. She and Mark are attracted to one another, and for Mark, being a caretaker means facing his own emotions as a son and as a young lover. Fiction.

Ryan, Jeanette Mines. **Reckless.** Flare Books, 1983.

Sixteen-year-old Jeannie Tanger, a good student, falls in love with Sam Bensen, a handsome boy from the wrong side of the tracks. Jean's family tries to keep her away from Sam, who drinks uncontrollably, drives fast, and manifests cruel moodiness. Jean resents the intrusion of these problems in her relationship with Sam but loves him anyway—until their relationship becomes so dangerous that it is almost too late to save either of them. Fiction.

Smith, Steven Phillip. **Firstborn.** Pocket Books, 1984.

Jake is forced to take on adult responsibilities in order to save his family from destruction when his recently divorced and very depressed mother falls victim to cocaine. Once he fully understands the situation, Jake takes charge of a plan to protect his mother from the dangerous characters who deal in drugs and to help her free herself from addiction. Based on the screenplay by Ron Koslow. Fiction.

Snyder, Anne. **First Step.** Signet Books, 1976.

Cindy Scott and her younger brother Brett live with a mother who has a serious drinking problem. At first, Cindy denies that her mother is an alcoholic, even though Cindy is ostracized at school and loses her best friend because of it. But the movies and a leading role in her high school's production of *Peter Pan* offer her a wonderful escape. So does the attention of Mitch, a handsome senior who introduces Cindy to an Alateen program where she finally learns how to cope with her mother's disease. Fiction.

Snyder, Anne. **My Name Is Davy—I'm an Alcoholic.** Signet Vista Books, 1978.

When he drinks, Davy finds life infinitely easier and more exciting, especially with Maxine, another heavy drinker who shares his wild parties and good times. Both attend AA meetings and try to confess that they are hooked. Maxine truly reforms, but Davy still doesn't think he has a problem. When he persuades Maxine to give in to alcohol "just once" at a beach party, the results are tragic. Fiction.

Weil, Andrew, and Winifred Rosen. **Chocolate to Morphine: Understanding Mind-Active Drugs.** Houghton Mifflin, 1983.

This definitive sourcebook on psychoactive drugs provides straightforward discussions of each substance's nature, how it is likely to affect the body, and the precautions necessary to limit potential harm. Nonfiction.

Easy Reading

Carlson, Dale. **The Frog People.** Illus. Michael Garland. Skinny Books, 1982.

A strange disease seems to be turning the residents of Proud Point into human-size frogs with green skins, bulging eyes, wide mouths, and webbed hands and feet. Ann Derry and her friend Dan race to discover the reason and a solution before everyone succumbs to the frightening transformation. Fiction.

Cohen, Daniel. **The Headless Roommate and Other Tales of Terror.** Illus. Peggy Brier. Bantam Books, 1982.

These nineteen tales are not new—some of them have been around for hundreds of years. But they are all part of urban folklore, those horror stories told around campfires or at slumber parties. Although the details may change with each telling, the stories always retain their blood and gore. Even the titles are frightening: "The Headless Roommate," "The Phantom Hitchhiker," and "The Moving Coffin" are just a few examples. Fiction.

Cohen, Daniel. **How to Test Your ESP.** Photographs by Joan Menschenfreund. Skinny Books, 1982.

Do you have ESP? Daniel Cohen gives the novice interested in extrasensory perception a bit of history about the subject, followed by several stories on clairvoyance, precognition, telepathy, and dreams. Included are a number of items which the reader can use to test his or her own ESP abilities. Nonfiction.

Cone, Molly. **Paul David Silverman Is a Father.** Photographs by Harold Roth. Skinny Books, 1983.

Paul David Silverman is sixteen and Cathy is a few months younger when they learn that they will be parents. Cathy, usually happy and always laughing, becomes sad and quiet. Paul David decides that he and Cathy should get married a little sooner than they had planned and that their marriage will be perfect. They will divide everything equally. But quickly they learn that there is one thing they cannot divide equally. Fiction.

Fortune, J. J. **Revenge in the Silent Tomb.** Laurel-Leaf Library, 1984.

Stephen suspects that there is something strange about his Uncle Richard. He never dreams, however, that Uncle Richard is a special agent who will suddenly whisk him off to a desert in North Africa. Stephen's escapade there is similar to a James Bond movie with all its tricks and hazards. The easy-to-read style propels the exciting adventure to a rapid conclusion. This story is the first in the Race against Time series. Fiction.

Giff, Patricia Reilly. **Suspect.** Illus. Stephen Marchesi. Skinny Books, 1982.

An icy night and a bus ride to a strange town begin the adventures of Paul Star, and lead to friendship, mystery, and murder. Although Paul is running from one problem, he finds himself in the middle of another—more dangerous than the one he has left behind. This whodunit keeps the reader guessing all the way. Fiction.

Gunning, Thomas G. **Amazing Escapes.** Dodd, Mead, 1984.

The title of this book gives the reader an indication of its content: nine true stories that portray the brave, dauntless lives of people escaping from danger to freedom. These action-packed dramas are told with exciting authenticity. Nonfiction.

Kelley, Leo P. **Alien Gold.** Illus. Cliff Spohn. Bantam Books, 1983.

Kinkaid, a falsely accused and convicted space commander; Karen, a knife-carrying kidnapper; Lor'l, a one-eyed friendly alien; and Zeno, a sharp-toothed angry alien; are prisoners on planet Earth. Adam Lane, founder of a new star, Alba, offers freedom and his spaceship to Kinkaid and the others if they will rescue Adam's kidnapped daughter Allison from the Albans. The crew experience many surprising adventures as they travel through space in the year 2183. Fiction.

Kelley, Leo P. **Night of Fire and Blood.** Illus. Ed Diffenderfer. Bantam Books, 1983.

Life is good for Marilyn: she is working, and she is in love. Then strange things begin to happen, and she realizes that someone is trying to hurt her. She can't understand what's going on until she reads *The Book of the Dead,* and then everything suddenly becomes clear. Fiction.

Knudson, R. R. **Speed.** Photographs by Linda Eber. Skinny Books, 1983.

Winning the Los Angeles City Track and Field Championship is important for the students of Watts High. Can a woman coach help? Ron, Luther, Hollywood, and Tyrone, members of the track team, are not sure. Coach Huey has proven that she can run, but can she teach them speed? And can running help Tyrone get over the pain of breaking up with his girlfriend? Coach Huey believes in the team; they only need to believe in themselves. Fiction.

McHargue, Georgess. **Meet the Vampire.** Illus. Stephen Gammell. Laurel-Leaf Library, 1983.

Here you'll read of vampires old and modern, east and west, horrible and more horrible, like Vlad the Impaler, the original Count Dracula. The last chapter provides possible explanations for vampires, and the book includes some gruesome black-and-white illustrations. Nonfiction.

McHargue, Georgess. **Meet the Werewolf.** Illus. Stephen Gammell. Laurel-Leaf Library, 1983.

Old tales and legends say that there are people who sometimes turn into wolves. The author uses case histories from around the world to support the existence of werewolves and tells you how to know a werewolf when you see one. Excellent illustrations. Nonfiction.

Nixon, Joan Lowery. **Days of Fear.** Photographs by Joan Menschen-freund. Skinny Books, 1983.

Life is going well for Eddie, Alma, and baby Paul, especially after an article appears in the newspaper concerning Eddie's success at work. Then one evening, Eddie's life is changed. He is robbed at gunpoint. Even though the bandit tries to hide his identity with a ski mask, Eddie recognizes him. The assailant is a fearful, mean person bent on terrorizing Eddie's neighborhood. What can Eddie do? What should he do? Fiction.

Otfinoski, Steven. **Village of Vampires.** Illus. Chris Kenyon. Bantam Books, 1982.

Dr. John Lawrence, his daughter Sandy, and Paul Ross, his young helper, find themselves in Taxacola, Mexico. They are seeking answers to the ancient problem of vampires and the mystery surrounding the animal and human inhabitants of this Mexican town. Fiction.

Platt, Kin. **The Ape inside Me.** Bantam Books, 1983.

Eddie Hill loses control easily. Kong—the voice inside him—is mean and nasty, urging him to strike out at the slightest provocation. But Eddie, at fifteen, is getting tired of hitting and being beaten by bigger kids. The trouble is that he doesn't know how to control Kong. Fiction.

Prager, Arthur, and Emily Prager. **World War II Resistance Stories.** Illus. Steven Assel. Laurel-Leaf Library, 1980.

These true stories of six brave patriots (both men and women) who fought in secret during World War II show the importance of undercover work. These resistance fighters' greatest desire was to help their country, but they were successful only because of the many everyday people who worked to help them accomplish their goals. Nonfiction.

Reuben, Liz. **Trading Secrets.** Photographs by Harold Roth. Laurel-Leaf Library, 1983.

In order to attract Danny's attention, Amy seeks the help of Jim, her best friend Carla's twin brother. This is the beginning of confusion, anger, and misunderstanding for all four individuals. Can they solve all their problems and still remain friends? Fiction.

Roy, Ron. **I Am a Thief.** Illus. Mel Williges. Unicorn Books, 1982.

Have you ever felt alone and outside of a group? If so, you can understand thirteen-year-old Brad's feelings. Because he's lonely, Brad is happy to become friends with the "supercool" Chet. When Brad becomes involved with Chet's shoplifting outfit, he realizes he's in with the wrong crowd, but he's not sure he can turn to his mother for help. Is conflict the price of friendship? Brad has to almost lose his life as a result of his involvement with Chet before he realizes how much his mother loves him. Fiction.

Sachs, Marilyn. **Beach Towels.** Illus. Jim Spence. Skinny Books, 1982.

Although Lore seems happy and carefree and Phil is lonely and depressed, they have something in common: each has a secret that needs to be told. This story of a teenage friendship that forms during a summer at the beach will leave lasting memories. Fiction.

Simon, Seymour. **Ghosts.** Illus. Stephen Gammell. Laurel-Leaf Library, 1984.

So you don't believe in ghosts? After reading these nine reports of poltergeists, ghostly hitchhikers, haunted houses, phantom dogs, and other unexplained phenomena, you may just change your mind. A title in the Eerie Series. Nonfiction.

Tregaskis, Richard. **Guadalcanal Diary.** Random House, 1984.

What is it like to be in the midst of an actual battle? Can the American army be successful when they are outnumbered and unfamiliar with the territory? These inquiries plagued journalist Richard Tregaskis during the battle of Guadalcanal. As an eye-witness to one of the most crucial battles of World War II, Tregaskis presents the drama of the operation with immediate excitement. First published in 1943. Nonfiction.

Weinberg, Larry. **The Hooded Avengers.** Photographs by Bill Cadge. Bantam Books, 1983.

In Ben's haste to become a real man, he is led into a world of stark reality—a world of cruelty, prejudice, and a secret order involving some of the most important people in a small town. The decision he must make to please and understand his cousin Willis is the most serious one he'll ever have to make. Fiction.

Education, Language, and Self-Improvement

Bear, John. **How to Get the Degree You Want: Bear's Guide to Non-Traditional College Degrees.** Ten Speed Press, 1982.

No matter what restrictions or limitations your life imposes, there is a way to get the degree you want painlessly. You just need to know where to go. Depending on the field and the type of degree you are seeking, you may never have to take a single traditional course. Nonfiction.

Birnbach, Lisa. **Lisa Birnbach's College Book.** Villard Books, 1984.

It's all here—from best to worst! Read everything imaginable about colleges and universities throughout the United States. Learn about dress codes, career choices, peer pressure, social scenes, dollars and cents, and nonsense happenings in the nation's best and worst institutions of higher learning. Nonfiction.

Booher, Dianna Daniels. **Help! We're Moving.** Julian Messner, 1983.

Moving is exciting and adventurous, but it is also traumatic and scary. It means leaving friends and familiar places and situations. But moving can also mean new opportunities, new friends and adventures, and new beginnings. With *Help! We're Moving,* coping with the transition from old to new is easier. Nonfiction.

Byrne, Josefa Heifetz (edited by Robert Byrne). **Mrs. Byrne's Dictionary of Unusual, Obscure, and Preposterous Words, Gathered from Numerous and Diverse Authoritative Sources.** Washington Square Press, 1984.

If you like the sound of words or enjoy knowing the meanings of uncommon words, this dictionary is for you. Where else can you find *giffgaff, fard, jupe, speigelschrift,* and *tesselated* in the same collection? The author's definitions are brief and concise, written to amuse and inform. From U.S. slang to foreign animals, this book gives you a new word for almost any occasion. Nonfiction.

Carlson, Dale, and Dan Fitzgibbon. **Manners That Matter: For People under Twenty-One.** E. P. Dutton, 1983.

This handy guide not only suggests proper etiquette for all social situations, but also includes several samples of useful business letters. It even tells you how to say no and how to accept no for an answer. Nonfiction.

Fields, Mike. **Getting It Together: The Black Man's Guide to Good Grooming and Fashion.** Photographs by Bert Andrews. Illus. Kenneth Hunter. Dodd, Mead, 1983.

As the first comprehensive guide to grooming and fashion for black men, this book treats all issues with finesse. Topics covered include body care and hygiene, hairstyling and conditioning, sports, diet, and choosing the appropriate fashion for any type of man, for any type of occasion, for any time of day or year. The fashion section is especially well illustrated, and the author interjects helpful hints from his own successful experience as a professional model. Nonfiction.

Fitzgibbon, Dan. **All about Your Money.** Illus. David Marshall. Atheneum, 1984.

Learn how to have common sense about dollars and cents. This book discusses the function and importance of money and how to manage personal finances, including such topics as saving, investing, checking accounts, credit cards, borrowing, and lending. Nonfiction.

Fixx, James F. **Games for the Superintelligent.** Warner Books, 1982.

Bored with television? These amazing math, logic, and word puzzles will snap you out of that TV trance and invade your mind for hours. These brain-teasers are unconditionally guaranteed to make you superintelligent if you aren't already—or to slowly drive you mad. Nonfiction.

Fixx, James F. **More Games for the Superintelligent.** Warner Books, 1982.

Puzzles and games can provide more pleasure than you can imagine, especially when you can solve them and your friends can't! Tease your brain and your friends' brains with fascinating, ingenious, and almost absurd perplexities. Answers are provided; you'll definitely need them. Nonfiction.

Fixx, James F. **Solve It!** Warner Books, 1983.

If you love to solve puzzles, you'll be mesmerized by this myriad of puzzles and riddles. Some are fun and unusual, while others are mind-boggling challenges even to the best of the problem solvers. You also have a slight edge: the answers are provided here. Here's a sample riddle: What word is spelled wrong in every dictionary? Nonfiction.

Fleming, Alice. **What to Say When You Don't Know What to Say.** Charles Scribner's Sons, 1982.

Learn how to talk your way through or out of any type of occasion, situation, calamity, or dilemma. The guide suggests how you can overcome shyness and tension no matter how awkward or unusual the situation. Nonfiction.

Gardner, John. **The Art of Fiction: Notes on Craft for Young Writers.** Alfred A. Knopf, 1984.

If you are eager to try your hand at fiction writing, you will find this book informative and helpful. Gardner explains that good fiction obeys laws and standards, and combines truth and interest. He helps you examine the intricacies of plot development, technique, and style. You are even given a selection of exercises to develop your writing skills. You'll sharpen your brain as well as your pencil. Nonfiction.

Gilbert, Sara. **How to Take Tests.** William Morrow, 1983.

Are you psyched about taking tests? Tests cause frustration, anxiety, and even anger, but there are ways you can relieve your uneasy feelings. Learn about more effective study methods, strategies, gimmicks, and hints that will increase your self-confidence and improve your test-taking ability. Nonfiction.

Gilbert, Sara. **What Happens in Therapy.** Lothrop, Lee and Shepard Books, 1982.

Psychotherapy is a treatment that helps you understand yourself better, particularly during an emotional crisis. Therapy can be a useful tool, but it demands trust and cooperation. It is not magic; it is an honest interaction between you and a skilled professional who can act as a needed support in your life. Gilbert explains clearly what goes on in different types of therapy and how to measure success. Nonfiction.

Goldstein, Sue. **The Underground Shopper's Guide to Off-Price Shopping.** Warner Books, 1984.

Are you looking for that special piece of merchandise at 80 percent off? This book is the best bargain in town. Every worthwhile discount outlet and bargain mail-order house is listed here with directions, merchandise descriptions, and prices. You can even join clubs that offer up to 90 percent discounts on anything and everything you could ever need or want. Nonfiction.

Gordon, Karen Elizabeth. **The Well-Tempered Sentence: A Punctuation Handbook for the Innocent, the Eager, and the Doomed.** Ticknor and Fields, 1983.

This guide to correct punctuation is a far cry from traditional grammar and usage handbooks. Although a separate chapter is devoted to each mark of punctuation, and the various related rules are clearly signaled, the true value of the book lies in its flavor: the many examples make delicious reading. In fact, one would probably be just as apt to read it for pleasure as to check on punctuation. Nonfiction.

Graham, Lawrence. **Conquering College Life: How to Be a Winner at College.** Washington Square Press, 1983.

This is probably the most candid and comprehensive manual you will ever read about attending and succeeding at college. There are strategies to attack every task and situation, to solve every problem, and to direct you in accomplishing almost any goal. Nonfiction.

Harrington, S. W. **How to Get Your Parents to Give You Everything You've Ever Wanted.** Atheneum, 1982.

Harrington combines common sense and psychology to create guidelines for young people who want more than what they have. Of course, with this advice you can learn the subtleties of charming persuasion and careful manipulation. Today, your parents; tomorrow, the world! Nonfiction.

Hirshon, Sheryl L. (with Judy Butler). **And Also Teach Them to Read (Y tambien enséñeles a leer).** Photographs by Larry Boyd. Lawrence Hill, 1983.

Sheryl Hirshon fought in Nicaragua's battle against illiteracy. In her gripping and sensitive story, she explains her crusade to teach rural teenagers how to read and how the social order was changed because of newly acquired literacy. Armed with pencils, notebooks, and rifles, soldiers of this crusade are still fighting. Nonfiction.

Houston, Jean. **The Possible Human: A Course in Extending Your Physical, Mental, and Creative Abilities.** J. P. Tarcher, 1982.

The human body and mind are capable of magnificent accomplishments. Through psychological and physical exercises, Houston shows how you can awaken your senses and release latent creative abilities. Nonfiction.

Leokum, Arkady. **The Curious Book.** Signet Books, 1978.

Experience the unusual and enjoy the absurd by investigating curious happenings and facts about people and places from all over the world. Packed with fascinating trivia and interesting illustrations, this book will give you hours of pleasure and many topics of conversation that will intrigue your friends. Nonfiction.

Lewis, Norman. **Instant Word Power.** Signet Books, 1982.

Would you like to improve your SAT scores and bedazzle your teachers with new and different words? Spice up your jargon with almost four hundred pages of interesting and unique ways to increase your vocabulary. Words are keys to understanding, success, and confidence. With practice and patience, you can be master of all you say. Nonfiction.

Marshall, Evan. **Eye Language: Understanding the Eloquent Eye.** New Trend Books, 1983.

People's eyes speak a language of their own to those who know how to read them. They can reveal various emotions, personality traits, and even the body's state of health. Included in this guide are photos of famous people and analyses of what their eyes tell us about them. Nonfiction.

Molloy, John T. **Dress for Success.** Warner Books, 1976.

How you look and, more importantly, how you dress can determine your chances for success in life. Fifteen years of research and interviews with thousands of professional men reveal the dos and don'ts of dressing to get that important job, to impress that special client, or to bedazzle that special person. Learn how to sell yourself with clothing and how to save money while creating your wardrobe. Nonfiction.

Rosenbaum, Alvin. **The Young People's Yellow Pages: A National Sourcebook for Youth.** Perigee Books, 1983.

This outstanding sourcebook contains factual information and references to directories on such subjects as success, sex, stress, drugs, nutrition, money, family problems, high school and college, community service, jobs and careers, runaways, health, religion, legal rights, and voting. Letting your fingers walk through these yellow pages is a real learning experience. Nonfiction.

Rydjord, John. **Indian Place-Names: Their Origin, Evolution, and Meanings, Collected in Kansas from the Siouan, Algonquian, Shoshonean, Caddoan, Iroquoian, and Other Tongues.** University of Oklahoma Press, 1982.

The author details how many political divisions and land features in Kansas came to have names which originated with Indian tribes living not only on the Great Plains but throughout much of our country. The chapters, organized by tribes or linguistic families, trace the evolution of the original Indian names to their present pronunciation and spelling. Nonfiction.

Schneider, Meg. **Romance! Can You Survive It? A Guide to Sticky Dating Situations.** Laurel-Leaf Library, 1984.

Problems of all sorts crop up once you begin to date—problems with the person you're dating, problems with other friends, and problems with parents. This guide offers sound advice on how to be sensitive to the needs of others while meeting your own needs. And it gives practical suggestions about what to say when you find yourself in predicaments you want to change. Nonfiction.

Sternberg, Patricia. **Speak to Me: How to Put Confidence in Your Conversation.** Lothrop, Lee and Shepard Books, 1984.

Learn how to turn effective listening into effective conversation. In order to be a good conversationalist you must listen creatively, ask open-ended questions, interpret and use body language, and practice. Sternberg explains how to put confidence into your conversation. Nonfiction.

Stewart, Marjabelle Young. **The Teen Girl's Guide to Social Success.** Signet Vista Books, 1982.

According to Stewart, social success during the teenage years depends on the particular social and personal style that a young woman develops. The author discusses such topics as groups, speech for all occasions, relationships with family and friends, etiquette, and money management. The guide is thorough, informative, and interesting. Nonfiction.

Ullyot, Joan L. **Running Free: A Guide for Women Runners and Their Friends.** Perigee Books, 1982.

This guide for women who like to run is a personal yet simple approach for beginners and marathoners alike. So that beginners can feel comfortable with its message, the book moves from a simple to a more complex understanding of running. The advice given here is encouraging, insightful, and beneficial. Nonfiction.

Vedral, Joyce L. **I Dare You: How to Use Psychology to Get What You Want out of Life.** Holt, Rinehart and Winston, 1983.

Dedicated to "all who want the best from life and are willing to take a chance," this book explains how you can get much more out of life if you set goals, plan strategies, and learn the psychology of getting what you want. The author explains how you can learn to be in control of your actions, not a victim of them, and learn to be honest about yourself, your abilities, your weaknesses, and your strengths. Nonfiction.

Wallach, Janet. **Working Wardrobe: Affordable Clothes That Work for You.** Illus. Christine Turner. Warner Books, 1982.

The Capsule Concept shows discerning and sensible young women how to plan and acquire an attractive, versatile, and affordable wardrobe. Mixing and matching, color coordinating, and careful selection can outfit you in any look for any occasion, dressy or casual. Wallach shows how you can make your wardrobe work for you. Nonfiction.

Essays

Anderson, Dave, editor. **The Red Smith Reader.** Random House, 1982.

In the first autobiographical piece included here, Smith admits that he had a lot of writing heroes and learned from all of them, mostly through a process of shameless imitation. Now Smith himself, who died in 1982, has become a model for anyone who cares about capturing the frantic and poignant moments of sports through carefully honed reporting. The reader of this collection will be able to go from season to season and from the Olympics to solitary fishing because Red Smith felt that sports were an important part of being human and that they deserved to be described in carefully crafted prose. Nonfiction.

Buchwald, Art. **While Reagan Slept.** G. P. Putnam's Sons, 1983.

Ronald Reagan's America is the subject of this topical and entirely partisan collection of essays. Buchwald's humorous attacks move from subtle satire to forthright bludgeoning. The book offers a hard-hitting and very personal perspective on our fortieth president's personality and policies. Nonfiction.

Calder, Nigel. **1984 and Beyond.** Penguin Books, 1984.

Nigel Calder brought together a symposium in 1964 on the topic "The World in 1984." Now that 1984 has come and gone, Calder has enlisted the aid of a supercomputer named O'Brien to help him review predictions and begin the process of hailing the advent of 2004 in a series of lively and provocative dialogues. Nonfiction.

Downs, Robert B. **Books That Changed the World.** Rev. ed. Mentor Books, 1983.

Beginning with the Bible, Downs traces the course of Western history by examining the greatest ideas published in both the humanities and the sciences. Several chapters are devoted to the contributions of the ancient Greeks and Romans, but more modern authors like Mary Wollstonecraft *(Vindication of the Rights of Women)*, Karl Marx *(Das Kapital)*, Charles Darwin *(Origin of Species)*, and Albert Einstein *(Relativity, the Special and General Theories)* are featured, too. The most recent work included is Rachel Carson's *Silent Spring*, her 1962 discussion of environmental pollution caused by pesticides. *Books That Changed the World* was originally published in 1956. Nonfiction.

Freilich, Morris, editor. **The Pleasures of Anthropology.** Mentor Books, 1983.

This collection of twenty-seven essays written by persons in anthropology or closely related fields is divided into eight sections dealing with such topics as fieldwork, reconstructing the past, sex and sex roles, culture, religion, politics, law, and war. The selections vary from popular to scholarly in style, and the book is of value either as a reference tool or for general reading. Nonfiction.

Greene, Bob. **American Beat.** Penguin Books, 1984.

If you really want to learn how to write, there is no better way to do it, certainly no more enjoyable way to do it, than to read Bob Greene's short pieces on everything from an interview with Nixon to an account of an abortion. Greene is a master at investing his writing with sharp emotional edges through the use of nuance. Nonfiction.

Grizzard, Lewis. **Kathy Sue Loudermilk, I Love You.** Warner Books, 1984.

Grizzard spins tales of the South with an obvious love for the Georgian twang, a hankering to explain down-home traditions, and an admiration for the Confederate disposition. All three come alive in this hilarious series of essays which depict the real South. Nonfiction.

Kael, Pauline. **Taking It All In.** William Abrahams Books, 1984.

Film critic for *The New Yorker,* Pauline Kael has been an authoritative voice for movie fans for many years. In this, her seventh collection of film reviews, Kael displays her insightful and witty opinions on dozens of recent films, including *Chariots of Fire, The Blues Brothers, Tex, The Road Warrior, Ordinary People, E.T., Fanny and Alexander, Sophie's Choice,* and *Fast Times at Ridgemont High.* Nonfiction.

Pizer, Vernon. **Eat the Grapes Downward: An Uninhibited Romp through the Surprising World of Food.** Dodd, Mead, 1983.

Delving into this book is as rewarding as a sampling of the culinary delights it describes. Offbeat, full of enriching tangents, this is a history of food and its improbable combinations and permutations written with wry humor and appetite-arousing sincerity. Nonfiction.

Powers, Thomas. **Thinking about the Next War.** Mentor Books, 1983.

Any thoughtful discussion of nuclear war will be enriched by the reading of Powers's collection of very articulate essays. He covers topics as diverse as "What to Tell the Kids" and "Crossing the Nuclear Threshold" in clear, graphic prose as he tries to educate readers about the realities of conflict in the 1980s. Nonfiction.

Rodriguez, Richard. **Hunger of Memory: The Education of Richard Rodriguez.** Bantam Books, 1983.

This collection of autobiographical essays covers a myriad of themes as Richard Rodriguez describes his growth from a little boy who enters school barely able to speak English to a man who achieves academic success with his work at the British Museum. Throughout the essays Rodriguez discusses the importance of language and the ways in which his assimilation into an English-speaking world has altered his life. His views on bilingual education in America are controversial and thought-provoking. Nonfiction.

Rooney, Andrew A. **A Few Minutes with Andy Rooney.** Warner Books, 1982.

Andy Rooney's book is a compilation of light and humorous yet sophisticated essays on everyday experiences shared by us all. Rooney has a comment on everything from the way we choose the soap we buy to the way we answer the telephone. His work is the short-essay version of the satire that is evident in his segment of "Sixty Minutes." Nonfiction.

Rooney, Andrew A. **And More by Andy Rooney.** Warner Books, 1983.

This is Rooney's second book of humorous essays on the human condition in America. Whether the author is commenting on old friends or the weather, sophisticated readers will find in every essay a fresh perspective on their own experiences. Nonfiction.

Royko, Mike. **Sez Who? Sez Me.** Warner Books, 1983.

This collection of short essays covers the range of Royko's concerns—which is considerable. Here he reflects on topics from "The

Great Fish, the Bullhead" to "How to Insult a Norwegian" in the style which has made him a journalistic institution in Chicago. Nonfiction.

Shanks, Ann Zane. **Busted Lives: Dialogues with Kids in Jail.** Photographs by author. Delacorte Press, 1982.

Thirteen young people reflect, from prison, on their families, friends, and choices, with a cross sampling of professionals adding illuminating commentary. The narratives, perfectly complemented by the stark images of the author's photographs, are bleak and candid. Nonfiction.

Shapiro, James E. **Meditations from the Breakdown Lane: Running across America.** Houghton Mifflin, 1983.

Though not the first person to do so, Jim Shapiro ran—alone— the three thousand miles from San Francisco to New York City during the summer of 1980. In telling the story of his run, he explores the essence of the nation as well as his own feelings about his lonely and sometimes painful effort. One reviewer called this book "*Walden Pond* on foot"; another named it "Zen and the art of psychomotor maintenance." Shapiro himself says he was merely "trying to learn how to wake up." Nonfiction.

Siner, Howard, editor. **Sports Classics: American Writers Choose Their Best.** Coward-McCann, 1983.

In this splendid collection of sports writing, Siner has brought together some of the best examples of how journalism enhances victory and defeat in covering athletic competition. Included are pieces from the *New York Post, The Saturday Evening Post, Sports Illustrated, Esquire,* and *The New Yorker.* Nonfiction.

Smith, Red. **To Absent Friends.** Plume Books, 1983.

There are 182 tributes in this collection, and every one of them immortalizes both its subject and its creator. Among the great sports figures described here are the well-known Vince Lombardi, Jim Thorpe, Babe Ruth, and Joe Louis, as well as lesser-known figures such as Clark Daniel Shaughnessy, Chalky Wright, and Joe Liebling. Smith's compassion and humor grace every page. Nonfiction.

Steinem, Gloria. **Outrageous Acts and Everyday Rebellions.** Plume Books, 1983.

In this collection Steinem unites many of her classic pieces into a continuum which traces the growth of consciousness—hers and ours. Some of the pieces are funny, all are moving, and in total they become authentic social history which carries a mandate for change and justice. Nonfiction.

Thomas, Lewis. **Late Night Thoughts on Listening to Mahler's Ninth Symphony.** Viking Press, 1983.

Style and intelligence mark this newest collection of essays by the award-winning Thomas on subjects as diverse as altruism, alchemy, and the Pentagon; the title of the work is taken from one of the essays. The style seems effortless and almost conversational, beguiling and amusing. Nonfiction.

Thompson, Hunter S. **The Great Shark Hunt: Strange Tales from a Strange Time.** Warner Books, 1982.

Thompson is a practitioner of "new journalism," and his prose is biting, satirical, and profane. Nevertheless, this collection of essays contains some of the most acute political reporting available, particularly on the McGovern campaign and on Watergate. Nonfiction.

Thoreau, Henry David. *Walden; or, Life in the Woods* **and** *On the Duty of Civil Disobedience.* Signet Classics, 1980.

Henry David Thoreau went to Walden Pond in the 1840s to live his life more fully. *Walden* is his naturalistic description of daily activities at the pond, of the animals there, and of his reflections on life. It is followed by "On the Duty of Civil Disobedience," Thoreau's essay on the need for a more effective government, in which he claims that principles are more important than the power of the majority, and that indeed, a person who is right constitutes a majority of one. Thoreau calls out to the people to follow their principles, even if they must face the possibility of going to jail— as he did. Some of Thoreau's poems are also included in this volume. Nonfiction.

Young, Louise B. **The Blue Planet.** Illus. Jennifer Dewey. Meridian Books, 1984.

In an artistic combination of fact, personal observation, and illustration, Young paints an elegant, almost magical picture of our planet. Its creation, its metamorphosis, its mysteries, its secrets, its evolution, and its future tantalize and fascinate. Nonfiction.

Ethnic Experiences

Anaya, Rudolfo A. **Heart of Aztlan.** Illus. Morton Levin. Editorial Justa, 1982.

This novel depicts the life of the Chávez family and their move from the security of their familiar land to the unknown city where their life-style changes drastically. The struggle for Roberto, Benjie, Jason, Ana, and Juanita to find their identities in a new society yet hold to their culture results in dramatic consequences. Fiction.

Angelou, Maya. **Shaker, Why Don't You Sing?** Random House, 1983.

Best known for her series of autobiographical works, especially *I Know Why the Caged Bird Sings,* which tells of her experiences as a black child in Arkansas and St. Louis, Angelou is also a talented poet. Sometimes dramatic and sometimes playful, her poems speak of love and parting, of Saturday night partying and the smells and sounds of Southern cities, of freedom and shattered dreams.

Asher, Sandy. **Daughters of the Law.** Laurel-Leaf Library, 1983.

Pretending to be part of Denise's family makes life more bearable for Ruth. Since her father's death, Ruth's mother has grown even more silent. Ruth knows that the silence has something to do with the dark, secret years spent in a Nazi concentration camp, but no one will talk to her about it. Learning the truth of her family's past helps Ruth make an important decision about her future. Fiction.

Bierhorst, John, editor. **The Sacred Path: Spells, Prayers and Power Songs of the American Indians.** William Morrow, 1983.

Beautifully laid out and thematically arranged, this collection includes chants and prayers about birth, love, hunting, farming, and death. Some typical examples are the exultant "Prayer of an Old Man at a Young Man's Change of Name" and the haunting "Prayer to the Ghost." Nonfiction.

Gaines, Ernest J. **A Gathering of Old Men.** Alfred A. Knopf, 1983.

Several old black men from the backwoods of Lousiana are given a second chance to prove their manhood. In flashbacks, events happen that allow them to establish a legacy for future generations. This story also portrays the determination of a young white woman to uphold justice however she can. Fiction.

Garver, Susan, and Paula McGuire. **Coming to North America: From Mexico, Cuba, and Puerto Rico.** Laurel-Leaf Library, 1984.

About fifteen million Hispanics live in the United States, the fifth largest population of Spanish-speaking people in the world. This book describes the history and life-styles of the three major groups: the Mexicans, the Cubans, and the Puerto Ricans. These peoples are different in many ways, but they all have shared the experience of rejection and discrimination in their chosen home. This sympathetic, easy-to-read account is made vivid with numerous quotes from contemporary letters and magazines and with interesting illustrations. Nonfiction.

Giovanni, Nikki. **Black Feeling, Black Talk.** 3d ed. Broadside Press, 1983.

Giovanni's gifts grace this collection of twenty-six poems which range over different facets of black experience. The imagery, language, and tone of these poems pierce the reader's sensibilities whether Giovanni is speaking about a relaxing evening at home with a friend or screaming in anger about revenge against oppression.

Hansen, Joyce. **Home Boy.** Clarion Books, 1982.

Marcus has come from a Caribbean island to the South Bronx. At first, his need to prove himself gets him into trouble again and again and earns him the nickname "Jamaica." With the help of Cassandra, a girl he meets in school, Marcus begins to straighten out his life—only to have things turn bad again when he plunges a knife into a boy who has been taunting him. Fiction.

Harris, Marilyn. **Hatter Fox.** Ballantine Books, 1983.

Hatter Fox, a seventeen-year-old Navajo girl, hates and is hated by the white community of Santa Fe, New Mexico, where she lives. Her young life is marred by involvement with drugs, prostitution, and crime, and Dr. Teague Summer is the only person who wants to help her. He tries to keep Hatter out of the mental institution, but he seems doomed to fail because, as he says, "there is something wrong in the world." Fiction.

Haskins, James. **The Guardian Angels.** Enslow, 1983.

This brief book relates the origins and development of the Guardian Angels, a volunteer organization that tries to prevent crime in the streets and the subways. Both positive and negative viewpoints are given on the multiethnic group which began in New York City in 1979. Nonfiction.

Hijuelos, Oscar. **Our House in the Last World.** Persea Books, 1983.

Alejo and Mercedes Santinio immigrated to the United States, their "last world," from Cuba in 1943. Their sons, Horacio and Hector, are influenced by another "last world"—their parents' sensuous, beautiful homeland, which is molding them as it did their parents. Hector's account of the Santinio family, beginning with his parents' courtship and ending shortly after his father's death, reveals the intimate thoughts of his family members and offers a realistic portrayal of immigrant life in America. Fiction.

Lester, Julius. **This Strange New Feeling.** Dial Press, 1982.

Based on true accounts, this set of three short stories revolves around three couples: Ras and Sally, Forrest and Maria, and William and Ellen. All have been slaves their entire lives, and all slowly taste a morsel of freedom with love as the motivating force. Fiction.

Morrison, Toni. **Tar Baby.** Signet Books, 1983.

Tar Baby is a complex novel that intermingles black males and females into the sophisticated lives of white millionaires. This contemporary story also gives the reader the opportunity to move geographically from Manhattan Island to the Southern plains and to a beautiful Caribbean island as the characters experience love, hope, excitement, sex, and adventure. Fiction.

Ruby, Lois. **Two Truths in My Pocket.** Viking Press, 1982.

This collection of six stories of adolescence as seen through the eyes of Jewish teenagers deals with love, family, friendship, and the complexity of being Jewish in today's world. Some sample titles are "Inscriptions on Stone," which tells the story of Micah's movement away from tradition, and "Strangers in the Land of Egypt," which is about Barry and Esther's struggle with the problems of interracial dating. Fiction.

Santiago, Danny. **Famous All Over Town.** Plume Books, 1984.

For fourteen-year-old Rudy "Chato" Madina, school is a bore. Street life, on the other hand, is exciting, though often dangerous. Chato's father is a tyrant but a hard worker who provides material comforts for his impoverished family; his mother is tolerant but on the verge of rebelling against her husband's indiscretions. Life in the Los Angeles barrio could destroy this young Chicano or help him rise above his peers. Chato's defiant behavior is both humorous and sad, and the outcome of his actions is uncertain. Fiction.

Stucky, Solomon. **For Conscience' Sake.** Herald Press, 1983.

Michael, a Mennonite, believes as his father and grandfather before him that war and killing are wrong. The government calls him a conscientious objector because he is against its policy in Vietnam. Michael is the product of his heritage, and the story of his ancestors helps him to stand by his convictions. Fiction.

Terry, Wallace. **Bloods: An Oral History of the Vietnam War by Black Veterans.** Random House, 1984.

In the years immediately after the Vietnam War, very little was written about the soldiers' experiences. Now, in the outpouring of stories about that confusing war comes *Bloods,* an account from twenty black veterans. In their own sensitive yet brutal, honest, and insightful words, we can see and feel the uncertainty, the fear, the pride, the horror, and the heroism of their experiences, along with the racial battles that plagued them in and out of the military. Nonfiction.

Thomas, Joyce Carol. **Marked by Fire.** Flare Books, 1982.

Abyssinia Jackson is born in an Oklahoma cotton field in the wake of a tornado that tears her family apart. But Abby's spirit is strong, and as she grows up, she learns the secrets of folk medicine from the healer Mother Barker and becomes a positive force in her community. The events are realistic and uncensored, but the language flows like lyrics to a song. Fiction.

Walker, Alice. **The Color Purple.** Washington Square Press, 1983.

In a series of letters to God and her sister Nettie, Celie tells the story of her checkered life—from the horrifying details of childhood sexual abuse to glorious material success as an adult. Sparing no details, Walker's Pulitzer Prize-winning novel vividly etches into the reader's experience what it means to be poor, to be abused, to be challenged, and to find self-worth. Fiction.

Wallin, Luke. **In the Shadow of the Wind.** Bradbury Press, 1984.

A sort of Indian-and-Anglo *Romeo and Juliet* set on the Georgia frontier in 1835, this novel explores the love between Pine Basket, a Creek Indian, and Caleb McElroy, the son of white settlers. Caleb is cast against his own people as the whites slowly but resolutely destroy the Indians' forests and sources of sustenance, finally forcing them along the Trail of Tears to distant Oklahoma. Amidst the fighting and the fear, the two sixteen-year-olds uncover the differences as well as the similarities between their peoples. Fiction.

Wartski, Maureen Crane. **A Long Way from Home.** Signet Vista Books, 1982.

In Vietnam, fifteen-year-old Kien had avoided school and learning, but now in America he has to deal with all sorts of uncomfortable things, including the school bully. Although his adopted sister and brother feel comfortable in their new home, Kien decides that his only hope is to run away to Travor, where there are other refugees. But once there, he finds himself caught in a battle between the immigrants and the local people who resent their presence. Why did he leave one place of hate and violence for another? Fiction.

Wonger, B. **Walg: A Novel of Australia.** Dodd, Mead, 1983.

In Australia the aborigines believe that the land is an extension of a person's body and soul. If the land is disturbed, life will cease. And the land is now being ravaged by whites in their search for uranium. Across this same land, Djumala and her unborn child travel back to her tribal country—her walg, or womb. She wishes to learn the secrets of motherhood that will prolong the life of her tribe. Fiction.

Family Conflicts

Adler, C. S. In Our House Scott Is My Brother. Bantam Books, 1982.

Thirteen-year-old Jodi feels that she and her dad do all right for themselves. She cannot help feeling jealous of her new stepmother, Donna. Donna wants to change everything—including Jodi's appearance, her room, and her diet. And Donna's son Scott is another change that Jodi finds hard to accept. Fiction.

Angell, Judie. Dear Lola; or, How to Build Your Own Family. Laurel-Leaf Library, 1982.

No one knows that Lola, of the syndicated advice column "Dear Lola," is really eighteen-year-old Arthur Beniker. This is an unusual job for a teenager, but it allows Arthur to sneak his "family" out of St. Theresa's Home and provide a place for all of them. Will the neighbors grow suspicious when they discover there are no adults living next door? Fiction.

Angell, Judie. What's Best for You. Laurel-Leaf Library, 1983.

Lee is angry that her parents seem to think they always know what is best. At fifteen, Lee knows a few things, too. She knows that she wants to live with her dad, that she fights too often with her mother, and that her sister Allison is too serious and sad. Divorce touches everyone in the family, and no one can have all the answers. Fiction.

Arrick, Fran. Nice Girl from Good Home. Bradbury Press, 1984.

When Dory's father loses his job and the family is forced to change their life-style and sell their home, everyone suffers. Dory chooses to hang around with the wrong group of friends and gets involved in a bomb threat at school. She feels so alone that she cannot see the disturbing change taking place in her mother. Fiction.

Asher, Sandy. Daughters of the Law. Laurel-Leaf Library, 1983.

Pretending to be part of Denise's family makes life more bearable for Ruth. Since her father's death, Ruth's mother has grown even more silent. Ruth knows that it has something to do with the dark, secret years spent in a Nazi concentration camp, but no one will talk to her about it. Learning the truth of her family's past helps Ruth make an important decision about her future. Fiction.

Bartholomew, Barbara. **Anne and Jay.** Signet Vista Books, 1982.

While their parents are away for a long-deserved vacation, the three Hollis sisters are on their own. Fifteen-year-old Anne, considered the baby, longs to prove herself, but she is not willing to use her new friendship with Jay to influence Jay's father. When an accident occurs, Anne suddenly has the opportunity to take charge. Fiction.

Berger, Fredericka. **Nuisance.** William Morrow, 1983.

Julie feels that she is a bother to her mother and new stepfather. She's having trouble adjusting to a different school and neighborhood, but her new friend Cal tries to help with his magical stories and quiet support. At Cal's urging, Julie decides to speak up for herself when it looks like her cat might be sent away to the county home. Fiction.

Boissard, Janine (translated by Elizabeth Walter). **A Matter of Feeling.** Fawcett Juniper Books, 1981.

Translated from the French, this is a sensitive story of four sisters growing up in a Parisian family and becoming young women, each with her own identity, in the tradition of *Little Women*. The central figure is Pauline, who discovers the bittersweet joy of first love with an older man, Pierre. He is willing to leave his wife and child for her. Is Pauline willing to allow this to happen? Fiction.

Bridges, Sue Ellen. **Notes for Another Life.** Bantam Books, 1982.

The summer Oren turns fourteen is a season of change for her and her brother Kevin. They realize then that their father might never be home for good from the mental hospital where they visit him. After their mother decides to get a divorce and move to Chicago alone, Oren and Kevin draw strength from their Grandmother Bliss, whose wisdom and music help them to accept the changes. Fiction.

Bunn, Scott. **Just Hold On.** Delacorte Press, 1982.

Charlotte Maag and Steven Herndon are two very lonely high school students. Each has few friends, a deeply troubled home life, and no one to talk to. As their relationship develops, they find comfort in each other even though they still cannot bring themselves to reveal their innermost secrets. In the process of finding love, they transform not only their lives but the lives of those around them as well. Fiction.

Burchard, Peter. **Sea Change.** Farrar, Straus and Giroux, 1984.

This intriguing three-part novel deals with special mother-daughter relationships over three generations. The universal episodes which bind mothers and their daughters together are examined in separate stories, each focusing on its own problems. Alice, Anne, and Lisa share their pain and happiness as they grow into adults and have daughters of their own. Fiction.

Byrd, Elizabeth. **I'll Get By.** Fawcett Juniper Books, 1982.

It is New York City during the Prohibition era, and there is a lot happening in Julie's life. At her fancy experimental school, she has plenty of friends, interesting acting classes, and an "older man" interested in taking her out. But she doesn't have her dashing father at home, and that is what she wants most of all. Should she grow up and resign herself to never seeing him again as her mother has done? Originally published in 1928. Fiction.

Calvert, Patricia. **The Hour of the Wolf.** Charles Scribner's Sons, 1983.

Jake Matthieson's father sends his "loner" son from their home in Minnesota to live with friends in Alaska with the hope that the wayward boy will become someone the whole family can be proud of. When Jake and his friend Danny Yumart, a native Alaskan, join a thirteen-hundred-mile dogsled race from Anchorage to Nome, Jake has an adventure that does, indeed, change him forever. Fiction.

Carter, Alden R. **Growing Season.** Coward-McCann, 1984.

Seventeen-year-old Rick is devastated when his family decides to move to a farm before he graduates from high school. Although Rick goes with his family out of a sense of obligation, once he is there he finds that life on a farm has something very valuable to teach him. Fiction.

Cavanna, Betty. **Storm in Her Heart.** Hiway Books, 1983.

Anne Dalton's parents divorce when she is seventeen. Unable to deal with the pain of choosing one parent over another, Anne accepts the role of live-in companion and aide to her rehabilitating alcoholic grandmother. Together Anne and Gram deal with a car accident and minister to tornado victims. Through their experiences of acting responsibly toward others and toward one another, they learn to cope with their own problems. Fiction.

Childress, Alice. **Rainbow Jordan.** Flare Books, 1982.

Rainbow is a fourteen-year-old black girl who feels that the world is a hostile, uncaring sort of place. She lives with Josie, an older woman, in an "interim home," while waiting for her mother to find time for her. All three women reveal their feelings as they size up the situation. The use of black dialect adds realism to the hard-hitting story of growing up defensively. Fiction.

Cleaver, Vera, and Bill Cleaver. **Where the Lilies Bloom.** Signet Books, 1974.

The Great Smoky Mountains are the stage for this touching story. Fourteen-year-old Mary Call is stubbornly determined to keep her small family together after the death of her father. She has no money and few resources except her strong will and Grandmother Cosby's wildcrafter's book. Fiction.

Cohen, Barbara. **Roses.** Illus. John Steptoe. Lothrop, Lee and Shepard Books, 1984.

Isabel's family is preoccupied with plans for her older sister Mimi's wedding, and Izzie feels on the outside. Her search for a summer job leads her to Leo, a hideously deformed man whose life as well as his body has been damaged in a tragic accident. Despite family pressures, Izzie knows she cannot walk away from him. Fiction.

Colman, Hila. **The Family Trap.** William Morrow, 1982.

Sixteen-year-old Becky Jones and her two sisters live alone because their father is dead and their mother is a permanent resident of a psychiatric hospital. When Becky's oldest sister Nancy decides she must be the parent in the household, Becky balks. She feels capable of living responsibly without Nancy's stern control. To resolve this problem, Becky is advised by a lawyer to petition the juvenile court to become an emancipated minor. Fiction.

Craven, Linda. **Stepfamilies: New Patterns in Harmony.** Julian Messner, 1983.

Teenagers normally experience many family problems; the potential for problems is even greater for those in stepfamilies. Using vignettes about real teenagers, Linda Craven examines all sorts of problems that can arise in stepfamilies and offers sensible ways to deal with them. Included are problems of getting along with a new parent, coping with feelings for a dead or absent parent, dealing with discipline, adjusting to a new baby, sharing with siblings, reacting to physical abuse, handling sexual urges, and finding help. Nonfiction.

Culin, Charlotte. **Cages of Glass, Flowers of Time.** Laurel-Leaf Library, 1983.

Deserted by her artist-father at thirteen, Clair is forced to live with her alcoholic and abusive mother. Clair is hungry, often bruised black and blue, and finds little solace in life. In spite of her loner attitude, two new friends try to help her deal with her problems. But Clair avoids telling them the truth about her situation, fearing her mother will send her off to an even worse fate—her abusive grandmother. Fiction.

Danziger, Paula. **The Divorce Express.** Laurel-Leaf Library, 1983.

Ninth-grader Phoebe lives a life split between Woodstock and New York City. She shuttles back and forth from her dad to her mother on the bus known as the Divorce Express. Phoebe is not alone. There are lots of other kids in similar situations—her new friend Rosie for one. Just when the girls think they have everything figured out, a new problem arises. Fiction.

Elfman, Blossom. **The Return of the Whistler.** Fawcett Juniper Books, 1982.

Arnie is an underachiever in an overachieving family. His only two talents—whistling and playing the harmonica—don't count for much. When he meets Francie, he finds in her a kindred soul, but her delicate mental state only adds to his problems. Through a series of violent incidents, Arnie finds a way to deal with the pressures he faces from all quarters—his family, his teachers, and his classmates. Fiction.

Eyerly, Jeannette. **He's My Baby, Now.** Archway Paperbacks, 1985.

Charles reads in the paper that his former girlfriend Daisy has just had a baby. Acknowledging that the baby is also his, Charles wants to be included in the decision of what should be done with the child. Objecting to Daisy's decision to put the baby up for adoption, Charles sees only one alternative: he must raise his son himself. Fiction.

First, Julia. **Look Who's Beautiful!** Laurel-Leaf Library, 1984.

Thirteen-year-old Connie Griswold knows she isn't exactly beautiful—her mother reminds her of it often enough. Connie is looking forward to getting away on the class trip to Washington, but first she must earn the money. She takes a job running errands for the elderly and becomes fast friends with eighty-five-year-old Mrs. Marston. For the first time in her life, Connie can talk to someone who understands her. Fiction.

Fox, Paula. **A Place Apart.** Signet Vista Books, 1982.

Victoria Finch is thirteen when her father dies, forcing her mother to sell their home and move from Boston to a small town. She feels estranged until she meets Hugh Todd, a gifted, spoiled, older boy who has few friends. Vicky doesn't care whether the others dislike Hugh, because when she is with him she feels special. Fiction.

Gerber, Merrill Joan. **Please Don't Kiss Me Now.** Signet Vista Books, 1982.

Leslie can't figure out how her life can be so wrong: her mother and father are divorced; her mother has several new boyfriends; her father is newly married; and a favorite teacher proves unreliable. Leslie's best friend and her new boyfriend only seem to add to her confusion. Then a great tragedy helps Leslie realize some important truths about life. Fiction.

Gilbert, Sara D. **How to Live with a Single Parent.** Lothrop, Lee and Shepard Books, 1982.

One-fifth of the children in the United States are living with only one parent. Divorce isn't the only reason; there are those who are widowed or who never marry. Life in a single-parent family presents some challenges for both children and parents. This book offers some ideas on turning potentially negative situations into positive ones. Written with the help of real parents and teens, it offers sound, practical advice. Nonfiction.

Guest, Judith. **Second Heaven.** Viking Press, 1982.

Gale Murray, a troubled teenager, runs away to the shelter of Cat Holtzman, a divorced woman and an unlikely foster parent.

Against the advice of her friend Mark, who agrees to represent the boy in court, Cat becomes increasingly more attached to the unhappy, disturbed Gale. This is a complex, contemporary novel of people helping people. Fiction.

Hall, Lynn. **Denison's Daughter.** Charles Scribner's Sons, 1983.

Sandy is sixteen and the youngest of John Denison's three daughters. Her life on a midwest cattle farm is relatively calm and safe. But Sandy is haunted by doubts that her father really loves her. She is tempted to seek affection from an older man who has been paying attention to her. Then a tragic farm accident occurs that brings her closer to her father. Fiction.

Hamilton, Virginia. **A Little Love.** Philomel Books, 1984.

Sheba's mother is dead, and her father disappeared when she was a baby. Although she has been raised by loving grandparents, she still has a need to find her father; his absence gnaws at her. *A Little Love* is the sensitive story of Sheba's journey in search of her father and of the characters who support and nurture her along the way. Fiction.

Hamilton, Virginia. **Sweet Whispers, Brother Rush.** Flare Books, 1983.

Fourteen-year-old Tree struggles to understand herself and her family. She is devoted to her retarded brother Dab, and spends many days alone trying to run the household, waiting for her mother to return home and ease the loneliness. Meanwhile she journeys into her past with Brother Rush, the ghost of a dead uncle, who gives her some answers and companionship. Fiction.

Heyman, Anita. **Final Grades.** Dodd, Mead, 1983.

Rachel has always been an *A* student, and she knows that her parents are expecting her to apply to the best schools. But Mrs. Baker, the Senior English teacher, is making assignments that frustrate and confuse Rachel. Given a second chance, Rachel still refuses to conform to the teacher's expectations. She is then forced to reconsider what she really would like to do with her life. Fiction.

Hill, Rebecca. **Blue Rise.** Penguin Books, 1984.

Jeannine Lewis's return to Blue Rise, Mississippi, brings back memories of typical deep Southern roots, family tradition, and religious fervor. In her return and her seeking, Jeannine comes to terms with who she was and who she is. Fiction.

Howe, Fanny. **Radio City.** Flare Books, 1984.

Aunt Bonnie and Uncle Charles seem preoccupied by their adoption of two orphaned babies, so fourteen-year-old Casey leaves for New York City to find her own father. He is everything she dreamed he would be. Although he is delighted to see her, he does not appear to want her around permanently. Casey must discover why before returning to Boston and the only family she has ever known. Fiction.

Hughey, Roberta. **The Question Box.** Delacorte Press, 1984.

Anne is in ninth grade now—old enough, she thinks, to wear makeup, to take a social relationships class, and to go on an overnight school trip. Unfortunately, her father disagrees. His overly strict rules are stifling Anne—until Genevra, the most popular and glamorous girl in the class, offers her a way out. But Anne soon discovers that Genevra's offer of friendship has hidden motives and painful consequences. Fiction.

Irwin, Hadley. **What about Grandma?** Margaret K. McElderry Books, 1983.

Sixteen-year-old Rhys is caught in the middle when her mother decides to sell Grandma Wyn's house and possessions and put Grandma in a nursing home. Grandma Wyn is opposed to moving—she wants to remain independent. The three women spend Grandma's last summer together working out old hurts and discovering new joys. Rhys learns a lot about herself and about first love while she competes with her mother for the attentions of an older man. Fiction.

Kerr, M. E. **The Son of Someone Famous.** Signet Vista Books, 1983.

Adam Blessing, at sixteen, lives in the shadow of his very famous father. In an effort to be his own person, Adam breaks all the rules and gets thrown out of several schools. Taking a new approach, Adam changes his last name, leaves his father, and moves in with his grandfather. There he meets Brenda Belle, another misfit, who lives in the shadow of her nagging and self-indulgent mother. Calling their relationship "Nothing Power," they hang on to one another, trying to ignore their respective worlds. Fiction.

Kidd, Ronald. **Who Is Felix the Great?** Lodestar Books, 1983.

Junior Tim Julian still thinks about his dad a lot even though it's been five years since his father's death. Tim also feels upset by his mother's new relationship, so he takes advantage of an English assignment to research an old-time baseball player long admired by his father. In the process, Tim learns much about himself. Fiction.

Klass, Sheila Solomon. **Alive and Starting Over.** Charles Scribner's Sons, 1983.

Jessica Van Norden, heroine of *To See My Mother Dance,* is fifteen and faced with new challenges. Her always feisty grandmother, now ill, is unable to continue living alone. Her friend Sylvia cannot cope with an overly critical stepmother. And Jess's new friend Peter is flirting with a serious health problem. Finally Jess learns that she must not give up on others too soon. Fiction.

Klass, Sheila Solomon. **To See My Mother Dance.** Fawcett Juniper Books, 1983.

Jessica resists her father's remarriage. In her mind, her mother is only away doing things like dancing, painting, and writing beautiful verse. She will not allow her stepmother Martha to replace that dream version of her missing mother. When Jessica accepts Martha's invitation to go to California and visit her natural mother, she is shocked by what she finds. Fiction.

Klein, Norma. **The Queen of the What Ifs.** Fawcett Juniper Books, 1982.

Robin's brother has dubbed her "the Queen of the What Ifs," and maybe she does worry too much about things that have not happened yet. But the prospects are grim: her father has left home, her mother feels inadequate, and her sister is seeing an older man. Is this any time to fall in love for the first time? Fiction.

Krementz, Jill. **How It Feels to Be Adopted.** Photographs by author. Alfred A. Knopf, 1982.

Like *How It Feels When Parents Divorce,* this book shares the heartfelt emotions of real children and teenagers. Ranging in age from eight to sixteen and from every social setting, they have two things in common: adoption and honesty. They tell their experiences so that others may better understand what adoption means and how it feels. Nonfiction.

Krementz, Jill. **How It Feels When Parents Divorce.** Photographs by author. Alfred A. Knopf, 1984.

This is a sensitive collection of photographs and interviews with children ages seven to sixteen who have experienced divorce. They share their stories in order to let other children like them know that the feelings they might have—shock, anger, confusion, pain, defiance, and understanding—have been felt by someone else. The message is that the feelings are all right; they are normal and appropriate. Nonfiction.

Landis, J. D. **Daddy's Girl.** William Morrow, 1984.

Jennie Marcowitz loves her father; they have a joyous, open relationship. How can she tell him that she has seen him kissing Susan Lacoutre? She can't discuss the problem with her mother, and her wacky friends are not much help either. Can Jennie save her parents' marriage? Fiction.

Leavitt, Caroline. **Meeting Rozzy Halfway.** Ballantine Books, 1982.

Bess and Rozzy are as different as any two sisters can be, but they somehow complement one another. Bess is conservative, practical, and sane, while Rozzy is unpredictable, whimsical, and quite mad. Her madness disrupts the whole family. Rozzie seems unaware of the private agonies faced by her parents, her sister, and her boyfriend as they try to understand her dark, secret self. Fiction.

Lee, Joanna, and T. S. Cook. **Mary Jane Harper Cried Last Night.** Signet Vista Books, 1978.

Mary Jane's mother, Rowena, abandoned by her husband, is young, spoiled, and unaccustomed to not having her way. Rowena takes her angry frustrations out on her baby girl. Mary Jane cries a lot, but no one who hears her seems to care much. Then Dr. Angela Buccieri recognizes signs of child abuse. She fights to bring the case to court, hoping someone will listen before it is too late to save Mary Jane. Fiction.

Lingard, Joan. **Strangers in the House.** Lodestar Books, 1983.

Calum resents his mother's remarriage and the family's move from the Scottish countryside to a cramped flat in Edinburgh. His new stepsister Stella dislikes the arrangement even more for having to share not only her father but her privacy as well. The two teenagers wage a silent war, little realizing that they are in the same situation. Fiction.

List, Julie Autumn. **The Day the Loving Stopped.** Fawcett Juniper Books, 1983.

Not content to become just another divorce statistic, Julie List writes about divorce from a daughter's point of view. This book is a compilation of her high school and college journals, her letters, and letters from her father as they work to understand their changing relationship. It is realistic, sad, and strangely consoling at the same time. Nonfiction.

Luger, Harriett. **The Un-Dudding of Roger Judd.** Viking Press, 1983.

Roger Judd is an entertaining, likable character who lives with his father, a new stepmother, and a half sister in California. In a series of journal entries, sixteen-year-old Roger reveals how he feels about first love, failing grades, and phony relationships. His reunion in New York City with his mother, a recovering alcoholic, is both tender and humorous. Fiction.

MacLeod, Charlotte. **Maid of Honor.** Atheneum, 1984.

This feminist novel contrasts two young women, Persis Green, a talented pianist, and her sister Lori, who is about to marry a wealthy young man. Completely absorbed in Lori's wedding preparations, their mother ignores Persis. When her musical ability wins her a prestigious scholarship, Persis feels so rejected that she does not tell her family. The disappearance of an expensive wedding present causes a family crisis that reveals some surprising truths about the Greens. Contemporary young women will find in Persis a heroine with whom they can identify. Fiction.

Major, Kevin. **Far from Shore.** Laurel-Leaf Library, 1983.

Dependent on alcohol and afraid to admit it, fifteen-year-old Chris Slade manages to find trouble in his life at every turn. His home life is in a shambles; he has just failed his sophomore year; and summer work seems impossible to find. He starts to hang out with the wrong crowd until, when in a drunken, blacked-out state, he is accused of a crime he can't remember committing. Fiction.

Maxwell, William. **So Long, See You Tomorrow.** Ballantine Books, 1981.

The unnamed narrator looks back in time to a violent crime and a childhood mistake that he still cannot forgive himself for. In retelling the incident, he chronicles the destruction of two families and the values of his Midwestern childhood. His memories are clear and powerful years later. Fiction.

Mays, Lucinda. **The Candle and the Mirror.** Atheneum, 1982.

At fifteen, Anne resents being left behind on her grandmother's farm while her mother lectures around the country. In 1895, Emily

Simmons is a true crusader whose most ardent cause is organizing the miners in the coal country. Later, when Anne joins her mother and sees the miners' pain and desperation for herself, she sets her own goals and comes to realize what she must do to make her own contribution. Fiction.

Mazer, Norma Fox. **Downtown.** William Morrow, 1984.

Living a double life causes problems for Pete Greenwood, alias Pax Connors, whose parents are sought by the FBI and charged with participating in a terrorist bombing. For eight years, Pete's Uncle Gene has been both father and mother to him. Theirs is a realistic relationship with the usual ups and downs. But Pete knows his uncle loves him, and when his mother comes back into his life, it is not easy for him to think of leaving the only home he has ever known. Fiction.

Mazer, Norma Fox. **Taking Terri Mueller.** William Morrow, 1983.

Terri remembers living only with her father, and moving from place to place with few friends and no relatives except Aunt Vivian. Her father is protective and loving, but he is also secretive and refuses to answer any of Terri's questions about her mother. At age fourteen Terri is devastated to learn that her mother is still alive. Terri's story is fiction, but every year in this country there are 25,000 cases of parental kidnapping like hers. Fiction.

Mazer, Norma Fox. **When We First Met.** Four Winds Press, 1982.

When seventeen-year-old Jennie Pennoyer first sees Rob Montana, she is immediately attracted to him. Later, when the two are falling in love, she discovers that his mother was the reckless driver who killed her older sister Gail two years before. Only gradually, through a series of emotionally charged scenes, do the various members of both families come to grips with Gail's death and the young couple's relationship. Fiction.

Miklowitz, Gloria D. **Close to the Edge.** Delacorte Press, 1983.

High school senior Jenny Hartley seems to have it all, yet she often feels lost and afraid. Her concern for her suicidal friend, Cindy, leads her to reevaluate her friendships, family, and interests. Through a volunteer assignment at the senior citizens' center, Jenny finds new hope and meaning for her life. Fiction.

Miklowitz, Gloria D. **The Day the Senior Class Got Married.** Delacorte Press, 1983.

Dr. Womer's economics class pairs off students as make-believe couples in a unit designed to explore the responsibilities of married life. For Lori and Rick the exercise is a serious one because they have announced their plans to marry right after graduation. Lori's painful realization that there are serious differences between them forces her to rethink her June plans. Fiction.

Moeri, Louise. **First the Egg.** E. P. Dutton, 1982.

Sarah Webster and David Hanna become "parents" of an egg for one week during their senior year, thanks to their Marriage and Family class. Their twenty-four-hour-a-day shared partnership is rocky from the start, with David's reluctance to get involved and Sarah's intense overinvolvement. Gradually, they come to a mutual realization that their time together with their egg has been more revealing and difficult than they could ever have imagined and that their worlds will never be the same. Fiction.

Mulligan, Kevin. **Kid Brother.** Lothrop, Lee and Shepard Books, 1982.

Brad realizes that he both loves and hates his older brother, Tom. He wishes he could be half as good as Tom is at the things he tries, but at the same time, he is tired of the constant comparison. It is Tom who is responsible for the single most embarrassing moment of Brad's life. But crazy Aunt Sheila in Albuquerque gives Brad a chance to be his own man, and to stop being Tom's kid brother. Fiction.

Myers, Walter Dean. **Won't Know Till I Get There.** Viking Press, 1982.

Fourteen-year-old Steve wants to show his new foster brother Earl that he's tough, so he spray-paints a subway car. But Earl is even tougher: he has a criminal record. Before they know it, Steve, Earl, and their friends are serving a sentence working in a retirement home. What they learn about the old people is news to all of them. Fiction.

Naylor, Phyllis Reynolds. **A String of Chances.** Atheneum, 1983.

Evie decides to spend her sixteenth summer with her married cousin Donna, who is expecting her first child. Donna's home is a stark contrast to Evie's own, where she has grown up never questioning her minister-father or the values shared by family members.

A sorrowful event causes Evie to rethink her own beliefs and to seek answers to some important questions. Fiction.

Newton, Suzanne. **I Will Call It Georgie's Blues.** Viking Press, 1983.

Neal Sloane's family lives in the public eye because his father is the Baptist minister in a small Southern town. Underneath a very proper exterior there are many problems tearing the family apart: Neal's sister may not graduate; Neal's younger brother Georgie is overwhelmed by emotional problems; and Neal's mother is constantly torn between her husband and her children. At fifteen, Neal himself finds comfort in jazz music, but he is afraid his interest will be misunderstood. Fiction.

Orgel, Doris. **Risking Love.** Dial Books, 1985.

Barnard College freshman Dinah Moskowitz sees a psychiatrist just to please her father. After all, it's his problem that he can't accept her decision to leave college to follow her boyfriend to Florida. Surprisingly, Dinah begins to listen to herself in therapy—and finds she must confront old feelings of conflicting love, anger, and hurt from her parents' divorce before she can find new strength and growth to risk love. Fiction.

Osborne, Mary Pope. **Love Always, Blue.** Dial Books for Young Readers, 1984.

Blue is a shy and self-conscious fifteen-year-old. She adores her playwright father, who lives in New York City. During the summer following her parents' separation, she convinces her mother to let her go to New York. There Blue is intrigued by the Greenwich Village scene, the open cafés, and the activity. But she is confused by her father's self-doubts and his deep sadness. He seems too far out of reach to help. Fiction.

Pevsner, Stella. **Lindsay, Lindsay, Fly Away Home.** Clarion Books, 1983.

Lindsay has spent most of her seventeen years abroad in exotic places. She suspects her father is sending her back to her aunt in the States to cool her romance with a handsome Indian youth, Rajee. Aunt Meg is nice enough, but Lindsay still has lots of questions about why she is being forced to leave India. Fiction.

Pfeffer, Susan Beth. **Starting with Melodie.** Four Winds Press, 1982.

Elaine envies her friend Melodie's glamorous life-style. But beneath the glitter of celebrity life, Melodie's family is troubled by an impending divorce and an unpleasant custody battle. Elaine quickly learns to appreciate her parents, her twin brothers, and the simple life they take for granted. Fiction.

Powell, Padgett. **Edisto.** Farrar, Straus and Giroux, 1984.

Edisto is a complex novel told from the point of view of an unusually sophisticated twelve-year-old. Simons Manigault has been trained to assume adult manners, speech, and company well before his time. Through Taurus, his mother's mysterious lover, he experiences his first date and witnesses his first boxing match. By the time Simons's father returns home and Taurus is forced to leave, Simons has learned much about love, life, and destiny. Fiction.

Powledge, Fred. **So You're Adopted.** Charles Scribner's Sons, 1982.

The writer was adopted forty-five years ago. He knows that while being adopted is only part of the person he is, that part is important and makes him special. In honest, thoughtful language, the writer discusses the idea of adoption, the feelings of everyone involved, and the reality of being one of the adopted. Nonfiction.

Radley, Gail. **The World Turned Inside Out.** Crown, 1982.

It is important to fifteen-year-old Jeremy Chase to understand why his brother Tyler drowned himself. But the family doesn't talk about the incident much except to toss blame around. Then Jeremy is offered a summer job at Seaside, the institution where Tyler was once a patient. Jeremy reluctantly takes the position and begins not only to understand what went wrong with Tyler, but also to discover what is right about himself. Fiction.

Reed, Kit. **The Ballad of T. Rantula.** Fawcett Juniper Books, 1981.

Fred's mother needs to find herself, and his dad needs to blame himself. Fred needs help holding it all together, so he invents T. Rantula, the spider-rock star. It's a joke shared by Fred and his two best pals. But the joke fades when the imaginary playmate becomes Fred's crutch in dealing with his life. Fiction.

Riley, Jocelyn. **Only My Mouth Is Smiling.** William Morrow, 1982.

Thirteen-year-old Merle is caught up in a long-running argument between her mother and her grandmother. Merle, her sister, and her brother accept their mother's mental illness but never give up hope that she will somehow get well on her own. When Mother suddenly takes them away to live in the wilds of northern Wisconsin, they try to start life anew. But the voices in Mother's head return, and the children are forced to deal with her bizarre behavior again. Fiction.

Robson, Bonnie. **My Parents Are Divorced, Too: Teenagers Talk about Their Experiences and How They Cope.** Everest House, 1980.

A child psychiatrist writes about her conversations with adolescents who have recently experienced divorce. The group members (paid volunteers, ages eleven to eighteen) demonstrate maturity and remarkable insight into adult problems. This book destroys the myth that teenagers are unaffected by divorced and separated parents. Nonfiction.

Rofes, Eric E., editor. **The Kids' Book of Divorce: By, for and about Kids.** Vintage Books, 1982.

Twenty school children from the Fayerweather Street School in Cambridge, Massachusetts, give advice on just about everything having to do with divorce, from not taking sides to adjusting to new relationships. They write from the heart and with their eyes wide open, and what they have to say is worth hearing by anyone touched by divorce. Nonfiction.

Roth, Arthur. **The Secret Lover of Elmtree.** Fawcett Juniper Books, 1981.

Greg rejects the story of his adoption until the Saturday when his natural father pulls into the garage driving a yellow Maserati. At seventeen he has to choose between the parents he has always called Mom and Dad and his real father, Peter March, who offers a future that is hard to pass up. Fiction.

Sams, Ferrol. **Run with the Horsemen.** Penguin Books, 1984.

Precocious Porter Osbourne grows up amid a houseful of relatives and other small-town characters all portrayed with affection and humor in this meandering memoir-novel of life in rural Georgia before and during the Great Depression. Race relations form the background of the story as Porter strives to become valedictorian of his high school and to come to terms with his hard-drinking, violent father, the county school superintendent. Fiction.

Samuels, Gertrude. **Run, Shelley, Run!** Signet Books, 1975.

Shelley Farber is a PINS—person in need of supervision. She is regarded as trouble by the court system, and there are people at the state training school who would like to break her spirit. But Shelley plans to run again to save herself, to find a place where trouble can't find her. Fiction.

Sebestyen, Ouida. **Far from Home.** Laurel-Leaf Library, 1983.

Salty must somehow get his great-grandmother to the Buckley Arms. That is where his mother had worked for fifteen years keeping house, and her last request was that he and Mam live there together. The note also directed him to love Tom Buckley. Salty is willing to work for his keep, but he isn't sure he will ever be fond of the man he suspects is his missing father. Fiction.

Shaw, Richard. **The Hard Way Home.** Laurel-Leaf Library, 1983.

Tired of having his father on his back, Gary decides to run away to show both his parents that he isn't a kid. But life on the road is difficult. Working to support himself, Gary discovers that everyone expects him to do his share. He is counting on his parents to come after him, but will they? Fiction.

Shepard, Jim. **Flights.** Alfred A. Knopf, 1983.

Thirteen-year-old Billy has problems he can't seem to deal with. His mom and dad continuously fight; his sister seems to hate him; he's not doing well at school; and, finally, a friend deserts him. To deal with his feelings of isolation and fear, Billy dreams of flying away from them—literally. After reading about flight and studying flight controls, all he needs is a plane. Fiction.

Shreve, Susan. **The Revolution of Mary Leary.** Alfred A. Knopf, 1982.

Mary Leary struggles to understand her relationship with her "smothering" mother. In the summer before her senior year, she leaves home to live with Dr. Sally Page and discovers that things are often not what they seem to be. Mary's comic sense and natural good humor lighten her more serious search for her own identity. Fiction.

Silsbee, Peter. **The Big Way Out.** Bradbury Press, 1984.

After Uncle Dick commits suicide and Paul's father is returned to the mental hospital, the family is split apart again. Paul's brother Tim defends their father but spends as much time as possible away from the house. When their mother finally flees to relatives in New York, Paul is left alone to try and find a way to save his family. Fiction.

Smith, Robert Kimmel. **Jane's House.** Pocket Books, 1984.

After the death of their mother, seventeen-year-old Hilary and her younger brother Bobby cannot continue living their own lives because they are imprisoned by their memories. Their troubles continue when their father brings his new wife into their home. Fiction.

Snyder, Anne, and Louis Pelletier. **Nobody's Brother.** Signet Vista Books, 1982.

Seventeen-year-old Josh and eleven-year-old Howie are as close as any two brothers could be. With his stepbrother, Josh doesn't stutter. But their parents are getting a divorce, and Howie will be going to live with his father in Skytop. What will it take to convince Josh's mother that the boys belong together? Fiction.

Snyder, Zilpha Keatley. **The Birds of Summer.** Atheneum, 1983.

Fifteen-year-old Summer loves her mother but lives in fear that she will one day disappear in search of the happiness she left behind in a San Francisco commune. Summer also dislikes her mother's new boyfriend and suspects that the two of them are involved in the cultivation of a marijuana crop, so she assumes responsibility for her younger sister. Summer seeks the help of her English teacher and her young friend, Nicky, and their advice helps keep her from making a disastrous mistake. Fiction.

Sweeney, Joyce. **Center Line.** Delacorte Press, 1984.

Five brothers are united against a common enemy—their abusive father. Shawn, the oldest brother, decides it is time for them to leave and risk the law coming after them. On their own, the brothers tire of the ` nture, and tensions start to pull them apart. But they must all stick together or they will all lose. Fiction.

Tamar, Erika. **Blues for Silk Garcia.** Crown, 1983.

At fifteen, Linda is a promising young guitarist who wants to be the best. She also wants to learn more about her deceased father, Silk Garcia, the jazz musician. People tell her that she resembles him. But Linda finds that the likeness is only skin deep as she begins to wish she had left her father's unspoken past alone. Fiction.

Terris, Susan. **No Scarlet Ribbons.** Flare Books, 1983.

Rachel wants to be part of a family again. She is delighted that she was responsible for her mother's meeting Norm, and that they got married, but a marriage doesn't make a family. Her stepfather doesn't seem to care about her, and her stepbrother thinks she is weird. The harder Rachel tries, the further apart they move. Her only happiness comes from the memory of her dead father and their magic times together. Fiction.

Thomas, Joyce Carol. **Bright Shadow.** Flare Books, 1983.

Twenty-year-old Abyssinia Jackson, a black college student in Oklahoma, finds love in this beautifully written short novel. But when her life is touched by an especially macabre murder, she must learn to cope with tragedy. In spite of the murder, this is not a story of death but of life and love. Fiction.

Thomas, Joyce Carol. **Marked by Fire.** Flare Books, 1982.

Abyssinia Jackson is born in an Oklahoma cotton field in the wake of a tornado that tears her family apart. But Abby's spirit is strong, and as she grows up, she learns the secrets of folk medicine from the healer Mother Barker and becomes a positive force in her community. The events are realistic and uncensored, but the language flows like lyrics to a song. Fiction.

Thompson, Julian F. **The Grounding of Group Six.** Flare Books, 1983.

Arriving at what they believe is an exclusive school, five sixteen-year-olds are unaware that they have been sent there to be exterminated and that their teacher is a murderer for hire. Fiction.

Tyler, Anne. **Dinner at the Homesick Restaurant.** Alfred A. Knopf, 1982.

Deserted by her salesman-husband, Pearl has raised her family alone, and her anger and possessiveness have colored all their lives. Now Pearl is dying, and her children are gathered together at her deathbed. Pearl's recollections carry the reader back thirty-five years to witness the growing pains of Cody, Jenny, and Ezra. Fiction.

Voigt, Cynthia. **Dicey's Song.** Atheneum, 1983.

Dicey Tillerman, from the novel *Homecoming,* faces the challenges of building a new life with her grandmother for herself and her sister and brothers. They cannot forget the mentally ill mother who abandoned them. Dicey herself finds it difficult to stop worrying about the children and to put her trust in Grandma. Fiction.

Voigt, Cynthia. **Homecoming.** Fawcett Juniper Books, 1983.

Dicey knows that her mother will not be coming back. She knows it is up to her to look out for James, Sammy, and Maybeth. Somehow she must get them to a safe place and get them there together. But it seems that every adult they meet is against them, so the children keep walking, sleeping in cemeteries, and hiding out, looking for a place to call home. Fiction.

Voigt, Cynthia. **A Solitary Blue.** Atheneum, 1983.

Jeff Green's mother left home when he was seven. Her note said that she had work to do in the world and that others needed her. Jeff grew up feeling very much alone, unable to communicate with his father, the professor. But it is this same man who is able to help Jeff heal his pain years later when his mother betrays him a second time. Fiction.

Whitt, Anne Hall. **The Suitcases.** Signet Books, 1983.

Three small sisters, Anne, Carolyn, and Betty, are old enough to realize that their mother is dead. But they cannot understand why they are being shuttled from foster home to foster home, waiting in vain for their father to come help. Against the backdrop of the South during the Great Depression, the girls search bravely for love and a place to unpack their suitcases once and for all. Nonfiction.

Wolitzer, Hilma. **Out of Love.** Farrar, Straus and Giroux, 1984.

Teddy stubbornly dreams about her parents getting back together. The love letters in her mother's closet are proof that they care. Teddy believes she can make her mother more attractive with makeup and exercises. Then her father will have second thoughts about leaving. Fiction.

Wolitzer, Hilma. **Wish You Were Here.** Farrar, Straus and Giroux, 1984.

Thirteen-year-old Bernie Segal can't reveal his secret plan to anyone—not even his grandfather, his best friend, or Mary Ellen. Bernie needs ninety-nine dollars to complete his plan. As he struggles to earn the money, he must also cope with his older sister, the problems of being short, passing algebra, and his feelings about his dead father. Fiction.

Wright, L. R. **The Favorite.** Pocket Books, 1983.

In this family story about love, death, and guilt, Margaret Kennedy, an aspiring actress, falls in love with and marries Ted Griffin, a young English professor. Marriage brings many changes in Margaret's life, but none is more significant than the birth of her daughter Sarah. For seventeen years Sarah is absolutely sure that she is her father's favorite, but when she herself falls in love, Ted's affection seems to turn to resentment. Then the family learns that he is dying of cancer. Fiction.

Zindel, Paul, and Crescent Dragonwagon. **To Take a Dare.** Bantam Books, 1984.

After thirteen-year-old Chrysta Perretti runs away from home to escape her self-indulgent mother and abusively critical father, she must make a life for herself in a hostile and exploitative world. With pluck and hard work she succeeds and finally settles in a small town in Arkansas, where she falls in love with Luke. Here also she befriends Dare, a homeless young boy. These relationships help Chrysta understand her own troubled family. Fiction.

Fantasy

Alexander, Lloyd. **The Beggar Queen.** E. P. Dutton, 1984.

In the last work in Alexander's trilogy (which also includes *West-mark* and *The Kestrel*), the government of Mickle (now Queen Augusta) collapses through the joint effects of internal bickering and meddlesome espionage. Like its predecessors, this novel confronts Theo and Mickle with the end products of what they think they want and traces out predictable developments in political thought and process. Fiction.

Alexander, Lloyd. **The Kestrel.** Laurel-Leaf Library, 1983.

Theo's nickname is "the Kestrel," which means a fierce and bloody captain who is famous for his swooping raids on the enemy. Those who remember the gentle, compassionate Theo from *Westmark* will be puzzled as to how Theo can have changed so much and still hold to the things that give life meaning for him, like his loyalty to his friends and his love for Mickle, now Queen Augusta. In fact, it's a paradox that threatens to destroy Theo, as well as Mickle and their friends. Fiction.

Asimov, Isaac, Martin H. Greenberg, and Charles G. Waugh, editors. **Wizards.** Signet Books, 1983.

A master of fantasy himself, Asimov and his coeditors have gathered here ten marvelous tales that feature wizards who duel, transpose, and escape. Some of fantasy's most honored authors are represented in this collection, which is the first volume of the series entitled Isaac Asimov's Magical Worlds of Fantasy. Fiction.

Beagle, Peter S. **The Last Unicorn.** Del Rey Books, 1983.

The lovely, immortal unicorn is no longer young when she realizes from overhearing a chance conversation that all the other unicorns have vanished long ago. She sets out to find them, drawing to her aid Schmendrick the Magician, whose spirit is as willing as his skills are weak, and the practical Molly Grue. There are familiar components to this tale, but with a new twist: for example, the band of outlaws in the Greenswood wants to go home, and the damsel in distress has a brother named Calvin. Slapstick alternates with tenderness in this gently satiric story of what may have been. Fiction.

Bell, Clare. **Ratha's Creature.** Margaret K. McElderry Books, 1983.

In a story that takes place twenty-five million years ago, Ratha tames fire, a victory that costs her the suspicion of her clan leader. No other of the Named, a group of highly intelligent and socially ordered cats, has ever done so, and even if the weapon might help the Named against the marauding Un-Named, the price seems too threatening to pay. Fiction.

Bethancourt, T. Ernesto. **The Tomorrow Connection.** Holiday House, 1984.

In *Tune in Yesterday,* Bethancourt gave us Richie Gilroy and Matty Owen—two musicians who traveled back in time. In this book, Richie and Matty are still stranded in 1906 and have asked the famous magician Harry Houdini for help in getting back to their own time. Houdini sends the boys across the country, posing as magician's helpers, to search for a gate to the past and the future. Unfortunately, they arrive in San Francisco just in time for the great earthquake. Fiction.

Bradley, Marion Zimmer. **City of Sorcery.** DAW Books, 1984.

This Darkover novel traces the quest of Magdalen Loone, who builds, through her life and journeying, a series of bridges that span experiences, cultures, and planets. *City of Sorcery* stresses the several and particular gifts of women acting alone and in community. Fiction.

Bradley, Marion Zimmer, editor. **Greyhaven: An Anthology of Fantasy.** DAW Books, 1983.

In the preface to this volume of short stories, Marion Zimmer Bradley introduces Greyhaven, the spiritual (and sometimes physical) home of a community of gifted writers of fantasy who present here eighteen tales of adventure and magic. The quality varies from story to story, but the best of them make the collection a fascinating addition to anyone's library. Fiction.

Bradley, Marion Zimmer. **Hawkmistress!** DAW Books, 1982.

Romilly's ability to identify with hawks and horses is the Mac Aran Gift. But as she struggles to find a place for herself in her father's world, Romilly sees the gift as a curse. Nevertheless, it forces her out into the hills, doubly dangerous for a girl trying to find stability in a time of anarchy and rebellion, until, unknowingly, she meets the true king and pledges to use her gifts to secure his throne. A Darkover novel. Fiction.

Bradley, Marion Zimmer, editor. **Sword and Sorceress: An Anthology of Heroic Fantasy.** DAW Books, 1984.

Bradley's aim in these fantasy tales is to present the reader with a familiar sword-and-sorcery tale told with a twist. The twist is that all the heroic figures in these fifteen stories are women. Fiction.

Bradley, Marion Zimmer, and the Friends of Darkover. **Sword of Chaos and Other Stories.** DAW Books, 1982.

The title story in this collection is by Bradley, but her influence permeates the rest of the tales, just as the environment of Darkover, the planet she created, sustains the lives of the characters who move through each short story. Fiction.

Bradshaw, Gillian. **In Winter's Shadow.** Signet Books, 1983.

In Winter's Shadow is the third volume of Bradshaw's Arthurian trilogy that begins with *Hawk of May* and *Kingdom of Summer.* Here, Queen Gwynhwyfar narrates the story of the fall of Camlann. She tells how she falls in love with Bedwyr, Arthur's perfect knight, and how this union, along with the evil plotting of Medraut, Arthur's bastard son, brings about the destruction of the kingdom. Fiction.

Bradshaw, Gillian. **Kingdom of Summer.** Signet Books, 1982.

An invaluable addition to a collection of fantasies generated by Arthurian legend, *Kingdom of Summer* tells the love story of Lord Gwlchmai, Arthur's kinsman and champion, following the events narrated in *Hawk of May.* Told from the point of view of Rhys, Gwlchmai's servant, the novel captures both the triumphs and the despair of war-torn Britain, circa 500 A.D. Fiction.

Carter, Lin. **Down to a Sunless Sea.** DAW Books, 1984.

Combining the features of love and adventure with fantastic creatures and settings, Carter gives us a rogue-hero in Brant, who has lived on the wrong side of the law and flees into a world he couldn't have imagined. There he is aided by outlaws and loses his previously impervious heart. Fiction.

Cherryh, C. J. **The Dreamstone.** DAW Books, 1983.

The forest of Ealdwood, which keeps a time different from elsewhere, is the last remaining place of magic that mortals have not destroyed. Arafel the Sidhe is the guardian of Ealdwood and one of the last of her kind—the faery folk. When she meets Niall, a human warrior, she grants him haven in her forest from the men who pursue him. When Niall himself relinquishes that haven to battle for a human king, Arafel is caught up in a fight that signals the end of her own epoch. Fiction.

Cherryh, C. J. **The Tree of Swords and Jewels.** DAW Books, 1983.

Picking up where *The Dreamstone* left off, *The Tree of Swords and Jewels* follows Ciaran Cuidean, Branwyn, and Arafel, the Lady of Trees, as the power of the Sidhe diminishes and the works of men increase. Branwyn's struggle forms the heart of the book; as wife and mother, she fears the source of power that intervenes in her family's destiny, but the child she once was never allows her to put aside her affection for Ealdwood and Arafel. Fiction.

Curry, Jane Louise. **Shadow Dancers.** Margaret K. McElderry Books, 1983.

Wrongfully accused of stealing a valuable moonstone, Lek the conjurer determines to enter the dread Shadowland, where the sun never shines, and search for the long-sought Opal Mountains, where he might find another stone with equally potent powers. Fraught with danger and suspense, *Shadow Dancers* exemplifies the lure of mythology in fantasy. Fiction.

Dank, Gloria Rand. **The Forest of App.** Greenwillow Books, 1983.

A crippled boy named Nob, left behind by his own people, a race of storytellers, is taken in by a witch-girl, an elf, and a dwarf, creatures of an ancient forest from which the magic has all but disappeared. Fiction.

Ende, Michael (translated by Ralph Manheim). **The Neverending Story.** Illus. Roswitha Quadflieg. Doubleday, 1983.

Bastian Balthazar Box is a boy with a problem, or rather, several problems. He's overweight, the other kids jeer at him, and his father seems indifferent. But one day he begins to read a book called *The Neverending Story,* and thus enters Fantastica, a world where fortunes and characters are reversed and remade. If you loved *The Wizard of Oz* and *E.T.,* you'll understand why this is called "a fantasy for all ages." Fiction.

Foster, Alan Dean. **The Day of the Dissonance.** Warner Books, 1984.

In this third novel to feature Jon-Tom, the Spellsinger, Clothahump can be saved from death only by rare medicinal powders. Jon-Tom embarks on the quest, complete with guides and his usual magnetic effect on winsome damsels. Fiction.

Foster, Alan Dean. **The Hour of the Gate.** Warner Books, 1984.

Once again would-be graduate student Jonathan Thomas Meri-weather (who doubles as a rock guitarist) joins with the wizard Clothahump (who doubles as a turtle) to repel the invasion of the Plated Folk. Aided by the valiant Mudge the Otter and the beautiful Talea, Jon-Tom alternately plays the roles of minstrel and crusader. Second book in the Spellsinger series. Fiction.

Foster, Alan Dean. **Shadowkeep.** Warner Books, 1984.

In this companion to the game of the same title, the power of Shadowkeep is challenged by the apprentice blacksmith, Practor Fime, who simultaneously undergoes a rigorous moral education. Fiction.

Foster, Alan Dean. **Spellsinger.** Warner Books, 1983.

Jonathan Thomas Meriweather thought his life as a graduate student was complex enough before he was summoned into another world to lead a struggle for freedom. It does not help his composure to learn that his destiny lies in the grasp of Clothahump, the wizard-turtle. Fiction.

Gedge, Pauline. **Stargate.** Penguin Books, 1983.

In the beginning, the Worldmaker made many beautiful worlds, each different and each ruled over by a sun-lord. Each sun-lord succumbs in turn to the temptation to know and control the future, and the world of each passes away, leaving only Dananion to watch the dawn of the age of mortals. The concepts of freedom, justice, and change are explored here through a complex cast of characters and a demanding story line. Fiction.

Goldman, William, reteller. **The Princess Bride: S. Morgenstern's Classic Tale of True Love and High Adventure.** Ballantine Books, 1982.

This is not your average fairy tale. For starters, its hero is named Westley, the heroine is Buttercup, and the villain is Humperdinck. Goldman claims that, in all modesty, this is not wholly his work, that he has lifted and strung together the "good parts" from the S. Morgenstern classic. The pace is hectic, the dialogue hilarious, and the characters endearing in the final product. This is possibly the only fairy tale around whose moral is that "life isn't fair. It's just fairer than death, that's all." Fiction.

Goldstein, Lisa. **The Red Magician.** Pocket Books, 1982.

Kicsi's world is real—in fact, too real and too terrifying. She lives in a town in Central Europe just before World War II. She is a Jew, and although the Rabbi rails against the talk of Vörös, who predicts disaster, Kicsi believes. But who is Vörös? Why does he protect Kicsi after the war, and what is the source of his frightening power? *The Red Magician* blends horror and fantasy, history and hope into a beautiful, prize-winning novel. Fiction.

Gordon, John. **The Edge of the World.** Margaret K. McElderry Books, 1983.

After thirteen-year-olds Kit and Tekker see a frightening ghost-creature near a cottage owned by Ma Grist, a strange old woman, Tekker develops some unusual powers. He can now move small objects using only his mind, and he can also turn the flat English countryside into a burning hot desert of red sand. But when Ma Grist draws them farther and farther into this desert world and threatens the life of Dan, Kit's fifteen-year-old brother, Kit and Tekker must enter upon a life-and-death mission to save Dan's life and to rescue someone trapped years ago in the scorching land. Fiction.

Harris, Geraldine. **The Children of the Wind.** Greenwillow Books, 1982.

As Prince Kerish and his companions continue their quest for the key to the seven citadels, where the savior of the Galkien empire is imprisoned, Kerish grows in both humility and patience. Second book in the Seven Citadels series. Fiction.

Harris, Geraldine. **Prince of the Godborn.** Greenwillow Books, 1982.

In this first book of the Seven Citadels series, we meet Prince Kerish and his steadfast brother, Lord Forollkin. Their quest is to free their promised savior, who has been imprisoned behind seven gates by seven sorcerers. Fiction.

Helprin, Mark. **Winter's Tale.** Pocket Books, 1984.

It is the year 2000 in New York City. When Peter Lake, master mechanic and burglar, tries to rob a mansion on the Upper West Side, he meets Beverly Penn, the daughter of the house, and they fall in love. Soon Peter decides to try "to stop time and bring back the dead." Will he be successful? Fiction.

Hill, Douglas. **The Huntsman.** Margaret K. McElderry Books, 1982.

As a baby, Finn Ferral was found abandoned in the wilderness. Fostered by Joshua, he exhibits an uncanny aptitude for each task he is given. When his foster family is kidnapped by the sinister Them, Finn must use both natural lore and supernatural powers to rescue them. Fiction.

Hindle, Lee J. **Dragon Fall.** Flare Books, 1984.

Everyone's childhood fears of monsters in the bedroom closet come startlingly true for seventeen-year-old Gabe Holden. He constructs human-size, lifelike monsters for a toy company—until late one night they come alive and attempt to kill him. With this chillingly convincing story, the eighteen-year-old author won the first Avon/ Flare contest for novels "written by teenagers about teenagers for teenagers." Fiction.

Hoban, Russell. **Riddley Walker.** Washington Square Press, 1982.

Set in England at a time far into the future, this unusual and mature novel is written totally in dialect. The story is told from the point of view of young Riddley Walker and begins just after Riddley has been initiated as a connection man, a sort of priest who interprets puppet shows performed by the government's traveling players. In a time of mystery and change, Riddley helps his society move from a hunting-gathering culture to the rediscovery of gunpowder and the future it will bring. Fiction.

Hodgell, P. C. **God Stalk.** Argo Books, 1983.

The three-faced God has made the Kencyrs a tool to use against the Darkling. Jame, a Kencyr, is deprived of home, kin, and memory. Inexplicably she begins to move against her background as she seeks refuge in the rich and depraved city of Tai-tastigon. As the forces of the great city expand Jame's own restless searching, she begins to learn who she is and what she must do. Fiction.

Lee, Tanith. **Anackire.** DAW Books, 1983.

There's more than a coincidental resemblance between *Anackire* and *Richard III:* both plots are dominated by fascinating, utterly remorseless villains, and both have scenes where madness seems the only possible response to injustice. Both ultimately uphold a pattern of poetic political justice working through suffering and bloodshed. In *Anackire,* redemption comes from unlikely sources, and if the reader can separate out character and place-names, the sheer density of the novel provides rewards for persistence. Fiction.

Lee, Tanith. **Cyrion.** DAW Books, 1982.

Each chapter details one of the many breathtaking adventures of Cyrion, who combines all the best qualities of Harry Houdini and Indiana Jones. Cyrion is never seen at a disadvantage with either women or his many enemies, and his sheer audacity makes him a candidate for the title "Rogue-Hero of the 1980s." Fiction.

Lee, Tanith. **Sung in Shadow.** DAW Books, 1983.

What if parallel worlds existed, and in them hauntingly familiar stories were acted out, with local variations? This is such a story, of Romulan and Iuletta, who live in a place like Renaissance Italy. They love each other in defiance of their feuding families, and tragedy stalks their fragile happiness. Fiction.

MacAvoy, R. A. **Tea with the Black Dragon.** Bantam Books, 1983.

When Martha Macnamara's daughter disappears into the world of computer crime, Martha is aided by Mayland Long, former Imperial Chinese dragon. The intrepid Martha and the formidable Long are marvelous characters in a novel as fast paced as it is imaginatively conceived. Fiction.

Malamud, Bernard. **God's Grace.** Farrar, Straus and Giroux, 1982.

In the not-too-distant future, the Djanks and the Druskies fight a war to end all wars which, in fact, almost does end all life on Earth. Only Calvin Cohn survives the war and subsequent flood, and Calvin's task is to beguile God once more with the fruits of creation, chiefly a chimpanzee named Buz and various other primates. Fiction.

Maxwell, Ann. **Dancer's Illusion.** Signet Books, 1983.

The two previous novels in this series, *Fire Dancer* and *Dancer's Luck,* introduced Rheba the fire dancer. In this continuation of the saga, Rheba and her friend Kirtn make a stop on the seductive and complex world of Yhelle and discover that its reputation for pleasure masks an encroaching evil. Fiction.

Mayhar, Ardath. **Lords of the Triple Moons.** Argo Books, 1983.

Johab and Ellora are all that is left of the Old Lords. Both children possess great power, and once they are fully grown, they begin to challenge the new dictators' hold on the land they love. In this way the two discover, as do their former captors, that what makes them superior is their ultimate willingness to be sacrificed. Fiction.

Mayhar, Ardath. **Runes of the Lyre.** Argo Books, 1982.

Yinri is in great peril when she finds the lyre on the tree branch. Playing it saves her from immediate crisis, but it also opens for her a new way of life as she throws her lot in with the Asyir, who have the power to protect the many worlds which together make one cosmos. Without Yinri, however, and the runes carved on the lyre, no alliance can withstand those whose aim it is to pillage and kill. Fiction.

McKinley, Robin. **The Blue Sword.** Greenwillow Books, 1982.

Harry, bored with her sheltered life in the remote orange-growing colony of Darta, discovers magic in herself when she is kidnapped by a native king with mysterious powers. Fiction.

McKinley, Robin. **The Hero and the Crown.** Greenwillow Books, 1985.

Aerin, with the guidance of the wizard Luthe and the help of the blue sword, contends victoriously with Maur, the Black Dragon. Thus she wins the birthright due her as the daughter of the Damarian king and a witchwoman of the mysterious, demon-haunted North, and alters forever the history of Damar. Fiction.

Norton, Andre. **'Ware Hawk.** Margaret K. McElderry Books, 1983.

Norton's Witch World stories have earned her an enthusiastic following among fantasy fans who like their far-away and long-ago conflicts to contribute something to life in the here and now. *'Ware*

Hawk presents Tirtha, whose family has been wiped out in a purge, and her uneasy alliance with a mercenary falconer, Neril. Together, they rescue the child Alon and trace their way to Hawkholme to reclaim Tirtha's shattered heritage. Fiction.

Rosenberg, Joel. **The Sleeping Dragon.** Signet Books, 1983.

Seven young college students, all addicts of fantasy games, are transported by their gamemaster to a land where the conditions of the game govern the perils. The characters, embodied according to their game roles, must struggle desperately to find their way home through the Gate between Worlds. Book one of the Guardians of the Flame series. Fiction.

Saha, Arthur W., editor. **The Year's Best Fantasy Stories: 10.** DAW Books, 1984.

The eleven stories in this collection range in length from the novella of Fritz Leiber to short stories by Tanith Lee, Avram Davidson, and Grania Davis. What the tales have in common is that they are all spellbinders and together provide a powerful demonstration of the lure and popularity of fantasy. Fiction.

Saxton, Mark. **Havoc in Islandia.** Houghton Mifflin, 1982.

Islandia is one of those imaginary places that make the realities of our own world more apparent. Bren, a young naval officer coming of age in Islandia, finds himself combatting a Catholic plot to influence the religious heritage of the royal dynasty. Fiction.

Shea, Michael. **The Color out of Time.** DAW Books, 1984.

This sequel to H. P. Lovecraft's *The Color out of Space* takes place in modern New England near an unnamed lake. There is something in that lake that is not of this world—an indescribable color that conveys a feeling of evil to all who see it. And the evil is growing quickly—will anyone be able to stop it in time? Fiction.

Shippey, T. A. **The Road to Middle-Earth.** Houghton Mifflin, 1983.

Shippey has written a very concise and illuminating guide to the works of J. R. R. Tolkien. If you're a big fan of *The Lord of the Rings* and *The Hobbit,* you'll find this book a useful and entertaining resource. Nonfiction.

Sucharitkul, Somtow. **Utopia Hunters: Chronicles of the High Inquest.** Bantam Books, 1984.

Jen-Jen is a weaver of light who comes to the attention of Ton Ellovan, the Inquestor. Through Jen-Jen's research, we learn the history of Ton Ellovan and the vision of the Inquest. But the safety of Jen-Jen's homeworld and of countless souls depends on whether Ton Ellovan has the capacity for human involvement as opposed to the compassion he cultivates. Fiction.

Tolkien, J. R. R. (edited by Christopher Tolkien). **Unfinished Tales of Númenor and Middle-Earth.** Houghton Mifflin, 1980.

For those who finished *The Lord of the Rings* and *The Hobbit* thirsting for more details about Middle-Earth, *Unfinished Tales* will be a necessity. It provides background, missing pieces of the puzzle, and another glimpse of the personalities that make Tolkien's stories so addictive. Fiction.

Wilder, Cherry. **A Princess of the Chameln.** Argo Books, 1984.

When the Mel'Nir invade the Chameln lands, Princess Aidris flees to safety disguised as a cavalry soldier. She works patiently at this discipline for years, and by the time her people are ready for her, she has grown as a woman and as a queen. Volume one of *The Rulers of Hylor.* Fiction.

Wilder, Cherry. **The Tapestry Warriors.** Argo Books, 1983.

Rovan's special gift of mind-linking makes him an invaluable recruit for the forces plotting to overthrow the traditions of Torin. Yet, even when his idolized older sister joins the rebels, Rovan cannot still his misgivings about turning the young as a weapon on the aged. So he carves out his own way, learning about responsibility and freedom as he goes, steering clear of simplistic solutions. Fiction.

Wolfe, Gene. **The Citadel of the Autarch.** Timescape Books, 1983.

In this fourth and last volume of *The Book of the New Sun,* the ultimate destiny of Severian the Torturer is revealed. As Severian continues his journey across the sands of Urth, an outcast wanderer who has been exiled from his own guild, he is hunted by strange creatures from beyond Urth and even offered a kingdom under the seas by the dwellers in the deep waters. But Severian's fate is tied up with the fate of all Urth—in the coming of the New Sun. Fiction.

Yolen, Jane. **Dragon's Blood.** Illus. George Buetel. Delacorte Press, 1982.

On the planet Austar IV, the economy revolves around pit dragon fights, and the social hierarchy is composed of masters and bondsmen. Jakkin, a bond boy working as a keeper in a dragon nursery, resolves to steal a dragon hatchling and use it to obtain his free-dom. But freedom turns out to be a thornier commodity than Jakkin anticipates. Fiction.

Yolen, Jane. **Heart's Blood.** Illus. Tom McKeveny. Delacorte Press, 1984.

Jakkin, the young hero of *Dragon's Blood,* has become a Dragon Master, and Heart's Blood, the hatchling he stole, has grown into a mature dragon with her own hatchlings. But instead of being able to train the new hatchlings for the gaming pits, Jakkin feels compelled to infiltrate a rebel group plotting to overthrow the Galaxian Federation, where he hopes to locate his missing beloved Akki in this action-packed second installment of the *Pit Dragons* trilogy. Fiction.

Handicaps—Physical and Emotional

Ames, Mildred. **The Silver Link, the Silken Tie.** Charles Scribner's Sons, 1984.

Tim has been seeing a psychiatrist to help him deal with a family tragedy that occurred when he was six. While working on the school paper, he meets fifteen-year-old Felice, who is seeking ways to resolve her feelings about the death of her parents and younger brother. Tim and Felice grow in the awareness that their lives are intertwined psychically through dreams and physically by friendship. Fiction.

Anaya, Rudolfo A. **Tortuga.** Editorial Justa, 1982.

Tortuga is the name given to a crippled Mexican boy. Sent to a hospital for the handicapped in Mexico, he is placed in a body cast that resembles a turtle's shell which he must spiritually and physically find the strength to shed. Fiction.

Bach, Alice. **Waiting for Johnny Miracle.** Bantam Books, 1982.

When seventeen-year-old Becky Maitland learns she has bone cancer, she experiences shock, then fear and denial. Her subsequent depression gives way to determination to fight against the inevitable. But along the way she also has to deal with her healthy twin sister, her unaccepting boyfriend, and a mother who suffers in her own way. Fiction.

Bauer, Marion Dane. **Tangled Butterfly.** Clarion Books, 1980.

This is a tale of mental illness and a family's reluctance to face it. Seventeen-year-old Michelle finds comfort in her grandmother, who is tucked away in her mind and comes out whenever Michelle wants her to. Robert, Michelle's older brother, plays the game with her for awhile, but their mother refuses to believe that there is anything different in Michelle's behavior until it's almost too late. Then Michelle is sent away to the Apostle Islands for a rest. There she meets Paul DuBois, a Native American writer, who is the first person to sense how deeply disturbed she really is. Fiction.

Cavallaro, Ann. **Blimp.** Lodestar Books, 1983.

Overweight Kim is mystified as to why gorgeous Gary Bellmore choses to spend his time with her instead of with one of the other girls in their high school. Their friendship becomes seriously strained when Kim learns of Gary's emotional problems. Fiction.

Froman, Katherine. **The Chance to Grow.** Everest House, 1983.

This book can be many things to many people, but most of all, it offers hope to the parents of handicapped children. Through the use of case studies, it offers insights into the many common types of handicaps resulting from genetic defects, birth or other injury, and/or prenatal problems. In addition, the book explains what a physical therapist does, and contains valuable appendices that list sources for additional information. Nonfiction.

Girion, Barbara. **A Handful of Stars.** Laurel-Leaf Library, 1983.

Julie Meyers starts her high school career with a bang. She's involved in drama, admired by a special basketball player, and popular with her new friends. Then, all of a sudden, Julie starts blacking out. Her friends start treating her differently, and she loses control of her life. No sudden treatment appears; no easy acceptance occurs. But Julie slowly learns to deal with her epilepsy. Fiction.

Greenberg, Jan. **No Dragons to Slay.** Farrar, Straus and Giroux, 1983.

Thomas was the star on the soccer team until the lump in his side turned out to be cancer. Now he must deal with his family and friends as well as with the pain. In this realistic story of personal growth, a positive ending emerges. Fiction.

Hallman, Ruth. **Breakaway.** Laurel-Leaf Library, 1983.

Rob loses his hearing in a diving accident during a high school swim meet, and his mother's reaction is to smother him with attention. Determined to get him away from his mother's influence, Rob's girlfriend Kate convinces him to run away with her. Out on their own, they face the task of teaching Rob to cope with the hearing world. Fiction.

Hautzig, Deborah. **Second Star to the Right.** Flare Books, 1982.

In spite of being a well-to-do fourteen-year-old living in one of the most exciting cities in the world, Leslie Hiller is an unhappy person who never feels in control unless she is dieting. The author lets us into the troubled mind of the anorexic, who is determined to control her weight—even if it kills her. Fiction.

Hull, Eleanor. **Alice with Golden Hair.** Signet Vista Books, 1982.

Alice is unable to explain her thoughts and feelings. After she is forced to leave her special school for the mentally retarded, her social worker finds a job for her in a convalescent home. Alice's honest compassion endears her to the patients but complicates her relationships with her coworkers. Fiction.

Josephs, Rebecca. **Early Disorder.** Fawcett Juniper Books, 1981.

At fifteen, Willa is a normal teenager until she decides to grow up and lose weight. But when she goes too far and becomes anorexic, her world begins to close in on her. She must then fight to find and love herself as well as to understand her family. Fiction.

Kata, Elizabeth. **A Patch of Blue.** Warner Books, 1983.

Selina, blinded at an early age, is intelligent though uneducated. Isolated by cruelty, poverty, and intolerance, she finds love with a man who has had his share of pain. Originally published as *Be Ready with Bells and Drums*. Fiction.

Kellogg, Marjorie. **Tell Me That You Love Me, Junie Moon.** 2d ed. Farrar, Straus and Giroux, 1984.

Warren is a paraplegic confined to a wheelchair; Arthur has an undiagnosable neurological disease that gets progressively worse; and Junie Moon has been horribly disfigured by an irate boyfriend who poured battery acid on her face. These three "misfits" decide to live together when they are released from the hospital because they have no place else to go. In this painful yet beautiful story, Kellogg shows us the indomitable spirit of three severely maimed people who learn to love. Fiction.

Kerr, M. E. **Little Little.** Bantam Books, 1983.

Little Little LaBelle is seventeen and beautiful but only three feet three inches tall. Sidney Cinnamon is three feet four-and-a-half inches tall and plays the role of the roach in a TV pest control commercial. These unusual "diminutives" find each other in a chain of wacky events concerning a group of teenage dwarfs in contemporary society. Fiction.

Levenkron, Steven. **The Best Little Girl in the World.** Warner Books, 1981.

Francessa has to be perfect. To be the person she wants to be, she renames herself Kessa and stops eating. The world of an anorexic, filled with obsessive rituals, fantasy, pain, and despair, is brought into sharp focus here. But can't Kessa see that the lack of love and attention from her parents and friends is killing her? Fiction.

Levy, Marilyn. **The Girl in the Plastic Cage.** Fawcett Juniper Books, 1982.

What with gymnastics, beginning high school, and Kurt, Lori felt that life had a great deal to offer her. One of the things she hadn't counted on, though, was scoliosis and wearing a brace from her chin to the middle of her back. Now she can no longer participate in gymnastics. In addition, she has to face trouble at home and at school and deal with a breakup with Kurt. Fiction.

Likhanov, Albert (translated by Richard Lourie). **Shadows across the Sun.** Harper and Row, 1983.

In this novel, originally published in the USSR, crippled Lena falls in love with Fedya, a young boy who keeps pigeons on the roof of the Moscow apartment next door to hers. Fedya has his problems, too: his father is an alcoholic. Eventually, the young people come to rely on one another. This sensitive story of a deepening relationship provides interesting glimpses of life in the Soviet Union. Fiction.

MacCracken, Mary. **City Kid.** Signet Books, 1982.

Mary MacCracken is a teacher who works with emotionally disturbed children. Luke, the seven-and-a-half-year-old city kid who sets fires and steals, is her toughest assignment. Nonfiction.

Neufeld, John. **Lisa, Bright and Dark.** Signet Books, 1970.

No one believes that sixteen-year-old Lisa is going crazy; her family denies that there is anything wrong. Lisa's friends know differently, and is it up to them to save her sanity? Fiction.

Oneal, Zibby. **The Language of Goldfish.** Fawcett Juniper Books, 1982.

Being talented in art and math just isn't enough to transform thirteen-year-old Carrie from a child into a teenager. When pressures overwhelm her, Carrie finds comfort in thinking about an island from her childhood. Pushing reality aside, her island looms larger and larger in her mind, until it threatens her sanity. Fiction.

Perske, Robert. **Show Me No Mercy: A Compelling Story of Remarkable Courage.** Abingdon Press, 1984.

Paralyzed in an accident that kills his wife and daughter, Andy Banks struggles to overcome his handicap. But that is not Andy's only problem: he also has a teenage son, Ben, who has Down's syndrome. Can Andy prevent Ben from being institutionalized? Fiction.

Platt, Kin. **The Ape inside Me.** Bantam Books, 1983.

Eddie Hill loses control easily. Kong—the voice inside him—is mean and nasty, urging him to strike out at the slightest provocation. But Eddie, at fifteen, is getting tired of hitting and being beaten by bigger kids. The trouble is that he doesn't know how to control Kong. Fiction.

Polikoff, Judy (as told to Michele Sherman). **Every Loving Gift: How a Family's Courage Saved a Special Child.** Signet Books, 1984.

Andy Polikoff was born with brain damage, and his family eventually embarked on the controversial technique called "programming." While this book details Andy's progress, it more impressively details the almost unbelievable emotional and financial strains put on Andy's parents and his two brothers. The Polikoff's story offers rare insights into the behavior of others toward the handicapped. Nonfiction.

Radley, Gail. **The World Turned Inside Out.** Crown, 1982.

It is important to fifteen-year-old Jeremy Chase to understand why his brother Tyler drowned himself. But the family doesn't talk about the incident much except to toss blame around. Then Jeremy is offered a summer job at Seaside, an institution where Tyler was once a patient. Jeremy reluctantly takes the position and begins not only to understand what went wrong with Tyler, but also to discover what is right about himself. Fiction.

Riley, Jocelyn. **Only My Mouth Is Smiling.** William Morrow, 1982.

Thirteen-year-old Merle is caught up in a long-running argument between her mother and her grandmother. Merle, her sister, and her brother accept their mother's mental illness but never give up hope that she will somehow get well on her own. When Mother suddenly takes them away to live in the wilds of northern Wisconsin, they try to start life anew. But the voices in Mother's head return, and the children are forced to deal with her bizarre behavior again. Fiction.

Sachs, Marilyn. **The Fat Girl.** E. P. Dutton, 1984.

Jeff is at first repulsed and then later obsessed with Ellen, the fat girl in his ceramics class. At the beginning of their relationship, Ellen is touchingly grateful for Jeff's attention. But when Jeff's obsession with her hinders her chances for personal growth, Ellen must make a painful decision about their friendship. Fiction.

Sallis, Susan. **Only Love.** Laurel-Leaf Library, 1982.

This realistic, funny, and satisfying love story pits spunky Fran Adamson, who is paralyzed from the waist down, against Lucas Hawkens, who enters the convalescent home after being injured in a motorcycle accident. When Lucas refuses to leave his room, Fran communicates with him by telephone and persuades him to care about others and about himself. Fiction.

Savitz, Harriet May. **Come Back, Mr. Magic.** Signet Vista Books, 1983.

Greg Martin earned the name "Mr. Magic" at seventeen because of his success in working with handicapped people at the rehabilitation center. Then a hit-and-run car accident leaves Greg in a coma in need of everyone else's support. By focusing on the responses of high school dropout Shelley and a young drifter named David, the author provides insights into physical therapy and the realities faced by teenage victims of debilitating accidents and illnesses. Fiction.

Savitz, Harriet May. **Run, Don't Walk.** Signet Vista Books, 1980.

After Samantha finds herself in a wheelchair following a diving accident, she tries not to stand out at Scot High School. But another wheelchair student, Johnny Jay, encourages her to become active—even to go so far as to try to enter a marathon race and to fight to make the school's facilities accessible for handicapped students. Fiction.

Silsbee, Peter. **The Big Way Out.** Bradbury Press, 1984.

After Uncle Dick commits suicide and Paul's father is returned to the mental hospital, the family is split apart again. Paul's brother Tim defends their father but spends as much time as possible away from home. When their mother finally flees to relatives in New York, Paul is left alone to try and find a way to save his family. Fiction.

Smith, Lee. **Black Mountain Breakdown.** Ballantine Books, 1982.

Sometimes a mental breakdown is unforseen, especially when a person is blessed with good looks, popularity, academic success, and even love. Crystal Spangler, an Appalachian native who manages to rise above her roots to become a beauty queen, seems to have it all. Yet somehow she finds herself disconnected and confused, a statistic among those who are mentally ill for no apparent reason. Fiction.

Snyder, Anne. **Goodbye, Paper Doll.** Signet Vista Books, 1980.

Having everything she could ever need, seventeen-year-old Rosemary is starving herself to death. In the process of trying to overcome anorexia nervosa, Rosemary has to deal with her social relationships, her relationship with her family, and her own sexuality. Fiction.

Snyder, Anne, and Louis Pelletier. **Nobody's Brother.** Signet Vista Books, 1982.

Seventeen-year-old Josh and eleven-year-old Howie are as close as any two brothers could be. When with his stepbrother, Josh doesn't stutter. But their parents are getting a divorce, and Howie will be going to live with his father in Skytop. What will it take to convince Josh's mother that the boys belong together? Fiction.

Terris, Susan. **Wings and Roots.** Farrar, Straus and Giroux, 1982.

Volunteer Jenny West finds that Kit Hayden, one of the patients at her uncle's hospital, is sarcastic, bitter, and angry. A victim of the 1950s polio epidemic, he vents his feelings in powerful poems which he posts around the hospital. Jenny is fascinated by him. They form a turbulent relationship that lasts for four years. Fiction.

Valens, E. G. **The Other Side of the Mountain.** Warner Books, 1977.

While training to be on the U.S. Olympic ski team, Jill Kinmont crashes into a tree at forty miles an hour and becomes permanently paralyzed from the shoulders down. Her determination to lead a meaningful and productive life is inspiring. Originally titled *A Long Way Up,* her story is continued in *The Other Side of the Mountain: Part 2.* Nonfiction.

Health and Physical Fitness

Akers, Keith. **A Vegetarian Sourcebook.** G. P. Putnam's Sons, 1983.

In this comprehensive book on vegetarianism, Akers presents the three main arguments for becoming a vegetarian: a vegetarian diet is healthier than a meat-oriented diet; a vegetarian diet is more efficient in its use of natural resources; and a vegetarian diet does not require the death and suffering of innocent animals. Includes an index and a bibliography. Nonfiction.

Arnold, Caroline. **Too Fat? Too Thin? Do You Have a Choice?** William Morrow, 1984.

Are you too fat or too thin? The author reveals here the reasons for these problems and gives a patient, sensitive approach for understanding your body and controlling your weight. Arnold discusses the latest studies and theories on weight control and emphasizes the role of heredity as well as habits in determining individual weight. Included is a chart that lists daily nutritional needs. Nonfiction.

Arnold, Peter (with Edward L. Pendagast, Jr.). **Emergency Handbook: A First Aid Manual for Home and Travel.** Illus. Charles McVicker. Plume Books, 1981.

This book covers all kinds of medical emergencies, including insulin shock, bee stings, choking, fainting, and strokes. Realistically, the reader is cautioned to be prepared and instructed here on how to take care of these situations that can arise either at home or away. Nonfiction.

Bayrd, Ned, and Chris Quilter. **Food for Champions: How to Eat to Win.** Houghton Mifflin, 1982.

Combining research findings from the fields of nutrition, medicine, and sports science, Bayrd and Quilter present a case for improving athletic performance by eating right. In other words, they tell you how to gain a competitive edge by maintaining the proper diet. All aspects of sports nutrition are covered, from assessing your nutritional needs, to the effects of steroids and megavitamins, to providing nutritional plans for basic training as well as for intensive competition. Nonfiction.

Diagram Group. **The Healthy Body: A Maintenance Manual.** Plume Books, 1982.

Presented in a simple, direct manner, *The Healthy Body* is a handy resource book that provides answers to questions about most health concerns, from pinkeye to pregnancy and head lice to hair transplants. The explicit diagrams, drawings, and charts add to the reader's understanding. The author warns, however, that this book is not a replacement for a medical doctor. Nonfiction.

Dominguez, Richard H., and Robert S. Gajda. **Total Body Training.** Warner Books, 1983.

Dominguez, a doctor specializing in sports medicine, and Gajda, a sports trainer, combine their expertise to present here a sensible approach to total body training. The correct methods for carrying out the activities of a coordinated program are demonstrated. Nonfiction.

Fretz, Sada. **Going Vegetarian: A Guide for Teenagers.** Illus. Eric Fretz. William Morrow, 1983.

This guide for teenagers will be an eye-opener for those who are not familiar with the reasons people become vegetarians. The author states her case clearly by presenting philosophical, practical, and nutritional aspects of vegetarianism. Fretz also includes over fifty meatless recipes and a bibliography of recommended cookbooks. Nonfiction.

Gillespie, Oscar. **Herpes: What to Do When You Have It.** Grosset and Dunlap, 1982.

Taking the reader step by step, Dr. Gillespie defines herpes and presents a calm, sane way of helping the reader cope with the myths and misinformation commonly associated with this disease. He talks about feelings, treatments, and resources that are available so that the patient's fears can be eliminated. Nonfiction.

Heidenstam, Oscar, editor. **The New Muscle Building for Beginners.** Arco, 1983.

The subject of this book is keeping one's body healthy and beautiful. In a simple style, Heidenstam describes how seven food supplements and exercises can keep one physically fit. The diet is simple, and the exercises are easy to perform. Along with the illustrations and diagrams, photographs of Mr. Universe and Olympian title winners are presented. Nonfiction.

Landau, Elaine. **Why Are They Starving Themselves? Understanding Anorexia Nervosa and Bulimia.** Julian Messner, 1983.

Being skinny, especially for girls, is a highly desired goal in our society. But for many teenagers, that goal leads to one of the related disorders of anorexia nervosa or bulimia, both of which can lead rapidly to an early death. By looking at examples of real teenagers, Elaine Landau shows the effects of these two contemporary disorders, issues underlying the personalities of those likely to suffer from food-related problems, treatments of these problems, and places where teenagers can seek help. Nonfiction.

Levenkron, Steven. **Treating and Overcoming Anorexia Nervosa.** Charles Scribner's Sons, 1982.

Anorexia nervosa is a disease that strikes one out of every 250 teenage girls. But teenagers are not the only victims: women from twenty to sixty-two as well as young men are also affected. Here Dr. Levenkron unravels the mystery of the disease and sympathetically answers many questions to help the reader to understand the doctor, the family, and the patient. The case studies are poignant, and the book itself is comprehensive. Nonfiction.

Mace, Nancy L., and Peter V. Rabins. **The Thirty-Six-Hour Day: A Family Guide to Caring for Persons with Alzheimer's Disease, Related Dementing Illnesses, and Memory Loss in Later Life.** Warner Books, 1984.

A resource about debilitating illnesses, including Alzheimer's disease, this book gives helpful hints on how to handle the behavior of family members who are affected with memory loss. This is a valuable tool for all persons faced with this health problem. Nonfiction.

McCoy, Kathy, and Charles Wibbelsman. **The Teenage Body Book.** Rev. ed. Illus. Bob Stover. Wallaby Books, 1984.

The Teenage Body Book discusses the female and male bodies, health, grooming, emotions, and many questions about sex. The easy-to-follow question-and-answer style is appealing. Nonfiction.

McGregor, Rob Roy, and Stephen E. Devereux. **EEVeTeC: The McGregor Solution for Managing the Pains of Fitness.** Illus. Bill Hoest. Houghton Mifflin, 1982.

Pronounced *ev-ah-tek,* the letters stand for *E*quipment, *E*nvironment, *Ve*locity, *Te*chnique, and *C*onditioning. This is the McGregor system for handling those five variables in sports as an alternative to playing in pain or quitting. Sports medicine pioneer and marathoner Dr. Rob Roy McGregor and tennis expert Stephen Devereux together provide hundreds of sensible tips that sports enthusiasts can use to avoid injury or to deal with it effectively if an injury does occur. Clever cartoons help convey the messages throughout this lively text. Nonfiction.

Miller, Peter M. **The Hilton Head Metabolism Diet.** Warner Books, 1983.

Dr. Miller begins by encouraging his readers to have a good self-image and not to feel guilty for weighing too much. The chapters are easy to read, and the author talks to the reader in a nonscientific way. This diet's focus is on losing weight sensibly by eating healthy meals and exercising moderately. Nonfiction.

Myers, Irma, and Arthur Myers. **Why You Feel Down—And What You Can Do about It.** Charles Scribner's Sons, 1982.

The teenage years are often the most difficult time in a person's life, and some teenagers find themselves frequently depressed. Speaking directly and candidly to readers, the authors explore the demands placed on teenagers, suggest ways to avoid depression, and offer activities and sources of help when depression occurs. Nonfiction.

Roth, Geneen. **Feeding the Hungry Heart: The Experience of Compulsive Eating.** Signet Books, 1983.

True stories from the author and other compulsive eaters tell how to overcome emotional hungers that cause secret food binges. The author's style makes it easy for the reader to believe the incidents and to take heart that there is help for food addicts. Nonfiction.

Squire, Susan. **The Slender Balance: Causes and Cures for Bulimia, Anorexia and the Weight-Loss/Weight-Gain Seesaw.** G. P. Putnam's Sons, 1983.

Squire defines bulimia, anorexia, and the weight-loss/weight-gain seesaw, offers some suggestions for correcting these eating disorders, and looks at case studies of both males and females who have these problems. Her sensitive approach to a clinical subject is comforting. Nonfiction.

Stabile, Toni. **Everything You Want to Know about Cosmetics; Or, What Your Friendly Clerk Didn't Tell You.** Dodd, Mead, 1984.

Called "the Ralph Nader of the cosmetic industry," Toni Stabile reveals here many facts you may not know about the products you use every day. Did you know, for example, that the term *cosmetics* refers not just to makeup, but to shampoo, toothpaste, bubble bath, talcum powder, mouthwash, and deodorant, too? And classified as cosmetics, these products escape most of the consumer safeguards we're accustomed to having on our food and drugs. Nonfiction.

Ullyot, Joan L. **Running Free: A Guide for Women Runners and Their Friends.** Perigee Books, 1982.

This guide for women who like to run is a personal yet simple approach for beginners and marathoners alike. So that beginners can feel comfortable with its message, the book moves from a simple to a more complex understanding of running. The advice given here is encouraging, insightful, and beneficial. Nonfiction.

Witt, Reni L., and Jeannine Masterson Michael. **Mom, I'm Pregnant.** Scarborough Books, 1982.

A realistic, objective guide for teenagers, this book supplies information on the issues surrounding an unplanned pregnancy, the alternatives, and their consequences. From the first sentence, "You are not alone," to the conclusion, the authors radiate empathy and offer sound advice for the over one million teenage girls who become pregnant each year. Also included are candid observations by pregnant teens, who share their feelings and offer their insights. Nonfiction.

Historical Fiction

Aiken, Joan. **The Girl from Paris.** Doubleday, 1982.

The social whirl of Paris in the 1860s changes twenty-one-year-old Ellen Paget's life after she is whisked from her prim and proper English boarding school to a post as governness to the Comte and Comtesse de la Ferte. Her experiences in Paris help her cope with life and love when family obligations force her to return to Victorian England. Fiction.

Aldrich, Bess Streeter. **A Lantern in Her Hand.** Signet Vista Books, 1983.

Abbie MacKenzie, a talented singer and aspiring artist, is nineteen when she marries Will Deal in 1865. Homesteading in Nebraska, Abbie and Will face droughts, dust storms, blizzards, and locust infestations. Abbie's courage and her love for Will and her children lead her to sacrifice her dreams for theirs. Originally published in 1928. Fiction.

Brown, Dee. **Killdeer Mountain.** Holt, Rinehart and Winston, 1983.

Sam Morrison, a journalist, travels on a steamer heading up the Missouri River in 1866 to a commemoration in honor of Charles Rawley, Civil War hero and Indian fighter. But Morrison has many questions about Rawley's identity and his actions. Did Rawley capture the hated Indian chief Spotted Horse, or was it the harmless Medicine Horse? Is he the hero of the battle of Killdeer Mountain or a coward? Is he Captain Rawley, son of the United States senator, or is he Drew Hardesty, "Galvanized Yankee" (a Confederate P.O.W. swearing allegiance to the Union)? This Western adventure by the author of *Bury My Heart at Wounded Knee* is filled with mistaken and/or disguised identities and a true feeling for the post–Civil War frontier. Fiction.

Carter, Forrest. **Watch for Me on the Mountain.** Laurel Editions, 1983.

The great Apache warrior Geronimo, whose name was feared throughout the Southwest, resists the effort of the U.S. government to place his tribe on reservations, which would force them to abandon their traditional lands and life-styles. Raising a small band of warriors, Geronimo keeps the U.S. Army fully occupied until his capture in 1877. Originally published as *Cry Geronimo!* Fiction.

Clavell, James. **Noble House: A Novel of Contemporary Hong Kong.** Dell, 1982.

The financial and political complexities caused by the dual Chinese/ British heritage of Hong Kong come to life when Linc Bartlett, a self-made American millionaire, and his beautiful associate, Casey Tcholok, arrive on the island in 1963 to attempt a business takeover of Noble House. Ian Dunross, *tai-pan* of Noble House, strives to save his crumbling financial empire, while his traditional rival, Quillan Gornt, manipulates matters to ensure its downfall. Linc and Casey play one rival against the other as they maneuver to dominate a business world where politics, espionage, and romance are intertwined. Fiction.

Farber, Norma. **Mercy Short: A Winter Journal, North Boston, 1692– 93.** Unicorn Books, 1982.

Mercy Short is a seventeen-year-old indentured servant caught in the hysteria surrounding the Salem witchcraft trials of 1692. Mercy fights her possession by demonic forces with the help of Cotton Mather, a Puritan clergyman who believes that "witches" can be treated with prayer and fasting. In her journal entries, Mercy describes her experiences when possessed and also recounts her captivity by Indians. She draws a strong contrast between the Indian life-style and that of the colonists. Fiction.

Foreman, Paul. **Quanah: The Serpent Eagle.** Northland Press, 1983.

Quanah Parker, son of a white captive and a Comanche chief, challenges Captain Ronald MacKenzie of the U.S. Army by leading his band of Indian warriors on innumerable raids on white settlers and army units. An intelligent and fearless chief, Quanah combines his Comanche expertise, his skill with horses, and his use of peyote to frustrate the army's efforts to resettle the Indians in accordance with the Medicine Lodge Treaty of 1867. Fiction.

Forrest, Anthony. **The Pandora Secret.** Hill and Wang, 1982.

In 1804, Robert Fulton, debonair American inventor, leaves Napo-leonic France to continue his work on a "plunging" boat or "sub-mersible" vessel for the British Admiralty. The Admiralty, realizing

Fulton's invention could change the course of modern naval warfare, assigns Captain John Justice to protect the *Pandora* and Fulton. Rich in period detail and historically accurate, this novel is the second volume in the Captain Justice adventure series. Fiction.

Geras, Adèle. **Voyage.** Atheneum, 1983.

The immigrant experience is captured here as three young Jewish girls—Minna, Golda, and Rachel—flee Eastern Europe for America in 1904. Sharing crowded steerage quarters, the girls find that despite their different reasons for leaving home, their troubles fade as they reveal their hopes for love and security in the new world. Fiction.

Guthrie, A. B., Jr. **Fair Land, Fair Land.** Houghton Mifflin, 1982.

Dick Summers marries a Blackfoot squaw, Teal Eye, and tries to recapture the independent and idyllic wilderness experience he knew as a mountain man in this sequel to *The Way West*. White settlers pouring into the upper Missouri during the 1850s fail to understand Indian values and culture, which leads to tragic consequences for Dick and his family. Fiction.

Heaven, Constance. **The Wildcliffe Bird.** Coward-McCann, 1983.

Fleeing Paris after her father's death, young and beautiful Juliet Prior is forced to take refuge with her Chartley relatives. Family secrets and love dominate this romance set in mid-nineteenth-century Yorkshire against the background of the Chartist labor movement in the pottery factories. Fiction.

Heidish, Marcy. **The Secret Annie Oakley.** Plume Books, 1984.

Annie Oakley, famous sharpshooter, is at the height of her career when newspaper articles published by William Randolph Hearst harm her reputation. Her partner, manager, and husband, Frank Butler, realizes he does not know the real Annie as the truth of her painful childhood comes to light. This biographical novel colorfully details the show business world of the late nineteenth century as well as the very courageous person the world knew as "Little Sure Shot." Fiction.

Herbert, Kathleen. **Queen of the Lightning.** St. Martin's Press, 1984.

After the sudden death of her brother, Riemmelth, a Celtic princess, becomes heiress of Cumbria. In an effort to protect her and her inheritance from warring tribes, her grandfather forces her to marry Oswy of Northumbria, an Englishman. But Riemmelth is in love with Elidir, a man without property who is below her rank. Taught to despise the English as crude and uncivilized, Riemmelth faces a most distasteful marriage in this action-packed romance set in seventh-century Britain. Fiction.

Hodges, Margaret. **The Avenger.** Charles Scribner's Sons, 1982.

Seeking revenge for a disservice dealt to his father, the ruler of Asini, Alexis, fifteen years old and an Olympic champion, is captured by pirates and sold into slavery along with his foe, Glaukon of Tiryn. Circumstances force the two boys together as they fight side by side at the Battle of Marathon during the Persian Wars in 490 B.C. Fiction.

Hurmence, Belinda. **Tancy.** Clarion Books, 1984.

Tancy, an eighteen-year-old house slave on the Gaither plantation in North Carolina, finds herself freed at the end of the Civil War. Determined to locate her real mother, who had been sold from the plantation, Tancy travels to Knoxville, works for the Freedman's Bureau, and copes with the problems of providing for herself after a life dependent on the wishes of other people. Fiction.

Jones, Douglas C. **Gone the Dreams and Dancing.** Holt, Rinehart and Winston, 1984.

Civil War veteran Liverpool Morgan, working as an army contract driver and Indian interpreter at Fort Sill in 1875, watches the surrender of Comanche chief Kwahadi and his people. Mutual respect between these two warriors leads to Liver's search for Kwahadi's white mother, Chosen, who was retaken by the Texas Rangers in 1854. While learning and adapting to the white world, Kwahadi instills in Liver an appreciation of the Indian way of life. Liver marries into the tribe and remains a friend and brother to The People as Oklahoma emerges into statehood. Fiction.

Kent, Alexander. **Success to the Brave.** G. P. Putnam's Sons, 1983.

This latest novel in the seafaring series featuring Richard Bolitho of the British Navy is set in 1802. Bolitho, promoted to vice admiral, is sent to Caribbean waters to carry out the terms of the Treaty of Amiens and give the island of San Felipe to the French. A dedicated and humane seaman, Bolitho is frustrated by his new rank, his orders, and his separation from his wife as he acts the role of warrior and diplomat while fighting a renegade British governor, the French, and the Spanish. Vivid scenes of sea battles, naval blockades, and close escapes characterize this authentic adventure tale. Fiction.

Leekley, John. **The Blue and the Gray.** Dell, 1982.

The fury of the Civil War forces two families, the Geysers and the Hales, to break the blood bond that existed between them. Famous Civil War battles are described through the eyes of John Geyser, an artist for the *Gettysburg Compiler,* in this companion to the television miniseries of the same title. Fiction.

Llywelyn, Morgan. **The Horse Goddess.** Houghton Mifflin, 1982.

Epona, daughter of a Celtic chief, is initiated into womanhood at fourteen. Gifted with telepathic powers with horses, Epona is pressured by the Druid high priest to become a Druid priestess. But she is determined to control her own life, so she flees her tribe and accompanies Kazhok, a Scythian warrior and prince of the wild horsemen, to his tribe on the eastern plains. Set in the eighth century B.C., this historic novel combines adventure and love. Fiction.

Lofts, Norah. **Madselin.** Doubleday, 1983.

During the Norman invasion of Anglo-Saxon England in 1066, Madselin, the seventeen-year-old wife of an aging Saxon landlord, is left a widow without a family, a home, or her former social position. To survive, Madselin, a girl with strong convictions and great pride, marries the conquering Norman, Rolf—the man responsible for her deprivations. Fiction.

McCunn, Ruthanne Lum. **Thousand Pieces of Gold.** Laurel Editions, 1983.

Lalu Nathoy is sold to bandits by her starving family in China. Her name changed to Polly Bemis, she is traded by the bandits into slavery, and then brought to America, where she works the saloons of the rough California gold mining towns. A remarkable woman who endures frontier hardships and the humiliations dealt to the Chinese in California in the late nineteenth and early twentieth centuries, Polly eventually marries and homesteads with the man who won her in a poker game. Fiction.

Michener, James A. **Poland.** Random House, 1983.

Over seven hundred years of Polish history, from the Tartar invasions of the thirteenth century to the current Communist regime,
are presented by melding the lineage and destinies of three families
from three different classes of society—the nobility, the gentry, and
the peasantry. Through all the tragedies and traumas of history—
constant invasions, occupations, and wars—the spirit, ideals, pride,
and resilience of the Polish people remain intact. Fiction.

Michener, James A. **Space.** Random House, 1982.

Covering a spectrum of political, scientific, and technical events,
this lengthy fictionalized account of the development and imple-
mentation of America's space program from the 1940s to today
includes appearances by many real historical figures. Fiction.

Moore, Ruth Nulton. **In Search of Liberty.** Illus. James Converse.
Herald Press, 1983.

Fourteen-year-old Jon Reed is given a 1794 Liberty penny by his
father as a good-luck piece prior to an operation. As the story
traces this nearly two-hundred-year-old coin's journey from its
original owner, Jeremy, a Philadelphia chimney sweep, to Vinh, a
Vietnamese refugee, it also traces significant events in this country's history, including slavery, the underground railroad, the settlement of the West, and the Nez Percé's trek to Canada with Chief
Joseph. Fiction.

Oates, Stephen B. **The Fires of Jubilee: Nat Turner's Fierce Rebellion.**
Mentor Books, 1976.

In 1831, in Southampton County, Virginia, Nat Turner, a deeply
religious man and a self-styled visionary, leads a band of discon-
tented slaves in one of the bloodiest rebellions in American history.
Nat's personality, his sense of mission, his struggle under slave
conditions, and the attitudes and feelings of Southern white slave
owners are carefully documented in this detailed account of this
tragic insurrection. Fiction.

Paterson, Katherine. **Rebels of the Heavenly Kingdom.** Lodestar Books,
1983.

During the Taiping Rebellion in China (1850–1864), a poor and
illiterate peasant, sixteen-year-old Wang Lee, is kidnapped by
Chinese bandits. Freed by Mei Lin, a woman warrior in the secret

society that is plotting to overthrow the Manchu emperor, Wang learns to read, to fight, and to love. Fiction.

Penman, Sharon Kay. **The Sunne in Splendour.** Penguin Books, 1984.

Fifteenth-century battle scenes, political intrigues, and family conflicts are richly detailed in this story of Richard Plantagenet. Richard, Duke of Gloucester, devoted and loyal to his brother Edward IV, becomes entangled in a power struggle for the throne of England after Edward's death when the question of the legitimacy of Edward's sons surfaces. Passionate, brave, and kindly, Richard III finds himself accused of murder and betrayed by former allies and friends. Long maligned in history, Richard's moral character is redeemed in this interpretation. Fiction.

Stone, Irving (edited by Jean Stone). **The Origin: A Biographical Novel of Charles Darwin.** Signet Books, 1982.

Introducing his theory of evolution into the nineteenth-century Victorian world, Charles Darwin rocked both scientific and social circles with a controversy that continues today. This lengthy biographical novel details Darwin's life, love, and scientific theories. Fiction.

Sutcliff, Rosemary. **Bonnie Dundee.** E. P. Dutton, 1984.

In seventeenth-century Scotland, teenager Hugh Herriott is at odds with his rebellious Covenanter family. Rejecting their beliefs, Hugh follows John Graham of Claverhouse (Bonnie Dundee), head of the King's Cavalry, as the cavalry tries to subdue the Scottish rebels. Hugh's love for the mysterious Darklis does not sway him from Claverhouse's side as Claverhouse battles to the death for King James against William and Mary. Fiction.

Turner, Ann. **The Way Home.** Crown, 1982.

During the spring of 1349, Anne, a teenager, is forced to flee her beloved English village. Lord Thomas's men are searching for her, claiming she is a witch who has caused Lord Thomas's death and created the great plague. For months, Anne is forced to live in the great marsh, waiting for the summer to end so she can return home. Fiction.

Vosper, Alice. **Rags to Riches.** Flare Books, 1983.

When Julie's father strikes it rich with a copper mine worth a million dollars, she goes through an exciting, almost overnight change from a poor hill-country girl to an elegant young woman whose possibilities for the future are endless. Julie meets each challenge of her new life and enjoys the advantages that wealth gives her in the 1880s. But, at the same time, she comes to realize that there are limitations to the happiness that wealth can bring. Fiction.

Wallin, Luke. **In the Shadow of the Wind.** Bradbury Press, 1984.

A sort of Indian and Anglo *Romeo and Juliet* set on the Georgia frontier in 1835, this novel explores the love between Pine Basket, a Creek Indian, and Caleb McElroy, son of white settlers. Caleb is cast against his own people as the whites slowly but resolutely destroy the Indians' forests and sources of sustenance, finally forcing them along the Trail of Tears to distant Oklahoma. Amidst the fighting and the fear, the two sixteen-year-olds uncover the differences as well as the similarities between their peoples. Fiction.

Wisler, G. Clifton. **Thunder on the Tennessee.** Lodestar Books, 1983.

Determined to uphold the family tradition of being in the front line of battle, sixteen-year-old Willie Delamer eagerly follows his father into the Second Texas Regiment in 1862. With little training, and armed with muskets left over from the 1845 Mexican War, the green Confederate troops engage the Yankees on the banks of the Tennessee. In a battle which history nicknames "Bloody Shiloh," Willie displays the courage, valor, and terror of the common soldier. Fiction.

History

Barzini, Luigi. **The Europeans.** Penguin Books, 1983.

What contributes to the character of a nation? Barzini presents portraits of what he describes as the quarrelsome French, the flexible Italians, the careful Dutch, and, in the annex to Europe, the baffling Americans. With these differences, is the dream of a united Europe possible? What role would America play in the future of Europe? This book provides insight into what generates national pride and national character. Nonfiction.

Blumenthal, Shirley, and Jerome S. Ozer. **Coming to America: Immigrants from the British Isles.** Laurel-Leaf Library, 1981.

Although the British subjects who settled in Virginia and Massachusetts in the seventeenth century called themselves colonists, they were really the first immigrants to a land already inhabited by Native Americans. These colonists, and the Welsh and Scottish immigrants who joined them later, left England for economic reasons or to escape religious and political persecution. In the 1840s, almost a million Irish came to America, fleeing from the poverty and disease caused by the potato famine. This third volume of the Coming to America series tells the story of all these immigrants from Great Britain. Notes, a bibliography, and a brief history of U.S. immigration laws are included. Nonfiction.

Bruce, Preston. **From the Door of the White House.** Lothrop, Lee and Shepard Books, 1984.

As doorman for five presidents, Preston Bruce had the opportunity to view and sometimes participate in some of the most important events in recent American history. Here he provides an insider's perspective on the personal and professional lives of Presidents Dwight D. Eisenhower, John F. Kennedy, Lyndon Johnson, Richard Nixon, and Gerald Ford, and tells of his role in such momentous events as the funeral of President Kennedy and the resignation of Richard Nixon. Nonfiction.

Davis, Burke. **The Civil War: Strange and Fascinating Facts.** Illus.
Raymond Houhlihan. Fairfax Press, 1982.

Every student knows the basic facts about the bloody confrontation
which began in 1861 between the North and the South. But did
you know that the first machine gun was used during the Civil War
by the Union troops? Did you know that the hero of Gettysburg
was a seventy-year-old man who joined the Union Army for only
a few hours on July 1, 1863? These and hundreds of other little-
known facts about the Civil War appear in Davis's fascinating
book. Originally published in 1960 as *Our Incredible Civil War.*
Nonfiction.

Davis, Daniel S. **Behind Barbed Wire: The Imprisonment of Japanese
Americans during World War II.** E. P. Dutton, 1982.

The relocation camps during World War II had high barbed wire
fences around them and soldiers on guard outside. Who was in
these camps? Not our enemies, but Americans of Japanese descent,
who were denied some of their most basic rights. *Behind Barbed
Wire* sheds light on what happened during some of America's
darkest days. Nonfiction.

Dawidowicz, Lucy S. **On Equal Terms: Jews in America 1881–1981.**
Holt, Rinehart and Winston, 1982.

"America is the land of freedom and opportunities whose streets
are paved in gold." Beliefs such as these served to draw huge
numbers of immigrants to the United States between 1870 and
1930. When these people arrived, they found a land that demanded
hard work, patience, and the ability to deal with hardships.
Dawidowicz's history of Jews in America begins with the assassination of the Russian czar Alexander II on March 31, 1881. She
catalogs the major events and influences on Jewish migration and
identity, and the relationship to the American ideals of freedom
and democracy. By recounting the levels of prejudice and hardships
faced by Jews, *On Equal Terms* is essentially a tale of the difficulties
overcome. Nonfiction.

Downs, Robert B. **Books That Changed the World.** Rev. ed. Mentor
Books, 1983.

Beginning with the Bible, Downs traces the course of Western
history by examining the greatest ideas published in both the
humanities and the sciences. Several chapters are devoted to the
contributions of the ancient Greeks and Romans, but more modern

authors like Mary Wollstonecraft *(Vindication of the Rights of Women)*, Karl Marx *(Das Kapital)*, Charles Darwin *(Origin of Species)*, and Albert Einstein *(Relativity, the Special and General Theories)* are featured, too. The most recent work included is Rachel Carson's *Silent Spring,* her 1962 discussion of environmental pollution caused by pesticides. *Books That Changed the World* was originally published in 1956. Nonfiction.

Ewers, John C. **The Blackfeet: Raiders on the Northwestern Plains.** University of Oklahoma Press, 1982.

First published in 1958, this two-hundred-year history of one of the strongest and fiercest tribes on the Western plains relies not just on historical facts but also on firsthand accounts which give the presentation an honesty and liveliness that make it highly readable. The text is accompanied by several informative drawings and photographs and followed by an extensive bibliography. A volume in the Civilization of the American Indian series. Nonfiction.

Ford, Barbara, and David C. Switzer. **Underwater Dig: The Excavation of a Revolutionary War Privateer.** William Morrow, 1982.

This account of the archaeological excavation of the Revolutionary War privateer *Defence,* which was sunk in Penobscot Bay, Maine, in 1779, provides a clear look at the new science of nautical archaeology. The six-year-long scientific undertaking shed new light on an often overlooked defeat in American naval history. Illustrated with photographs and diagrams. Nonfiction.

Gard, Wayne. **The Chisholm Trail.** Illus. Nick Eggenhofer. University of Oklahoma Press, 1984.

Cowboys herding cattle from Texas to railroads in Kansas between 1867 and 1884 often used the Chisholm Trail. The trip was always exciting and filled with danger from rattlesnakes, Indians, snowstorms, lightning, river crossings, rustlers, and the longhorns themselves. But the end of the trail always promised riches and places in which to spend them—saloons, gambling parlors, and dance halls. This book looks at the truth behind the legends of the famous trail. Nonfiction.

Josephy, Alvin M., Jr. **Now That the Buffalo's Gone: A Study of Today's American Indians.** University of Oklahoma Press, 1984.

This detailed study looks at Native Americans from their early settlements across the United States (primarily during the 1500s when Spanish and French explorers clashed with already existing tribes) to the present. The author attempts to explain the historical reasons for the conflicts between whites and Native Americans and to explore the nature of the Indian in America. Nonfiction.

Leuthner, Stuart. **The Railroaders.** Photographs by Lawson Little. Random House, 1983.

Carl A. Peterson knew from a very early age that the only place he wanted to work was on the railroad. In 1911 he began his career with the New York Central Railroad, a career which he would end as an engineer some forty-six years later. This unique book represents the lives and views of Peterson and thirty-two other railroaders as they describe their aspirations, memories, and hopes for the future of rail travel. Each man or woman interviewed recalls the numerous special events that made his or her railroad career memorable. Nonfiction.

Lyttle, Richard B. **The Games They Played: Sports in History.** Illus. by author. Atheneum, 1982.

Have you ever wondered what the original Olympic games were like? What individual and team events took place at that time? This book describes the development of the Olympics in the context of Greek history. The author also traces other individual and team sports back to their beginnings, looking at archaeological evidence of sports such as lacrosse and polo. Nonfiction.

Lyttle, Richard B. **The Golden Path: The Lure of Gold through History.** Illus. by author. Atheneum, 1983.

Gold has influenced all peoples, from ancient Egyptians and Sumerians to the modern gold rushers of North America, South America, Australia, and Africa. Even the earliest civilizations developed intricate techniques for working with gold in jewelry, statuary, cloth, religious symbols, and lavishly decorated architecture. The foundations of modern physics and chemistry are but one of several by-products of the "lure of gold" highlighted here. Nonfiction.

Perrin, Linda. **Coming to America: Immigrants from the Far East.** Laurel-Leaf Library, 1981.

Compiled partly from letters, diaries, and interviews, this fourth book in the Coming to America series examines the problems of Chinese, Japanese, Filipino, and Vietnamese immigrants in adjusting to life in the United States, and documents the prejudice and discrimination they found when they got here. The author examines the changing history of Asians in America from 1849, when news of the Gold Rush in California reached China, to the resettlement of the Vietnamese "boat people" in 1979. Photographs, chapter notes, separate bibliographies for each group, and a brief history of U.S. immigration laws make this carefully researched book worthwhile reading. Nonfiction.

Rips, Gladys Nadler. **Coming to America: Immigrants from Southern Europe.** Laurel-Leaf Library, 1982.

This book describes the tide of immigrants from Italy, Greece, Portugal, and Spain who brought their talents, fears, hopes, and customs to America as they came looking for a better life. If your relatives came from these countries, you will learn much about them and your heritage here. Nonfiction.

Robbins, Albert. **Coming to America: Immigrants from Northern Europe.** Laurel-Leaf Library, 1982.

This second volume in the Coming to America series tells the story of the Dutch, French, German, and Scandinavian immigrants who explored and settled the land from Pennsylvania to Oregon and produced many well-known politicians and industrialists like Rockefeller, Roosevelt, Van Buren, Eisenhower, Heinz, Westinghouse, and Du Pont. The book includes illustrations, a bibliography, an index, and a brief history of U.S. immigration laws. Nonfiction.

Ruby, Robert H., and John A. Brown. **Indians of the Pacific Northwest: A History.** University of Oklahoma Press, 1982.

Ruby and Brown detail the history of the Indians of the Pacific Northwest, describing their life-styles, beliefs, art, first dealings with whites, and life on the reservations between 1750 and 1900. For the first time, the history of more than one hundred tribes in fifteen language groups is brought together to form a composite portrait. Revealing photographs and drawings accompany the scholarly text. Nonfiction.

Salisbury, Harrison E. **China: One Hundred Years of Revolution.** Holt, Rinehart and Winston, 1983.

For most Americans, China remains a country of beauty and mystery. Since the Chinese opened their doors to the Western world some ten years ago, we have had a greater opportunity to read about their customs, history, and leaders such as Sun Yat-sen, Chiang Kai-shek, and Mao Tse-tung. The last one hundred years of Chinese history are traced by Salisbury in a well-documented and concise text accompanied by over 125 pictures. Salisbury uses his firsthand knowledge to help the reader to understand Chinese politics, literature, and revolutions. Nonfiction.

Selden, Bernice. **The Mill Girls: Lucy Larcom, Harriet Hanson Robinson, Sarah G. Bagley.** Atheneum, 1983.

As the first planned industrial community, the textile mills of Lowell, Massachusetts, set the scene for subsequent American industrial development. Unique in its efforts to assist its employees, the mill system in turn educated, emancipated, and appalled working women. Focusing on the lives of Lucy Larcom, Harriet Hanson Robinson, and Sarah G. Bagley, who shared the Lowell experience as weavers and dressers during different periods of the nineteenth century, this book cites their contributions as educators and labor reformers to raising the consciousness of the American working woman. Nonfiction.

Stefansson, Evelyn, and Linda C. Yahn. **Here Is Alaska.** 4th ed. Charles Scribner's Sons, 1983.

Now in its fourth edition, *Here Is Alaska* presents a wide-ranging view of our forty-ninth state. The history of the oil rush of 1968–79 reveals the changing face of Alaska and the efforts made to maintain its natural beauty. The central figures in this book are the Alaskan people, and the story is set against the backdrop of facts and fables about this great state, all of which reveal the uniqueness of Alaska. Nonfiction.

Sullivan, George. **Return of the Battleship.** Dodd, Mead, 1983.

A fascination for the sea is reflected in Sullivan's book about the largest of the fighting ships—the battleship. Beginning with the ironclad ships of the Civil War and ending with the reemergence of battleships in the 1980s, he depicts the unique place battleships and aircraft carriers have had in naval history. He explains why battleships have a role in today's navy, even with nuclear submarines and guided missiles. Nonfiction.

Tateishi, John. **And Justice for All: An Oral History of the Japanese American Detention Camps.** Random House, 1984.

Manzanar. Minidoka. Topaz. Tule Lake. Heart Mountain. Beautiful-sounding place names. But it was in these places that over

115,000 Americans of Japanese ancestry living on the West Coast of the United States were confined during World War II. Although much has been written about their experiences, these people have never before spoken out for themselves. From recorded interviews, Tateishi, who was himself confined at the Manzanar camp from the age of three, lets the victims recount their bitter and poignant memories. Nonfiction.

Wallace, Terry. **Bloods: An Oral History of the Vietnam War by Black Veterans.** Random House, 1984.

In the years immediately after the Vietnam War, very little was written about the soldiers' experiences. Now, in the outpouring of stories about that confusing war comes *Bloods,* an account from twenty black veterans who survived. In their own sensitive yet brutal, honest, and insightful words, we can see and feel the uncertainty, the fear, the pride, the horror, and the heroism of their experiences, along with the racial battles that plagued them in and out of the military. Nonfiction.

Underhill, Ruth M. **The Navajos.** University of Oklahoma Press, 1983.

Forced into submission when Kit Carson and his soldiers defeated them in 1864, the once-proud Navajos have struggled to regain their pride and status. This comprehensive history, first published in 1956, is accompanied by photographs and an extensive bibliography. Nonfiction.

Van Dyk, Jere. **In Afghanistan: An American Odyssey.** Coward-McCann, 1983.

To investigate the story behind the newspaper headlines, Jere Van Dyk, an American, traveled to Afghanistan and wrote a first-person account of the country, its people, and its spirit. Current events will seem more human when seen through the eyes of the author. Nonfiction.

White, Theodore H. **America in Search of Itself: The Making of the President, 1956–1980.** Warner Books, 1983.

Pulitzer Prize-winning author Theodore H. White has written three previous books about the presidency in which he analyzed the campaigns of Kennedy, Johnson, and Nixon. Now he takes a broader look at the American chief executive office and describes presidents since 1956: Eisenhower, Kennedy, Johnson, Nixon, Ford, Carter, and Reagan. He explains how forces in American and world affairs influenced these presidents, and, in turn, how their programs and personalities shaped American society. Nonfiction.

Wilroy, Mary Edith, and Lucie Prinz. **Inside Blair House.** Doubleday, 1982.

Mary Edith Wilroy, former manager of Blair House, the U.S. president's guest house, recounts her most fascinating experiences in planning for state visits from leading heads of state who visited Washington between 1961 and 1975. Among the guests you can read about are the Shah of Iran, Golda Meir, Indira Gandhi, Pierre Trudeau, and Leonid Brezhnev. Nonfiction.

Wulforst, Harry. **Breakthrough to the Computer Age.** Charles Scribner's Sons, 1982.

Although today's computers are built by large corporations, that has not always been the case. The history of electronic computing includes the work of scientists, many working independently, who developed the concepts that led to the building of these remarkable machines. Today's modern computers would not exist if it had not been for the work of these little-known individuals. Nonfiction.

Hobbies and Crafts

Alkema, Chester J. **Mask Making.** Sterling, 1983.

With text and photos, this art book shows you how you can make creative masks from such materials as paper, plastic foam, and egg cartons. Step-by-step instructions are included. Nonfiction.

Fixx, James F. **Games for the Superintelligent.** Warner Books, 1982.

Bored with television? These amazing math, logic, and word puzzles will snap you out of that TV trance and occupy your mind for hours. These brainteasers are unconditionally guaranteed to make you superintelligent if you aren't already—or to slowly drive you mad. Nonfiction.

Fixx, James F. **More Games for the Superintelligent.** Warner Books, 1982.

Puzzles and games can provide more pleasure than you can imagine, especially when you can solve them and your friends can't! Tease your brain and your friends' brains with fascinating, ingenious, and almost absurd perplexities. Answers are provided; you'll definitely need them. Nonfiction.

Fixx, James F. **Solve It!** Warner Books, 1983.

If you love to solve puzzles, you'll be mesmerized by this myriad of puzzles and riddles. Some are fun and unusual, while others are mind-boggling challenges even to the best of the problem solvers. You also have a slight edge: the answers are provided here. Here's a sample riddle: What word is spelled wrong in every dictionary? Nonfiction.

Hay, Henry. **The Amateur Magician's Handbook.** 4th ed. Photographs by Audrey Alley. Signet Books, 1983.

A professional magician provides solid advice on performing magic for small or large audiences. Hay illustrates dozens of tricks using cards, coins, balls, and "mentalism." Additional sections tell you how to stage a magic show and how to perform for children. Nonfiction.

Korn, Ellen. **Teach Yourself Calligraphy: For Beginners from Eight to Eighty.** Illus. Boche Kaplan. William Morrow, 1982.

This introduction to calligraphy covers the basics using clear and simple instructions. Requiring few supplies but time and patience, calligraphy is a satisfying hobby. Nonfiction.

Roessler, Carl. **Mastering Underwater Photography.** William Morrow, 1984.

With the aid of brilliantly colored photographs, Carl Roessler offers professional techniques and personal tips for amateur divers to successfully photograph what they see underwater. Included are chapters on cameras, lighting, diving skills, dangers, use of human models, and development of an individual style. Nonfiction.

Sheridan, Jeff. **Nothing's Impossible! Stunts to Entertain and Amaze.** Photographs by Jim Moore. Lothrop, Lee and Shepard Books, 1982.

Clear black-and-white photos illustrate basic but clever tricks in a way that helps to ensure your success with any stunt in this book. Using free or inexpensive materials, you can learn such stunts as balancing a quarter on the edge of a dollar bill, slicing a banana without removing the peel or cutting through it, and mysteriously moving the label from the outside to the inside of a bottle. Nonfiction.

Smith, Ray. **How to Draw and Paint What You See.** Alfred A. Knopf, 1984.

In this book, the author takes a serious approach to a wide range of techniques in drawing and painting in several media, including oil, acrylic, and watercolor. Style and color techniques are covered as well. Nonfiction.

Stine, G. Harry. **Handbook of Model Rocketry.** Arco, 1983.

An invaluable handbook to the fascinating hobby of model rocketry, this comprehensive guide covers every aspect of the subject. Included are instructions in the use of computers (using the BASIC language) and calculators to design and fly original rockets. Nonfiction.

Stolzenberg, Mark. **Clown for Circus and Stage.** Photographs by Neil Sapienza. Sterling, 1983.

Action photos of male and female professional clowns reveal the skills needed to become a clown. Staging routines, makeup techniques, and costuming are included in a step-by-step format, helping to make this guide indispensable for anyone interested in clowning. Nonfiction.

Stolzenberg, Mark. **Exploring Mime.** Photographs by Jim Moore. Sterling Publishers, 1983.

This step-by-step instruction book will start you working in mime immediately. It includes tips on doing warm-up exercises, performing mime, inventing routines, putting on makeup, and creating your own shows. Nonfiction.

Van Wormer, Joe. **How to Be a Wildlife Photographer.** Lodestar Books, 1982.

After twenty years as a wildlife photographer, Joe Van Wormer knows what he's talking about. Here he gives direct and easy-to-understand pointers about where and how to find animals to photograph. He also includes information on composition, background, lighting, and viewpoint, as well as some tips on inexpensive cameras that are good for photographing wildlife. Nonfiction.

Holocaust

Degens, T. **The Visit.** Viking Press, 1982.

Set in present-day Berlin, this gripping reconstruction of Kate's aunt's involvement with the Hitler Youth movement in 1943 is revealed through the diary that Kate finds in the attic. Fiction.

Karmel-Wolfe, Henia. **Marek and Lisa.** Dodd, Mead, 1984.

After Marek and Lisa marry, they change their names to avoid deportation by the Nazis. They're eventually turned in by an informer, however, and sent to different concentration camps. Both survive the war, but separately. Lisa awakens in a hospital, recovering from being shot in the leg. When Marek searches for her, he is told that she didn't survive. But the two refuse to forget one another, and they are eventually reunited through a string of chances as improbable and nerve-racking as the war they have survived. Fiction.

Keneally, Thomas. **Schindler's List.** Penguin Books, 1983.

This is a fictionalized account of the life of Oskar Schindler, a German industrialist who saved Jews from the gas chambers through his ingenious factory-camp. He single-handedly masterminded a scheme to employ Jews in his factory, which doubled as a prison camp, right under the eyes of the Nazis. Fiction.

Oberski, Jona (translated by Ralph Manheim). **Childhood.** Plume Books, 1984.

Thirty years after he was awakened in the middle of the night in his Amsterdam home, Jona Oberski describes his childhood experiences in Bergen-Belsen where, at the age of five, he was imprisoned with his parents. In this brief but terrifying story, he gives us a child's-eye view of life in a concentration camp, where his youth and naïveté prevent him from understanding the atrocities that are all too clear in retrospect. Nonfiction.

Rashke, Richard. **Escape from Sobibor.** Houghton Mifflin, 1982.

Sobibor, one of three Nazi death camps in eastern Poland, was the site of the biggest prisoner escape of World War II. Since the Nazis destroyed all of the physical evidence and all but three documents about the camp, very little has been said about the six hundred Jews who revolted against their guards. Rashke, a non-Jew, tracked down the thirty survivors and recreated this piece of history with the help of their memoirs, diaries, notes, and testimony at war criminal trials, and through personal interviews. Nonfiction.

Rhue, Morton. **The Wave.** Laurel-Leaf Library, 1981.

Based on a true incident which occurred in a California high school, this novelization from a television movie shows one teacher's attempt to dramatically illustrate the powerful group pressures that have influenced many historic movements, especially those in Nazi Germany. Laurie and David are two students who recognize the threat to their individual rights and try to stop the experiment before it is too late. Teleplay by Johnny Dawkins, based on a short story by Ron Jones. Fiction.

Rothchild, Sylvia. **Voices from the Holocaust.** Meridian Books, 1982.

Culled from the William E. Wiener Oral History Library of the American Jewish Committee, this compilation of the memories of Holocaust survivors living in America is divided into life before, during, and after the Holocaust. These stories reflect the culture, ideas, and issues of the Jews of pre–World War II Europe, detail the horrors of death and destruction in the ghettos and concentration camps, and chronicle the hardships of survival throughout and after the war. Nonfiction.

Siegal, Aranka. **Upon the Head of the Goat: A Childhood in Hungary, 1939–1944.** Signet Vista Books, 1983.

Piri Davidowitz is nine at the start of this autobiography and fourteen when she and her family leave the ghetto bound for the Nazi death camp Auschwitz in 1944. In between are her vivid memories of growing up in the countryside and cities of Hungary, as well as surviving in the ghetto in the weeks before deportation. This Newbery Honor Book is a gripping, inspiring story. Nonfiction.

Zyskind, Sara (translated by Marganit Inbar). **Stolen Years.** Signet Books, 1983.

In this autobiogoraphical memoir, the author recreates her life in Poland from 1939 to 1945. She realistically details her six years of suffering, survival, and courage as she moves from an innocent eleven-year-old in pigtails to a concentration camp survivor in her teens. Nonfiction.

Horror, Witchcraft, and the Occult

Aiken, Joan. **A Whisper in the Night: Tales of Terror and Suspense.** Delacorte Press, 1984.

In this collection of thirteen eerie tales for Aiken fans, each story involves young people's encounters with the suspenseful, the horrifying, or the supernatural. Some sample titles are "Finders Weepers," "The Windowbox Waltz," and "Homer's Whistle." Fiction.

Bloch, Robert. **Twilight Zone: The Movie.** Warner Books, 1983.

An extension of the television series and the recent movie, this book presents four stories based on the original film screenplay. Fans of Rod Serling's journeys into dimensions not only of sight and sound, but also of mind, can take another trip into the imaginative twilight zone. Fiction.

Brunn, Robert. **The Initiation.** Laurel-Leaf Library, 1982.

Adam Maxwell discovers that Blair Prep School is being run by a vampire-headmaster. He confides his story to Loren, only to find that many of the Blair students are also part of the vampire plot—a plot to take over the school, the community, and the world. This is the third volume of the Twilight series. Fiction.

Cohen, Daniel. **The Encyclopedia of Ghosts.** Dodd, Mead, 1984.

This encyclopedia draws from a wide variety of sources—parapsychology, psychic research, and ancient ghost stories. Famous ghosts, strange hauntings, poltergeists, and apparitions are featured in written and photographic accounts. Hoaxes such as the Amityville Horror and classic cases such as the Hydesville (New York) Haunting make for intriguing reading. Nonfiction.

Cohen, Daniel. **Masters of Horror.** Clarion Books, 1984.

Horror-film fans will delight in this close-up account of the classic actors and actresses featured in many frightening movies. Writers and stars like Stephen King, Boris Karloff, Steven Spielberg, Bela

Lugosi, and many others are profiled to help you better understand the horror of it all. Nonfiction.

Hoke, Helen, editor. **Demonic, Dangerous and Deadly.** Lodestar Books, 1983.

In this anthology of stories of horror and the supernatural, noted authors such as Roald Dahl, Ambrose Bierce, and Robert Bloch head the list, and a special story by Winston Churchill is also included. Fiction.

Hoke, Helen, editor. **Uncanny Tales of Unearthly and Unexpected Horrors.** Lodestar Books, 1983. Fiction.

Included in this collection are stories by Ray Bradbury, Patricia Highsmith, and other horror authors. The offerings feature elements of the supernatural, the ghastly, the terrifying, the eerie, and the shocking. They are guaranteed to make your imagination run wild and your flesh crawl. Fiction.

Howe, Imogen. **Vicious Circle.** Laurel-Leaf Library, 1983.

The children of Maple Ridge Estates are disappearing one after another, only to be found later in a dazed condition. Jenny suspects the strange Hurch house has something to do with the ominous force clutching the town. Only she and her boyfriend Simon can save Jenny's little sister, Andrea. Thirteenth in the Twilight series. Fiction.

Jones, Diana Wynne. **Witch Week.** Greenwillow Books, 1982.

"Someone in this class is a witch," said the note passed in Mr. Crossley's class at the Larwood House in England. Quickly the orphaned residents begin the search, only to secretly find that they all possess some form of supernatural powers. Does this mean certain death for everyone, or can the old magician Chrestomanci help them survive? Fiction.

Jordan, Lee. **Cat's Eyes.** Signet Books, 1983.

Rachel Chater's husband flies to California on business, leaving Rachel alone in the English countryside with their new child. Each night Rachel awakens in a cold sweat, hearing a tapping at the window and seeing the flash of green cat's eyes watching her every move. Rachel's new friend Celia dismisses everything as mere nightmares. But then Rachel begins to wonder about Celia. Fiction.

Kelley, Leo P. **Night of Fire and Blood.** Illus. Ed Diffenderfer. Bantam Books, 1983.

Life is good for Marilyn: she is working and she is in love. Then strange things begin to happen, and she realizes that someone is trying to hurt her. She can't understand what's going on until she reads *The Book of the Dead,* and then everything suddenly becomes clear. Fiction.

King, Stephen. **Christine.** Viking Press, 1983.

Arnie Cunningham, Leigh Cabot, and Dennis Guilder, three high school students from Pittsburgh, become involved with a super-natural car named Christine, whose dark forces slowly begin to come alive and take over their lives. Dennis and Leigh then face death as they try to break Christine's terrifying hold on Arnie. The use of street language is realistic. Fiction.

King, Stephen. **Cujo.** Signet Books, 1982.

Cujo is Stephen King's chilling story about a rabid St. Bernard who terrifies a mother and her son in Castle Rock, Maine. All kinds of monsters and demons are unleashed as the tale unfolds. Fiction.

King, Stephen. **Different Seasons.** Viking Press, 1982.

Horror author Stephen King demonstrates his versatility in this collection of four short stories. Fans of King will enjoy his "Summer of Corruption" and "Fall from Innocence" tales as he takes his readers through life-or-death adventures in the Maine woods and into the hideous past of his characters. Cliff-hanging plots will satisfy readers seeking mystery and suspense. Fiction.

King, Stephen. **Pet Sematary.** Signet Books, 1984.

Dr. Creed, his wife, and their two small children move into an old house next to an ancient Indian burial ground, the special powers of which soon make Dr. Creed a believer in the resurrection of the dead. The harrowing story involving the little boy Gage will give you goose bumps and shivers. Fiction.

Koontz, Dean R. **Phantoms.** G. P. Putnam's Sons, 1983.

The quiet town of Snowfield, California, is mysteriously being consumed by a strange beast from the past. Dr. Jennifer Paige and her younger sister, Lisa, soon become trapped by the dark, chilling force. Government specialists and local sheriffs battle for their lives in this horrifying adventure. Fiction.

Livingston, Myra Cohn, editor. **Why Am I Grown So Cold? Poems of the Unknowable.** Margaret K. McElderry Books, 1983.

Have you ever had the hair on the back of your neck rise? Or felt cold breezes in windowless spaces? This collection of poems charts how poets have sought to describe and explain the inexplicable, the eerie, and the supernatural. Nonfiction.

McHargue, Georgess. **Meet the Vampire.** Illus. Stephen Gammell. Laurel-Leaf Library, 1983.

Here you'll read of vampires old and modern, east and west, horrible and more horrible, like Vlad the Impaler, the original Count Dracula. The last chapter provides possible explanations for vampires, and the book includes some gruesome black-and-white illustrations. Nonfiction.

McHargue, Georgess. **Meet the Werewolf.** Illus. Stephen Gammell. Laurel-Leaf Library, 1983.

Old tales and legends say that there are people who sometimes turn into wolves. The author uses case histories from around the world to support the existence of werewolves and tells you how to know a werewolf when you see one. Excellent illustrations. Nonfiction.

Phipson, Joan. **The Watcher in the Garden.** Margaret K. McElderry Books, 1983.

Fifteen-year-old Kitty finds a special attachment to a beautiful garden and its owner, an old blind man. Their relationship cannot be understood by anyone except themselves and a violent neighborhood boy, Terry. A struggle comes when Kitty realizes that she can read Terry's mind and that he is a danger to the old man. Fiction.

Poe, Edgar Allan. **The Fall of the House of Usher and Other Tales.** Signet Classics, 1980.

Fourteen gothic tales of terror are presented in this Poe collection. In "The Fall of the House of Usher," the narrator leads us to the family estate of Roderick Usher, where he meets Roderick's sister Madeline and senses the death and decay of the Usher family. What follows, as the morbid figure of Usher unfolds, is an eerie story of cataleptic seizures, premature entombment, and death. Fiction.

Riland, George. **The New Steinerbooks Dictionary of the Paranormal.** Warner Books, 1982.

This reference guide to the psychic, mystic, cosmic, and occult fields is in a dictionary format. Many of the entries are the length of encyclopedia articles, containing both past and present information on subjects ranging from "abracadabra" to "Zen." Nonfiction.

Shelley, Mary; Bram Stoker; Robert Louis Stevenson. *Frankenstein; Dracula; Dr. Jekyll and Mr. Hyde.* Signet Classics, 1978.

The first novel in this collection of classic horror stories introduced by Stephen King is Mary Shelley's eighteenth-century gothic romance, *Frankenstein.* Here, Victor Frankenstein discovers the secret of creating life and fashions a creature out of materials collected from butchers and dissection labs. When the creature later turns into a monster, Victor must spend his final days in pursuit. *Dracula* is the nineteenth-century tale of a vampire who survives on the blood of his victims as he is hunted throughout dreary castles and open graves. The third novel, *Dr. Jekyll and Mr. Hyde,* is about a good man, Dr. Henry Jekyll, who is turned evil by a potent drug. When the evil Mr. Hyde's personality becomes stronger, Dr. Jekyll must find a way to destroy him. Fiction.

Tenny, Dixie. **Call the Darkness Down.** Margaret K. McElderry Books, 1984.

Morfa Owen, an American girl studying at a college in Wales, attempts to locate her Welsh grandparents. Her actions set into motion a series of events that are tinged with the supernatural. Containing much information on Welsh folklore, this novel deals with both good and evil witches. Fiction.

Towne, Mary. **Paul's Game.** Laurel-Leaf Library, 1983.

Julie's ability to receive mental messages from her friend Andrea fascinates the mysterious Paul Deveraux. Soon Paul has Julie attempting all kinds of mind manipulation activities to the point that Andrea wonders if Paul may actually be controlling Julie's mind for his own purposes. With time running out, Andrea must find a way to stop Paul's evil scheme. Fiction.

Wagner, Karl Edward. **In a Lonely Place.** Warner Books, 1983.

This collection of seven frightening stories is sure to bring out the cold sweats in its readers. "In the Pines" and ".220 Swift" by this master horror author will stir the imagination and keep readers away from dark and lonely places. Fiction.

Wagner, Karl Edward, editor. **The Year's Best Horror Stories.** Series X. DAW Books, 1982.

These nerve-racking horror stories by ghostly greats include those of Ramsey Campbell, Harlan Ellison, and M. John Harrison. Campbell's lead story, "Through the Walls," will bring you goose bumps as you begin your journey into eerie worlds. Fiction.

Wagner, Karl Edward, editor. **The Year's Best Horror Stories.** Series XII. DAW Books, 1984.

Here are nineteen stories of horror from the psychological, science fiction, and contemporary realms. Featured writers like Stephen King, Roger Johnson, and Tanith Lee will delight those who love to be frightened out of their skins or taken to worlds not yet discovered. Fiction.

Webster, Joanne. **Gypsy Gift.** Lodestar Books, 1981.

Cassie is given the gift of second sight by Rollo, her part-gypsy boyfriend who cares deeply about her. She finds out, however, that this gift is not always fun and exciting when she begins to see future disasters. Fiction.

Westall, Robert. **Break of Dark.** Greenwillow Books, 1982.

Five stories start out normally, but each ends up intertwined somehow with the supernatural, changing the lives of such ordinary people as a Scottish college student camping by himself, a World War II bombardier, two couples, a police sergeant, and a clergyman. Fiction.

Wright, Betty Ren. **The Dollhouse Murders.** Holiday House, 1983.

A haunted dollhouse is the focal point of this brief novel of the supernatural. Thirteen-year-old Amy and her retarded sister unravel the mystery of the moving dolls and solve a pair of forty-year-old murders. Fiction.

Human Rights

Arrick, Fran. **Chernowitz!** Signet Vista Books, 1983.

For two years all that Bobby Cherno hears from Emmett Sundback is vicious name-calling whenever the two pass each other in Middleboro High. Soon Emmett convinces others to bother Bobby. Bobby is able to take the harassment quietly until even his best friends start calling him names. Then when Emmett's meanness hurts Bobby's parents, Bobby decides to teach Emmett a lesson. But the plan for revenge becomes more complicated than Bobby expects. Fiction.

Ashabranner, Brent. **Morning Star, Black Sun: The Northern Cheyenne Indians and America's Energy Crisis.** Photographs by Paul Conklin. Dodd, Mead, 1982.

For nearly a hundred years the Northern Cheyenne Indians have struggled to survive on their small reservation in Montana. Then recently, energy companies discovered large coal deposits just beneath the surface of their precious land. The Northern Cheyennes now find themselves in the most challenging struggle of their lives: instant wealth is at hand, but only if their land is destroyed. Ashabranner provides a sensitive history of the people and an insightful analysis of their attempts to determine their future. Nonfiction.

Asher, Sandy. **Summer Begins.** Bantam Books, 1982.

Summer Smith has to contribute an article to the eighth-grade class newspaper. She writes an editorial that she doesn't think will be very interesting. But her choice of what she thinks is a "safe" topic turns out to be anything but that. When her article is published there is such a furor that her teacher resigns in protest and Summer finds herself in the midst of the greatest controversy of her life. Fiction.

Corcoran, Barbara. **Strike!** Atheneum, 1983.

Barry and his father, a member of the local school board, seem to disagree on almost everything, but when the teachers decide to go on strike and Barry supports them, the gap becomes even wider. The central issue in the strike is control of the books that are part of the curriculum. In a day of direct confrontation between the two opposing views in the town, Barry must put his values on the line. Fiction.

Engel, Beth Bland. **Big Words.** Lodestar Books, 1982.

The troubled South in the 1960s is the setting for this human drama which unites a twelve-year-old white girl and a black youth charged with murder. From the moment Sandy discovers Will hiding in her tree house, she believes in his innocence and in her right to shelter him. Her decision is not made any easier knowing that she cannot count on support from her father or much of the rest of the white community. Fiction.

Fugard, Athol. **"Master Harold" . . . and the Boys.** Penguin Books, 1984.

Set in South Africa, *"Master Harold" . . . and the Boys* explores the experiences of a young man who has been lovingly raised by black servants. At the play's end, he finds that he must choose between accepting the societal demands of apartheid, which would require him to assert his superiority over his black friends and advisors, or to continue to live as an equal with the people who have given him both love and dignity.

Harris, Marilyn. **Hatter Fox.** Ballantine Books, 1983.

Hatter Fox, a seventeen-year-old Navajo girl, hates and is hated by the white community of Sante Fe, New Mexico. Her young life is marred by involvement with drugs, prostitution, and crime, and Dr. Teague Summer is the only person who wants to help her. He tries to keep Hatter out of the mental institution, but he seems doomed to fail because, as he says, "there is something wrong in the world." Fiction.

Haskins, James. **The Guardian Angels.** Enslow, 1983.

This brief book relates the origins and development of the Guardian Angels, a volunteer organization that tries to prevent crime in the streets and the subways. Both positive and negative viewpoints are given on the multiethnic group which began in New York City in 1979. Nonfiction.

Hentoff, Nat. **The Day They Came to Arrest the Book.** Laurel-Leaf Library, 1983.

Barney Roth, editor of the high school newspaper, believes he must take a stand when a group of students and parents decide that *The Adventures of Huckleberry Finn* should be removed from the school library. The group finds the book offensive to blacks and insists that it be omitted from school reading lists. The question is, where does censorship end? What stops the next group from finding another book offensive to someone else's sensibilities? Fiction.

Hentoff, Nat. **Does This School Have Capital Punishment?** Laurel-Leaf Library, 1983.

Sam Davidson had never been successful in school, but Burr Academy seems to offer him a new chance—until Sam is framed for possession of marijuana by an unpopular student. That student's refusal to confess the truth raises timely questions about fairness and justice. Although this novel is a sequel to *This School Is Driving Me Crazy,* it can be understood and appreciated on its own. Fiction.

Hurmence, Belinda. **A Girl Called Boy.** Clarion Books, 1982.

Blanche Overtha Yancey, or Boy, is a pampered eleven-year-old who dislikes her slave heritage. While on a family outing in the North Carolina mountains, Boy becomes lost. She is transported back in time to the 1850s and taken captive by a pair of slave traders. As she struggles to return to her family and to the present, Boy gains an appreciation for her slave ancestors. Fiction.

Lee, Harper. **To Kill a Mockingbird.** Warner Books, 1982.

Jem and Scout are raised by their father, Atticus Finch, in a dusty little town in the pre–civil rights South. Atticus's defense of a black man, Tom Robinson, in an alleged rape case creates a stir and teaches the children and the adults of the town a lesson in justice and common decency. Originally published in 1960. Fiction.

Magubane, Peter. **Black Child.** Photographs by author. Alfred A. Knopf, 1982.

Black photographer Peter Magubane has assembled a photographic essay on growing up in South Africa under apartheid. His introduction explains the history of apartheid, the frustration it causes, and the eternal hope that things may change. The story is made more dramatic by his camera's focus on the most vulnerable of South Africans—the black children. Nonfiction.

Marzollo, Jean. **Do You Love Me, Harvey Burns?** Dial Books for Young
Readers, 1983.

Lisa likes Harvey Burns. He's good looking, intelligent, and understanding. The only problem is that he is so concerned with being
Jewish that it influences his whole life, including his relationship
with Lisa. The novel becomes mysterious as someone in the town
of Bar Ferry creates a series of bizarre occurrences that seem
designed to separate them. Lisa's confidence is shaken as she comes
to realize that nobody is to be trusted. Fiction.

Mays, Lucinda. **The Candle and the Mirror.** Atheneum, 1982.

At fifteen, Anne resents being left behind on her grandmother's
farm while her mother lectures around the country. In 1895, Emily
Simmons is a true crusader whose most ardent cause is organizing
the miners in the coal country. Later, when Anne joins her mother
and sees the miners' pain and desperation for herself, she sets her
own goals and comes to realize what she must do to make her own
contribution. Fiction.

Neufeld, John. **A Small Civil War.** Fawcett Juniper Books, 1982.

Ava feels caught in the middle of a debate that is rapidly taking
on the dimensions of a civil war in the small town of Owanka.
Councilman Brady wants to remove *The Grapes of Wrath* from
tenth-grade literature study. His most vocal opponent is Ava's
younger sister, Georgia. Ava's parents, friends, and her boyfriend
(who happens to be the councilman's son) are all divided. Should
Ava write her editorial and take her own stand? Fiction.

Norwick, Kenneth P., editor. **Lobbying for Freedom in the 1980s: A
Grass-Roots Guide to Protecting Your Rights.** Wideview/Perigee
Books, 1983.

Norwick writes a handbook for the "citizen lobbyists" who care
about issues and want to let elected officials know how they feel
in order to bring about change. The book is a resource for sample
materials and discusses the status of such major areas of individual
freedom as reproductive freedom, women's rights, gay rights, drug
laws, and censorship. Nonfiction.

Pfeffer, Susan Beth. **A Matter of Principle.** Laurel-Leaf Library, 1983.

Becca Holtz is a good student, active on her high school newspaper.
But she and her close friends quit the *Sentinel* when they are
censored one too many times by their advisor and by the principal.

The group decides to go underground and really speak out on the issues. No one is prepared for the battle which follows as the students argue their constitutional freedoms. Fiction.

Rhue, Morton. **The Wave.** Laurel-Leaf Library, 1981.

Based on a true incident which occurred in a California high school, this novelization from a television movie shows one teacher's attempt to dramatically illustrate the powerful group pressures that have influenced many historic movements, especially those in Nazi Germany. Laurie and David are two students who recognize the threat to their individual rights and try to stop the experiment before it is too late. Teleplay by Johnny Dawkins, based on a short story by Ron Jones. Fiction.

Samuels, Gertrude. **Run, Shelley, Run!** Signet Books, 1975.

Shelley Farber is a PINS—person in need of supervision. She is regarded as trouble by the court system, and there are people at the state training school who would like to break her spirit. But Shelley plans to run again to save herself, to find a place where trouble can't find her. Fiction.

Stedman, Raymond William. **Shadows of the Indian: Stereotypes in American Culture.** University of Oklahoma Press, 1982.

Stedman looks at the distorted image of the stereotyped Indian found everywhere in popular culture and its transformations in art, literature, and history. He seeks a better understanding and recognition of the Indian as a vital force in the modern world. Nonfiction.

Stucky, Solomon. **For Conscience' Sake.** Herald Press, 1983.

Michael, a Mennonite, believes as his father and grandfather before him that war and killing are wrong. The government calls him a conscientious objector because he is against its policy in Vietnam. Michael is the product of his heritage, and the story of his ancestors helps him to stand by his convictions. Fiction.

Walter, Mildred Pitts. **The Girl on the Outside.** Lothrop, Lee and Shepard Books, 1982.

Based on a real incident that took place at Central High School in Little Rock, Arkansas, in 1957, the story celebrates those individuals destined to pave the way for integration in Southern schools. Sophia, the daughter of a wealthy white family, and Eva, one of nine black students to register at previously all-white Chatman High, dramatize the fear and emotions shared by young people on both sides. Fiction.

Wilkins, Roy (with Tom Mathews). **Standing Fast: The Autobiography of Roy Wilkins.** Viking Press, 1982.

This autobiography of Roy Wilkins tells less of his personal life and more of the civil rights movement in this century. Insights are given into the attitudes and actions toward blacks by each of the presidents from Franklin D. Roosevelt to Jimmy Carter. The role of the NAACP is clearly defined, and the development of newer black groups is also covered. Nonfiction.

Humor and Satire

Adams, Douglas. **The Hitchhiker's Guide to the Galaxy.** Pocket Books, 1981.

Adams turns the end of the world into a hilarious novel which features outlandish events, making the end a lot more fun than the reader might expect. This sophisticated comedy itemizes the Creator's "mistakes," deals with the disappearance of McDonald's, and explains why the universe is a lot safer if you bring a towel. It should be enjoyed by anyone who likes satire. Fiction.

Angell, Judie. **Suds.** Bradbury Press, 1983.

In this soap opera spoof, Sue Sudley decides to sell the family estate, Suddenly, and become a "real teenager" by moving in with her Aunt Paige and Uncle Nick. Orphaned by the midair collision of her parents' planes, Sue shares a series of misfortunes with her governess, her family, and her newfound friends. A gutsy survivor, Sue overcomes each dilemma in fine soap-heroine style. Fiction.

Buchwald, Art. **While Reagan Slept.** G. P. Putnam's Sons, 1983.

In this topical and entirely partisan collection of essays on Ronald Reagan's America, Buchwald's humorous attacks move from subtle satire to forthright bludgeoning. The book offers a hard-hitting and very personal perspective on our fortieth president's personality and policies. Nonfiction.

Feiffer, Jules (edited by Steven Heller). **Jules Feiffer's America: From Eisenhower to Reagan.** Alfred A. Knopf, 1982.

The world of political humor is explored by famous satirist and cartoonist Jules Feiffer. Presidents past and present fall prey to Feiffer's razor-sharp pen-and-ink drawings and sarcastic impressions. Nonfiction.

Grizzard, Lewis. **Kathy Sue Loudermilk, I Love You.** Warner Books, 1984.

Grizzard spins tales of the South with an obvious love for the

Georgian twang, a hankering to explain down-home traditions, and an admiration for the Confederate disposition. All three come alive in this hilarious series of essays which depict the real South. Nonfiction.

Kiesel, Stanley. **The War between the Pitiful Teachers and the Splendid Kids.** Flare Books, 1982.

This novel is a wacky and imaginative spoof on school administrators, high school rules and events, educational jargon, and creative adult hocus-pocus which attempts to save kids from themselves. A wild series of events is concluded by a farcical battle in which "bad teachers" and their diabolic ditto machines are propelled down a sewer pipe to Much City, and rebellious students are fed "Status Quo Solidifiers" in their peanut butter in order to make them respectable, courteous, and conforming young adults. Fiction.

Petersen, P. J. **Here's to the Sophomores.** Delacorte Press, 1984.

Michael is looking forward to a good sophomore year at Hendley High. His friend Warren has decided to return to Hendley rather than go away to prep school, and Michael has a new interest in his old friend Margaret. But by the end of the first week of school, Michael and Margaret find themselves in a situation they're not sure they'll be able to handle. Fiction.

Pinkwater, Daniel. **Slaves of Spiegel.** Four Winds Press, 1982.

Steve Nickelson and his assistant Norman work at the Magic Moscow, a bizarre gourmet, health food, and ice cream restaurant. Both men, needless to say, are quite surprised when their place of employment disappears. They later discover that fat pirates from the planet Spiegel have transported the restaurant through space to compete in an intergalactic junk-food cooking contest. One of the Magic Moscow stories. Fiction.

Pinkwater, Daniel. **The Snarkout Boys and the Avocado of Death.** Signet Vista Books, 1983.

Genghis Khan High School and its bizarre surroundings are the setting for a *Mad Magazine-* or *National Lampoon*-type version of the adventurous lives of 1980s high school students. The book introduces us to the students' Darth Vader-like friends, to detectives in the style of Remington Steel, and even to a life-saving avocado. The author enjoys manipulating and poking fun at silly stereotypes that pervade our everyday news and fictional media. Fiction.

Powers, John R. **The Last Catholic in America.** Warner Books, 1982.

A brief exchange of pleasantries with a fellow passenger on an airplane opens this fictional, first-person memoir about the narrator's experiences as a Catholic school student in Chicago in the 1950s. The narrator recalls, with a pleasantly ironic nostalgia, subjects of both trauma and joy, such as his first confession, the local pastor's attitude toward his unruly flock, and the nuns around whom school life revolved. Fiction.

Rooney, Andrew A. **A Few Minutes with Andy Rooney.** Warner Books, 1982.

Andy Rooney's book is a compilation of light and humorous yet sophisticated essays on everyday experiences shared by us all. Rooney has a comment on everything from the way we choose the soap we buy to the way we answer the telephone. His work is the short-essay version of the satire that is evident in his segment of "Sixty Minutes." Nonfiction.

Rooney, Andrew A. **And More by Andy Rooney.** Warner Books, 1983.

This is Rooney's second book of humorous essays on the human condition in America. Whether the author is commenting on old friends or the weather, sophisticated readers will find in every essay a fresh perspective on their own experiences. Nonfiction.

Inspiration

Augsburger, David. **Caring Enough to Hear and Be Heard.** Herald Press, 1982.

David Augsburger, a professor at a Mennonite seminary, stresses that careful listening is the keystone of good communication. The six chapters of this book are packed with many relevant suggestions that are designed to improve all types of relationships. Biblical references and group exercises are included at the end of each chapter. Nonfiction.

Barrett, William E. **The Lilies of the Field.** Illus. Burt Silverman. Warner Books, 1982.

Homer Smith, a young black man recently discharged from the army, comes upon a group of immigrant nuns who are trying to build a chapel in the desert. Smith's role in this undertaking and its eventual outcome are the basis for this short novel that is both inspirational and moving and that was extremely popular in the early 1960s. Fiction.

Ching, Lucy. **One of the Lucky Ones.** Doubleday, 1982.

This inspiring autobiography tells of a blind Chinese girl's fight for an education and a future. When Lucy Ching was born in the 1930s, a blind girl in China was an outcast with no future other than begging or prostitution. Her family did not throw her out or sell her, but they did ignore her. It was her *amah* (nanny), Ah Wor, who helped Lucy find a productive life that resulted in her helping many other blind Chinese. Nonfiction.

Deford, Frank. **Alex: The Life of a Child.** Signet Books, 1984.

Alex died of cystic fibrosis shortly after her eighth birthday, and this is her father's description of her life and death. He does not follow a strictly chronological format, but deals extensively with the emotional impact his daughter's illness had on her family as well as on her schoolmates, teachers, nurses, doctors, and the community at large. These events led the whole Deford family to examine their individual beliefs in God and heaven. Nonfiction.

De Santo, Charles P. **Dear Tim.** Herald Press, 1982.

This collection of letters, written by a minister to his college-age son, is designed to be an explanation of the basic tenets of Protestant Christianity. Specific biblical references are given to support the points made by the author. Nonfiction.

Froman, Katherine. **The Chance to Grow.** Everest House, 1983.

This book can be many things to many people, but most of all, it offers hope to the parents of handicapped children. Through the use of case studies, it offers insights into the many common types of handicaps resulting from genetic defects, birth or other injury, and/or prenatal problems. In addition, the book explains what a physical therapist does, and contains valuable appendices that list sources for additional information. Nonfiction.

Kaufman, Barry Neil. **Son Rise.** Photographs by author. Warner Books, 1979.

Barry and Suzi Kaufman become aware that their son is autistic. Finding no help in conventional medical circles, they embark on their own program to bring their son into the mainstream of life. *Son Rise* details their struggles and their eventual triumph. Kaufman also devotes a goodly portion of the book to his personal philosophy of life. Nonfiction.

Phillips, Carolyn E. **Michelle.** Signet Books, 1982.

Michelle Price, the subject of this book, is a real girl who was stricken with bone cancer when she was eight. How she fought to overcome the effects of chemotherapy and the amputation of her leg is a moving story. A recurrent theme in this account is Michelle and her family's deep faith in God and their belief that she had divine help in her recovery. Several pages of photographs add to the story. Nonfiction.

Polikoff, Judy (as told to Michele Sherman). **Every Loving Gift: How a Family's Courage Saved a Special Child.** Signet Books, 1984.

Andy Polikoff was born with brain damage, and his family eventually embarked on the controversial technique called "programming." While this book details Andy's progress, it more

impressively details the almost unbelievable emotional and financial
strains put on Andy's parents and his two brothers. The Polikoff's
story offers rare insights into the behavior of others toward the
handicapped. Nonfiction.

Music and Dance

Bentley, Toni. **Winter Season: A Dancer's Journal.** Random House, 1982.

Toni Bentley was a dancer with the New York City Ballet in 1979, but her dancing and her life were not going well. In 1980, she began writing this journal to describe the joys and pains of dancing. It will be of special interest to students considering a career in the arts. Nonfiction.

Bethancourt, T. Ernesto. **T.H.U.M.B.B.** Holiday House, 1983.

Now in high school, Tom and Aurelio, the inseparable buddies from *New York City Too Far from Tampa Blues,* find themselves in trouble for performing their music in a bar. They then hit on a zany scheme to turn the school's fife-and-drum corps into a marching band—not just any marching band, but one with amplified instruments and a rolling bandstand, accompanied by the Godzilla Brothers gang and a squad of karate experts, and preceded by six of the loveliest baton twirlers in school. It's T.H.U.M.B.B.—The Hippest Underground Marching Band in Brooklyn. Fiction.

Busnar, Gene. **Superstars of Country Music.** Julian Messner, 1984.

How much do you know about Hank Williams, Johnny Cash, and Tammy Wynette? *Superstars of Country Music* describes the careers of nine of America's great country music performers, portraying the struggle that each of them went through to become a star. Nonfiction.

Denyer, Ralph (with Isaac Guillory and Alastair M. Crawford). **The Guitar Handbook.** Alfred A. Knopf, 1982.

This handbook and reference guide has been written for anyone interested in guitar music. It covers topics such as guitar innovators, acoustic guitars, electric guitars, and how to play rhythm, melodic, or harmonic guitar. An extensive supply of pictures and charts accompanies the practical advice on maintenance, customizing, amplification, and recording. Nonfiction.

185

Gordon, Suzanne. **Off Balance: The Real World of Ballet.** Photographs by Earl Dotter. Pantheon Books, 1983.

As with any artistic or athletic activity, the good performers make ballet look easy. But behind the beauty and grace of ballet are painful realities seldom seen or even heard about by the general public. Here Suzanne Gordon exposes "the real world of ballet"— life in the ballet schools, the daily strain of being part of a dance company, the constant struggle to remain thin, the injuries that must be endured, and the physical and psychological strain of competition. Nonfiction.

Greene, Bette. **Them That Glitter and Them That Don't.** Alfred A. Knopf, 1983.

Carol Ann Delaney cherishes a dream of becoming a composer and country-western singer when she finishes high school. Her considerable talent goes unrecognized, however, until she sings before the school assembly and realizes her power to move others and win their approval. Jean McCaffrey, Carol Ann's music teacher, encourages her to look beyond the small world of Baines-ville, Arkansas, and her gypsy parents to the larger world of Nash-ville, where she can make her dream come true. Fiction.

Haskins, James. **I'm Gonna Make You Love Me: The Story of Diana Ross.** Laurel-Leaf Library, 1982.

From her birth in 1944 in a Detroit ghetto to her superstar status of today, Diana Ross reveals her tenacity in her climb to the top. Haskins traces Ross's musical beginnings with the Primettes to her move to Motown with the Supremes to movie stardom. Although professional success does not always ensure personal satisfaction for Ross, her personal life is enriched by family love, friends, and understanding. Nonfiction.

Hentoff, Nat. **Jazz Country.** New ed. Laurel-Leaf Library, 1983.

Tom has learned to play the trumpet, but he's not yet acquainted with jazz. Once he meets the jazz musicians, he becomes obsessed with the soul of their music. Then he must make a decision: a jazz career or college. This novel acquaints readers with jazz greats and the music world, although its examples and language reflect the mid-1960s when it was first published. Fiction.

Newton, Suzanne. **I Will Call It Georgie's Blues.** Viking Press, 1983.

Neal Sloane's family lives in the public eye because his father is the Baptist minister in a small Southern town. Underneath a very proper exterior there are many problems tearing the family apart: Neal's sister may not graduate; Neal's younger brother Georgie is overwhelmed by emotional problems; Neal's mother is constantly torn between her husband and her children. At fifteen, Neal himself finds comfort in jazz music, but he is afraid his interest will be misunderstood. Fiction.

Strasser, Todd. **Rock 'n' Roll Nights.** Laurel-Leaf Library, 1983.

For Gary Spector, making it to the top of the music business is what matters. But so much stands in the way: his cantankerous keyboard player, his drummer's weird mother, his attraction to the female bass player (who also happens to be his cousin), and competition from groups like Deranged and the Zoomies. What does it take to get the Electric Outlet sparking? Fiction.

Strasser, Todd. **Turn It Up!** Delacorte Press, 1984.

Turn It Up! continues the struggle of Gary Spector and his band from *Rock 'n' Roll Nights* as they exchange an inept manager for the hollow promises of Barney Star. As the Coming Attractions drift into financial difficulties, Gary seems preoccupied with an attractive ballet dancer, and Allison is the only one with an idea of how to help the band survive. Fiction.

Switzer, Ellen. **Dancers! Horizons in American Dance.** Photographs by Costas. Atheneum, 1982.

Switzer begins by noting that in the early 1980s more people attended dance performances than went to baseball games. For those who enjoy dance performances of all kinds, especially ballet, Switzer provides a brief history and a glimpse into the makeup and philosophy of today's important dance companies, such as the New York City Ballet, the Alvin Ailey Company, and the Dance Theatre of Harlem. She includes personal comments from young dancers as well as from star performers such as Mikhail Baryshnikov and Natalia Makarova. Nonfiction.

Tyler, Anne. **A Slipping-Down Life.** Berkley Books, 1983.

Evie Decker has never been interested in rock music until she hears an interview with Drumstrings Casey on the radio and wants to see him perform at a local night spot. The unsuccessful Drum doesn't notice the unattractive high school junior until she carves his name into her forehead, thus linking them in a very odd way. The unusual relationship between these two misfits moves slowly but inexorably toward self-realization. Originally published in 1970. Fiction.

Mysteries, Spies, and Crime

Adler, C. S. **The Evidence That Wasn't There.** Clarion Books, 1982.

Kim, a high school sophomore, is sure that her favorite teacher, Ms. Davis, and her mother, Emma Davis, are being swindled. However, convincing them or the police is another matter. Before the truth is out, Kim finds herself in real danger and learns a great deal about herself and the two boys in her life. Fiction.

Adler, C. S. **Shadows on Little Reef Bay.** Clarion Books, 1984.

A cross between "Magnum, P.I." and a Nancy Drew story, *Shadows on Little Reef Bay* is a mystery novel set in the Caribbean that pits fifteen-year-old Stacy against a band of drug traffickers. In her search for evidence to clear her friend of smuggling charges, Stacy finds that the real criminals may work in the very hotel where she and her mother are living. Fiction.

Bennett, Jay. **The Executioner.** Flare Books, 1982.

High school senior Bruce Kendall is one of three survivors of an automobile accident that killed the driver, Raymond Warner. Realizing that someone is out to avenge Raymond's death by murdering the survivors, Bruce tries to identify the avenger before he becomes a victim. Fiction.

Bennett, Jay. **Slowly, Slowly I Raise the Gun.** Flare Books, 1983.

Seventeen-year-old Chris Gordon finds that his lead role in *Hamlet* has real-life ramifications when an unsigned note implicates his father in Chris's mother's death. The young man's life is endangered as he tries to find out the truth in this short, suspense-filled novel. Fiction.

Bethancourt, T. Ernesto. **Doris Fein: Legacy of Terror.** Holiday House, 1984.

Eighteen-year-old Doris Fein, a wealthy West Coast heiress and newspaper owner, goes to Chicago to meet the man claiming to be the real heir to her fortune. She almost loses her life as she unravels a puzzle that originated in the mob-dominated Roaring Twenties. This short, fast-paced novel is filled with distinctive characters. Fiction.

Bograd, Larry. **Bad Apple.** Farrar, Straus and Giroux, 1982.

Nicky has never had it easy. His family lives in a run-down building, and he's not very successful in school. When the chance for some easy cash comes along, Nicky considers not taking it, but decides to go ahead. However, neither Nicky nor his friend Prune are prepared for the consequences of their actions. Nicky's realistic struggle to give his life meaning is as upsetting as it is thought-provoking. Fiction.

Bograd, Larry. **The Kolokol Papers.** Laurel-Leaf Library, 1983.

Lev Kolokol's father is a famous Russian dissident. Sixteen-year-old Lev races time and the authorities to write his story of his father's arrest and the family's persecution. He hopes that if the story is smuggled out, it will generate worldwide support. Lev's story is a mixture of terror, tenderness, and suspense, right to the final page. Fiction.

Bonham, Frank. **Premonitions.** Holt, Rinehart and Winston, 1984.

Sixteen-year-old Kevin Spicer is intrigued with Anni, a French girl in his class. After some false starts, they begin to date, but her strong extrasensory powers endanger their relationship and her happiness. Also casting a pall over their friendship is the unexplained drowning of her popular brother the year before. Fiction.

Carroll, James. **Family Trade.** Signet Books, 1983.

In 1960, Jake McKay, son of a CIA official, is a college freshman whose world is falling apart as this hard-hitting spy drama opens. The novel flashes back to the fall of Berlin in World War II and then moves to the present for a tense, exciting, and slightly unexpected conclusion. Fiction.

Cavanna, Betty. **Stamp Twice for Murder.** Tempo Books, 1983.

Sixteen-year-old Janice Nelson, her brother Tony, and their parents arrive in France to see the cottage that her mother unexpectedly inherited from an elderly French uncle whom she had never met. The cottage, deserted and in a state of disrepair, is not at all the way the Nelsons pictured it, and, temporarily, their dreams are dashed. However, they decide to stay for the summer as planned, and while enjoying an exciting and romantic vacation, they solve the mystery of a hidden treasure and an old murder. Fiction.

Chambers, Kate. **Danger in the Old Fort.** Signet Vista Books, 1983.

Diana Winthrop is a seventeen-year-old detective in the tradition of Nancy Drew. In this book, which is more sophisticated than others in the series, her father has her come to Puerto Rico to act as an undercover agent on the set of a TV miniseries with which he is involved. There has been a series of accidents and delays that threaten to ruin the project. Diana and the man in her life, Brad Ferriers, solve the mystery—but at great personal risk. Fiction.

Chambers, Kate. **The Secrets on Beacon Hill.** Signet Vista Books, 1984.

Diana goes to Boston to spend Christmas with her grandmother on Beacon Hill. A string of very valuable family pearls disappears, and it is up to Diana to solve the mystery. This easy-to-read mystery is a little more sophisticated than some of the earlier titles in the Diana Winthrop mystery series. Fiction.

Cody, Liza. **Bad Company.** Warner Books, 1984.

Anna Lee, detective-heroine of *Dupe,* is kidnapped along with a frightened teenage girl. The bulk of the story deals with Anna's coworkers' attempts to find her before it is too late and with Anna's own attempts to escape. Fiction.

Cody, Liza. **Dupe.** Warner Books, 1983.

Scotland Yard calls Deirdre Jackson's death an accident. Her parents believe otherwise and hire Anna Lee, a member of a London private detective agency, to find out the truth. As Anna looks into the dead woman's past, an exciting and tangled story of London's unsavory film industry unfolds. Fiction.

Cohen, Jamey. **The Night Chasers.** Signet Books, 1983.

The night chasers are three gorillas who play a key role when the young scientist working with them is kidnapped in this tale of suspense set in modern Africa. Terrorism and political unrest combine with science, compassion, and love in this very different novel. Fiction.

Coker, Carolyn. **The Other David.** Dodd, Mead, 1984.

Andrea Perkins is a young American serving as an assistant museum curator in Florence, Italy, when a previously unknown masterpiece by Michelangelo surfaces. It serves as the catalyst for a sophisticated tale of suspense, murder, and romance. Fiction.

Collins, Wilkie. **The Moonstone.** Signet Classics, 1984.

The moonstone in the title of this mystery novel is a rare yellow diamond complete with a curse and three Indian guardians who are sworn to protect it. Stolen from a shrine in India, the gem and its ill-starred owners produce a story told from several viewpoints. This novel first appeared in 1868 and is considered a classic in the mystery novel genre. Fiction.

Cross, Amanda. **The James Joyce Murder.** Ballantine Books, 1983.

Kate Fansler is an English professor who is responsible for over-seeing the sorting of some letters written by James Joyce to his publisher. While she is doing this, her thoroughly unpleasant next-door neighbor is shot. Will Kate be able to solve the murder? Fiction.

Cross, Gillian. **Born of the Sun.** Holiday House, 1984.

Paula is suddenly taken out of boarding school by her explorer-adventurer father in order to go on a long-dreamed-of expedition to Peru in search of a lost Inca city. The hastily conceived journey is plagued by misfortune and by the erratic behavior of Paula's father. Many discoveries are made on the trip, the least of which are archaeological. Fiction.

Deighton, Len. **Berlin Game.** Alfred A. Knopf, 1984.

There is a traitor at the very highest level of British Intelligence, and Bernard Samson finds himself in the middle of the problem. A high-ranking member of the intelligence community, he is requested to help an agent escape from East Berlin. However, his life and the lives of all the agents in the East Berlin network are in danger unless he can identify the traitor. Fiction.

Dodson, Susan. **Shadows across the Sand.** Lothrop, Lee and Shepard Books, 1983.

Sixteen-year-old Billie Lowe unexpectedly ends up in Hibiscus, a very small Bayside Florida town, to spend Christmas with her great-uncle. She soon realizes that he and his retired show-business friends are being terrorized. Billie's search for the terrorists is suspense filled and successful. Fiction.

Doyle, Sir Arthur Conan. **The Adventures of the Speckled Band and Other Stories of Sherlock Holmes.** Signet Classics, 1965.

"The Adventures of the Speckled Band" is the first of twelve stories highlighting the shrewd detective Sherlock Holmes. Characterized by his cool analytical skills, his keen powers of observation, and his brilliant inductive reasoning, Holmes solves the seemingly unsolvable. In one story after another, the reader is invited to walk through nineteenth-century England along with Holmes and his faithful companion, Dr. Watson, as the two discuss the clues of a case. Fiction.

Eberhart, Mignon G. **Another Man's Murder.** Warner Books, 1983.

Another Man's Murder is set in Florida, where the hero, Cayce, is suspected of his uncle's murder, an event which occurs when Cayce returns after six years. The reader is kept guessing in this fast-paced yarn. Fiction.

Eberhart, Mignon G. **Postmark Murder.** Warner Books, 1983.

Laura cares for a little Polish refugee girl who may or may not be an heiress to a large fortune in this mystery set in post–World War II Chicago. There is a pair of murders, and Laura is the prime suspect. She has to fight for her life before the real murderer is found. First published in 1955. Fiction.

Eberhart, Mignon G. **Unidentified Woman.** Warner Books, 1983.

The American South just prior to the start of World War II is the setting for this tightly plotted novel. Victoria Steane is cleared of one murder, but more follow, and the finger of suspicion points to her again. Suspense, romance, jealousy, and embezzlement are all story elements in this reprint of a popular 1943 novel. Fiction.

Eberhart, Mignon G. **Witness at Large.** Warner Books, 1983.

A fog-shrouded island is the setting for this mystery novel. The reader knows that Sister did not kill Sahib, but who did? The surprising answer comes at the end of an exciting and tense tale which is complete with boat sinkings and a chase through the tall marsh grasses. Originally published in 1966. Fiction.

Francis, Dick. **Twice Shy.** G. P. Putnam's Sons, 1982.

First Jonathan Derry and then his younger brother William become involved in this suspense-filled tale involving a foolproof system for betting on horse races, a set of computer tapes, murder, and assorted mayhem. The book is set in present-day England and covers a fifteen-year time span. An understanding of racing and betting are necessary for maximum enjoyment. Fiction.

Gardner, John. **Icebreaker.** G. P. Putnam's Sons, 1983.

This James Bond spy thriller involves agents from several normally unfriendly countries allegedly working together to stop the rise of a new Hitler. It has all the usual trappings of the 007 stories: amazing weapons, beautiful women, dangerous agents, thrilling chases, and a breathtaking climax. Fiction.

Giff, Patricia Reilly. **Suspect.** Illus. Stephen Marchesi. Skinny Books, 1982.

An icy night and a bus ride to a strange town begin the adventures of Paul Star, and lead to friendship, mystery, and murder. Although Paul is running from one problem, he finds himself in the middle of another—more dangerous than the one he has left behind. This whodunit keeps the reader guessing all the way. Fiction.

Goulart, Ron, editor. **The Great British Detective.** Mentor Books, 1982.

These fifteen detective stories star such famous sleuths as Sherlock Holmes, Hercule Poirot, Father Brown, and Lord Peter Wimsey, as well as a variety of lesser-known men and women. A good general introduction, introductions to each story, and a reading list at the end of the collection all add to the volume's value and the reader's pleasure. The selections included were written between the 1890s and the 1960s. Fiction.

Guy, Rosa. **New Guys around the Block.** Delacorte Press, 1983.

Sixteen-year-old Imamu Jones spends a summer alone in a rat-infested Harlem apartment while his mother fights for her health in a nearby hospital. Trying to lift Mom's spirits, Imamu paints the apartment in preparation for her homecoming and to keep himself off the streets. Meanwhile, the police are heatedly trying to catch a phantom burglar and Imamu is a prime suspect. He, however, suspects that his new friends might be the very thieves the police are looking for. Fiction.

Hitchcock, Alfred, editor. **Alfred Hitchcock's Daring Detectives.** Random House, 1982.

Eight tales of clever detective work make up this anthology featuring well-known detectives, such as Ellery Queen and Hercule

Poirot, as well as rank amateurs. All stories pose a challenging riddle and, after the reader has solved an array of confusing clues, a satisfying solution. Fiction.

Hitchcock, Alfred, editor. **Alfred Hitchcock's Sinister Spies.** Random House, 1982.

In this collection of ten spy stories, Hitchcock has drawn on the work of several authors, ranging from Somerset Maugham and Lord Dunsany to Eric Ambler. In some, like "Code Two" and "The Problem Solver and the Spy," the reader may well solve the mystery long before the final paragraph. Other stories, however, are baffling to the very end. The wide variety provides spy yarns for every taste. Fiction.

Jackson, Shirley. **We Have Always Lived in the Castle.** Penguin Books, 1984.

This is a very sophisticated and frightening tale of a family's murder by arsenic and the effects of the murder on the remaining three family members, one of whom is accused of the crime. Especially forceful are the actions that the community takes against the survivors. First published in 1962. Fiction.

Jaffe, Rona. **Mazes and Monsters.** Dell Books, 1982.

Four bright young college students start playing Mazes and Monsters, a game similar to Dungeons and Dragons. Gradually the game assumes more and more control over their lives until it becomes all important—with tragic results. The reader will easily become involved with the characters in this rapidly moving novel. Fiction.

James, P. D. **The Black Tower.** Warner Books, 1982.

Adam Dalgliesh of Scotland Yard, a policeman and a published poet, is featured in this mystery novel set in a private hospital for the physically handicapped. Dalgliesh is brought to the scene by the death of an old friend, and the murders continue right up to the unexpected conclusion. This long and complex novel will prove rewarding to the sophisticated reader. Fiction.

James, P. D. **Innocent Blood.** Warner Books, 1982.

Philippa Palfrey, the adopted daughter of a successful university professor and writer, decides she wants to locate her blood parents. After she finds them, she becomes involved in a cat-and-mouse game that has her natural mother as its target. The suspense mounts to a startling conclusion in this long novel set in modern London. Fiction.

James, P. D. **A Mind to Murder.** Warner Books, 1982.

Adam Dalgliesh is again featured in this novel of greed and murder set in a psychiatric clinic. In typical James style, the novel is long and complex and poses a challenging puzzle for reader and detective to solve. Fiction.

James, P. D. **The Skull beneath the Skin.** Warner Books, 1983.

Cordelia Gray, one of P. D. James's two detective creations, is hired to protect the life of Clarissa Lisle, a well-known actress who is to play the lead in a private theatrical performance on an island estate. Cordelia's life is endangered as she learns the startling truth about a series of letters received by the star of the play. Fiction.

Johnston, Velda. **The Other Karen.** Dodd, Mead, 1983.

Catherine Mayhew, an aspiring but unsuccessful actress, is hired by Eunice and Brian Andexter to impersonate their niece Karen, who had run away eight years before at the age of eighteen. The supposed reason for the masquerade is to make Karen's dying grandmother happy during her final days, but Catherine soon begins to suspect a more sinister motive. A search for the truth brings her both love and danger. Fiction.

Johnston, Velda. **Voice in the Night.** Dodd, Mead, 1984.

Carla Baron fled from Arizona to New York after the drowning death of her husband. There she is making a new life for herself and her daughter and even has a new love interest. Then one night, four years after her arrival, the phone rings and over it comes the voice of her dead husband. After two more such calls, Carla returns to Arizona to determine who is at the bottom of her problems. She faces excitement and danger before the novel comes to an unexpected conclusion. Fiction.

L'Engle, Madeleine. **Dragons in the Waters.** Laurel-Leaf Library, 1982.

A curse, a prophecy, a murder, an attempted murder, a sinister cousin, and a valuable portrait of Simón Bolívar combine to plague thirteen-year-old Simon Renier on a freighter trip to modern Caracas. His shipboard friends, fourteen-year-old Polly and her psychic twelve-year-old brother Charles, are just two of a colorful collection of characters who help Simon uncover past secrets and solve present problems. Fiction.

Leonard, Constance. **Aground.** Dodd, Mead, 1984.

In this Tracy James mystery, Tracy flies from Florida to her parents' summer home in Maine, where it soon becomes apparent that there have been many changes in the years since she left. O'Day, a lobsterman and an old friend, has had a series of accidents and misfortunes that have turned him into a bitter and unhappy man. Tracy, at great personal risk, finds out what's really going on in this swiftly moving suspense novel. Fiction.

Leonard, Constance. **Stowaway.** Dodd, Mead, 1983.

Tracy James is sailing in convoy with Pete Sturtevant and his wealthy charter passengers to the Bahamas. A stowaway child on Tracy's boat greatly changes the trip. Modern-day smugglers, a storm, and personal conflicts all contribute to the suspense in this rapidly moving novel. Fiction.

Levy, Elizabeth. **The Dani Trap.** William Morrow, 1984.

Sixteen-year-old Dani Nelli is concerned about the amount of drinking some of her friends are doing. Because of this concern, she volunteers to work undercover with the police in an effort to trap liquor store owners who are selling to underage buyers. But when Dani is framed as an accomplice in a liquor-store holdup, the story turns tense. Fiction.

Lindsey, Robert. **The Falcon and the Snowman.** Pocket Books, 1985.

Christopher Boyce and Daulton Lee came from upper-middle-class, stable homes. Growing up in the turbulent sixties, they turned to drugs and to values different from those of their parents. This turning away eventually led to their becoming spies for the Soviet Union and turning over valuable secrets dealing with satellites and other space programs. This book—which provided the basis for the film of the same name—covers the young men's lives, their spy activities, their eventual capture, and their trial. Nonfiction.

Lockhart, Robin Bruce. **Reilly: Ace of Spies.** Penguin Books, 1984.

Sigmund Rosenblum, alias Sidney Reilly, was considered by many to be one of the most brillant spies of this century. Active starting in the period prior to World War I through the mid-1920s, Reilly performed incredible feats of espionage. This book relates what is known of his colorful personal life as well as his undercover activities, and formed the basis for a series on public television. Nonfiction.

Lyall, Gavin. **The Conduct of Major Maxim.** Viking Press, 1983.

Major Harry Maxim is drawn into a tangled web of murder, secret agents, and cold-war double-dealing. He not only lacks the support of his superiors, but he faces outright antagonism from them. This is a classic spy story with twists, turns, and a startling conclusion. Fiction.

MacKellar, William. **Terror Run.** Dodd, Mead, 1982.

Mark Simmons finds evil, terror, and murder waiting for him in the sleepy Scottish town where he and his stepfather go for a vacation. Mark not only finds a solution to the mysteries they encounter there, but also makes some new friends and gains a better understanding of his relationship with his stepfather. Fiction.

MacLeod, Charlotte. **Cirak's Daughter.** Atheneum, 1983.

A legacy from the famous cinematographer-father who deserted her as a baby starts nineteen-year-old Jenny on a search to find out what he was like and how he died. Her search takes her to Meldrum, Rhode Island, where Harriet Compton, a mature, sophisticated woman, turns up on Jenny's doorstep and helps her find the totally unexpected answers to her questions. Fiction.

Marston, Elsa. **The Cliffs of Cairo.** Signet Vista Books, 1982.

Sixteen-year-old Tabby Sherwood is living temporarily in Cairo, Egypt, with her geologist-father, her mother, and her younger brother. Tabby's purchase of an icon for her Aunt Barbara triggers a series of sinister events involving both Tabby and her family. Nabil, a handsome young Egyptian whom she meets on an excursion to an ancient mosque, adds an element of romance to this fast-paced novel. The resolution of the story involves a mysterious cult which has its roots in Egypt's past. Fiction.

McCullough, David Willis, editor. **Great Detectives: A Century of the Best Mysteries from England and America.** Pantheon Books, 1984.

This hefty volume includes two novels, a novella, and sixteen short stories by some of the best English and American mystery writers of the last century. McCullough frequently selects some of the lesser-known but equally good stories by the writers in the collection, thus setting it apart from similar anthologies. Fiction.

McDonald, Gregory. **Fletch and the Man Who.** Warner Books, 1983.

Fletch is hired to be press representative for Governor Caxton Wheeler, a candidate for president. A series of murders that occur when Wheeler's group is on the scene makes Fletch's job more difficult. He must discover the truth before the deaths put an end to Wheeler's candidacy. Fiction.

Murphy, Jim. **Death Run.** Clarion Books, 1982.

Brian and his buddies play a trick on a classmate, but when the trick backfires, the victim dies. *Death Run* details Detective Sergeant Robert Wheeler's search for the killers and Brian's torment as he must decide whether to hide or to confess. The eventual outcome is helped along by Wheeler's daughter, Susan, and her friend, the editor of the high school newspaper. Fiction.

Myers, Walter Dean. **Tales of a Dead King.** William Morrow, 1983.

John Robie goes to Aswan, Egypt, to join his great-uncle, Dr. Erich Leonhardt, on an archaeological dig. There he meets Karen Lacey, another American high school student, who joins the expedition. When Dr. Leonhardt is missing, it is up to Karen and John to find him. In this short, easy-to-read adventure, the teenagers also discover a plot to rob a pharaoh's tomb. Fiction.

Nash, Jay Robert. **Bloodletters and Bad Men, Book 1: Captain Lightfoot to Jesse James.** Warner Books, 1984.

Nash has assembled here photographs and accounts of many of the outstanding male and female lawbreakers of the past. The accounts, in alphabetical order, range from one paragraph in length for the lesser-known criminals to some thirty pages in the case of Jesse James. Eighteenth- and nineteenth-century bad men and women are covered in this book, which is the first in a series of three. The photographs, obtained from many sources, include some of dead criminals with their fatal wounds. Nonfiction.

Nash, Jay Robert. **Bloodletters and Bad Men, Book 2: Butch Cassidy to Al Capone.** Warner Books, 1984.

This collection follows the same format as the first volume in the series and covers criminals of the late nineteeth and early twentieth centuries. As in the first book, there are many photographs from a wide variety of sources. Nonfiction.

Nash, Jay Robert. **Bloodletters and Bad Men, Book 3: Lucky Luciano to Charles Manson.** Warner Books, 1984.

This third and final book in Nash's series covers twentieth-century criminals. The author once again follows the same format, using photographs and cross-referencing. The set forms a concise but complete encyclopedia of criminals. Nonfiction.

Nixon, Joan Lowery. **The Specter.** Delacorte Press, 1982.

Dina, a seventeen-year-old orphan with Hodgkin's disease, is wrapped up in her own problems until nine-year-old Julie is put in her hospital room. Dina's concern over Julie, who was orphaned in an automobile accident, almost results in Dina's death before the mystery of the strange little girl is solved. Fiction.

Okimoto, Jean Davies. **Who Did It, Jenny Lake?** Pacer Books, 1984.

Jenny Lake, an orphan and a junior at an exclusive boarding school, spends her spring vacation at an expensive resort owned by her guardian in Hawaii. Freddie, her best friend from school, goes with her. Shortly after their arrival, Mrs. Van Pelte, a friend of Jenny's guardian, dies in a mysterious fashion. Freddie and Jenny help to solve the mystery. Fiction.

Peck, Richard. **Through a Brief Darkness.** Laurel-Leaf Library, 1982.

Sixteen-year-old Karen Beatty desperately tries to avoid facing the fact that her father is a mobster. Finally, in London, she realizes that not only is her father a criminal but that his activities may cost her her life. A friend from her past, Jay Fielding, proves a valuable ally as Karen fights for her future. Fiction.

Roy, Ron. **I Am a Thief.** Illus. Mel Williges. Unicorn Books, 1982.

Have you ever felt alone and outside of a group? If so, you can understand thirteen-year-old Brad's feelings. Because he's lonely, Brad is happy to become friends with the "supercool" Chet. When Brad becomes involved with Chet's shoplifting outfit, he realizes he's in with the wrong crowd, but he's not sure he can turn to his mother for help. Is conflict the price of friendship? Brad has to almost lose his life as a result of his involvement with Chet before he realizes how much his mother loves him. Fiction.

Sheldon, Sidney. **The Naked Face.** Warner Books, 1984.

Judd Stevens, a psychoanalyst, realizes that he is the target of a murderer. The police, rather than believing this, suspect him of the murders of two people with whom he is closely connected. Concluding that one of his patients must be involved, Dr. Stevens tries to find the murderer before he becomes the third victim. This rather long story, first published in 1970, takes many turns before the tense and unexpected conclusion. Fiction.

Sleator, William. **Fingers.** Atheneum, 1983.

Is it a touch of the supernatural or just a series of weird coincidences that leads to the startling conclusion of this unusual story? Humphrey, a former child prodigy on the piano, has come to the end of his career. In an attempt to revive it, his ambitious mother gets his brother, eighteen-year-old Sam, to write some music that Humphrey is tricked into believing was dictated to Sam by a dead gypsy pianist. The fraud is a resounding success—but with unforeseen results. Fiction.

St. George, Judith. **Do You See What I See?** Signet Vista Books, 1983.

After his parents' divorce, seventeen-year-old Matt Runyon is unhappily transplanted from his native Colorado to his mother's former summer home on Cape Cod. There he becomes suspicious of the new tenants in a nearby cottage and almost loses his life when he stumbles onto the truth about them. Julie Chamberlain helps him both to solve the mystery and to learn to like the Cape. Fiction.

Tenny, Dixie. **Call the Darkness Down.** Margaret K. McElderry Books, 1984.

You may not believe in witches before reading this exciting novel, but by the end you might not be so sure. Morfa Owen, an American studying at a college in Wales, attempts to track down her Welsh grandparents. Her search makes her the target of an evil force in this tale that builds to a suspenseful and shocking climax. Fiction.

Truman, Margaret. **Murder in the White House.** Warner Books, 1984.

If anyone should be able to write convincingly about the White House, it is a former occupant. Margaret Truman shows an insider's knowledge in this tale of the murder of a secretary of state in the private quarters of the White House. Young attorney Ron Fairbanks is asked by the president to oversee the murder investigation. Ron's search turns up many things, including a few presidential family skeletons, before finding the startling truth. Fiction.

Truman, Margaret. **Murder on Capitol Hill.** Warner Books, 1984.

When a prominent senator is murdered at his own testimonial dinner, attorney Lydia James is selected by his family to head an investigation. An earlier murder, the power of a religious cult, and stiff-necked family pride are all elements that combine to keep the reader guessing until the surprising conclusion. Fiction.

Weinberg, Larry. **The Hooded Avengers.** Photographs by Bill Cadge. Bantam Books, 1983.

In Ben's haste to become a real man, he is led into a world of stark reality—a world of cruelty, prejudice, and a secret order involving some of the most important people in a small town. The decision he must make to please and understand his cousin Willis is the most serious one he'll ever have to face. Fiction.

Weisman, John. **Watchdogs.** Viking Press, 1983.

This suspense novel brings together the dedicated head of the presidential protection detail of the Secret Service, a South Korean cult, a Jewish president-elect, an assassination plot, and some ruthless, cutthroat TV reporters. The plot abounds with betrayals, seductions, infighting, murders, and posthypnotic suggestions. This is one book where it is vital that you read chapter headings carefully. Fiction.

Wells, Rosemary. **The Man in the Woods.** Dial Books for Young Readers, 1984.

When fourteen-year-old Helen investigates what she considers the false arrest of a classmate, she receives some terrifying death threats. Even worse, no adult will take her seriously. New Bedford, Massachusetts, is the setting for this modern-day suspense novel whose solution is found only by digging into the past. Fiction.

White, Ellen Emerson. **Friends for Life.** Flare Books, 1983.

Prep school senior Susan McAllister and her family return to Boston after a three-year absence. Sue looks forward to being with her best friend, Colleen, and with Patrick Finnegan, the boy in her life. But then tragedy strikes when Colleen dies from a drug overdose. Was it an accident or murder? Sue risks her life and Patrick's love to find out in this fast-paced mystery novel. Fiction.

Whitney, Phyllis A. **Emerald.** Doubleday, 1983.

Carol Hamilton takes her son and flees to Palm Springs to escape her powerful and cruel ex-husband. She turns to her only relative, recluse Monica Arlen, her great-aunt and a former movie star. Carol's attempts to protect her son, her discovery of a new love, and her unraveling of the mystery surrounding Monica and Saxon Scott, Monica's former lover, combine to create suspense and surprise. Fiction.

Woolrich, Cornell. **Black Alibi.** Ballantine Books, 1982.

Set in South America, this tense novel involves a mysterious jaguar who attacks five women, killing four of them. The suspense builds as press agent Jerry Manning desperately tries to find the lair of the super-powerful beast before it kills again. This book, which first appeared in 1942 and was made into a successful movie called *The Leopard Man,* has stood the test of time well. Its explosive climax is still exciting. Fiction.

Wright, Betty Ren. **The Dollhouse Murders.** Holiday House, 1983.

A haunted dollhouse is the focal point of this brief novel of the supernatural. Thirteen-year-old Amy and her retarded sister unravel the mystery of the moving dolls and solve a pair of forty-year-old murders. Fiction.

Yep, Laurence. **Liar, Liar.** William Morrow, 1983.

Sean Pierce believes that the car accident that killed his friend Marsh resulted from someone's tampering with the brakes. Unfortunately, because of Sean's past, no one believes him. This fact almost costs Sean his life before the killer is unmasked in this short but exciting story. Fiction.

Yep, Laurence. **The Mark Twain Murders.** Four Winds Press, 1982.

Mark Twain teams up with a fifteen-year-old street urchin in this mix of fact and fantasy. Together they share adventures, track a murderer, and stumble onto a Confederate plot in this novel set in San Francisco during the Civil War. Mark Twain's reputation as an unreliable reporter almost causes their undoing in this fast-paced yarn. Fiction.

Yep, Laurence. **The Tom Sawyer Fires.** William Morrow, 1984.

Set during the Civil War, this mystery features the Duke of Bay-
water and Mark Twain, who was a cub reporter at that time. The
Tom Sawyer of the title is based on a real fireman of the period.
Mark, Tom, and the fifteen-year-old narrator uncover the plot of
a Confederate arsonist in San Francisco. While not strictly a sequel
to *The Mark Twain Murders*, *The Tom Sawyer Fires* is more enjoyable if the earlier book is read first. Fiction.

Yolen, Jane. **The Stone Silenus.** Philomel Books, 1984.

Sixteen-year-old Melissa Stanhold cannot recover from her poet-
father's drowning death the year before. Her father's works dealt
with fauns and satyrs, and when Melissa meets a strange boy who
is faunlike in appearance and who resembles her father, she thinks
her father may have returned. Fiction.

Myths, Legends, and Folklore

Abrahams, Roger D., reteller. **African Folktales: Traditional Tales of the Black World.** Pantheon Books, 1983.

This comprehensive anthology is a good introduction to the ancient tradition of storytelling in which tales are passed down orally from generation to generation. These yarns will give you a look at ancient customs, rituals, concerns, and superstitions of peoples from one end of the African continent to the other.

Andersen, Hans Christian (translated by R. P. Keigwin). **Eighty Fairy Tales.** Illus. Vilhelm Pedersen and Lorenz Frølich. Pantheon Books, 1982.

In addition to such well-known tales as "The Princess and the Pea" and "The Ugly Duckling," this attractively illustrated collection of Andersen's Danish tales contains a number of lesser-known stories, some of which are mystical, others satirical, and some prophetically visionary, clearly illustrating that his tales were not written just for children. Fiction.

Asbjørnsen, Peter Christen, and Jørgen Moe (translated by Pat Shaw and Carl Norman). **Norwegian Folk Tales.** Illus. Erik Werenskiold and Theodor Kittelsen. Pantheon Books, 1982.

More than two dozen Norwegian folktales comprise this powerful anthology selected from a collection of tales first published in 1845. The book presents and preserves the romantic splendor, folk humor, and realistic view of life that characterize the Norwegian people. Fiction.

Bierhorst, John, editor. **The Hungry Woman: Myths and Legends of the Aztecs.** William Morrow, 1984.

In this collection of myths and legends from the sixteenth-century Aztec culture, several themes emerge. Among them are humanity's desire to understand its beginnings, the importance of the woman in Aztec folklore, and the people's desire to understand the forces of good and evil and God's triumph over Satan.

Braymer, Marjorie. **Atlantis: The Biography of a Legend.** Margaret K. McElderry Books, 1983.

Braymer tells two stories in this book. The first is the history of the lost city of Atlantis and the legends that follow the city first written about by Plato. The second story describes the recent archaeological excavations at Thera, in the Aegean Sea, where thirty buildings—destroyed by a volcanic eruption—have been unearthed since 1967. Could Thera prove to be the legendary Atlantis? Nonfiction.

Brunvand, Jan Harold. **The Vanishing Hitchhiker: American Urban Legends and Their Meanings.** W. W. Norton, 1981.

If you've heard and then retold the story of the man with the hook who terrorizes teenagers along a lover's lane, you are one of millions who spread urban legends. Brunvand has collected a number of these legends, including "The Babysitter and the Man Upstairs," "The Kentucky Fried Rat," and "Alligators in the Sewers." He traces their origins, discusses their variations, and attempts to explain their meanings and importance in American folklore. Nonfiction.

Calvino, Italo, reteller (translated by George Martin). **Italian Folktales.** Pantheon Books, 1981.

Almost everyone knows of the collections of folktales from Hans Christian Andersen and the Brothers Grimm. To those legendary collections is now added this large volume retold by Italo Calvino. As in other cultural collections, included here are tales of monsters and dragons, sleeping beauties and enchanted palaces, ugly witches and wily sorcerers. Most interesting are the Italian versions of "Cinderella," "The Three Little Pigs," and "Snow White." Fiction.

Cohen, Daniel. **The Encyclopedia of Monsters.** Dodd Mead, 1982.

Readers who are interested in monsters will find this an authoritative guide that can be read for either reference or enjoyment. Classified as humanoids, land monsters, phantoms, sea monsters, or weird creatures, such exotic beings as the vampire, the abominable snowman, the giant sloth, the sea serpent, and the zeuglodon are described here. Authentic claims of witnesses add to the romance, excitement, and mystery of these unforgettable creatures. Nonfiction.

de France, Marie (translated by Jeanette Beer). **Medieval Fables.** Illus. Jason Carter. Dodd, Mead, 1983.

Jeanette Beer's translation of Marie de France's fables welcomes the reader to a world of magic and fantasy. This impressive group of fables, beautifully and colorfully illustrated, represents a fine selection of the author's work. Fiction.

Erdoes, Richard, and Alfonso Ortiz, editors. **American Indian Myths and Legends.** Pantheon Books, 1984.

The vibrant folklore tradition of the North American Indian is magnificently depicted in this collaboration between an anthropologist and a storyteller, who have gathered together 166 myths and legends from tribal societies stretching from the Northeast to the Far West. While some of the familiar legends have been retold in a contemporary style, many others have never before been recorded. Imagination, humor, courage, and spiritual beliefs pervade these tales about creation, grisly monsters, heroes, warriors, tricksters, and the spirit world.

Evslin, Bernard. **Hercules.** Illus. Jos. A. Smith. William Morrow, 1984.

Evslin retells the folktale of the demigod Hercules in an exciting, easy-reading style. As Hercules struggles to accomplish seemingly impossible tasks, the gallantry, excitement, and adventure of the characters bring the story alive with creative imagery.

Garden, Nancy, reteller. **Favorite Tales from Grimm.** Illus. by Mercer Mayer. Four Winds Press, 1982.

The tales first written by Jacob and Wilhelm Grimm have enchanted people of all ages for nearly two centuries. This newest edition makes several of the Grimms' fairy tales, as retold by Nancy Garden, more attractive than ever because of the exquisite and sensitive full-color illustrations by Mercer Mayer. Fiction.

Graves, Robert. **Greek Myths.** Doubleday, 1981.

This beautifully illustrated volume is divided into seven sections: "In the Beginning"; "The Olympians"; "Of Heroes, Gods and Men"; "Minos and Theseus"; "Thebes and Mycenae"; "Heracles"; and "The Argonauts and Medea." The book organizes the history of myths in a developmental fashion and gives the reader an exciting explanation of the wonders of our universe.

Grinnell, George Bird, compiler (edited by John Bierhorst). **The Whistling Skeleton: American Indian Tales of the Supernatural.** Illus.
Robert Andrew Parker. Four Winds Press, 1982.

These easy-to-read mystery tales are thrilling and suspenseful and
evoke an understanding of Native American culture. The main
character in each of the stories is led by a supernatural being that
brings either good or bad fortune. Through these tales the reader
can learn about Native American customs of child rearing, marriage, hunting, warfare, treatment of illness, and home life.

Johnston, Norma. **The Days of the Dragon's Seed.** Atheneum, 1982.

At a time when Oedipus should have been the happiest, the haunting chant of a tavern song changes the course of his life. It is
important for him to find out his identity and fulfill the truth of
the Oracle. This account of the life of Oedipus is adventurous and
suspenseful and leaves the reader with many questions. Notes and
a glossary add to the book's value.

Hughes, Langston, and Arna Bontemps, editors. **The Book of Negro
Folklore.** Dodd, Mead, 1983.

The folklore in Hughes and Bontemps's anthology is African in
origin and was transplanted to meet the needs and anxieties of the
slaves as they coped with their plight in America. The material
ranges from animal tales, ghost stories, spirituals, rhymes, and
ballads to jazz and blues and much more.

Nolan, Paul T. **Folk Tale Plays round the World.** Plays, Inc., 1982.

This collection presents an insight into the folklore of both the
Eastern and the Western world in short play format. The plays
offer an understanding of basic customs and discuss themes which
peoples of all lands have in common, such as clan rivalry and the
need for goals and dreams.

Porter, Jane (edited by Kate Douglas Wiggin and Nora A. Smith). **The
Scottish Chiefs.** Illus. N. C. Wyeth. Charles Scribner's Sons, 1956.

It's the time of Scotland's defeat under King Edward of England,
a time of bravery and love for God, country, and truth. Sir William
Wallace, King Edward, and Ladies Marion, Helen, and Mary are
some of the characters who bring excitement to these tales of love
and adventure. Based on a true story. Fiction.

Rosa, Joseph G. **The Gunfighter: Man or Myth?** University of Oklahoma Press, 1982.

Settlement of the land west of the Mississippi in the last half of the nineteenth century created the legend of the coolheaded, pistol-packing, straight-shooting gunfighter, and Western literature and movies have contributed to the myth. In this well-documented study, the author distinguishes fact from fiction as he pits the myths about gunfighters against the authentic recorded accounts of their exploits. Nonfiction.

Outdoor Life and Travel

Duncan, David James. **The River Why.** Sierra Club Books, 1983.

An interest in fishing and a love of the outdoors will make this novel about an avid angler, Augustine "Gus" Hale-Orviston, more enjoyable to the reader. A slightly off-the-wall sense of humor is even more important. Mature high school readers will find *The River Why* a different and thought-provoking book. Fiction.

Durrell, Gerald (with Lee Durrell). **The Amateur Naturalist.** Alfred A. Knopf, 1983.

Famed naturalist Gerald Durrell leads the reader on a verbal and visual tour of seventeen natural habitats including meadows, woodlands, deserts, tundras, grasslands, mountains, ponds, streams, and coastal regions. From bugs to birds, from mosses to shrubs, from plant life to animal life, this beautifully illustrated book vividly describes each environmental area, intertwining the author's expert scientific knowledge with his deep love of, appreciation for, and experience with the outdoor world. There are suggestions on how to study nature, including a discussion of the techniques and equipment necessary to do so. Nonfiction.

Fletcher, Colin. **The Complete Walker III: The Joys and Techniques of Hiking and Backpacking.** 3d ed. Illus. Vanna Prince. Alfred A. Knopf, 1984.

In this complete revision of the definitive book on backpacking and hiking, the author thoroughly discusses any and all equipment related to the sport, from boots to bedding. His love for the outdoors is obvious, and his philosophy on how to protect and enjoy our environment is clearly stated in the introduction and conclusion of the book. Appendices give a checklist for equipment as well as lists of mail-order retailers and organizations that promote walking. Nonfiction.

Hart, John. **Walking Softly in the Wilderness: The Sierra Club Guide to Backpacking.** Rev. ed. Sierra Club Books, 1984.

This Sierra Club guide to backpacking covers not only the basic equipment necessary for comfortable, safe hiking but also discusses the various wilderness areas in the eastern and western United States. Explicit in the author's message is the need to treat wilderness areas with great care to protect our remaining open spaces. Coverage of trip planning, compass and map skills, overnight and long-term camping, and skills necessary to cope with emergencies will guide both novice and veteran backpackers. Nonfiction.

LaBastille, Anne. **Women and Wilderness.** Sierra Club Books, 1984.

Excitement, adventure, and commitment mark the lives and careers of the fifteen women naturalists profiled in this book. From white-water rafting to Olympic monitoring and Alaskan home-steading, the lives of these vital modern women embracing the outdoors are vastly different from the roles women have historically played in the wilderness. These former roles are detailed in brief case studies of pioneer women on the American frontier, and, as a contrast, the book also explores the opening of new and varied career options for women interested in outdoor occupations. Nonfiction.

McGinniss, Joe. **Going to Extremes.** Signet Books, 1982.

This descriptive account of the state of Alaska focuses not only on the beauty and isolation of the wilderness areas, but also on the frontier spirit which entices people to seek solace or fortune in our fiftieth state. Nonfiction.

Moon, William Least Heat (William Trogdon). **Blue Highways: A Journey into America.** Photographs by author. Fawcett Crest Books, 1984.

Having lost his job and his wife, the author decides to set out in his van to travel the circumference of the United States using secondary roads (the "blue highways" of the title) whenever he can. This is his description of the countryside and the people he meets along the way. Nonfiction.

Peterson, Lee Allen. **A Field Guide to Edible Wild Plants of Eastern and Central North America.** Illus. by author and Roger Tory Peterson; photographs by author. Houghton Mifflin, 1977.

Designed for practical field use, this guide provides succinct descriptive information about 373 of the better-known species of edible plants. A separate section lists various habitats in which the species are found, including seashore, bogs, meadows, woods, and tundras. Plants described in the guide have been categorized into

twenty-two food-use categories with basic cooking directions provided. A volume in the Peterson Field Guide series. Nonfiction.

Thum, Marcella, and Gladys Thum. **Exploring Military America.** Atheneum, 1982.

This selective state-by-state guidebook is a listing of battle sites,
forts, military museums, statues, and monuments which commem-
orate the wars fought by Americans from the Colonial period to
Vietnam. Part I of the guide is a summary of U.S. military history;
Part II gives locations of the memorials, a short history of each,
and travel directions. Nonfiction.

Warner, William W. **Distant Water: The Fate of the North Atlantic
Fisherman.** Penguin Books, 1984.

Warner's purpose for writing this book is to document the final
days of the factory trawlers. His principal characters are the sailors
and ships of five nations—the United States, Great Britain, West
Germany, Spain, and the Soviet Union—all in search of cod and
herring in the North Atlantic. With sensitivity, he describes the
daily occurrences and the nightly stories of an industry "doomed
by its own remarkable efficiency." Nonfiction.

Poetry

Adoff, Arnold. **All the Colors of the Race.** Illus. John Steptoe. Lothrop, Lee and Shepard Books, 1982.

Told through a child's eyes, Adoff uses his own family's experience of multiracial identity to explore in poetry what about skin colors appears to separate us and what actually unites us.

Angelou, Maya. **Shaker, Why Don't You Sing?** Random House, 1983.

Few modern writers have proved as at home in both poetry and autobiography as the multitalented Maya Angelou, whose wry poetry never lacks for the authentic pulse-hold on human experience. This is a good accompaniment to the author's series of autobiographical works.

Bierhorst, John, editor. **The Sacred Path: Spells, Prayers, and Power Songs of the American Indians.** William Morrow, 1983.

Beautifully laid out and thematically arranged, this collection includes chants and prayers about birth, love, hunting, farming, and death. Some typical examples are the exultant "Prayer of an Old Man at a Young Man's Change of Name" and the haunting "Prayer to the Ghost."

Bishop, Elizabeth. **The Complete Poems: 1927–1979.** Farrar, Straus and Giroux, 1984.

Containing fifty hitherto unpublished poems, this collection of Bishop's work clearly illustrates her sharp eye and perfectly controlled tone by presenting a range of moods and effects, beginning with works written at Vassar in 1927, and including works translated from Portuguese and Spanish.

Bodecker, N. M. **Pigeon Cubes and Other Verse.** Illus. by author. Margaret K. McElderry Books, 1982.

Graced with wry line drawings, Bodecker's poetry is bright, witty, and highly quotable, and will be most savored by those who like their verse short and bittersweet.

Frost, Robert (edited by Edward Connery Lathem). **North of Boston: Poems.** Illus. J. J. Lankes. Dodd, Mead, 1983.

Containing some of the most famous of Frost's poems, this edition is graced with mood-complementing woodcuts that catch the patience and austerity of the landscape of this New England poet. In simple language, Frost makes often profound statements using familiar objects, such as stone walls, blueberries, apple trees, and, of course, New Englanders.

Giovanni, Nikki. **Black Feeling, Black Talk.** 3d ed. Broadside Press, 1983.

Giovanni's gifts grace this collection of twenty-six poems which range over different facets of black experience. The imagery, language, and tone of these poems pierce the reader's sensibilities whether Giovanni is speaking about a relaxing evening at home with a friend or screaming in anger about revenge against oppression.

Glenn, Mel. **Class Dismissed! High School Poems.** Photographs by Michael J. Bernstein. Clarion Books, 1982.

This is a kind of *Spoon River Anthology* set in an American high school, peopled with thoughtful, perplexed, angry, and joyous adolescents who put the complexity of their lives into verse and come before us to testify what growing up is like.

Janeczko, Paul B., editor. **Poetspeak: In Their Work, about Their Work.** Bradbury Press, 1983.

In an accessible, stimulating format, this mixture of poems and commentary by sixty-two modern poets ranges across many themes and experiences. The most fascinating aspect of the book is the parallel view one gets of what actually goes into the writing of certain poems by hearing the poet speak both as critic and as creator.

Janeczko, Paul B., editor. **Strings: A Gathering of Family Poems.** Bradbury Press, 1984.

Janeczko has a gift for establishing a central theme around which he gathers some of the best of modern poetry. This collection—about parents, grandparents, cousins, brothers and sisters, and husbands and wives—is moving, funny, and gentle.

Livingston, Myra Cohn, editor. **Why Am I Grown So Cold? Poems of the Unknowable.** Margaret K. McElderry Books, 1983.

Have you ever had the hair on the back of your neck rise? Or felt cold breezes in windowless spaces? This collection of poems charts how poets have sought to describe and explain the inexplicable, the eerie, and the supernatural.

Merriam, Eve. **If Only I Could Tell You: Poems for Young Lovers and Dreamers.** Illus. Donna Diamond. Alfred A. Knopf, 1983.

Anyone who has ever been in love or plans to be will find in Merriam's glowing verse an exploration of all the moods that this emotion creates. More than fifty poems catch and hold up love for us to recognize.

Piercy, Marge. **Circles on the Water.** Alfred A. Knopf, 1982.

Piercy's poetry is always insightful and charged with the voltage of disciplined feelings. Some of the poems have appeared elsewhere, but their arrangement here makes it possible to trace both the poet's development and her concerns.

Plotz, Helen, compiler. **Eye's Delight: Poems of Art and Architecture.** Greenwillow Books, 1983.

An offbeat collection of poems inspired by the forms of art and architecture, *Eye's Delight* contains over one hundred poems through which artists celebrate the different faces of creativity while themselves creating structures with words.

Plotz, Helen, compiler. **Saturday's Children: Poems of Work.** Greenwillow Books, 1982.

A fine thematic anthology, this volume brings together poetic reflections on work and the worker over the ages and from all over the world. Divided into four sections, the poems deal with rural occupations, women's work, child labor and unemployment, and work as a special calling.

Smith, William Jay, compiler. **A Green Place: Modern Poems.** Illus. Jacques Hnizdovsky. Merloyd Lawrence Books, 1982.

Many subjects and poetic forms are mirrored in this collection which focuses on bringing examples of superb modern poetry before a new readership. If Eve Merriam's "Rainbow Writing" or

Randall Jarrell's "Bats" doesn't catch your fancy, perhaps Elizabeth Hodges's "Persimmons and Plums" will. Or Phil George's "Battle Won Is Lost." Or Elizabeth Morgan's "Caravati's Junkyard." Or Richard McCann's "The Fat Boy's Dream."

Politics and Law

Bernstein, Carl, and Bob Woodward. **All the President's Men.** Warner Books, 1976.

In this classic, stranger-than-fiction account of investigative news reporting, Bernstein and Woodward tell the exciting and suspenseful story of the Watergate investigation from the time of the break-in to a year later when newly elected President Nixon delivered his State of the Union message. By this time,,the reporters' persistence, with the aid of the mysterious Deep Throat, had laid bare the links between the burglary of the Democratic Headquarters and the Oval Office, writing a dramatic new chapter in the history of the American presidency. Nonfiction.

Capra, Fritjof, and Charlene Spretnak (with Rüdiger Lutz). **Green Politics: The Global Promise.** E. P. Dutton, 1984.

An important new political party has emerged in Europe: the Greens. Their original support came from groups of antinuclear demonstrators in West Germany. While the party's chief concerns are protection of the environment and nuclear disarmament, it also supports decentralization of government, redistribution of wealth, and nonviolence. This sympathetic account describes the movement, its leaders, and its principles, and analyzes its future in the United States and other parts of the world. Nonfiction.

Dolan, Edward F., Jr. **Protect Your Legal Rights: A Handbook for Teenagers.** Julian Messner, 1983.

Presented in question-and-answer form, this book focuses on the points of law that the author considers of greatest interest to young people. The volume stresses that the law differs from state to state, but readers may be interested in knowing that in all states, parents and school officers, who are deemed to be acting *in loco parentis,* have extensive authority over young people; parents even have a right to the earnings of minors. This book is part of the Teen Survival Library. Nonfiction.

Feiffer, Jules (edited by Steven Heller). **Jules Feiffer's America: From Eisenhower to Reagan.** Alfred A. Knopf, 1982.

The world of political humor is explored by famous satirist and cartoonist Jules Feiffer. Presidents past and present fall prey to Feiffer's razor-sharp pen-and-ink drawings and sarcastic impressions. Nonfiction.

Garver, Susan, and Paula McGuire. **Coming to North America: From Mexico, Cuba, and Puerto Rico.** Laurel-Leaf Library, 1984.

About fifteen million Hispanics live in the United States, the fifth largest population of Spanish-speaking people in the world. This book describes the history and life-styles of the three major groups: the Mexicans, the Cubans, and the Puerto Ricans. These peoples are different in many ways, but they all have shared the experience of rejection and discrimination in their chosen home. This sympathetic, easy-to-read account is made vivid with numerous quotes from contemporary letters and magazines and with interesting illustrations. Nonfiction.

Laski, Harold J. **Harold J. Laski on *The Communist Manifesto.*** Mentor Books, 1982.

Introduced by British political scientist Harold Laski, the text of *The Communist Manifesto* is that of the authorized English translation of 1888, edited and annotated by Friedrich Engels. Laski's most important contribution is to distinguish the theories of Marx and Engels from their manifestation in Soviet Russia. He writes, "The spirit of the Communist Movement since the Russian Revolution has been in a grave degree a denial of the spirit of the *Manifesto.*" Nonfiction.

Miller, Arthur R. **Miller's Court.** Plume Books, 1983.

What does the law say about issues like school prayer, abortion, self-defense, teenagers' rights, and sports violence? In an effort to demystify the law, Miller has written on over a dozen such topics in a clear and readable manner. This introduction to thinking like a lawyer is the basis of a public television series called *Miller's Court.* Nonfiction.

Nixon, Richard. **Leaders.** Warner Books, 1983.

In this collection of short biographies, former President Nixon provides personal insights into the character and behavior of influential statesmen he met during his long political career. Included here are accounts of the lives of Winston Churchill, Charles de Gaulle, Douglas MacArthur, Shigeru Yoshidida, Nikita Khrushchev, Zhou Enlai, and others. Reflecting de Gaulle's remark, "Nothing great is done without great men," these biographies offer an interesting commentary on the ways of greatness as perceived and reported by a controversial president. Nonfiction.

Olney, Ross R., and Patricia J. Olney. **Up against the Law: Your Legal Rights as a Minor.** Lodestar Books, 1985.

Written in a lively case-study approach, this book encourages young people to know and protect their rights. It is a valuable guide for teenagers who want to understand their rights regarding issues such as employment, marriage, birth control, abortion, school searches, dress codes, and accidents. There is a chapter on how to fight city hall and another on what to do if accused of a crime. Also included are a glossary of terms and a list of organizations that are prepared to help defend the civil rights of minors. Nonfiction.

Osborn, John Jay, Jr. **The Paper Chase.** Warner Books, 1983.

Employing a shifting point of view, this novel presents the struggles of a group of first-year Harvard Law School students. It focuses on Hart, an able student preoccupied with understanding his dictatorial professor Kingsfield, and on the professor's rebellious daughter. This book is the basis of the movie and the television series of the same name. Fiction.

Smith, David. **Marx's *Kapital* for Beginners.** Illus. Phil Evans. Pantheon Books, 1983.

Das Kapital, Karl Marx's life's work, the book in which he fully set out his theory of communism, was one of the most influential works of the nineteenth century. This lavishly and amusingly illustrated introduction to it may appear to take a tongue-in-cheek attitude toward Marx's ideas because it includes such offbeat items as a fictitious diary entry. It is, however, serious in its advocacy of Marxian social democracy. Nonfiction.

Thompson, Hunter S. **The Great Shark Hunt: Strange Tales from a Strange Time.** Warner Books, 1982.

Thompson is a practitioner of "new journalism," and his prose is biting, satirical, and profane. Nevertheless, this collection of essays contains some of the most acute political reporting available, particularly on the McGovern campaign and on Watergate. Nonfiction.

White, Ellen Emerson. **The President's Daughter.** Flare Books, 1984.

Fifteen-year-old Meghan Powers is attractive and popular, living a normal life in Massachusetts with her father and two younger brothers. Although her mother is an esteemed senator, Meghan enjoys no special privileges. When the rumors about her mother running for president become a reality, Meghan worries about being the daughter of the first woman president of the United States. She can handle the primaries, the debates, even the campaigning, but after moving to the White House, her life changes. She now has to deal with the increased attention, constant bodyguards, and doubts about the motives of her peers at her new school. Fiction.

White, Theodore H. **America in Search of Itself: The Making of the President, 1956–1980.** Warner Books, 1983.

Pulitzer Prize-winning author Theodore H. White has written three previous books about the presidency in which he analyzed the campaigns of Kennedy, Johnson, and Nixon. Now he takes a broader look at the American chief executive office and describes presidents since 1956: Eisenhower, Kennedy, Johnson, Nixon, Ford, Carter, and Reagan. He explains how forces in American and world affairs influenced these presidents, and, in turn, how their programs and personalities shaped American society. Nonfiction.

Recreation

Bavier, Robert N., Jr. **Keys to Racing Success.** Dodd, Mead, 1982.

Experienced sailor Robert Bavier defines the keys to racing success that winners have observed. Interesting anecdotes, diagrams, and photographs help to clarify his advice. This book will appeal to those at any level of sailing ability; it is clearly written and conversational in style. Nonfiction.

Briggs, Carole S. **Sport Diving.** Photographs by Carter M. Ayres. Lerner, 1982.

The author gives the reader a brief history of scuba diving before explaining the fundamentals of learning how to dive. Diving safety is informatively presented as well, with a discussion of the buddy system and the effects of water pressure. The book concludes with brilliantly colored photos of a diving trip to Moorea, a small island near Tahiti, where divers explored a coral reef. Part of the Superwheels and Thrill Sports series. Nonfiction.

Butterfield, John, Philip Parker, and David Honigmann. **What Is Dungeons and Dragons?** Warner Books, 1984.

If you want expert advice on playing the roles in the fantasy game of Dungeons and Dragons, this book is worth reading. Written for the experienced player, it is not a rule book and does not contain everything you need to know in order to play, but it does logically explain some complicated procedures that will improve your skills. Nonfiction.

Coombs, Charles. **Be a Winner in Windsurfing.** William Morrow, 1982.

Written in a simple and straightforward style, this short book provides a glimpse of the combination sport of surfing and sailing. Every lesson, including those on selecting a sailboard and becoming acquainted with nautical safety rules and various surfing feats, is illustrated for clarity with photographs and diagrams. Nonfiction.

Coombs, Charles. **BMX: A Guide to Bicycle Motocross.** William Morrow, 1983.

Interested in BMX biking? Here, Charles Coombs tells you how to choose and care for this special bicycle. Pages filled with pictures and a plain, readable style make it easy for you to learn how to perform stunts that are an important part of this sport. A glossary explains various terms, and a bibliography gives suggestions for further reading. Nonfiction.

Coombs, Charles. **Ultralights: The Flying Featherweights.** William Morrow, 1984.

Inform yourself about the new recreational craft—the ultralight— by reading this uncomplicated introduction to the low-flying, slow-moving airplane. Nearly every page contains photographs and/or diagrams that further explain instructions on the ultralight's controls. Nonfiction.

Gordon-Watson, Mary. **The Handbook of Riding.** Alfred A. Knopf, 1982.

Experienced riders will appreciate this heavily illustrated manual of horsemanship that covers learning to ride and advanced riding, as well as training and keeping a horse. This carefully compiled reference, written by an Olympic gold medalist, is accompanied by numbered instructions and diagrams to aid the equestrian. Nonfiction.

Hargrove, Jim, and S. A. Johnson. **Mountain Climbing.** Photographs by John Yaworsky. Lerner, 1983.

Curious about beginning mountain climbing? Necessary preparation, including getting in physical condition and obtaining the proper gear, is clearly explained here. Also helpful is a glossary of mountaineering terms and a record of various mountain-climbing teams from all over the world. One of the Superwheels and Thrill Sports series. Nonfiction.

Livingstone, Ian. **Dicing with Dragons.** Plume Books, 1983.

For those interested in improving their skill at role-playing games, including the popular fantasy game Dungeons and Dragons, this book is a useful guide. Fascinatingly illustrated, *Dicing with Dragons* can be helpful to the experienced player who appreciates that the cooperation of combined skills, rather than competition, is the main motivation. Nonfiction.

Marino, John, Lawrence May, and Hal Z. Bennett. **John Marino's Bicycling Book.** J. P. Tarcher, 1981.

Marino's book will familiarize you with bicycle mechanics, equipment, and accessories. Thoroughly and interestingly written, this book provides information about safety, training, and racing for the serious cyclist. Nonfiction.

Perry, Dave. **Winning in One-Designs.** Illus. Brad Dellenbaugh. Dodd, Mead, 1984.

An Olympic contender known for his teaching as well as his sailing, Dave Perry clearly imparts his knowledge of all aspects of sailing competition. He describes approaches already tried in his racing seminars that have proved to be understandable and helpful. Anecdotes that clarify various tactics and rules also make this book valuable reading for both the racing enthusiast and the novice sailor. Nonfiction.

Shapiro, James E. **Meditations from the Breakdown Lane: Running across America.** Houghton Mifflin, 1983.

Though not the first person to do so, Jim Shapiro ran—alone— the three thousand miles from San Francisco to New York City during the summer of 1980. In telling the story of his run, he explores the essence of the nation as well as his own feelings about his lonely and sometimes painful effort. One reviewer called this book "*Walden Pond* on foot"; another named it "Zen and the art of psycho-motor maintenance." Shapiro himself says he was merely "trying to learn how to wake up." Nonfiction.

Twelveponies, Mary. **There Are No Problem Horses—Only Problem Riders.** Houghton Mifflin, 1982.

Mary Twelveponies offers solutions for safe riding based on her knowledge of both the physical capability of the horse and the way the horse thinks. She says that rider-horse communication is essential. Safe for beginners, her advice covers the problems of negative behavior (runaways, biting, kicking, shying, etc.) as well as problems of handling (trailer loading, leading, and tying). The author includes many colorful incidents from her varied experiences, described in a comfortable conversational style. Nonfiction.

White, Rick. **Catamaran Racing: Solutions, Secrets, Speed.** Dodd, Mead, 1983.

A useful book for the beginning racer, *Catamaran Racing* includes not only the author's advice, but advice from several other experts on catamaran racing whose separate chapters are included as well. Understandable instructions are numbered and accompanied by diagrams, and a glossary defines various sailing terms. Nonfiction.

Religion and Cults

Appel, Willa. **Cults in America: Programmed for Paradise.** Holt, Rinehart and Winston, 1983.

This serious study of cults explains the lures that they use to attract young people into their world. Covered also are the history of cults and the personal power and wealth they bring to their leaders. The author details as well brainwashing techniques which cults use to ensure that any attempts to deprogram their members will be painful and often unsuccessful. Nonfiction.

Arrick, Fran. **God's Radar.** Bradbury Press, 1983.

Roxie Cable has difficult choices to make when she moves to a small Southern town where religious beliefs and conservative attitudes dominate almost everyone's actions. Although she attended church back in Syracuse, she is not ready for the religious rebirth of her parents, the strict behavior rules of her Christian high school, or the charismatic hold that Dr. Caramana seems to have on everyone in his congregation and in his television audience—everyone, that is, except for the free-spirited Jarrell Meek. Fiction.

Asheri, Michael. **Living Jewish: The Lore and Law of Being a Practicing Jew.** 2d ed. Dodd, Mead, 1983.

Questions about Judaism? Interested in understanding its customs and laws? Answers and explanations are covered in this thorough reference. Nonfiction.

De Santo, Charles P. **Dear Tim.** Herald Press, 1982.

This collection of letters, written by a minister to his college-age son, is designed to be an explanation of the basic tenets of Protestant Christianity. Specific biblical references are given to support the points made by the author. Nonfiction.

Gaeddert, LouAnn. **Daffodils in the Snow.** E. P. Dutton, 1984.

Eleanor no longer understands her childhood friend Marianne, who is now more interested in church than she is in high school activi-

ties, dating, or college plans. And when Marianne becomes pregnant and insists that her child's father is God, Eleanor is not the
only one who finds it hard to believe. As the controversy rages
over Marianne's baby, the two girls draw closer together, and
Eleanor finds that her life is tied to the fate of Marianne and the
child. Fiction.

Gillespie, Paul F., editor. **Foxfire 7.** Anchor Press, 1982.

Accompanied by numerous photographs, *Foxfire 7* provides a fascinating look at religion centered around the American mountain
culture. Mountain people talk candidly about their Christian
beliefs, covering each sect's principles and how they practice their
chosen religion. Topics include snake handling, camp meetings,
gospel songs, revivals, and more. Nonfiction.

Goldreich, Gloria. **A Treasury of Jewish Literature from Biblical Times
to Today.** Holt, Rinehart and Winston, 1982.

This sampling of Jewish literature comes from a variety of great
writings, such as the Torah, the Talmud, the Siddur, and the Kab-
balah, as well as from contemporary writers like Arthur Miller and
Philip Roth. Each selection is prefaced with notes on the historical
setting and insights into these writings. Jewish pride and history
are seen as the people struggle from generation to generation to
understand and accept the wisdom of the past and present.

Kerr, M. E. **What I Really Think of You.** Signet Vista Books, 1983.

Opal Ringer is a PK—preacher's kid. She dreads being singled out
as strange by her classmates who come to watch her father's service. They don't understand; they snicker and call her a Holy
Roller. It might take a miracle, but Opal will have her day. Fiction.

Miklowitz, Gloria D. **The Love Bombers.** Laurel-Leaf Library, 1982.

Jenna's brother has joined the Church of the World, a religious
cult, so Jenna and her friend Rick go to Berkeley to discover what
is going on. Will Jenna be strong enough to resist the cult's "love
bombing" and save her brother? Fiction.

Reader's Digest Editors. **Atlas of the Bible: An Illustrated Guide to
the Holy Land.** Reader's Digest Association, 1981.

Maps, up-to-date archaelogical finds, artifacts, and clear color photographs contribute to a fascinating look at the life and times of
the people of the Bible. Nonfiction.

Romance

Adler, C. S. **Roadside Valentine.** Pacer Books, 1984.

Jamie Landes and Louisa Murphy, two sensitive and appealing seniors, are good friends. The complicating factor is that Jamie loves Louisa. Adding to Jamie's troubles is that his mother has died and he cannot seem to live up to his father's expectations. As the year passes, both teenagers discover that they must be true to themselves rather than to what others want them to be, and this knowledge draws them closer together. Fiction.

Aks, Patricia. **A Dreamboy for Katie.** Fawcett Juniper Books, 1983.

Sophomore Katie Granger is immediately attracted to the handsome Reggie Hunter when she meets him at a country club barbecue. Even though they have little in common, she does not want to lose him. But as she gradually comes to realize that he is using her, she must decide just how important dating Reggie is. Fiction.

Aks, Patricia. **A New Kind of Love.** Fawcett Juniper Books, 1983.

Valerie Weill, at seventeen, has little patience with her eight-year-old sister, who always seems to be doing the wrong thing at the wrong time. When Val's new boyfriend, Bill, is ready to drop her because of the way she treats Jenny, Val feels misunderstood. Only after a series of unforeseen events does Val come to appreciate Bill's sensitivity and realize that she must sometimes put the welfare of others ahead of her own happiness. Fiction.

Aldrich, Bess Streeter. **A White Bird Flying.** Signet Vista Books, 1983.

Laura Deal had shared with her grandmother the dream that someday she would become a successful writer. Now, some years later, Laura sets out to fulfill this dream, still vowing that nothing, not even love, will keep her from it. Then she meets Allen Rinemiller and suddenly finds herself having to choose between pursuing her career and following her heart. Fiction.

Beckman, Delores. **Who Loves Sam Grant?** Laurel-Leaf Library, 1984.

Although Sam Grant, a high school sophomore, has been dumped by Bogie Benson, she still loves Bogie. So when he asks her to hide something he has stolen, Sam reluctantly agrees. As events unfold, she begins to question Bogie's character and reexamine her values. Fiction.

Bennett, Jay. **I Never Said I Loved You.** Flare Books, 1984.

Peter Martin, a high school senior, always intended to follow in his father's footsteps and become a lawyer. Then he meets Alice, who tries to convince him that he is not listening to his heart. Now Peter is faced with the dilemma of how to pursue his chosen career without losing Alice's love. Fiction.

Berry, Liz. **Easy Connections.** Viking Press, 1983.

Until Cathy Harlow stumbles into the world of Paul Devlin, lead guitarist of the rock group Easy Connection, her life is carefully arranged. As a first-year student at a prestigious London art school and a rising star in the art world, the seventeen-year-old's future is bright. But her confrontation with beautiful, violent Dev changes everything. Captivated by Cathy's beauty and innocence, Dev is determined to possess her—and he is used to getting what he wants. When Cathy's friends and family encourage Dev's pursuit of her, Cathy begins to doubt her ability to maintain her independence. Fiction.

Bonham, Frank. **Premonitions.** Holt, Rinehart and Winston, 1984.

Sixteen-year-old Kevin Spicer is intrigued with Anni, a French girl in his class. After some false starts, they begin to date, but her strong extrasensory powers endanger their relationship and her happiness. Also casting a pall over their friendship is the unexplained drowning of her popular brother the year before. Fiction.

Bunn, Scott. **Just Hold On.** Delacorte Press, 1982.

Charlotte Maag and Steven Herndon are two very lonely high school students. Each has few friends, a deeply troubled home life, and no one to talk to. As their relationship develops, they find comfort in each other even though they still cannot bring themselves to reveal their innermost secrets. In the process of finding love, they transform not only their lives but the lives of those around them as well. Fiction.

Byrd, Elizabeth. **It Had to Be You.** Viking Press, 1982.

Sixteen-year-old Kitty Craig is an irrepressible romantic even in the midst of the Great Depression. And although she dates other boys, she spends many of her waking hours dreaming about the handsome Johnny Aiken, a high school senior. When she finally has the chance to go out with him, she learns that the real Johnny does not measure up to the one of her dreams. Fiction.

Carr, Nicole. **Worthy Opponents.** Warner Books, 1984.

As spring approaches, Jill Farrell, an attractive, intelligent high school junior who has had many dates but no special boyfriend, finds herself attracted to Toby Martin, a handsome and clever classmate. When Jill has just about decided to run for class president, Toby tells her he is running for the same office. For the remainder of this book, you decide how the story will turn out. Each decision you make leads the heroine in a different direction. This title is third in the Make Your Dreams Come True series. Fiction.

Carr, Philippa. **Knave of Hearts.** G. P. Putnam's Sons, 1983.

When Lottie moves to France with her parents during the height of Louis XV's reign, she leaves behind both the enchanting English countryside and Dickon, the young man she loves. Eventually Lottie marries a wealthy Frenchman, but she never forgets Dickon. When her husband is killed, Dickon once more becomes her suitor, and she must decide just where her loyalties and obligations lie. Fiction.

Claypool, Jane. **Jasmine Finds Love.** Westminster Press, 1982.

Jasmine Chan's father is protective, refusing to let her see Tom Wu, the boy she thinks she loves. So she is surprised when her father actually encourages her to spend time with Sammy, a boy she likes but in whom she has no romantic interest. The climax occurs when Jasmine disobeys her father and sneaks out to a luau to meet Tom. While there, she sees, for the first time, beyond Tom's good looks and learns which personal qualities are truly important. A Floweromance. Fiction.

Colman, Hila. **Don't Tell Me That You Love Me.** Archway Paperbacks, 1983.

Fifteen-year-old Melissa becomes confused and cynical when her father leaves home to be with another woman. Even after his return, she refuses to trust any males, believing that women cannot depend on them. When Jimmy becomes interested in her, Melissa's problems are compounded. By wanting to be her friend, Jimmy is asking for more than she is ready to give. Fiction.

Cooney, Caroline B. **I'm Not Your Other Half.** Pacer Books, 1984.

When Fraser, a high school junior, first dates Michael, everything seems perfect. But after a while, she begins to realize that in spending so much time with Michael, she is surrendering herself rather than sharing her life. Fraser's problems increase when she encounters resistance from several quarters as she sets out to bring more balance to their relationship. Fiction.

Elfman, Blossom. **The Return of the Whistler.** Fawcett Juniper Books, 1982.

Arnie is an underachiever in an overachieving family. His only two talents—whistling and playing the harmonica—don't count for much. When he meets Francie, he finds in her a kindred soul, but her delicate mental state only adds to his problems. Through a series of violent incidents, Arnie finds a way to deal with the pressures he faces from all quarters—his family, his teachers, and his classmates. Fiction.

Eyerly, Jeannette. **More Than a Summer Love.** Archway Paperbacks, 1983.

When Casey's aunt and uncle are involved in a car accident, Casey has to change her plans and spend her seventeenth summer in Shady Rock, Iowa. Anticipating an unexciting summer, she instead meets Lance, the son of the local bank president, and Joe, a hardworking young man who is saving his money for college. Later, the whole town comes alive when Casey inadvertently uncovers embezzlement at the bank. Fiction.

Ferris, Jean. **Amen, Moses Gardenia.** Farrar, Straus and Giroux, 1983.

Fifteen-year-old Farrell Cunningham has everything going for her—she is smart and attractive and her parents provide her with all the clothes and gifts she could ever want. But Farrell still feels like a misfit everywhere but in the kitchen with Earl Mae, family housekeeper, gourmet cook, and good listener, who gives Farrell what she can't get from her mother—acceptance and understanding. Then Ted Kittredge, class president and star athlete, invites

Farrell to a New Year's Eve party and the evening turns out to be the best of her life. When Ted continues to see her, Farrell begins to feel good about herself—until a surprise confrontation destroys her contentment and she has to contrive a desperate plan to solve her problems. Fiction.

Foley, June. **It's No Crush, I'm in Love!** Laurel-Leaf Library, 1983.

Anne Cassidy falls in love with David Angelucci, her English teacher. Anne, the narrator of the novel, also has to cope with the numerous obligations she has to her widowed mother. The novel leads up to the moment when Anne has a chance to confess her love to Mr. Angelucci. A volume in the Young Love series. Fiction.

French, Michael. **Lifeguards Only beyond This Point.** Pacer Books, 1984.

When sixteen-year-old Max Riley goes to work as a waiter at a New Hampshire resort, he thinks the world can be his if only he goes after it. And when the beautiful and wealthy Annabelle Livingston is attracted to him, he sees his dreams of luxury coming true. But fate—in the form of a rich young lifeguard—and Max's own limitations intervene. Then Max finds he must struggle to make his dreams come true. Fiction.

Girion, Barbara. **In the Middle of a Rainbow.** Charles Scribner's Sons, 1983.

When Corrie Dickerson and Todd Marcus, high school seniors, fall in love, it is a magic time for them. But Corrie faces problems firmly grounded in reality: she's in love with someone who comes from a much wealthier family, she must somehow find money for college, and she also has to deal with her mother, who has been afraid to enter a relationship ever since Corrie's father was killed years ago. Corrie's dreams and her real world often collide, forcing her to examine her life and to grow in understanding. Fiction.

Goudge, Eileen. **Too Much Too Soon.** Laurel-Leaf Library, 1984.

To everyone but her three best friends, Kit appears to be a flirtatious and somewhat wild high school senior. But underneath, Kit is afraid of love and of becoming too involved. When she falls in love with Justin Kennerly, her fears intensify, and in an attempt to overcome them, she finds herself in a situation she can barely handle. A volume in the Seniors series. Fiction.

Greenwald, Sheila. **Blissful Joy and the SATs: A Multiple-Choice Romance.** Laurel-Leaf Library, 1983.

Uppermost in sixteen-year-old Bliss Bowman's mind is doing well on the SATs so she'll be able to get into Vassar. Then suddenly her world is turned upside down when two young men and a lost dog enter her life. Bliss finds herself misjudging the motives of the people close to her, and only after she is hurt is she finally able to separate deception from truth. Fiction.

Heaven, Constance. **The Wildcliffe Bird.** Coward-McCann, 1983.

Fleeing Paris after her father's death, young and beautiful Juliet Prior is forced to take refuge with her Chartley relatives. Family secrets and love dominate this romance set in mid-nineteenth-century Yorkshire against the background of the Chartist labor movement in the pottery factories. Fiction.

Holmes, Marjorie. **Saturday Night.** Laurel-Leaf Library, 1982.

Growing up in a small Midwestern town holds little excitement for Carly Williams—until the handsome Danny Keller begins to take an interest in her. At first, what appears to be his carefree attitude appeals to her. Only through a series of incidents does she come to understand that Danny is not the person she thought he was. Fiction.

Holmes, Marjorie. **Sunday Morning.** Laurel-Leaf Library, 1982.

In this sequel to *Saturday Night,* Carly Williams becomes pinned to Chuck. But when her former boyfriend Danny returns, Carly finds she must make a choice between the two boys. Originally titled *Love Is a Hopscotch Thing.* Fiction.

Hopper, Nancy J. **Lies.** Lodestar Books, 1984.

Allison Witner, a high school junior, has one major character flaw—she tells lies that turn into webs of deceit. In trying to attract Jerry Hamilton, a handsome new boy in town, she tells several whoppers and then incurs his anger when he begins to discover the truth. Finally, Allison is forced to face the problems she has created. Fiction.

Howe, Fanny. **Yeah, But.** Flare Books, 1982.

When Casey's aunt moves to a wealthy section of Boston, Casey must go with her. There she must come to grips with their being the only black family in the area and with losing her boyfriend Willie, who has decided she is both too rich and too young for his tastes. Then she meets and becomes attracted to Treat, a handsome blond who reminds her of her long-lost father. Fiction.

Johnston, Norma. **Timewarp Summer.** Atheneum, 1983.

Scott, Bettina, and Laura form a love triangle in this unusual story about people living—or reliving—their seventeenth summer. Bettina, the girl next door, and Laura, a scientist at the lab where all three work, help Scott to fulfill his dream of making a film during summer vacation. While they are caught up in this project, all three become involved in relationships that are as intense as they are dangerous. Fiction.

Kaplan, Janice. **If You Believe in Me.** Flare Books, 1984.

Moving from New York City to a small town in Florida and attending an all-girls parochial school does not appeal to fifteen-year-old Toby Lewis. Then she meets David Jarrell, who goes to a public school and spends much of his free time at the Jewish Community Center. Toby falls in love with David and is faced with new problems. Fiction.

Knudsen, James. **Just Friends.** Flare Books, 1982.

Junior Blake Webb has been lonely, so when he becomes best friends with Libby, the funniest girl in his class, and with a new senior, Spencer Frederick, he is delighted. But after several months, Blake realizes that their friendship is becoming strained. As Blake comes to grips with the faltering relationship, he begins to see his friends in a more realistic light, and he develops a new relationship with a girl he has previously ignored. Fiction.

Lee, Mildred. **The People Therein.** Signet Vista Books, 1982.

Long before Drew Thorndike, a handsome young man from Boston, arrives in the Great Smoky Mountains hamlet of Dewfall Gap, eighteen-year-old Lanthy Farr has convinced herself that no man wants a lame girl as his wife. But as the mountain people begin to accept Drew, he and Lanthy are drawn to each other. As their relationship develops, their happiness blinds them to other people's reactions, and only when it is almost too late do they realize they must reckon with the consequences of their love. Fiction.

L'Engle, Madeleine. **And Both Were Young.** Laurel-Leaf Library, 1983.

After Phillippa Hunter's mother is killed, her father's travel forces him to send Phillippa to a Swiss boarding school. At first she feels sorry for herself. But as her friendship with Paul turns to love, she becomes involved in helping him to confront his devastating childhood experiences and thus gains an understanding of herself and those around her. Fiction.

L'Engle, Madeleine. **Camilla.** Laurel-Leaf Library, 1982.

Fifteen-year-old Camilla Dickinson is baffled by the growing tension in her wealthy parents' marriage. When she falls in love with Frank, her best friend's brother, she comes to understand better her relationship with her parents and their relationship with each other. Fiction.

Levitin, Sonia. **The Year of Sweet Senior Insanity.** Atheneum, 1983.

Leni's senior year in high school is a frantic one. She has fallen in love with Blair, a college sophomore, and has difficulty finding time to meet her commitments to her family, friends, and extracurricular activities. Her problems finally come to a head when her parents take a trip to Hawaii and she invites Blair to spend the week at her house. Then Leni must decide just what is important to her. Fiction.

Levy, Elizabeth. **Double Standard.** Flare Books, 1984.

Collette Gordon and Abby Klein are best friends and high school rock singers. Ian Mitchell and Jim Abernathy, also good friends, are attracted to the girls. But problems develop until Collette and Ian finally realize that everyone applies different standards to friendship and to love. Fiction.

Likhanov, Albert (translated by Richard Lourie). **Shadows across the Sun.** Harper and Row, 1983.

In this novel, originally published in the USSR, crippled Lena falls in love with Fedya, a young boy who keeps pigeons on the roof of the Moscow apartment next door to hers. Fedya has his problems, too: his father is an alcoholic. Eventually, the young people come to rely on one another. This sensitive story of a deepening relationship provides interesting glimpses of life in the Soviet Union. Fiction.

Lyle, Katie Letcher. **Dark But Full of Diamonds.** Bantam Books, 1983.

Life begins to look better to sixteen-year-old Scott Dabney when he learns that Hilah Brown, a young woman who took special interest in him during the summer his mother died, is returning to teach at his high school. But his hopes of Hilah's returning his romantic interest are shattered when he discovers that she and his father are falling in love. Fiction.

Mazer, Norma Fox. **When We First Met.** Four Winds Press, 1982.

When seventeen-year-old Jennie Pennoyer first sees Rob Montana, she is immediately attracted to him. Later, when the two are falling in love, she discovers that his mother was the reckless driver who killed her older sister Gail two years before. Only gradually, through a series of emotionally charged scenes, do the various members of both families come to grips with Gail's death and the young couple's relationship. Fiction.

Miklowitz, Gloria D. **The Day the Senior Class Got Married.** Delacorte Press, 1983.

Dr. Womer's economics class pairs off students as make-believe couples in a unit designed to explore the responsibilities of married life. For Lori and Rick the exercise is a serious one because they have announced their plans to marry right after graduation. Lori's painful realization that there are serious differences between them forces her to rethink her June plans. Fiction.

Murphy, Barbara Beasley. **One Another.** Laurel-Leaf Library, 1984.

When Paul Montague, a French exchange student, comes to spend three weeks in America, he changes Melissa Pelikan's life. Shy and never having experienced a serious romance, Melissa blossoms as their relationship turns from friendship to love. It is a time of heightened emotions made all the more intense as Melissa and Paul realize they will soon be separated, at least for a while. Fiction.

Norby, Lisa. **Just the Way You Are.** Warner Books, 1984.

Things do not go well when Molly Becker first meets Stephen Malcolm, a foreign exchange student from England. Subsequent encounters go no better, yet Molly feels curiously drawn to him. It is only shortly before Stephen must return to England that they straighten out their misunderstandings and come to see each other as they really are. This romance, part of the Two by Two series, is actually two stories in one. One half of the book tells the girl's side of the story, and the other relates what happens from the boy's point of view. Fiction.

Osborne, Mary Pope. **Best Wishes, Joe Brady.** Dial Books, 1984.

Life in a small town is dull for eighteen-year-old Sunny Dickens until Joe Brady, a famous soap opera star, comes to do a play at the dinner theater where she is a waitress. When he pays her special attention, she is filled with both anticipation and apprehension. And as he turns her world upside down, she experiences the joy and heartbreak which almost inevitably accompany first love. Fiction.

Peck, Richard. **Close Enough to Touch.** Delacorte Press, 1983.

The sudden death of his sweetheart Dory leaves Matt Moran desolate, unable to cope with life at school or at home. To escape his pain, Matt tries alcohol and then long-distance running, but nothing helps much until he meets Margaret Chasen. Older than Matt, strong-willed Margaret puzzles and intrigues him. Eventually Matt must make a decision that reflects a sensitive young man's attitude toward the loss and renewal of love. Fiction.

Pevsner, Stella. **I'll Always Remember You . . . Maybe.** Archway Paperbacks, 1982.

Darien Holmes is a senior, and her boyfriend Paul Leonard has gone off to college. She cannot understand why Paul thinks they should be free of commitments to each other after two years of going steady. And even though rock superstar Ryley DeWitt enters her life, Darien cannot forget Paul. The year turns out to be one filled with both good times and bad, one in which she leaves childhood behind and becomes an adult. Fiction.

Ransom, Candice F. **Amanda.** Scholastic, 1984.

In 1846, sixteen-year-old Amanda Bentley's life changes drastically when her father announces they are leaving their comfortable Boston existence and crossing the Oregon Trail. As time passes, things go from bad to worse. The elements become more extreme, her father becomes increasingly disenchanted, and her misunderstandings with Ben, a handsome young fellow traveler, intensify. As Amanda learns to deal with each of these obstacles to her happiness, she turns into a fiercely independent and strong young woman. Part of the Sunfire series, a collection of historical romances. Fiction.

Savitz, Harriet May. **Summer's End.** Signet Vista Books, 1984.

As the only living child of a couple who survived the Holocaust, Jay Hansky feels pressured by his parents to fulfill the dreams they could not. When he spends the summer at an ocean resort, he finds unexpected happiness in the form of Ali Templeton. But even though she loves him, she has dreams of her own to pursue, and Jay, like his parents, must learn not to pressure the one he loves. Fiction.

Schneider, Meg. **Romance! Can You Survive It? A Guide to Sticky Dating Situations.** Laurel-Leaf Library, 1984.

Problems of all sorts crop up once you begin to date—problems with the person you're dating, problems with other friends, and problems with parents. This guide offers sound advice on how to be sensitive to the needs of others while meeting your own needs. And it gives practical suggestions about what to say when you find yourself in predicaments you want to change. Nonfiction.

Scoppettone, Sandra. **Long Time between Kisses.** Bantam Books, 1984.

A sophisticated, wisecracking sixteen-year-old, Billie James feels that she needs to make a statement about herself. So she cuts off her long brown hair and dyes the stubble purple. When she meets Robert Mitchell, a victim of multiple sclerosis, their relationship helps Billie to estabish an identity that is not dependent on purple hair. The novel vividly describes the inhabitants and flavor of Billie's neighborhood, the Soho section of lower Manhattan. Fiction.

Sharmat, Marjorie. **He Noticed I'm Alive . . . and Other Hopeful Signs.** Delacorte Press, 1984.

In the two years that have passed since her mother left to find herself, fifteen-year-old Jody Kline has not been happy. Her father is dating Gossamer Green, a woman Jody tolerates but does not want for a stepmother. When Jody meets Mrs. Green's son Matt, they immediately are attracted to each other, but they both fear that their dating may further solidify their parents' relationship. The young couple's attempts to solve this problem result in both humorous and more serious moments. Fiction.

Sharmat, Marjorie. **How to Meet a Gorgeous Guy.** Delacorte Press, 1983.

It is hard for Shari to believe that she will be the subject of her cousin Lisa's article in a popular teen magazine. Shari will be the focus of an experiment and an article entitled "How to Meet a Gorgeous Guy." Her problem is holding on to the gorgeous guy once she meets him. Fiction.

Springstubb, Tricia. **The Moon on a String.** Laurel-Leaf Library, 1984.

After graduating from high school, Deidre Shea decides that she wants more from life than marrying her boyfriend of four years and settling down in the country. She moves to Boston, where she meets Tad, a young man who holds values very different from her own. As Deidre tests her independence and develops her relationship with Tad, she comes to understand what in life is really important to her. Fiction.

Sunshine, Tina. **An X-Rated Romance.** Flare Books, 1982.

When Sara decides that boys her own age are immature, she becomes infatuated with Mr. Garfield, her eighth-grade English teacher. Spurred on by her best friend Emily, Sara sets out to seduce Mr. Garfield. During the months that follow, she and Emily concoct a number of schemes which result in humorous complications. Fiction.

Wheaton, Philip D. **The Best Is Yet to Be.** Dodd, Mead, 1983.

Raised during the Great Depression, Willie and Penny think they are brother and sister until one terrible day, as young teenagers, they learn otherwise. As the years pass, they go their separate ways, trying to make lives for themselves. When their respective romances fail, they are once again drawn to each other, and their relationship takes on a whole new meaning. Fiction.

Williamson, Amy. **Star Light, Star Bright.** Fawcett Juniper Books, 1982.

Seventeen-year-old Betsy Alexander is having a dull senior year. Then Patrick Groves, a handsome young movie star, returns to Apple Valley to take over his mother's drama and speech classes while she recuperates from a heart attack. Betsy is enamored with Patrick and mistakes his attention for romantic interest. She eventually discovers that she has a lot to learn about love and the go-getters of this world. Fiction.

York, Carol Beach. **Where Love Begins.** Ace Tempo Books, 1983.

> When Rachael Carey turns seventeen, she definitely feels more mature. So when one of her birthday presents turns out to be tickets to the circus, she somewhat hesitantly decides to use them. There she meets Tony Zorini, an acrobat who becomes her friend and, in the six days the circus is in town, shows her he understands that turning seventeen has made a difference. Fiction.

Zalben, Jane Breskin. **Here's Looking at You, Kid.** Farrar, Straus and Giroux, 1984.

> After Eric Fine, a high school senior, moves to Long Island, he finds himself attracted to two girls. He enjoys Enid's quick wit, but he has feelings of a very different sort for Kimberly. When his relationships with both girls begin to deteriorate, he is forced to examine who he is and what he wants. Fiction.

Zindel, Paul. **The Girl Who Wanted a Boy.** Bantam Books, 1982.

> Fifteen-year-old Sibella Cametta begins to worry that her ambition to own a gas station is keeping boys from becoming interested in her. Then she finds the boy of her dreams in a newspaper photo and immediately falls in love with him. In trying to develop a relationship with him, she suffers rejection and heartache but emerges a stronger and wiser young woman. Fiction.

Science

Anderson, Madelyn Klein. **Oil in Troubled Waters.** Vanguard Press, 1983.

The author paints a descriptive, honest, and alarming picture of the effects of oil spills in our ecosystem. She also presents an optimistic view of what technology and concerned people can do to try to prevent the problem and to deal with it once it has occurred. The message is clear, however: when headlines don't proclaim huge oil spills, public interest is low; but oil still enters the world's waters, resulting in death for all of nature. Nonfiction.

Asimov, Isaac, George Zebrowski, and Martin H. Greenberg, editors. **Creations: The Quest for Origins in Story and Science.** Crown, 1983.

Bringing together science fiction, science, and the Bible may provide some of the answers as to how life and the solar system began. Even after all the available facts are explained, all the formulas are calculated, and all the references are researched, there is only one real explanation. Fiction and nonfiction.

Audubon Society. **The Audubon Society Field Guide to North American Fishes, Whales, and Dolphins.** Alfred A. Knopf, 1983.

Designed for quick identification of aquatic animals, this single-volume field guide includes North America's most common freshwater and saltwater fishes as well as forty-five species of whales, dolphins, and porpoises. Clear directions are provided for use of the thumb tab guide and key. Over six hundred color photos are cross-referenced with the text to provide a bright and easy-to-use guide. Nonfiction.

Bornstein, Sandy, and Jerry Bornstein. **New Frontiers in Genetics.** Julian Messner, 1984.

Although genetics is a relatively new, complex, and ever-changing science, the Bornsteins—one, a geneticist and the other, a journalist—provide a clear and highly informative presentation of what is going on today in the field. The authors investigate the relationships among disease, pollutants, the environment, nuclear energy, cancer, and mutations of genes and look at how these relationships ultimately affect how we grow and develop. Nonfiction.

Brenner, Martha. **Fireworks Tonight!** Hastings House, 1983.

In easy-to-understand terms and with black-and-white photographs and illustrations on nearly every other page, this little book tells you everything worth knowing about fireworks: their history, how they are manufactured and displayed, fireworks trivia (the biggest dud, the worst disaster, the most expensive display), state laws, and types of fireworks you can use at home. There is even a guide to help you identify fireworks patterns you observe. Nonfiction.

Brown, Michael H. **Laying Waste: The Poisoning of America by Toxic Chemicals.** Washington Square Press, 1981.

As the title indicates, this is a strongly pro-environment book. According to the author, our entire environment is being poisoned, mutated, and destroyed by buried toxic wastes, aerial and water pollutants, and other invisible chemicals that have become a symbol of technical advancement and progress. The book's message: we must assume responsibility and be the watchdogs of our world, or we will surely lie in the waste. Nonfiction.

Bruun, Ruth Dowling, and Bertel Bruun. **The Human Body: Your Body and How It Works.** Illus. Patricia J. Wynne. Random House Library of Knowledge, 1982.

Take a vivid and accurate visual adventure into the structure and function of the workings of your body. Read about the hundreds of processes the human body experiences daily and learn how your body is more complex than even the most advanced computer. Nonfiction.

Croall, Stephen. **Nuclear Power for Beginners.** Illus. Kaianders. Pantheon Books, 1983.

Captivating comic illustrations along with an informative text explain the serious and controversial issues surrounding nuclear energy in a witty, satirical, and comprehensible manner. Formerly titled *The Anti-Nuclear Handbook,* this sophisticated comic book traces the history of nuclear weapons, exposes the problems of nuclear power, and suggests safe alternatives and solutions to contemporary energy problems. Nonfiction.

Darwin, Charles. **The Origin of Species.** Mentor Books, 1982.

Originally published in 1859, Charles Darwin's *Origin of Species* is still a magnificent testament to the importance of persistent observation and careful hypothesis. This classic recounts Darwin's revolutionary investigation into the science of evolution and reveals his genius, acute perception, and inspired vision of where humanity has been and where it is going. Nonfiction.

Dempsey, Michael W., editor. **Illustrated Fact Book of Science.** Arco, 1983.

Broad categories, clear and colorful illustrations, a comprehensive glossary, and a brief section devoted to scientists make this book a small reference library in itself. There is even a unit which explains interesting facts about and uses for all the chemical elements in the periodic table. Even a nonscientist will enjoy this one. Previously published as the *Rainbow Fact Book of Science.* Nonfiction.

Diagram Group. **The Brain: A User's Manual.** Perigee Books, 1982.

With its lucid illustrations, this exceptional guide to current scientific information makes the study of the brain an exciting adventure. The manual answers questions about awareness, instinct, psychoses, biofeedback, mind manipulation, and deception. Nonfiction.

Durrell, Gerald (with Lee Durrell). **The Amateur Naturalist.** Alfred A. Knopf, 1983.

Famed naturalist Gerald Durrell leads the reader on a verbal and visual tour of seventeen natural habitats including meadows, woodlands, deserts, tundras, grasslands, mountains, ponds, streams, and coastal regions. From bugs to birds, from mosses to shrubs, from plant life to animal life, this beautifully illustrated book vividly describes each environmental area, intertwining the author's expert scientific knowledge with his deep love of, appreciation for, and experience with the outdoor world. There are suggestions on how to study nature, including a discussion of the technique and equipment necessary to do so. Nonfiction.

Ford, Daniel F. **Three Mile Island: Thirty Minutes to Meltdown.** Penguin Books, 1982.

In 1976, Deputy Secretary of Energy John F. O'Leary stated that because of the massive safety issues associated with the generation of nuclear power, sooner or later, a major nuclear catastrophe would certainly occur. As early as October 1977, malfunctions in the main feedwater system were evident at Three Mile Island— Dr. O'Leary's prophecy was becoming reality. Here, Daniel F. Ford explains the alarming facts about Three Mile Island and how the potential for catastrophe is always present in our efforts to develop the most powerful renewable energy source of our age. Nonfiction.

Freedman, Russell. **Can Bears Predict Earthquakes? Unsolved Mysteries of Animal Behavior.** Prentice-Hall, 1982.

Many fascinating mysteries about animals and their behaviors are explored in this book. Scientists hope that by investigating these behaviors we may be able to answer questions about our own lives. There are stimulating ideas to ponder throughout the entire book, such as, can people hibernate? Nonfiction.

Gadd, Laurence D., and World Almanac Editors. **The World Almanac Book of the Strange No. 2.** Signet Books, 1982.

Escape into the fascinating, bizarre, and weird world around you. Reverse evolution, clones, psi phenomena, and cryonics are no longer just topics entertained by science fiction writers; these are verified factual occurrences that are becoming more common all the time. Bibliographies are provided should you wish to further investigate these phenomena. Originally titled *The Second Book of the Strange*. Nonfiction.

Gardner, Robert. **The Whale Watchers' Guide.** Illus. Don Sineti. Julian Messner, 1984.

Whale watching is becoming a very popular pastime on both American coasts. While it may present some difficulty for the whales, it is providing an abundance of data for the scientists and developing a network of concerned, excited watchers. This guide contains enough information to allow you to identify twenty-six different species of whales. Nonfiction.

Golden, Frederic. **The Trembling Earth: Probing and Predicting Quakes.** Charles Scribner's Sons, 1983.

How about a return engagement for the San Francisco earthquake? Building on this fictional premise, Golden explores what we know about earthquakes, from their terminology to the seismologists who predict them, all in straightforward prose. A helpful bibliography is included. Nonfiction.

Goldstein, Thomas. **Dawn of Modern Science.** Houghton Mifflin, 1980.

Goldstein takes a very human look at science during the Renaissance period. Designed for a nonscientific audience, *Dawn of Modern Science* tastefully and sensitively combines scientific thought with history and cultural evolution. You can almost see, feel, and hear the participants in this beautifully told narration of fact and discovery. Nonfiction.

Gosner, Kenneth L. **A Field Guide to the Atlantic Seashore: Invertebrates and Seaweeds of the Atlantic Coast from the Bay of Fundy to Cape Hatteras.** Illus. by author. Houghton Mifflin, 1978.

Part of the Peterson Field Guide series sponsored by the National Wildlife Federation, this guide is comprehensive and easy to use for both the newcomer and the expert. Over a thousand plant and animal species are described using correct scientific terms. Plentiful illustrations and detailed habitat descriptions allow for quick, accurate identification while in the field. Nonfiction.

Haines, Gail Kay. **Test-Tube Mysteries.** Dodd, Mead, 1982.

Test-Tube Mysteries highlights the art of scientific discovery as it has taken shape since the investigations of Louis Pasteur. You hypothesize, experiment, and discover insulin, the noble gases, atomic fission, carbon-14 dating, pulsars, and other wonders right along with the scientists. In addition to examining hard facts, you catch a glimpse of the personal side of the great men and women who have advanced technology, medicine, and life because of their genius and persistence. Nonfiction.

Hendrich, Paula. **Saving America's Birds.** Lothrop, Lee and Shepard Books, 1982.

In an attempt to make a better world, humans have destroyed or endangered much of the wildlife, especially the birds, of the United States. Hendrich shows how people are trying to rectify past mistakes by making valiant efforts to provide refuge for uprooted birds, to monitor and replenish diminishing populations, and to treat injured and diseased birds. Nonfiction.

Hitching, Francis. **The Neck of the Giraffe: Darwin, Evolution, and the New Biology.** Mentor Books, 1983.

No scientific theory is more disputed than Charles Darwin's theory of evolution. With research more enlightening and lucid than ever, scientists and creationists are posing questions that dispute the theory. In a series of panels, many questions are asked and debated. For example, why does the giraffe have such a long neck? Nonfiction.

Hyde, Margaret O., and Lawrence E. Hyde. **Cloning and the New Genetics.** Enslow, 1984.

Science fiction describes wild notions about future life, particularly about cloning. But is a human clone truly possible? Although fascinating and great sci-fi material, a human clone is probably impossible and, at best, boring. Learn about the facts of new genetics; it is a science of investigation, truth, and vision, a vision of a better life for all humanity. Nonfiction.

Jastrow, Robert. **God and the Astronomers.** Warner Books, 1984.

In a unique and fascinating intertwining of religion and science, Jastrow explores the idea of creation and our expanding universe. Using the work of Slipher, de Sitter, Einstein, Hubble, and Humason, Jastrow explains that in the final analysis scientists will reach the same conclusions the theologians have held all along: Big Bang and Genesis are one and the same. Nonfiction.

Jastrow, Robert. **Until the Sun Dies.** Warner Books, 1984.

Human nature dictates that as we evolve intellectually, we will choose to leap beyond the boundaries of the solar system. Our search will take us to other galaxies, possibly inhabited by new and different life forms, some less and others more advanced than we are. Jastrow calls this a new Darwinism—a quest that will continue "until the sun dies." Nonfiction.

Kiefer, Irene. **Nuclear Energy at the Crossroads.** Illustrations and photographs by Judith Fast. Atheneum, 1982.

Today the nuclear energy question is crucial and extremely controversial. Exhausted natural resources, manipulation of the world oil supply by OPEC, and increased energy demands make nuclear energy a more apparent and necessary option for the present. With its use, however, serious and possibly disastrous problems arise. Are there any solutions? Nonfiction.

Koebner, Linda. **Forgotten Animals: The Rehabilitation of Laboratory Primates.** Lodestar Books, 1984.

Millions of animals are used by laboratory scientists, and some of them are kept under inhumane conditions or treated cruelly. While the animals may serve to assist medical research, should they be treated in this manner? And what happens to these animals when they are no longer needed? The author uses chimpanzees, now an endangered species, to discuss her concern. Koebner also suggests some alternatives to using live animals in scientific research. Nonfiction.

Lampton, Christopher. **DNA and the Creation of New Life.** Arco, 1983.

Since the initial discovery of the double helix, our understanding of life has evolved into a new and frightening age—the age of genetic engineering and biological manipulation. Now that scientists have found, shaped, and sold the gene, where will they take us next? Lampton examines these controversial issues in this serious and complex book. A volume in the Arco How It Works series. Nonfiction.

Leon, George de Lucenay. **Energy Forever: Power for Today and Tomorrow.** Arco, 1982.

Is there an unending supply of energy that will adequately service the world's needs? The answer lies in renewable energy sources, according to Leon. What they are, when the nonrenewable resources will run out, and what is being done about the problem are the vital issues examined here. Nonfiction.

Ludlum, David M. **The American Weather Book.** Houghton Mifflin, 1982.

Weather enthusiasts and budding meteorologists will enjoy this potpourri of weather facts and figures. Learn about the great natural menaces and how they have baffled and destroyed. Listed are all the major record breakers in weather history, as well as brief but meaty explanations of all weather forms. What is a chinook? Is the blizzard of 1978 the worse snowstorm Boston has ever experienced? Find the answers to these and other weather questions right here. Nonfiction.

Maurer, Alan. **Lasers: Light Wave of the Future.** Arco, 1982.

Delve into the versatile and incredible uses of the laser—Light Amplification by Stimulated Emission of Radiation. Investigate how lasers work, who invented them, and how they are used in surgery, communications, and war. Learn how laser space stations and laser-propelled spaceships are no longer science fiction, but a real part of your future. A volume in the Arco How It Works series. Nonfiction.

McPhee, John. **In Suspect Terrain.** Farrar, Straus and Giroux, 1983.

With geologist Anita Harris, the author explores the Appalachian system from the New Jersey Highlands to the Indiana Dunes. This journal-like presentation of their findings includes paleontological and historical background for the many observations they make on their journey. Extensive geological information on New York is also provided. Nonfiction.

Miller, Jonathan. **Darwin for Beginners.** Illus. Borin Van Loon. Pantheon Books, 1982.

This biography is probably unlike any you have ever read. The combination of humor, fact, and sophistication make this a must not only for the Darwin enthusiast but for everyone else as well. The illustrations are clever and fascinating, and the content is informative and enjoyable. Nonfiction.

Milne, Lorus J., and Margery Milne. **Nature's Great Carbon Cycle.** Illus. Bruce Hiscock. Atheneum, 1983.

Did you know that when a diamond is heated in the presence of oxygen, it changes into carbon dioxide gas and the diamond vanishes? *Nature's Great Carbon Cycle* guides you through the versatile, intricate, and fascinating roles carbon atoms play in your life. Coal, diamonds, human and plant growth, and even starlight depend on carbon, an indispensable element of life. Nonfiction.

Milne, Lorus, and Margery Milne. **A Time to Be Born: An Almanac of Animal Courtship and Parenting.** Illus. Sarah Landry. Sierra Club Books, 1982.

The behavior of mammals is biologically regulated by a master clock and influenced by seasonal and environmental changes. The authors consider these factors as they review animal courtship and parenting of over one hundred species of mammals on six continents. The wealth of fascinating details and illustrations helps us understand how these animals have survived by adapting over the centuries. Nonfiction.

Nicholls, Peter, editor. **The Science in Science Fiction.** Alfred A. Knopf, 1983.

What seems incredible and impossible as presented in science fiction may not be as farfetched as you think. As you explore the scientific facts in fiction, you will find out that what seems unreal and preposterous has probably already happened and that truth is often stranger than fiction. Nonfiction.

Nilsson, Lennart (text by Hans Krook). **Close to Nature: An Exploration of Nature's Microcosm.** Pantheon Books, 1984.

Take the most exhilarating and visually stimulating photographic excursion of your life as you explore the deepest crevices and hidden worlds of insects and plant life. Through electron microscopy and photography you observe decay, a mite's anatomy, roundworms' habits, germination, and fungi, just to mention a few of nature's wonders. What you see will amaze and fascinate you. Nonfiction.

Peterson, Lee Allen. **A Field Guide to Edible Wild Plants of Eastern and Central North America.** Illus. by author and Roger Tory Peterson. Photographs by author. Houghton Mifflin, 1977.

Designed for practical field use, this guide provides succinct descriptive information about 373 of the better-known species of edible plants. A separate section lists various habitats in which the species are found, including seashore, bogs, meadows, woods, and tundras. Plants described in the guide have been categorized into twenty-two food-use categories with basic cooking directions provided. A volume in the Peterson Field Guide series. Nonfiction.

Pringle, Laurence. **Radiation: Waves and Particles/Benefits and Risks.** Enslow, 1983.

Radiation is as potentially destructive as it is beneficial. One of science's most advanced tools, radiation can cause the same life-threatening disease it often cures. Ionizing radiation—natural and synthetic, its uses and misuses, its risks and benefits—is the focus of the research. This text also presents provocative information about the common uses of radiation in everyday life. The author makes you take a careful look at these invisible waves and particles. Nonfiction.

Purcell, John. **From Hand Ax to Laser: Man's Growing Mastery of Energy.** Illus. Judy Skorpil. Vanguard Press, 1982.

The author traces humans' use of energy from Australopithecus's utilization of bones as tools to our present use of lasers in industry and medicine. Purcell explains how the harnessing of energy and fabrication of energy-using tools directly relate to our cultural evolution. This resource is an interesting and informative account of anthropology's relationship to the science of energy. Nonfiction.

Restak, Richard M. **The Brain: The Last Frontier.** Warner Books, 1980.

Embark on a sophisticated, stylish, and in-depth exploration of the human brain. In addition to learning about the brain's anatomy and physiology, you can explore this organ of emotion and sensitivity. Investigate how the brain organizes information to enable us to speak and understand language. The brain is unlike any other structure in the universe, and in this volume Dr. Restak reveals some of its mystery. Nonfiction.

Ritchie, David. **The Ring of Fire.** Mentor Books, 1982.

The disasters Ritchie describes are not fiction. They represent historically and geologically accurate accounts of the devastation wrought by volcanoes, earthquakes, and tidal waves. All events share a common origin: they all emanate from "the ring of fire." Nonfiction.

Sattler, Helen Roney. **Fish Facts and Bird Brains: Animal Intelligence.** Illus. Giulio Maestro. Lodestar Books, 1984.

Many people do not consider animals to be intelligent. Scientists now believe, however, that animals do have some kind of intelligence. Helen Roney Sattler discusses how animals' intelligence can be measured and how this knowledge will help us better understand human intelligence. Nonfiction.

Settle, Mary Lee. **Water World.** Lodestar Books, 1984.

Journey beneath the sea which covers three-quarters of the earth. The author describes primitive myths about the sea and the beginning of the science of oceanography. The ocean itself is probed to reveal lush underwater meadows and deep black holes. Nonfiction.

Silverstein, Alvin, and Virginia B. Silverstein. **Futurelife: The Biotechnology Revolution.** Illus. Marjorie Thier. Prentice-Hall, 1982.

Along with the revolutionary biotechnological discoveries of the 1980s, such as the PET Scan, the artificial heart, bionic vision, computerized limbs, clones, and test-tube offspring, come some difficult choices. The Silversteins take a hard look at these biotechnological wonders as well as at the moral issues and "bioethics" which are critical by-products of this scientific revolution. Nonfiction.

Simpson, George Gaylord, editor. **The Book of Darwin.** Washington Square Press, 1983.

Autobiographical in nature, the text gives a sensitive and keen insight into Darwin the researcher, the biologist, the collector, and the man. Darwin opened up new avenues of thought, and although much of his research is obsolete, these avenues are still open to travel. Nonfiction.

Sullivan, George. **Inside Nuclear Submarines.** Dodd, Mead, 1982.

A devastating power greater than all the bombs dropped during World War II can be housed on just one nuclear submarine. With the development of the *Nautilus,* the *Triton,* and even the *Thresher,* great strides have been made in antisubmarine attacks, communications, speed, and nuclear warfare. This book contains well-illustrated facts, figures, history, and adventures about nuclear submarines—our country's main defense. Nonfiction.

Thomas, Lewis. **The Youngest Science: Notes of a Medicine-Watcher.** Viking Press, 1983.

Lewis Thomas, author of *The Lives of a Cell,* presents here a history of medicine as much as the story of his professional life. Beginning with his childhood memories of his father's medical practice during the 1920s, Thomas describes the early medical practitioner who made house calls and established a personal relationship with the patient. When Thomas entered medical school, medicine moved from art to science. Using his personal experiences, he chronicles the changes in the medical profession with the advent of technology and its promises for research and practice. Nonfiction.

Thompson, Ida. **The Audubon Society Field Guide to North American Fossils.** Photographs by Townsend P. Dickinson. Alfred A. Knopf, 1982.

This Audubon publication is a comprehensive, practical, and beautifully illustrated guide to North American fossils. Whether you're a hiking enthusiast, seashore lover, or backyard investigator, this invaluable tool will surely enhance your appreciation of the life around you, where it came from, and where it all may go. This field guide is an excellent resource for the expert as well as the amateur. Nonfiction.

West, Beverly Henderson, Ellen Norma Griesbach, Jerry Duncan Taylor, and Louise Todd Taylor. **The Prentice-Hall Encyclopedia of Mathematics.** Prentice-Hall, 1982.

Explore angles and area, induction and infinity, and vectors and volume in this comprehensive mathematics reference book. There is even a section on computer programming. No operation remains unexplained, and no theorem remains unproven. Nonfiction.

World Almanac Editors. **The World Almanac Book of the Strange.** Signet Books, 1977.

Delve into the bizarre, the incredible, the astounding, and the strange. Killer bees, psychic phenomena, UFOs, animal mimicry, hypnosis, and even hiccups are the fascinating and amazing subjects investigated in this collection of weird wonders. Nonfiction.

Young, Louise B. **The Blue Planet.** Illus. Jennifer Dewey. Meridian Books, 1984.

In an artistic combination of fact, personal observation, and illustration, Young paints an elegant, almost magical picture of our planet. Its creation, its metamorphosis, its mysteries, its secrets, its evolution, and its future tantalize and fascinate. Nonfiction.

Science Fiction

Abbott, Edwin A. **Flatland: A Romance of Many Dimensions.** Illus. by author. Signet Classics, 1984.

In this book, gentlemen are squares, women are triangles, and sons are usually born with one side more than their fathers. Welcome to Flatland, a world second only to Gulliver's Laputa in its humorous vision of the laws, customs, and life-styles indigenous to our great sphere, Earth. Adventure into a land of lines and angles where talk of a third dimension is pointless and punishable by execution, and where it's "in" to be square. Fiction.

Asimov, Isaac, and Martin H. Greenberg, editors. **Isaac Asimov Presents the Great Science Fiction Stories.** Vol. 7, 1945. DAW Books, 1982.

Although the use of nuclear energy in 1945 would eventually create results stranger than fiction, Asimov has selected for this volume stories that reflect the chaos and uncertainty of this troubled time in history. These stories feature mutations from the literal to the abstract, in our society and from light years away. In science fiction as well as in history, 1945 was a momentous year. Fiction.

Asimov, Isaac, and Martin H. Greenberg, editors. **Isaac Asimov Presents the Great Science Fiction Stories.** Vol. 9, 1947. DAW Books, 1983.

Create your own clone. Will the real robot please stand up? The new human race is a race of mutants! These ideas are all found in this collection of amusing, ironic, prophetic, and horrifying stories from 1947. The best are assembled in this collection. Fiction.

Asimov, Isaac, and Martin H. Greenberg, editors. **Isaac Asimov Presents the Great Science Fiction Stories.** Vol. 10, 1948. DAW Books, 1983.

Nineteen forty-eight was a year of assassinations, political surprise, establishment of new free states and new regimes, revolutionary scientific discoveries, and marvelous accomplishments in the arts.

Such "stuff" motivated the themes of the science fiction stories presented here. Fiction.

Asimov, Isaac, and Martin H. Greenberg, editors. **Isaac Asimov Presents the Great Science Fiction Stories.** Vol. 11, 1949. DAW Books, 1984.

These are the best stories from 1949. Plots include a completely fissioned nuclear power plant, a watchful eye that misses no one, a stranger with extraordinary talents, and a dead man standing in the jungle. Asimov has selected tales that will surely thrill, frighten, excite, and mystify you. Fiction.

Asimov, Isaac, Martin H. Greenberg, and Charles G. Waugh, editors. **Caught in the Organ Draft: Biology in Science Fiction.** Farrar, Straus and Giroux, 1983.

These twelve science fiction stories take biological themes and develop them far beyond what we might imagine and often far beyond our worst fears. Mutants, biological experimentation, plagues, germ warfare, and hostile organisms are only some of the topics found in this collection. Fiction.

Asimov, Isaac, Martin H. Greenberg, and Charles G. Waugh, editors. **Intergalactic Empires.** Signet Books, 1983.

History is marked by the birth, expansion, and destruction of great empires, and so is the realm of science fiction. These stories explore the birth and death, the laws and penal systems, and the security and defense of these vast imaginary empires. This is the first in the series called Isaac Asimov's Wonderful Worlds of Science Fiction. Fiction.

Asimov, Isaac, Martin H. Greenberg, and Charles G. Waugh, compilers. **Science Fiction A to Z: A Dictionary of the Great S.F. Themes.** Houghton Mifflin, 1982.

Every possible science fiction theme appears in the tales collected in this reference book, including time travel, robots, alien invasions, insane scientists, computers, and much more. This is a science fiction collector's dream. Fiction.

Asimov, Isaac, Martin H. Greenberg, and Charles G. Waugh, editors. **Supermen.** Signet Books, 1984.

What is your definition of a "superman"? An avenging angel of death? A corrupted, bloodthirsty warrior? A man of average

strength but extraordinary determination and guts? A creature
with infinite life? Here you will meet every possible kind of superman, from hero to villain, from fact to fantasy, from heaven to
hell. Escape into the supernatural realm of the supermen! Third
of the Isaac Asimov's Wonderful Worlds of Science Fiction series.
Fiction.

Asimov, Isaac, and J. O. Jeppson, editors. **Laughing Space.** Houghton
Mifflin, 1982.

Welcome to the lighter side of science fiction. Assembled here are
poems, cartoons, anecdotes, short stories, and tales that will make
you chuckle and grin. Who says science fiction isn't funny? Fiction.

Asimov, Isaac, and Alice Laurance, editors. **Speculations.** Houghton
Mifflin, 1982.

Test your science fiction knowledge and guess who wrote each of
the stories in this anthology. A number code is given and the editors
present clues in each introduction, but it's up to you to figure out
who wrote about the postcard from William Shakespeare, who
wrote about the men who strip off age like a garment, as well as
who thought up the many other strange occurrences in these science fiction stories. Fiction.

Asimov, Isaac, Charles G. Waugh, and Martin H. Greenberg, editors.
Hallucination Orbit: Psychology in Science Fiction. Farrar, Straus
and Giroux, 1983.

Science fiction depicts absurd, bizarre, and incredible happenings
and the mind's reactions to these events. The stories assembled in
this anthology focus on the multifaceted reactions of people to the
surprises of the unknown. These responses often reflect the health
of the person's psyche. How would you have reacted in these
unusual situations? Fiction.

Asimov, Isaac, George Zebrowski, and Martin H. Greenberg, editors.
Creations: The Quest for Origins in Story and Science. Crown,
1983.

Bringing together science fiction, science, and the Bible may provide some of the answers as to how life and the solar system began.
Even after all the available facts are explained, all the formulas
are calculated, and all the allusions and references are researched,
there is only one real explanation. Fiction and nonfiction.

Brunner, John. **Total Eclipse.** DAW Books, 1975.

As Ian Macauley steps onto the now-deserted, Earth-like planet of Sigma Draconis, he can only wonder what happened to its inhabitants. Investigation reveals that they were different—all geniuses who erred only once, who never lied, but who may have been destroyed by a mutation that their biological know-how should have detected and changed in a nanosecond. What really devastated these brilliant Draconians, and will it destroy the rest of humanity? Fiction.

Bunting, Eve. **Strange Things Happen in the Woods.** Archway Paperbacks, 1984.

John begins to think that his girlfriend Cindy and his friend Bleecher are acting very strangely, so he and his grandfather set out to find the reasons for the changes. Originally titled *The Cloverdale Switch*. Fiction.

Carlson, Dale. **The Frog People.** Illus. Michael Garland. Skinny Books, 1982.

A strange disease seems to be turning the residents of Proud Point into human-size frogs with green skins, bulging eyes, wide mouths, and webbed hands and feet. Ann Derry and her friend Dan race to discover the reason and a solution before everyone succumbs to the frightening transformation. Fiction.

Cherryh, C. J. **Forty Thousand in Gehenna.** DAW Books, 1984.

The forty thousand who set out for Gehenna, a seemingly uninhabited but ominous planet, intend to investigate, record, report, and colonize. But these pioneers are not alone on Gehenna; calibans—huge, burrowing, lizard-like creatures—inhabit the planet. Forsaken and deserted, the pioneers are assimilated into the lizard race, and soon new species emerge. There is war and devastation, but then, more than two hundred years later, starmen arrive and marvel at what they see. Fiction.

Christopher, John. **New Found Land.** E. P. Dutton, 1983.

While Brad is visiting his friend Simon in England, the two of them are plunged into the past. There, accompanied by two new Roman friends, they encounter territories and peoples of the past, such as the Algonquins, the Vikings, and the Aztecs. While among the Aztecs, the time travelers even become a championship basketball team, Aztec-style. Each of the adventures in this sequel to *Fireball* has its share of dangers, however, and some of them are inescapable. Fiction.

Clarke, Arthur C. **2010: Odyssey 2.** Del Rey Books, 1982.

Is Dave Bowman still alive? Will Hal foil Spacecraft *Leonov*'s mission to Jupiter? In this successor to *2001: A Space Odyssey,* the Tycho monolith that baffled *Discovery I* gives only an inkling of the peril and scientific paradoxes that confront the unlikely American and Soviet crew of the *Leonov* as they attempt to continue the race to control this solar system. Fiction.

Correy, Lee. **Manna.** DAW Books, 1984.

Alexander Sandhurst Baldwin is a crackerjack U.S. pilot who is hired to put his skills to the ultimate test. The mission is like the most challenging video game he has ever played: Russians, explosions, saucers, invaders, aliens, torture chambers, even brainwashing. The only difference is that it's real! No quarters necessary. Fiction.

Crispin, A. C. **V.** Pinnacle Books, 1984.

Whether you saw or missed the TV showing of this thriller, the novel delivers added delights in abundance. The plot—the takeover of Earth's water supply by human-looking "Visitors"—and the characters, ranging from exhausted freedom fighters to villainous aliens—combine to produce a theme that looks at power, oppression, and the springs of resistance. Fiction.

del Rey, Lester. **Attack from Atlantis.** Del Rey Books, 1982.

While testing the capabilities of a nuclear-powered submarine, Don Miller, a young communications expert, notices very strange bubbles outside the ship. It turns out that the bubbles are moved by people who have adapted to life underwater, and moments after Don first sees them, the ship is mysteriously trapped by these bubble people. If the *Triton* doesn't surface soon, nuclear war will be triggered. Time is running out. Fiction.

Dick, Philip K. **UBIK.** DAW Books, 1983.

If you think life is complicated, try half-life. Telepath Joe Chip, second in command of Glen Runciter's Prudence Organization, finds this state especially complex; he can't tell if he's in life or half-life. Plunged into 1939 from 1992, Joe sees his friends dead one minute and alive the next. Something is terribly wrong. But there's a solution: UBIK—the answer to all problems. Fiction.

Duane, Diane. **My Enemy, My Ally.** Pocket Books, 1984.

In this *Star Trek* novel, the Romulans have created a way to clone Vulcan genetic materials, and if this discovery is not destroyed, all hopes for peace in the universe will be lost. In a daring and unorthodox joint venture, Romulan Commander Ael and Captain Kirk embark on a bizarre scheme to save the future. Is this plan really in the name of honor, or is it a deceptive Romulan plot to gain control of the *Enterprise* once and for all? Fiction.

Duprey, Richard, and Brian O'Leary. **Spaceship Titanic.** Dodd, Mead, 1983.

It is only two minutes and thirty-one seconds after lift-off when Houston orders the *Titan,* the ultimate in luxury space-age transportation, to return to the launch site. But a return is impossible, so astronauts Sager and Pepper take control. They plan to join *Space Lab,* transfer the women and children, and then land somewhere in Mexico. Everything proceeds as planned—until panic and mutiny set in, and Pepper dies. Sager and the new copilot, Judy Langenberg, hold in their hands not only the safety of their passengers, but the future of space travel as well. Fiction.

Dvorkin, David. **The Trellisane Confrontation.** Pocket Books, 1984.

In this *Star Trek* novel, a simple mission to retrieve prisoners from the planet Trellisane in the Neutral Zone throws the *Enterprise* into the midst of intergalactic war. It turns out that Trellisane, in the spirit of peace, has advanced Sealon technology and caused Sealon's alliance with the warlike Klingons. The prisoners from Trellisane capture the *Enterprise,* and Kirk must ally himself with the Klingons in order to recapture his ship and avoid all-out war with the Romulans. Fiction.

Farmer, Philip José. **Gods of Riverworld.** G. P. Putnam's Sons, 1983.

The Ethical Council of Twelve, members of an alien race, have created the planet called Riverworld and resurrected there thirty-five billion people who died on Earth between 99,000 B.C. and A.D. 1983. Now such diverse characters as Mark Twain, Hermann Göring, and Cyrano de Bergerac are wandering along the banks of a ten-million-mile-long river, searching for their makers and trying to learn why they are there. Fifth and final volume in the Riverworld series. Fiction.

Ferman, Edward L., editor. **The Best from Fantasy and Science Fiction.** 24th series. Charles Scribner's Sons, 1982.

Many successful and prominent science fiction writers have contributed to this unusual collection of literary works and readers' contributions to contests published in the *Magazine of Fantasy and Science Fiction.* Subjects of the stories vary from future worlds, robotics, and mind control to a fantasy involving household appliances and one about housewives' unusual problems. There is even a section on the most entertaining but unwieldy fifty-words-or-less titles for science fiction books. A *Magazine of Fantasy and Science Fiction* book. Fiction.

Gunn, James, editor. **The Road to Science Fiction No. 4: From Here to Forever.** Mentor Books, 1982.

In his fourth volume of science fiction, Gunn assembles stories that emphasize literary style rather than just adventure and imagination. He calls it "new wave" science fiction writing—with an emphasis on dress, behavior, actions, and setting. Vinge, Herbert, Keyes, Wilhelm, and Bishop are just a few of the great authors represented in this collection. Fiction.

Haldeman, Joe, editor. **Nebula Award Stories Seventeen.** Holt, Rinehart and Winston, 1983.

Some of the best and most exciting science fiction stories from 1981 are assembled in this collection. Tales of prophetic dreams, suspended animation, panhandling, and resurrection will provoke, madden, puzzle, and entertain you. Most of the stories begin in common places and ordinary times, but all possess that strange twist or bizarre plot that is so characteristic of science fiction. Fiction.

Heinlein, Robert A. **Citizen of the Galaxy.** Del Rey Books, 1982.

Young Thorby is sold as a slave on a remote planet and becomes an outlaw while working for a master who seems to be nothing more than a crippled beggar. His attempts to escape from the unjust space authorities force him into a web of political intrigue and adventures. Fiction.

Heinlein, Robert A. **The Number of the Beast.** Gold Medal Books, 1982.

> A party in California brings together four geniuses who are trying to escape alien forces. Zeb, Hilda, Jake, and Deety travel through time and the universe in Zeb's secret transporter as they try to locate a safe place to live. The imaginative worlds they discover in other time warps provide an exciting tour of our unknown universe. Fiction.

Hill, Douglas. **Alien Citadel.** Margaret K. McElderry Books, 1984.

> The Slavers have finally trapped the elusive Finn Ferral in this third volume of the trilogy that begins with *The Huntsman* and *Warriors of the Wasteland.* Enclosed inside the evil Citadel, Finn must outwit the horrid Cacinnix, an oozing and reeking machine of damp and baggy folds, or he will never see the outside world again. Fiction.

Hill, Douglas. **Planet of the Warlord.** Margaret K. McElderry Books, 1982.

> As the last surviving legionary of the planet Moros, Keill Rander must find and eliminate the evil Warlord who has destroyed his planet. But the Warlord is protected by the Deathwing, an elite group of agents highly skilled in destruction and death. Only the demise of the Warlord and his servants can free Keill to pursue his quest throughout the universe. Fiction.

Hill, Douglas. **Warriors of the Wasteland.** Margaret K. McElderry Books, 1983.

> Finn Ferral the huntsman and his Bloodkin friend Baer are captured by the evil Slavers of Earth and kept under guard by the Claw. Having escaped, but still pursued by the Claw, Finn and Baer head for the Wasteland, a flatland full of deformed beasts. There they join with comrades to battle the Slavers in hopes of finding Finn's foster sister Jena and the rest of his family. Fiction.

Hill, Douglas. **Young Legionary.** Margaret K. McElderry Books, 1983.

> In order to prove his manhood, twelve-year-old Keill Rander must embark on a lonely quest that leads him through lands inhabited by dangerous carnivores. Once through this ordeal, he becomes a Young Legionary with the responsibility of protecting others against evil and destruction. How he deals with the sinister Haxxarians will prove whether he is worthy of his title. Fiction.

Hoover, H. M. **The Bell Tree.** Viking Press, 1982.

The beautiful and unusual metallic scrolls give only an inkling of the treasures and magic that await Jenny and her dad, Dr. Sadler, when they reach the planet Tonin. Are these discoveries true artifacts of a once-magnificent society? Are the mysterious occurrences in the ghostly caves real or just tricks of the imagination? Jenny must decide whether it is right to disturb and exploit another's creations and culture for the sake of scientific discovery and advancement. Fiction.

Huddy, Delia. **The Humboldt Effect.** Greenwillow Books, 1982.

Tom Humboldt's time reversal machine works! In fact, it works too well. When it's tested on a submarine in the stormy Mediterranean, a crew member is lost at sea and a man from the fourth century B.C. is taken on board. He turns out to be Jonah, from the biblical story of Jonah and the whale. Fiction.

Hughes, Monica. **The Keeper of the Isis Light.** Bantam Books, 1984.

Sixteen-year-old Olwen Pendennis has lived almost her entire life on the planet Isis, alone except for the faithful companionship of her guardian robot. Having adapted physically and emotionally to the beautiful solitude and the sometimes harsh nature of Isis, she is not pleased when visitors from Earth come to colonize her home. Then she meets and is strongly attracted to a young settler whose reaction causes her world to fall apart. Fiction.

Irwin, Walter, and G. B. Love, editors. **The Best of *Trek* No. 6: From the Magazine for *Star Trek* Fans.** Signet Books, 1983.

Beam aboard the USS *Enterprise* and learn the deep, dark secrets of *Star Trek II: The Wrath of Khan.* Also find out what fans like you thought about the second *Star Trek* movie. All information is taken directly from *Trek* magazine. Fiction and nonfiction.

Jackson, Steve. **Starship Traveller.** Illus. Peter Andrew Jones. Laurel-Leaf Library, 1984.

Become a galactic traveler and battle the unknown! You control the weaponry, make major decisions, develop strategy, and keep score. In the style of Buck Rogers, Luke Skywalker, and Captain Kirk, you are a starship traveler. Fiction.

Kamerman, Sylvia E., editor. **Space and Science Fiction Plays for Young People.** Plays, Inc., 1983.

This collection of easy-to-produce, one-act, royalty-free plays focuses on young people caught up in adventures that are filled with astronauts, extraterrestrials, robots, and outer-space travel. Each play includes production notes on sets, costumes, lighting, sound effects, and properties.

Karl, Jean E. **But We Are Not of Earth.** Laurel-Leaf Library, 1984.

Romula, Bitsy, Gloust, and Waver are the Terrible Four. Orphaned in infancy, these children are unlike others of their planet and know they will not be content until they are allowed to be Discoverers. They find exploring the new planet Ariel exciting and fascinating until they are surrounded by large, strange, and terrifying animals and people who do not want them to leave. Fiction.

Kelley, Leo P. **Alien Gold.** Illus. Cliff Spohn. Bantam Books, 1983.

Kinkaid, a falsely accused and convicted space commander; Karen, a knife-carrying kidnapper; Lor'l, a one-eyed friendly alien; and Zeno, a sharp-toothed angry alien; are prisoners on planet Earth. Adam Lane, founder of the new star Alba, offers his spaceship and freedom to Kinkaid and the others if they will rescue his kidnapped daughter Allison from the Albans. The crew experience many surprising adventures as they travel through space in the year 2183. Fiction.

Lightner, A. M. **Star Dog.** Scholastic Book Services, 1983.

A UFO sighting and a dead six-legged dog make it impossible for Holt Dane to study for his science exam. But that's only the beginning; soon his dog Mitzie gives birth to a puppy with hair-like fur and a telepathic mind, who quickly becomes the focus of animal behaviorists and the brass ring for local criminals. Who knows? The strange canine may be the key to a peaceful alliance between Earthlings and aliens. Fiction.

Llewellyn, Edward. **Prelude to Chaos.** DAW Books, 1983.

There was never a prison quite like the Federal Penitentiary of the United States, comfortable and almost enjoyable, but magnificently controlled and inescapable. Unjustly incarcerated there, Gavin and Judith must escape to halt the mass production of a biological time bomb that will cause humanity's extinction. But is it already too late? Fiction.

Llewellyn, Edward. **Salvage and Destroy.** DAW Books, 1984.

Lucien the Ult disguises himself as a human in order to observe behaviors of the Earthlings. His superior Primates are threatened and amazed by a people that have developed nuclear power within three decades. Now he must learn about them, salvage what he can, and ultimately destroy this puzzling race. Lucien learns, however, that he is more human than he wants to admit. Fiction.

May, Julian. **The Golden Torc.** Houghton Mifflin, 1982.

Step back into the future as Aiken Drum and the other members of Green Group finally reach their destination: the medieval world of the Pliocene. Thrust into war between two extraterrestrial tribes, Aiken seizes an opportunity to use his psychic powers to gain dominance over all. His final test comes in the Grand Combat: will he be able to make himself worthy of the golden torc? Fiction.

Meluch, R. M. **Wind Child.** Signet Books, 1982.

East is a servant from Aeolis, a paradise for wealthy aristocrats. Laure is a beautiful and mysterious Earthwoman, the only person remaining who can talk to the winds. Together they create Daniel, the only hope left to bring the winds back to Aeolis and to free their planet from the evil control of the *cuyane* and give it back to the Kristaalians, the wind people. Fiction.

Nolane, Richard D., editor. **Terra SF II: The Year's Best European SF.** DAW Books, 1983.

In one story in this collection, only imprisonment in the hospital will help you escape the Disease. In another, Mother Earth is destroyed like a planet in a video game. These plots and many more—all unusual and exciting—are presented in this anthology of imaginative works from some of Europe's best science fiction authors. Fiction.

Palmer, David R. **Emergence.** Bantam Books, 1984.

Candy, Adam, Kim, and Lisa are a new breed, *Homo post hominem,* a species that is physiologically, psychologically, and intellectually equipped to handle everything that comes its way. After a bionuclear war, these three alone must reconstruct, restore, and preserve a new world which is to emerge out of the mistakes and rubble the *Homo sapiens* have left behind. Fiction.

Pinkwater, Daniel. **Slaves of Spiegel.** Four Winds Press, 1982.

Steve Nickelson and his assistant Norman work at the Magic Moscow, a bizarre gourmet, health food, and ice cream restaurant. Both men, needless to say, are quite surprised when their place of employment disappears. They later discover that fat pirates from the planet Spiegel have transported the restaurant through space to compete in an intergalactic junk-food cooking contest. One of the Magic Moscow stories. Fiction.

Pohl, Frederik. **Demon in the Skull.** DAW Books, 1984.

The verdict at Chandler's trial: not guilty by reason of possession. But Chandler is not the only one possessed; an alien intelligence has invaded the minds of millions and taken over their bodies. The result is a rash of the most evil atrocities ever perpetrated in society. In order to beat these aliens, Chandler must join them, learn how they control his mind, and then destroy them. Fiction.

Shaw, Bob. **The Ceres Solution.** DAW Books, 1984.

In exchange for perfect beauty, Gretana leaves Mollan, a planet where inhabitants have almost reached immortality, to spy on Earthlings. In exchange for independence and worthy employment, Denny Hargate leaves Earth to work on the planet Aristotle. Their paths fortuitously cross, and they discover a terrible plot to destroy Earth—but they may be too late to stop it. Fiction.

Shwartz, Susan, editor. **Habitats.** DAW Books, 1984.

In the stories in this science fiction collection, survivors of the future gather in caverns, on the desert, on the slopes, on astral planes, or in tree houses to battle the age-old enemy, the environment. In each story, the characters try to create new civilizations, but most importantly, they endeavor to make themselves a home and a life, no matter how short-lived. Fiction.

Silverberg, Robert, Charles G. Waugh, and Martin Harry Greenberg, editors. **The Science Fictional Dinosaur.** Flare Books, 1982.

Escape into the worlds of dinosaurs past and future. In this collection, the best science fiction writers place you in frightening and unusual situations. In one story, you will find yourself battling the most gruesome creature possible, while in the next setting you are saved by another grotesque but friendly creation. Fiction.

Simak, Clifford D. **Our Children's Children.** DAW Books, 1983.

Millions of visitors who claim they are from five hundred years into the future are streaming out of tree trunks, emerging from time tunnels, and coming out of the woodwork. They are fleeing from the end of the human race, and they need help. Do we build time tunnels to transport these refugees farther into the future or farther into the past? Or do we destroy them before they destroy us? Fiction.

Snodgrass, Melinda. **The Tears of the Singers.** Pocket Books, 1984.

In what is perhaps the most enchanting and magical *Star Trek* adventure, Captain Kirk and Klingon Commander Kor must band together to discover the musical formula of the "Great Song," a phenomenon that could destroy the universe. Fiction.

Sullivan, Mary W. **Earthquake 2099.** Lodestar Books, 1982.

Alone in strange living quarters, eleven-year-old Philip and his newly arrived cousins, Vita and No Name, battle the devastation and terror of a major earthquake. Accustomed to a life of efficient and advanced technology, Philip learns from Vita that when technology is destroyed, humans must turn to nature, the ultimate source of survival. Fiction.

Trebor, Robert. **An XT Called Stanley.** DAW Books, 1983.

Who is Stanley, or rather, *what* is Stanley? An advanced civilization sends cosmic signals to New Hope, signals which communicate the design of the most magnificent computer intelligence this world has ever seen—Stanley. Stanley seems friendly enough, but scientists and military powers think he's a spy. Has Stanley come in peace or for destruction? Fiction.

Vinge, Joan D. **Eyes of Amber and Other Stories.** Signet Books, 1979.

Although these stories are set in typical science fiction realms, their main characters are developed with a sensitivity and a uniqueness that make them more appealing than the run-of-the-mill alien or intergalactic hero. The stories offer varied themes and wide appeal, but "Tin Soldier," a love story that spans all galaxies and time, and "To Bell the Cat," a situation in which the manipulated alien displays admirable qualities (unlike his manipulator), are musts. Fiction.

Vinge, Joan D. **The Outcasts of Heaven Belt.** Signet Books, 1982.

They came from the distant planet called Morningside on a desperate quest for aid from Heaven Belt, the asteroid system that, according to legend, is lined with golden streets and rich bounty for all. But before the starship *Ranger* can even explain its mission, it is attacked by the people of the outermost asteroid and partially destroyed. Without sufficient hydrogen, the *Ranger* can't return home, and so it gravitates to the gas giant Discus, a hellish planet. Soon what began as a mission of hope for the crew of the *Ranger* becomes a breathtaking race for survival. Fiction.

Vinge, Joan D. **Psion.** Delacorte Press, 1982.

Life in Oldcity is a nightmare of abuse and starvation for a green-eyed, sixteen-year-old named CAT. Suddenly CAT awakens among others like himself—psions, humans and half-humans endowed with powers of telepathy, teleportation, and telekinesis. Together they must destroy an organization of criminal psions led by Rubiy, a master. CAT's help is crucial: he has the power; he is the chosen one. Fiction.

Van Vogt, A. E. **Computerworld.** DAW Books, 1983.

A computer that looks at a human and sees its soul? Preposterous! But in this world where every household has at least one computer for surveillance and where there have been no babies born in twelve years, technology is in total control. The narrator of the story, an omniscient Eye-O computer that has ultimate control, decides, however, that there is something to be said for the human spirit and the soul. Fiction.

Walker, Irma. **Portal to E'ewere.** Argo Books, 1983.

The Northeast has become a community of citizens disciplined to act and feel aloof even though they live in crowded conditions. But AMitY wants more out of life; she wants to experience the beauty of being close to people. Marriage to ConCord is her only chance for this experience, but his father was responsible for the death of AMitY's parents. ConCord can help AMitY find herself and paradise, but her guilt may prevent her from realizing her dreams. Fiction.

Webb, Sharon. **Earthchild.** Argo Books, 1982.

The Monat-Gari process has worked, and now the children are immortal. A gifted oboist at fifteen, Kurt Kraus, now five years older, has grown disinterested in music; after all, he can always return to it in the next century. But as he listens to his mortal brother play, he painfully realizes that immortality destroys creativity. Maybe the colony of Renascence will have the answer to his problem. Fiction.

Webb, Sharon. **Earth Song.** Argo Books, 1983.

In this sequel to *Earthchild,* humanity has come a long way; in fact, everyone except the deformed or misfits can now live forever. But with immortality comes a loss of motivation to excel, especially in the arts. There is a solution: an Earth colony called Renascence. Here some choose creativity at the expense of immortality; they die so that others may enjoy the beauty and genius of the creative spirit. Fiction.

Wollheim, Donald A., editor (with Arthur W. Saha). **The 1983 Annual World's Best SF.** DAW Books, 1983.

Wollheim has assembled a collection of unusual short stories from 1983. The tales all have bizarre twists and unexpected endings, and the settings vary from Pike's Peak to a typical shopping plaza and even an abbey. A kidnapping, an undelivered letter, and an obsession with video games are just a few of the plots that give you a taste of 1983's best. Fiction.

Wollheim, Donald A., editor (with Arthur W. Saha). **The 1984 Annual World's Best SF.** DAW Books, 1984.

Although labeled science fiction, some of these stories could unfortunately take place right in our backyard. Some of the frighteningly plausible topics include genetic engineering geared to produce telepaths, a national lottery where people literally gamble away their lives to control overpopulation, and people who are dying of starvation and cold because they are old and ineligible for welfare. Fiction.

Wollheim, Donald A., editor (with Arthur W. Saha). **Wollheim's World's Best SF.** Series 7. DAW Books, 1977.

Some of the most bizarre science fiction stories ever written were produced in 1977. The stories assembled here challenge your imagination far beyond what you might expect. They are intriguing, beautifully conceived and written, and exciting. Fiction.

Wylie, Philip. **The End of the Dream.** DAW Books, 1984.

The content of this science fiction novel will shake you into the wretched realization of what our world may be like before the middle of the next century. Crop devastation, genetic mutations, rampant murder, uncontrollable and incurable disease, biological warfare, and ultimate horrifying chaos are all possible. Fiction.

Sexuality

Asher, Sandy. **Things Are Seldom What They Seem.** Delacorte Press, 1983.

When Debbie's sister Maggie and Debbie's best friend Karen enter high school and join the Drama Club, they mysteriously change. Mr. Carraway, the drama coach, seems to have a strange power over them, which distances them from Debbie. Feeling left out, Debbie befriends Murray, a very short but exciting companion who willingly shares loyalty, laughter, and vulnerabilities with Debbie. Together they discover the nature of Mr. Carraway's hold on the girls in Drama Club and courageously disclose the teacher's sexual abuses. Fiction.

Blume, Judy. **Forever . . . .** Pocket Books, 1982.

Together, with tenderness and trembling, Michael and Katherine experience their first sexual encounter. Her parents, fearing that their daughter is getting too seriously involved, send her to camp after graduation while Michael is off in North Carolina. Katherine is certain their love is forever . . . until her grandfather dies and she encounters Theo. Fiction.

Corsaro, Maria, and Carole Korzeniowsky. **STD: A Commonsense Guide to Sexually Transmitted Diseases.** Owl Books, 1982.

This down-to-earth guide straightforwardly explains the many sexually transmitted diseases that are in existence today. Each description includes information on symptoms, testing, and treatment. The glossary, appendices, and diagrams add to the usefulness of this nonjudgmental handbook. Nonfiction.

Ecker, B. A. **Independence Day.** Flare Books, 1983.

Although Mike has a girlfriend, plays soccer, and seems like many other sixteen-year-olds, he is filled with conflicting emotions inside. For some time he has known that he is "different," and he has come to realize that his feelings for his close friend Todd are more than just friendship. Now he wonders how his decision to announce those feelings to Todd on the Fourth of July will affect the rest of his life. Fiction.

Garden, Nancy. **Annie on My Mind.** Farrar, Straus and Giroux, 1982.

Told in flashbacks by Liza during her freshman year at MIT, this story of two high school seniors, Liza and Annie, who fall in love and learn how to deal with the consequences of their controversial relationship, is frank, loving, and joyous. In their quest to be together, they face up to their choice of life-style, one which isn't easily accepted by their peers, parents, or even themselves. Fiction.

Klein, Norma. **Beginners' Love.** Hillside Books, 1983.

Shy, insecure, seventeen-year-old Joel falls passionately in love with assertive, outgoing Leda, and both begin a first-time sexual involvement that eventually leads to pregnancy, abortion, and the end of their relationship. Joel's musings on his relationship with his family, his best friend, and Leda ring true, as do the explicit descriptions of sexual activities and abortion. Fiction.

Major, Kevin. **Thirty-Six Exposures.** Delacorte Press, 1984.

The last few weeks of high school are momentous ones for Lorne. In his small seaside town in Canada, he develops his photographic skills, lets loose with his uninhibited friend Trevor, leads a student strike against an unfair teacher, and explores his growing sexuality with a new girlfriend. In brief chapters, like snapshots, the reader watches as Lorne learns, in sometimes harsh terms, that "you can't just play it safe all the time." Fiction.

Mazer, Harry. **I Love You, Stupid!** Flare Books, 1983.

Marcus Rosenbloom is a seventeen-year-old high school senior who feels he's ready for sex. Wendy Barrett is his childhood friend who has moved back to town to finish her senior year at his high school. The two of them rekindle their friendship and move on to become first-time lovers in this humorous, down-to-earth portrayal of teenage sexuality, friendship, and feelings told from a male (and sometimes female) point of view. Fiction.

Mazer, Norma Fox. **Someone to Love.** Delacorte Press, 1983.

When Nina Bloom, a college sophomore, and Mitchell Beers, a college-dropout-turned-housepainter, fall in love, they're both ecstatic that they've finally found one another. But once they decide to live together, delight turns to distrust, secretive behavior, betrayal, daily quarrels, and a gradual realization that falling blindly in love is quite different from staying in love. Fiction.

Mazer, Norma Fox. **Up in Seth's Room.** Laurel-Leaf Library, 1982.

When fifteen-year-old Finn falls in love with nineteen-year-old Seth, she has to struggle with her parents' strict rules, her budding sexuality, Seth's escalating demands, and her own conflicting feelings. Fiction.

McGuire, Paula. **It Won't Happen to Me: Teenagers Talk about Pregnancy.** Delacorte Press, 1983.

Fifteen young women tell about becoming pregnant and how their decision to continue or terminate their pregnancies affected and changed their lives. Also included in this group of candid interviews are the ideas and opinions of social workers, a physician, and one girl's mother. Nonfiction.

Mulford, Philippa Greene. **If It's Not Funny, Why Am I Laughing?** Delacorte Press, 1982.

In addition to having to deal with continual rejection from her absent mother and trying to care for her injured elderly neighbor, fifteen-year-old Mimi Canfield must face the prospect of her own sexuality. Her best friend is involved in an unhappy promiscuous relationship, Mimi's latest boyfriend has been pressuring her for more than kisses, and she has the knack of giggling at all the wrong times. Fiction.

Munro, Alice. **Lives of Girls and Women.** Plume Books, 1983.

In this novel about growing up in Canada during World War II, we meet Del, an innocent ten-year-old, and watch her progress through the years into a curious and original young woman. The novel traces her dreams, the changes in her life, and her search for sexual experiences and love. Fiction.

Stephensen, A. M. **Unbirthday.** Flare Books, 1982.

Louisa and Charlie, both high school seniors, must deal with the consequences of Louisa's unplanned pregnancy. Her carefully researched decision to have an abortion is made with the help of a volunteer at the local college Women's Center, who provides her with factual information, the name of a clinic, and constant support. Charlie is portrayed as understanding, loyal, loving, and supportive. Fiction.

Short Stories

Aiken, Joan. **A Whisper in the Night: Tales of Terror and Suspense.** Delacorte Press, 1984.

In this collection of thirteen eerie tales for Joan Aiken fans, each story involves young people's encounters with the suspenseful, the horrifying, or the supernatural. Some sample titles are "Finders Weepers," "The Window Waltz," and "Homer's Whistle." Fiction.

Asimov, Isaac, and Martin H. Greenberg, editors. **Isaac Asimov Presents the Great Science Fiction Stories.** Vol. 7, 1945. DAW Books, 1982.

Although the use of nuclear energy in 1945 would eventually create results stranger than fiction, Asimov has selected for this volume stories that reflect the chaos and uncertainty of this troubled time in history. These stories feature mutations from the literal to the abstract, in our society and from light years away. In science fiction as well as in history, 1945 was a momentous year. Fiction.

Asimov, Isaac, and Martin H. Greenberg, editors. **Isaac Asimov Presents the Great Science Fiction Stories.** Vol. 9, 1947. DAW Books, 1983.

Create your own clone. Will the real robot please stand up? The new human race is a race of mutants! These ideas are all found in this collection of amusing, ironic, prophetic, and horrifying stories from 1947. The best are assembled in this collection. Fiction.

Asimov, Isaac, and Martin H. Greenberg, editors. **Isaac Asimov Presents the Great Science Fiction Stories.** Vol. 10, 1948. DAW Books, 1983.

Nineteen forty-eight was a year of assassinations, political surprise, establishment of new free states and new regimes, revolutionary scientific discoveries, and marvelous accomplishments in the arts. Such "stuff" motivated the themes of the science fiction stories presented here. Fiction.

Asimov, Isaac, and Martin H. Greenberg, editors. **Isaac Asimov Presents the Great Science Fiction Stories.** Vol. 11, 1949. DAW Books, 1984.

These are the best from 1949. Plots include a completely fissioned nuclear power plant, a watchful eye that misses no one, a stranger with extraordinary talents, and a dead man standing in the jungle. Asimov has selected tales that will surely thrill, frighten, excite, and mystify you. Fiction.

Asimov, Isaac, Martin H. Greenberg, and Charles G. Waugh, editors. **Caught in the Organ Draft: Biology in Science Fiction.** Farrar, Straus and Giroux, 1983.

These twelve science fiction stories take biological themes and develop them far beyond what we might imagine and often far beyond our worst fears. Mutants, biological experimentation, plagues, germ warfare, and hostile organisms are only some of the topics found in this collection. Fiction.

Asimov, Isaac, Martin H. Greenberg, and Charles G. Waugh, editors. **Intergalactic Empires.** Signet Books, 1983.

History is marked by the birth, expansion, and destruction of great empires, and so is the realm of science fiction. These stories explore the birth and death, the laws and penal systems, and the security and defense of these vast imaginary empires. This is the first in the series called Isaac Asimov's Wonderful Worlds of Science Fiction. Fiction.

Asimov, Isaac, Martin H. Greenberg, and Charles G. Waugh, compilers. **Science Fiction A to Z: A Dictionary of the Great S.F. Themes.** Houghton Mifflin, 1982.

Every possible science fiction theme appears in the tales collected in this reference book, including time travel, robots, alien invasions, insane scientists, computers, and much more. This is a science fiction collector's dream. Fiction.

Asimov, Isaac, Martin H. Greenberg, and Charles G. Waugh, editors. **Supermen.** Signet Books, 1984.

What is your definition of a "superman"? An avenging angel of death? A corrupted, bloodthirsty warrior? A man of average strength but extraordinary determination and guts? A creature with infinite life? Here you will meet every possible kind of superman, from hero to villain, from fact to fantasy, from heaven to hell. Escape into the supernatural realm of the supermen! Third of the Isaac Asimov's Wonderful Worlds of Science Fiction series. Fiction.

Asimov, Isaac, Martin H. Greenberg, and Charles G. Waugh, editors. **Wizards.** Signet Books, 1983.

A master of fantasy himself, Asimov and his coeditors have gathered here ten marvelous tales that feature wizards who duel, transpose, and escape. Some of fantasy's most honored authors are represented in this collection, which is the first volume of the series entitled Isaac Asimov's Magical Worlds of Fantasy. Fiction.

Asimov, Isaac, and Alice Laurance, editors. **Speculations.** Houghton Mifflin, 1982.

Test your science fiction knowledge and guess who wrote each of the stories in this anthology. A number code is given and the editors present clues in each introduction, but it's up to you to figure out who wrote about the post card from William Shakespeare, who wrote about the men who strip off age like a garment, as well as the authors who thought up the many other strange occurrences in these science fiction stories. Fiction.

Asimov, Isaac, Charles G. Waugh, and Martin H. Greenberg, editors. **Hallucination Orbit: Psychology in Science Fiction.** Farrar, Straus and Giroux, 1983.

Science fiction depicts absurd, bizarre, and incredible happenings and the mind's reactions to these events. The stories assembled in this anthology focus on the multifaceted reactions of people to the surprises of the unknown. These responses often reflect the health of the person's psyche. How would you have reacted in these unusual situations? Fiction.

Beattie, Ann. **Distortions.** Warner Books, 1983.

These nineteen stories were written as if the author eavesdropped on the lives of her characters (children and adults, young and old) and then rushed to her typewriter to get everything down as it happened. The characters are recognizable as people we would know today, filled with questions about life and love. Fiction.

Bradley, Marion Zimmer, editor. **Greyhaven: An Anthology of Fantasy.** DAW Books, 1983.

In the preface to this volume of short stories, Marion Zimmer

Bradley introduces Greyhaven, the spiritual (and sometimes physical) home of a community of gifted writers of fantasy who present here eighteen tales of adventure and magic. The quality varies from story to story, but the best of them make the collection a fascinating addition to anyone's library. Fiction.

Bradley, Marion Zimmer, editor. **Sword and Sorceress: An Anthology of Heroic Fantasy.** DAW Books, 1984.

Bradley's aim in these fantasy tales is to present the reader with a familiar sword-and-sorcery tale told with a twist. The twist is that all the heroic figures in these fifteen stories are women. Fiction.

Bradley, Marion Zimmer, and the Friends of Darkover. **Sword of Chaos and Other Stories.** DAW Books, 1982.

The title story in this collection is by Bradley, but her influence permeates the rest of the tales, just as the environment of Darkover, the planet she created, sustains the lives of the characters who move through each short story. Fiction.

Cormier, Robert. **Eight Plus One.** Bantam Books, 1982.

Although Robert Cormier is known for his hard-hitting novels about some of the more unpleasant aspects of teenage life, this collection of nine stories reveals a completely different side of him. These are heartwarming stories about friendships, father-daughter relationships, first love, and a boy's first mustache. Accompanying each story is the author's explanation of how he came to write the story and the emotions that went with it. Fiction.

Doyle, Sir Arthur Conan. **The Adventures of the Speckled Band and Other Stories of Sherlock Holmes.** Signet Classics, 1965.

"The Adventures of the Speckled Band" is the first of twelve stories highlighting the shrewd detective Sherlock Holmes. Characterized by his cool analytical skills, his keen powers of observation, and his brilliant inductive reasoning, Holmes solves the seemingly unsolvable. In one story after another, the reader is invited to walk along with Holmes and his faithful companion Dr. Watson as the two discuss the clues of a case. Fiction.

Gallo, Donald R., editor. **Sixteen: Short Stories by Outstanding Writers for Young Adults.** Delacorte Press, 1984.

This unique collection of sixteen original short stories features such popular authors of novels for young adults as Cormier, Kerr, Lipsyte, Peck, and Mazer. The stories, ranging from science fiction to realistic fiction, fall into one of five categories: Friendship, Turmoils, Loves, Decisions, or Families. Questions are provided at the end of the book to allow the reader to explore each story in more depth. Fiction.

Gardam, Jane. **The Hollow Land.** Illus. Janet Rawlins. Greenwillow Books, 1981.

Nine short stories merge to tell the ongoing saga of the Teesdales, Cumbrian farmers, and their London summer tenants, the Batemans. Bell Teesdale, eight years old at the outset, befriends four-year-old Harry Bateman, and their friendship, adventures, and loyalty join both families to the lore and land of Light Trees Farm. Fiction.

Girion, Barbara. **A Very Brief Season.** Charles Scribner's Sons, 1984.

Ten short stories cover adolescence from freshman year in high school up through college, that time of one's life which can be looked back on as "a very brief season" in the scheme of things to come. Touched on are instances involving shoplifting, parental discord, romance, and college and high school achievement—all familiar themes to today's young adults. Fiction.

Gold, Robert S., editor. **Stepping Stones.** Laurel-Leaf Library, 1982.

This companion anthology to *Point of Departure* contains seventeen stories which deal with adolescents coming to terms with themselves as they interact with the adults in their lives. Fiction.

Goulart, Ron, editor. **The Great British Detective.** Mentor Books, 1982.

These fifteen detective stories star such famous sleuths as Sherlock Holmes, Hercule Poirot, Father Brown, and Lord Peter Wimsey, as well as a variety of lesser-known men and women. A good general introduction, introductions to each story, and a reading list at the end of the collection all add to the volume's value and the reader's pleasure. The selections included were written between the 1890s and the 1960s. Fiction.

Gunn, James, editor. **The Road to Science Fiction No. 4: From Here to Forever.** Mentor Books, 1982.

In his fourth volume of science fiction, Gunn assembles stories that emphasize literary style rather than just adventure and imagination. He calls it "new wave" science fiction writing—with an emphasis on dress, behavior, actions, and setting. Vinge, Herbert, Keyes,

Wilhelm, and Bishop are just a few of the great authors represented in this collection. Fiction.

Haldeman, Joe, editor. **Nebula Award Stories Seventeen.** Holt, Rinehart and Winston, 1983.

Some of the best and most exciting science fiction stories from 1981 are assembled in this collection. Tales of prophetic dreams, suspended animation, panhandling, and resurrection will provoke, madden, puzzle, and entertain you. Most of the stories begin in common places and ordinary times, but all possess that strange twist or bizarre plot that is so characteristic of science fiction. Fiction.

Hitchcock, Alfred, editor. **Alfred Hitchcock's Daring Detectives.** Random House, 1982.

Eight tales of clever detective work make up this anthology featuring well-known detectives, such as Ellery Queen and Hercule Poirot, as well as rank amateurs. All stories pose a challenging riddle and, after the reader has solved an array of confusing clues, a satisfying solution. Fiction.

Hitchcock, Alfred, editor. **Alfred Hitchcock's Sinister Spies.** Random House, 1982.

In this collection of ten spy stories, Hitchcock has drawn on the work of several authors, ranging from Somerset Maugham and Lord Dunsany to Eric Ambler. In some, like "Code Two" and "The Problem Solver and the Spy," the reader may well solve the mystery long before the final paragraph. Other stories, however, are baffling to the very end. The wide variety provides spy yarns for every taste. Fiction.

Hoke, Helen, editor. **Demonic, Dangerous and Deadly.** Lodestar Books, 1983.

Noted authors like Roald Dahl and Robert Bloch head the list of writers of these stories of horror and the supernatural, and a special story by Winston Churchill is also included. Fiction.

Hoke, Helen, editor. **Uncanny Tales of Unearthly and Unexpected Horrors.** Lodestar Books, 1983.

Included in this collection are stories by Ray Bradbury, Patricia Highsmith, and other horror authors. The offerings feature elements of the supernatural, the ghastly, the terrifying, the eerie, and the shocking. They are guaranteed to make your imagination run wild and your flesh crawl. Fiction.

King, Stephen. **Different Seasons.** Viking Press, 1982.

Horror author Stephen King demonstrates his versatility in this collection of four short stories. King fans will enjoy "Summer of Corruption" and "Fall from Innocence" as they delve into life-or-death adventures in the Maine woods and into the hideous past of the characters. Cliff-hanging plots will satisfy readers seeking mystery and suspense. Fiction.

Lester, Julius. **This Strange New Feeling.** Dial Press, 1982.

Based on true accounts, this set of three short stories revolves around three couples: Ras and Sally, Forrest and Maria, and William and Ellen. All have been slaves their entire lives, and all slowly taste a morsel of freedom with love as the motivating force. Fiction.

Mazer, Norma Fox. **Summer Girls, Love Boys and Other Short Stories.** Delacorte Press, 1982.

All set in the same neighborhood, these nine stories of love and adventure affectionately portray young women ages twelve to twenty as they deal with the problems of growing up. In "Avie Loves Ric Forever," Richie falls in love with her best friend Stevie; twelve-year-old Marlene runs away to teach her mother a lesson in "How I Run Away and Make My Mother Toe the Line"; and a high school assignment leads Mary Beth to discover a surprising incident in her mother's past in "Carmella, Adelina, and Florry." Fiction.

Nolane, Richard D., editor. **Terra SF II: The Year's Best European SF.** DAW Books, 1983.

In one story in this collection, only imprisonment in the hospital will help you escape the Disease. In another, Mother Earth is destroyed like a planet in a video game. These plots and many more—all unusual and exciting—are presented in this anthology of imaginative works from some of Europe's best science fiction authors. Fiction.

Poe, Edgar Allan. **The Fall of the House of Usher and Other Tales.** Signet Classics, 1980.

Fourteen gothic tales of terror are presented in this Poe collection. In "The Fall of the House of Usher," the narrator leads us to the family estate of Roderick Usher, where he meets Roderick's sister Madeline and senses the death and decay of the Usher family. What follows, as the morbid figure of Usher unfolds, is an eerie story of cataleptic seizures, premature entombment, and death. Fiction.

Ruby, Lois. **Two Truths in My Pocket.** Viking Press, 1982.

This collection of six stories of adolescence as seen through the eyes of Jewish teenagers deals with love, family, friendship, and the complexity of being Jewish in today's world. Some sample titles are "Inscriptions on Stone," which tells the story of Micha's movement away from tradition, and "Strangers in the Land of Egypt," which is about Barry and Esther's struggle with the problems of interracial dating. Fiction.

Saha, Arthur W., editor. **The Year's Best Fantasy Stories: 10.** DAW Books, 1984.

The eleven stories in this collection range in length from the novella of Fritz Leiber to short stories by Tanith Lee, Avram Davidson, and Grania Davis. What the tales have in common is that they are all spellbinders and together provide a powerful demonstration of the lure and popularity of fantasy. Fiction.

Shwartz, Susan, editor. **Habitats.** DAW Books, 1984.

In the stories in this science fiction collection, survivors of the future gather in caverns, on the desert, on the slopes, on astral planes, or in tree houses to battle the age-old enemy, the environment. In each story, the characters try to create new civilizations, but most importantly, they endeavor to make themselves a home and a life, no matter how short-lived. Fiction.

Silverberg, Robert, Charles G. Waugh, and Martin Harry Greenberg, editors. **The Science Fictional Dinosaur.** Flare Books, 1982.

Escape into the worlds of dinosaurs past and future. In this collection, the best science fiction writers place you in frightening and unusual situations. In one story, you will find yourself battling the most gruesome creature possible, while in the next setting you are saved by another grotesque but friendly creation. Fiction.

Singer, Isaac Bashevis. **The Collected Stories of Isaac Bashevis Singer.** Farrar, Straus and Giroux, 1982.

Singer believes that good short stories should not only have "the magical power of merging causality with purpose, doubt with faith, the passions of the flesh with the yearnings of the soul" but also be "unique and general, national and universal, realistic and mystical." This collection of forty-seven stories, chosen from more than a hundred by the Nobel Prize-winning author, illustrates those exact qualities and does so with humor and joy. Fiction.

Tuska, Jon, editor. **The American West in Fiction.** Mentor Books, 1982.

The romance, myth, and reality of the American West from the early frontier period to the present day are captured in this anthology of short stories which includes authors ranging from Mark Twain and Willa Cather to Luke Short and Louis L'Amour. Fiction.

Vinge, Joan D. **Eyes of Amber and Other Stories.** Signet Books, 1979.

Although these stories are set in typical science fiction realms, their main characters are developed with a sensitivity and a uniqueness that make them more appealing than the run-of-the-mill alien or intergalactic hero. The stories offer varied themes and wide appeal, but "Tin Soldier," a love story that spans all galaxies and time, and "To Bell the Cat," a situation in which the manipulated alien displays admirable qualities (unlike his manipulator), are musts. Fiction.

Wagner, Karl Edward. **In a Lonely Place.** Warner Books, 1983.

This collection of seven frightening stories is sure to bring out the cold sweats in its readers. "In the Pines" and ".220 Swift" by this master horror author will stir the imagination and keep readers away from dark and lonely places. Fiction.

Wagner, Karl Edward, editor. **The Year's Best Horror Stories.** Series X. DAW Books, 1982.

These nerve-racking horror stories by ghostly greats include those of Ramsey Campbell, Harlan Ellison, and M. John Harrison. Campbell's lead story, "Through the Walls," will bring you goose bumps as you begin your journey into eerie worlds. Fiction.

Wagner, Karl Edward, editor. **The Year's Best Horror Stories.** Series XII. DAW Books, 1984.

Here are nineteen stories of horror from the psychological, science fiction, and contemporary realms. Featured writers like Stephen King, Roger Johnson, and Tanith Lee will delight those who love to be frightened out of their skins or taken to worlds not yet discovered. Fiction.

Westall, Robert. **Break of Dark.** Greenwillow Books, 1982.

Five stories start out normally, but each ends up intertwined some-how with the supernatural, changing the lives of such ordinary people as a Scottish college student camping by himself, a World War II bombardier, two couples, a police sergeant, and a clergy-man. Fiction.

Wollheim, Donald A., editor (with Arthur W. Saha). **The 1983 Annual World's Best SF.** DAW Books, 1983.

Wollheim has assembled a collection of unusual short stories from 1983. The tales all have bizarre twists and unexpected endings, and the settings vary from Pike's Peak to a typical shopping plaza and even an abbey. A kidnapping, an undelivered letter, and an obses-sion with video games are just a few of the plots that give you a taste of 1983's best. Fiction.

Wollheim, Donald A., editor (with Arthur W. Saha). **The 1984 Annual World's Best SF.** DAW Books, 1984.

Although labeled science fiction, some of these stories could unfor-tunately take place right in our backyard. Some of the frighteningly plausible topics include genetic engineering geared to produce tele-paths, a national lottery where people literally gamble away their lives to control overpopulation, and people who are dying of star-vation and cold because they are old and ineligible for welfare. Fiction.

Wollheim, Donald A., editor (with Arthur W. Saha). **Wollheim's World's Best SF.** Series 7. DAW Books, 1977.

Some of the most bizarre science fiction stories ever written were produced in 1977. The stories assembled here challenge your imag-ination far beyond what you might expect. They are intriguing, beautifully conceived and written, and exciting. Fiction.

Social Situations

Anaya, Rudolfo A. **Heart of Aztlan.** Illus. Morton Levin. Editorial Justa, 1982.

This novel depicts the life of the Chávez family and their move from the security of their familiar land to the unknown city where their life-style changes drastically. The struggle for Roberto, Benjie, Jason, Ana, and Juanita to find their identities in a new society yet hold to their culture results in dramatic consequences. Fiction.

Anderson, Mary. **That's Not My Style.** Atheneum, 1983.

John has always considered himself the next great American novelist. In searching for material for his novel, he comes across a likable ex-convict, Cliff Karlbach. When John begins "studying" Cliff in order to make him the main character of a novel, John's devotion to his subject leads to a number of comic situations, including his family's belief that he has turned to a life of crime. Fiction.

Anderson, Mary. **You Can't Get There from Here.** Atheneum, 1982.

Regina Whitehall, a senior from upper-middle-class Larchmont, runs away from her family problems—a recent divorce, a mother who has pursued a mid-life career, and an older brother far away at college. She joins the Studio, a live-in theater workshop, where the Stanislavski method is carried one step too far by the resident playwright and teacher, Adam Bentley. The glitter and glamour of New York theater life seem to be a haven from personal problems and confronting one's identity. But Regina soon finds out that she can't bury herself behind a stage persona and that her drama teacher is less than honest. Fiction.

Arrick, Fran, **God's Radar.** Bradbury Press, 1983.

Roxie Cable has difficult choices to make when she moves to a small Southern town where religious beliefs and conservative attitudes dominate almost everyone's actions. Although she attended church back in Syracuse, she is not ready for the religious rebirth of her parents, the strict behavior rules of her Christian high school, or the charismatic hold that Dr. Caramana seems to have on everyone in his congregation and in his television audience—everyone, that is, except for the free-spirited Jarrell Meek. Fiction.

Asher, Sandy. **Summer Begins.** Bantam Books, 1982.

Summer Smith has to contribute an article to the eighth-grade class newspaper. She writes an editorial that she doesn't think will be very interesting. But her choice of what she thinks is a "safe" topic turns out to be anything but that. When her article is published there is such a furor that her teacher resigns in protest and Summer finds herself in the midst of the greatest controversy of her life. Fiction.

Beckman, Delores. **Who Loves Sam Grant?** Laurel-Leaf Library, 1984.

Although Sam Grant, a high school sophomore, has been dumped by Bogie Benson, she still loves Bogie. So when he asks her to hide something he has stolen, Sam reluctantly agrees. As events unfold, she begins to question Bogie's character and reexamine her values. Fiction.

Bradford, Richard. **Red Sky at Morning.** Washington Square Press, 1969.

Moved to a small town in rural New Mexico from Mobile, Alabama, while his father is off fighting in World War II, Joshua Arnold makes friends with a doctor's son, a minister's daughter, and the daughter of the family's Mexican cook. In learning about other life-styles and cultures while coping with his alcoholic mother, Josh—with great humor and insight—learns to understand himself and to cope with life's tragedies. Fiction.

Brancato, Robin F. **Facing Up.** Alfred A. Knopf, 1984.

Charming and popular Jep and his conservative best friend Dave do everything together. But Jep's gorgeous girlfriend soon has eyes for Dave. Dave measures his friendship with Jep and makes a decision—but he is too late. Fiction.

Callan, Jamie. **Over the Hill at Fourteen.** Signet Vista Books, 1982.

Becoming a famous model like Brooke Shields and Margot Hemingway is the dream of thousands of high school girls. Encouraged by a pushy mother and a flattering mirror, Sylvia Eisenstein fights to make that dream come true. By fourteen, Sylvia finds herself a successful model, a sex goddess, and, unfortunately, a spoiled and nasty brat. When gorgeous twelve-year-old Tammy topples Sylvia from her too easily gained success, Sylvia dreams up a fabulous tale to regain favor. Fiction.

Clements, Bruce. **Coming About.** Farrar, Straus and Giroux, 1984.

New to Oxbridge, New Hampshire, and to Burgess High School, fifteen-year-old Bob Royle decides that it is best for him to just blend in until he has the place figured out. But on Bob's first day of school, he meets Carl Reimer, who exerts a strange influence over Bob and takes over his life. Carl gets Bob to run for school office, go after the most beautiful girl in his class, rebuild a broken-down iceboat, and even break into the principal's office. But does Bob really want Carl to absorb all his time? Fiction.

Colman, Hila. **Not for Love.** William Morrow, 1983.

Totally engrossed in lazy summers, shopping sprees, and gossip, sixteen-year-old Jill Wells lives the life of an ordinary middle-class teenager. Then she meets antinuke activist Toby, who opens Jill's eyes to the world of political involvement. She works hard and idealistically for the cause but ultimately realizes that resolution of problems, no matter how important or immediate, is impossible without compromise. Fiction.

Conford, Ellen. **To All My Fans, with Love, from Sylvie.** Archway Paperbacks, 1983.

Fifteen-year-old Sylvie runs away from her third foster home and sets out for Hollywood. She hopes to find fame and fortune, but the way isn't paved with gold and adventure. Rather, she continues to face a cruel, difficult, and abusive world. Although the story takes place in the 1950s, it contains a very current message on sexual abuse. Fiction.

Corcoran, Barbara. **Strike!** Atheneum, 1983.

Barry and his father, a member of the local school board, seem to disagree on almost everything, but when the teachers decide to go on strike and Barry supports them, the gap becomes even wider. The central issue in the strike is control of the books that are part of the curriculum. In a day of direct confrontation between the two opposing views in the town, Barry must put his values on the line. Fiction.

Crutcher, Chris. **Running Loose.** Greenwillow Books, 1983.

For senior Louie Banks, living by what is right is much more important than being popular. When his football coach instructs the team to "play dirty" against an outstanding player on a rival team, Louie walks off the field. That turns out to be the most important decision of his life, because he then has to face the ridicule of his former teammates, the disappointment of his parents, the insinuations from his classmates, and his own self-image. Fiction.

Danziger, Paula. **There's a Bat in Bunk Five.** Laurel-Leaf Library, 1983.

An invitation from a former teacher to serve as a counselor at a creative-arts camp provides Marcy with a chance to get away from her parents for the summer. This sequel to *The Cat Ate My Gymsuit* provides a humorous yet authentic view of Marcy's growing up during one eventful summer. Fiction.

Davis, Terry. **Vision Quest.** Bantam Books, 1985.

Anyone who has ever puffed and sweated and strained to get into shape will understand part of what drives eighteen-year-old Louden Swain in his quest to reach 147 pounds so he can be a champion high school wrestler. But there is more to Louden's life than workouts: there are the antics of his half-Indian friend and teammate Kuch, the excitement of his sexually active live-in girlfriend Carla, and the pleasures of taking quiet hikes in the wilderness or pondering the issues in great books. As Louden grows stronger, wiser, more sensitive, and more mature, he begins to feel invincible. Fiction.

Elfman, Blossom. **The Return of the Whistler.** Fawcett Juniper Books, 1982.

Arnie is an underachiever in an overachieving family. His only two talents—whistling and playing the harmonica—don't count for much. When he meets Francie, he finds in her a kindred soul, but her delicate mental state only adds to his problems. Through a series of violent incidents, Arnie finds a way to deal with the pressures he faces from all quarters—his family, his teachers, and his classmates. Fiction.

Grace, Fran. **A Very Private Performance.** Bradbury Press, 1983.

Max Murphy is a mime and a marathon runner and is well known at Mira Vista High School as both. Mira Vista is a school where the performing arts are respected, but there has never been a student as famous as the newly arrived Burke Lindstrom, who has given violin solos with a symphony orchestra. In this often humorous novel, both Max and Burke learn about love and friendship. Fiction.

Grant, Cynthia D. **Hard Love.** Atheneum, 1983.

Although Stephen is only seventeen years old, he looks older. There are two important people in Stephen's life during his senior year: one is his friend Paulie, who is going crazy; the other is Molly, a twenty-three-year-old who thinks she is too old for Stephen. As a result of his relationships with these two people, Stephen's life changes greatly. Fiction.

Greenberg, Jan. **The Pig-Out Blues.** Farrar, Straus and Giroux, 1982.

Jody is a fifteen-year-old girl who is overweight, a fact her mother rarely lets her forget. The possibility of a part in a school play prompts Jody to go on a crash diet. However, when things go wrong, Jody sees food as the solution to her problems and begins eating more than ever. It takes the combined efforts of a number of people to help Jody realize her problem and start to develop some real solutions. Fiction.

Greene, Bette. **Them That Glitter and Them That Don't.** Alfred A. Knopf, 1983.

Carol Ann Delaney cherishes a dream of becoming a composer and country-western singer when she finishes high school. Her considerable talent goes unrecognized, however, until she sings before the school assembly and realizes her power to move others and win their approval. Jean McCaffrey, Carol Ann's music teacher, encourages her to look beyond the small world of Bainesville, Arkansas, and her gypsy parents to the larger world of Nashville, where she can make her dream come true. Fiction.

Greenwald, Sheila. **It All Began with Jane Eyre.** Laurel-Leaf Library, 1981.

When Franny reads a book, she lives it. She begins keeping a journal, but when nothing worth writing about happens in her own life, she begins to use her imagination. Her observations serve as a light-hearted "spoof" on novels about teenage problems. Fiction.

Guernsey, JoAnn Bren. **Five Summers.** Clarion Books, 1983.

During five crucial summers on her family's Minnesota farm, Mandy grows from an impatient teenager into a mature young woman able to deal with her grandmother's death, an orphaned cousin, her first love, and her mother's cancer. Fiction.

Hansen, Joyce. **Home Boy.** Clarion Books, 1982.

Marcus has come from a Caribbean island to the South Bronx. At first, his need to prove himself gets him into trouble again and again and earns him the nickname "Jamaica." With the help of Cassandra, a girl he meets in school, Marcus begins to straighten out his life—only to have things turn bad again when he plunges a knife into a boy who has been taunting him. Fiction.

Harris, Marilyn. **Hatter Fox.** Ballantine Books, 1983.

Hatter Fox, a seventeen-year-old Navajo girl, hates and is hated by the white community of Sante Fe, New Mexico. Her young life is marred by involvement with drugs, prostitution, and crime, and Dr. Teague Summer is the only person who wants to help her. He tries to keep Hatter out of the mental institution, but he seems doomed to fail because, as he says, "there is something wrong in the world." Fiction.

Jacobs, Anita. **Where Has Deedie Wooster Been All These Years?** Laurel-Leaf Library, 1983.

Life at fourteen seems to thrust too many problems at Deedie Wooster. First, her older brother dies, making her an only child. At school she's a dawdler and an underachiever. At parties she gets stuck having to wear clothes her mother picks out, and she is usually trapped dancing with Joey Falcaro, who is a head shorter than she and who calls her "Piano Legs." The only solution, Deedie decides, is to write about her troubles—but then she finds that writing comes with its own peculiar set of problems. Fiction.

Kellogg, Marjorie. **Tell Me That You Love Me, Junie Moon.** 2d ed. Farrar, Straus and Giroux, 1984.

Warren is a paraplegic confined to a wheelchair; Arthur has an undiagnosable neurological disease that gets progressively worse; and Junie Moon has been horribly disfigured by an irate boyfriend who poured battery acid on her face. These three misfits decide to live together when they are released from the hospital because they have no place else to go. In this painful yet beautiful story, Kellogg shows us the indomitable spirit of three severely maimed people who learn to love. Fiction.

Kerr, M. E. **Little Little.** Bantam Books, 1983.

Little Little LaBelle is seventeen and beautiful but only three feet three inches tall. Sidney Cinnamon is three feet four-and-a-half inches tall and plays the role of the roach in a TV pest control commercial. These unusual diminutives find each other in a chain of wacky events concerning a group of teenage dwarfs in contemporary society. Fiction.

Kerr, M. E. **What I Really Think of You.** Signet Vista Books, 1983.

Opal Ringer is a PK—preacher's kid. She dreads being singled out as strange by her classmates who come to watch her father's service. They don't understand; they snicker and call her a Holy Roller. It might take a miracle, but Opal will have her day. Fiction.

Levoy, Myron. **A Shadow Like a Leopard.** Signet Vista Books, 1982.

Joining a gang is the only way Ramon Santiago can save his fourteen-year-old skin. To do so, he must show how macho he is by robbing an old man. But when he encounters seventy-six-year-old Arnold Glasser, Ramon has other thoughts. Mr. Glasser's paintings open up a whole new set of possibilities for Ramon, and the bargain they strike changes both their worlds. Fiction.

Lipsyte, Robert. **Summer Rules.** Bantam Books, 1983.

Bobby Marks, the once-fat hero of *One Fat Summer* has been anticipating the excitement of his sixteenth summer. But Bobby is pressured by his father to be a counselor at Happy Valley Day Camp. Who wants to watch out for dumb kids at a crummy camp? Then along comes ten-year-old Harley, who is nothing but trouble; gorgeous, green-eyed Sheila, who works in the kitchen and drives Bobby wild; and an arsonist—creating for Bobby more excitement than he can handle. Fiction.

Major, Kevin. **Thirty-Six Exposures.** Delacorte Press, 1984.

The last few weeks of high school are momentous ones for Lorne. In his small seaside town in Canada, he develops his photographic skills, lets loose with his uninhibited friend Trevor, leads a student strike against an unfair teacher, and explores his growing sexuality with a new girlfriend. In brief chapters, like snapshots, the reader watches as Lorne learns, in sometimes harsh terms, that "you can't just play it safe all the time." Fiction.

McClanahan, Ed. **The Natural Man.** Farrar, Straus and Giroux, 1983.

Harry Eastep, a senior at Burdock County High School, has recently developed strong feelings toward "Oodles" Ockerman. Then Monk McHorning—who refers to himself as "the natural man"—moves to this Kentucky high school to improve their basketball team. Associating with Monk has a profound influence on Harry's life. Fiction.

McDonnell, Margot B. **My Own Worst Enemy.** Pacer Books, 1984.

Todd Richardson's life begins to fall apart at the start of his sophomore year. A new boy, Robbie, has moved into town, and Todd has lost his girlfriend to him as well as his position on the baseball team. Certainly Todd does not want to be friends with this boy, but Robbie has other ideas. Fiction.

McNamara, John. **Revenge of the Nerd.** Delacorte Press, 1984.

Bertram is the smartest kid in his ninth-grade class, but he's a nerd and everyone knows it. He has a crush on the very attractive Louise Baker, but everything he does seems to go wrong. One of the reasons for this is Bertram's enemy, Mike. In a series of very humorous incidents, Bertram finally gets his revenge when his science project enables him to invade other people's homes via their television screens. Based on the movie of the same name. Fiction.

Meyer, Carolyn. **The Summer I Learned about Life.** Margaret K. McElderry Books, 1983.

Fifteen-year-old Teddie Schneider does not want to spend the summer of 1928 learning how to become a good wife and mother, which is what her family expects. She wants to learn about *life*. Teddie wants to be an aviator, like Amelia Earhart, and baking pies and ironing all summer are not going to bring her closer to her dream. What Teddie does not realize is that her involvement in two romances during the summer will teach her more about life, and herself, than she expected to learn. Fiction.

Miller, Frances A. **Aren't You the One Who . . .?** Atheneum, 1983.

Although sixteen-year-old Matt McKendrick was not responsible for his sister's murder, he can't seem to convince anyone of that.

He is afraid to meet new people because eventually they find out about his sister's death and then their feelings toward him change. Matt takes a chance at friendship with the Schuylers, a motherless family from a few blocks away, always dreading the day they'll find out about him. It turns out that Matt has a few things to find out about the Schuylers. Sequel to *The Truth Trap*. Fiction.

Morrison, Toni. **Sula.** Plume Books, 1982.

This poetic novel traces the lives of two small-town black girls— Sula Peace and Nel Wright, as they confront their feelings, view the sometimes strange actions of their families, seek their places in the world, and examine their relationship with each other as they become adults and grow old. One stays in the place of her birth and raises a family; the other, more rebellious, leaves for college and to see the world before returning home. From the harshness of their realistically portrayed lives come two mature women with very different strengths. Fiction.

Murphy, Barbara Beasley, and Judie Wolkoff. **Ace Hits the Big Time.** Laurel-Leaf Library, 1982.

Horace "Ace" Hobart is nervous when he enrolls in a New York City high school. He is afraid of the Purple Falcons, the toughest gang around. Needless to say, he is surprised when, rather than beat him up, they ask him to join them. Joining plunges Ace into a whole new set of problems, not the least of which is with a rival gang. His humorous, first-person narration reflects the fears and insecurities of a peace-loving teenager who is thrust into a potentially violent situation. Fiction.

Oppenheimer, Joan. **Working on It.** Laurel-Leaf Library, 1983.

Shyness is common among high school students, but Tracy is unusually timid. Terrified of entering high school, she gathers the nerve to enroll in a drama course to appease her mother. But her worst fears prove true when Wylie Babcock and other members of the class begin to tease her mercilessly. Will she gather the courage to fight back? Fiction.

Peck, Richard. **Representing Super Doll.** Laurel-Leaf Library, 1982.

Darlene Hoffmeister is so beautiful that things always seem to go right for her. It is therefore not surprising that she becomes a shallow person, though she is still envied by her friend Verna, who is not beautiful. Darlene is chosen as Teen Super Doll and sent from her small Midwestern town to New York City, accompanied by Verna. There both girls learn important lessons about themselves. Fiction.

Perlberg, Deborah. **Heartaches.** Fawcett Juniper Books, 1983.

After fourteen-year-old Sandy Morse has a fight with her parents, she and her best friend Deanie run off to New York City. There they hope to meet a music promoter who can get their rock and roll group, the Heartaches, on national television. Sandy and Deanie are so determined to make it as musicians that they'll try almost anything for a chance at success. Then one day their big break finally comes—but from a very unexpected source. Fiction.

Petersen, P. J. **The Boll Weevil Express.** Delacorte Press, 1983.

Fifteen-year-old Lars is a misfit who dreams of escaping his environment. His classmates, who make fun of his quiet, solitary nature and his never-ending farm chores, only fortify his dreams. When Lars meets up with Doug, who is escaping from a local orphanage, his dreams come true. Together, Doug, Lars, and Doug's tagalong sister Cindy make their way to San Francisco, where they soon find out that street life is rough and frightening and that often the price of teenage freedom is fear and hardship. Fiction.

Petersen, P. J. **Here's to the Sophomores.** Delacorte Press, 1984.

Michael is looking forward to a good sophomore year at Hendley High. His friend Warren has decided to return to Hendley rather than go away to prep school, and Michael has a new interest in his old friend Margaret. By the end of the first week of school, Michael and Margaret find themselves in a situation they're not sure they'll be able to handle. Fiction.

Petersen, P. J. **Would You Settle for Improbable?** Laurel-Leaf Library, 1983.

After being released from juvenile hall, Arnold Norberry enrolls at Marshall Martin Junior High. Gradually, three classmates become Arnold's friends, and it begins to look as if they will all graduate together. Just when things seem to be going well, Arnold is accused of a crime that could send him back to juvenile hall. Is he guilty? Will he betray his friends? Excerpts from the characters' notebooks are woven into the narrative. Fiction.

Pevsner, Stella. **Lindsay, Lindsay, Fly Away Home.** Clarion Books, 1983.

Lindsay has spent most of her seventeen years abroad in exotic places. She suspects her father is sending her back to her aunt in the States to cool her romance with a handsome Indian youth, Rajee. Aunt Meg is nice enough, but Lindsay still has lots of questions about the reasons why she is forced to leave India. Fiction.

Pfeffer, Susan Beth. **A Matter of Principle.** Laurel-Leaf Library, 1983.

Becca Holtz is a good student, active on her high school newspaper. But she and her close friends quit the *Sentinel* when they are censored one too many times by their advisor and by the principal. The group decides to go underground and really speak out on the issues. No one is prepared for the battle which follows as the students argue their constitutional freedoms. Fiction.

Powell, Padgett. **Edisto.** Farrar, Straus and Giroux, 1984.

Edisto is a complex novel told from the point of view of an unusually sophisticated twelve-year-old. Simons Manigault has been trained to assume adult manners, speech, and company well before his time. Through Taurus, his mother's mysterious lover, he experiences his first date and witnesses his first boxing match. By the time his father returns home and Taurus is forced to leave, Simons has learned much about love, life, and destiny. Fiction.

Sachs, Marilyn. **Beach Towels.** Illus. Jim Spence. Skinny Books, 1982.

Although Lore seems happy and carefree and Phil is lonely and depressed, they have something in common: each has a secret that needs to be told. This story of a teenage friendship that forms during a summer at the beach will leave lasting memories. Fiction.

Santiago, Danny. **Famous All Over Town.** Plume Books, 1984.

For fourteen-year-old Rudy "Chato" Medina, school is a bore. Street life, on the other hand, is exciting, though often dangerous. Chato's father is a tyrant but a hard worker who provides material comforts for his impoverished family; his mother is tolerant but on the verge of rebelling against her husband's indiscretions. Life in the Los Angeles barrio could destroy this young Chicano or help him rise above his peers. Chato's defiant behavior is both humorous and sad, and the outcome of his actions is uncertain. Fiction.

Savitz, Harriet May. **If You Can't Be the Sun, Be a Star.** Signet Vista Books, 1982.

Sixteen-year-old Candy Miller decides to take on the world when she finally becomes disgusted with the rundown condition of her school and her neighborhood. In her zealous reform efforts, she dresses in wild costumes to attract the school newspaper editor, becomes estranged from her best friend Linda, feuds with her mother, finds support and romance with Flip, and eventually gets involved in a real effort to establish a neighborhood crime watch. Fiction.

Scoppettone, Sandra. **Long Time between Kisses.** Bantam Books, 1984.

A sophisticated, wisecracking sixteen-year-old, Billie James feels that she needs to make a statement about herself. So she cuts off her long brown hair and dyes the stubble purple. When she meets Robert Mitchell, a victim of multiple sclerosis, their relationship helps Billie to establish an identity that is not dependent on purple hair. The novel vividly describes the inhabitants and flavor of Billie's neighborhood, the Soho section of lower Manhattan. Fiction.

Seidler, Tor. **Terpin.** Farrar, Straus and Giroux, 1982.

Terpin Taft's careless lie contributes to a man's suicide. As a result, Terpin resolves never again to speak or act except truthfully. That policy repeatedly causes trouble for him, sometimes with comic results. The trouble finally becomes so severe that he leaves his hometown. Thirty years later he returns to the town, this time as a hero. But Terpin is curious to find out if things have really changed. Fiction.

Sharmat, Marjorie. **He Noticed I'm Alive . . . and Other Hopeful Signs.** Delacorte Press, 1984.

In the two years that have passed since her mother left to find herself, fifteen-year-old Jody Kline has not been happy. Her father is dating Gossamer Green, a woman Jody tolerates but does not want for a stepmother. When Jody meets Mrs. Green's son Matt, they immediately are attracted to each other, but they both fear that their dating may further solidify their parents' relationship. The young couple's attempts to solve this problem result in both humorous and more serious moments. Fiction.

Sharmat, Marjorie. **How to Meet a Gorgeous Guy.** Delacorte Press, 1983.

It is hard for Shari to believe that she will be the subject of her cousin Lisa's article in a popular teen magazine. Shari will be the focus of an experiment and an article entitled "How to Meet a Gorgeous Guy." Her problem is holding on to the gorgeous guy once she meets him. Fiction.

Slepian, Jan. **The Night of the Bozos.** E. P. Dutton, 1983.

Was that girl crazy? Why would anyone lie in the middle of the road, playing dead? Everything would have been so different for thirteen-year-old George and his uncle, Hibbie, if Lolly hadn't stopped their car in this odd fashion. But now that they have met this exotic tattooed girl from the visiting carnival and have been introduced to the mysterious world of the Bozos, their lives will never be the same again. Fiction.

Snyder, Anne, and Louis Pelletier. **Two Point Zero.** Signet Vista Books, 1982.

Cheating is not wrong unless you get caught—that's the basic philosophy of Eddie Kopke, the star college football kicker who is failing freshman composition and looking for well-written papers to keep him eligible. Kate Fleming agrees to write those papers for desperately needed money. This arrangement is threatened when Kate becomes involved with Doug, an aspiring journalist who coincidentally is writing an exposé on college cheating. When Kate realizes that her much-dreamed-of future at law school could be totally destroyed by her foolish actions, she scrambles to cover her tracks. Fiction.

Stanek, Lou Willett. **Megan's Beat.** Dial Books for Young Readers, 1983.

Megan Morgan is a farm girl. When she was young that didn't bother her, but when she gets to high school she wants to be part of the exciting life that the students from town seem to have. A series of events that culminate with being asked out by a handsome basketball star convinces Megan that she has made it. But when her relationships with the sophisticated kids from town threaten her old friendships, she begins to wonder whether it has all been worth it. Fiction.

Strasser, Todd. **Workin' for Peanuts.** Delacorte Press, 1983.

Life becomes complicated for Jeff, a vendor at a baseball stadium, when he falls in love with an attractive customer who turns out to be the daughter of the family that operates the concessions. In coming to terms with the differences in their social status, Jeff has to face a lot of things about himself and his goals in life. Fiction.

Stretton, Barbara. **The Truth of the Matter.** Alfred A. Knopf, 1983.

Jenny's and Andrea's lives change the day that Mr. Georgescu, their new history teacher, comes into their lives. Mr. G's charismatic qualities turn "gray Mondays" into something to look forward to. However, Peter, Andrea's jealous boyfriend, childishly decides that everyone is paying too much attention to the new teacher. Peter hears a tidbit of gossip about Mr. Georgescu and embarks on a quest of blackmail and scandal to rid the school of this unique and mysterious teacher who is getting a lot of attention. Fiction.

Tchudi, Stephen. **The Burg-O-Rama Man.** Laurel-Leaf Library, 1983.

At first, it seems that the arrival of the Burgo-O-Rama man and his promise to use students from Crawford High School in a series of television commercials can mean only good things for the school. But much to the surprise of Karen Wexler, the editor of the school paper, the chance at fame and fortune is too much for many of the students to handle. Friends begin to turn against one another in a mad scramble for stardom. Karen learns an important lesson that has little to do with hamburgers. Fiction.

Tyler, Anne. **A Slipping-Down Life.** Berkley Books, 1983.

Evie Decker has never been interested in rock music until she hears an interview with Drumstrings Casey on the radio and wants to see him perform at a local night spot. The unsuccessful Drum doesn't notice the unattractive high school junior until she carves his name into her forehead, thus linking them in a very odd way. The unusual relationship between these two misfits moves slowly but inexorably toward self-realization. Originally published in 1970. Fiction.

Wartski, Maureen Crane. **A Long Way from Home.** Signet Vista Books, 1982.

In Vietnam, fifteen-year-old Kien had avoided school and learning, but now in America he has to deal with all sorts of uncomfortable things, including the school bully. Although his adopted sister and brother feel comfortable in their new home, Kien decides that his only hope is to run away to Travor, where there are other refugees. But once there, he finds himself caught in a battle between the immigrants and the local people who resent their presence. Why did he leave one place of hate and violence for another? Fiction.

Zindel, Paul. **The Girl Who Wanted a Boy.** Bantam Books, 1982.

Fifteen-year-old Sibella Cametta is so interested in electronics and auto mechanics that she hasn't had time for boys. Deciding that it is time she had a boyfriend, she chooses a handsome boy whom she has seen in a newspaper photo. As she sets out to get him, she falls in love with him—with very interesting results. Fiction.

Zindel, Paul. **The Pigman's Legacy.** Bantam Books, 1984.

Several months after the death of their friend the Pigman, John and Lorraine return to his house and discover an unusual old man living there. In alternating chapters, John and Lorraine describe how they befriend Colonel Glenville, learn of his exciting past, fix him up with the female custodian from their school, and get involved in a zany gambling spree in Atlantic City. Sequel to *The Pigman*. Fiction.

Sociology

Abbott, Shirley. **Womenfolks: Growing Up Down South.** Ticknor and Fields, 1983.

Abbott examines her own life as a woman growing up in Arkansas in the 1940s, as well as the lives of her mother, aunts, grandmothers, and other female relatives. Interwoven with her personal recollections are historical, religious, and mythological fragments which fill out this quest for the ingredients that go into the makeup of Southern females. Nonfiction.

Coolidge, Grace. **Teepee Neighbors.** University of Oklahoma Press, 1984.

Originally published in 1917, these stories about the Arapaho and Shoshone Indians of Wyoming, as seen through the eyes of a white Episcopalian missionary, are vividly told. The reservation is depicted as an inhospitable home for a people accustomed to a different way of life. The poverty, lack of food and jobs, inadequate medical care, and government-controlled schooling are all presented in an unflattering light, giving us a seldom-seen glimpse into life on the reservation. Nonfiction.

Dolan, Edward F., Jr., and Shan Finney. **Youth Gangs.** Julian Messner, 1984.

Who are the young men who join gangs and why do they join? This account helps to uncover some of the real reasons. Those who think they know all about gangs will learn something new in this factual account. Nonfiction.

Francis, Dorothy B. **Vandalism: The Crime of Immaturity.** Lodestar Books, 1983.

This book is an interesting and intelligent examination of vandalism, its causes, and its cost—both to victim and criminal. Special emphasis is given to what individuals and the community can do to protect themselves from becoming victims. Nonfiction.

Goode, Stephen. **Violence in America.** Julian Messner, 1984.

A look at the broad expanse of American violence from earliest times to the present, this book includes such chapters as "The American Obsession with Violence"; "White Men and Indians"; "Violence against Blacks"; "Labor Violence"; "Black Power and Radical New Left Violence"; "Homicide, Rape and Robbery"; and "Family Violence." The author has a particular viewpoint about the origins and continued trend of violence in America that provides fertile ground for discussion and interpretation. Nonfiction.

Hirshon, Sheryl L. (with Judy Butler). **And Also Teach Them to Read (Y tambien enséñeles a leer).** Photographs by Larry Boyd. Laurence Hill, 1983.

Sheryl Hirshon fought in Nicaragua's battle against illiteracy. In her gripping and sensitive story, she explains her crusade to teach rural teenagers how to read and how the social order was changed because of newly acquired literacy. Armed with pencils, notebooks, and rifles, soldiers of this crusade are still fighting. Nonfiction.

Morrison, Joan, and Charlotte Fox Zabusky. **American Mosaic: The Immigrant Experience in the Words of Those Who Lived It.** Meridian Books, 1982.

Morrison and Zabusky provide an oral history of the memories of 140 immigrants who now live in America. They reflect on the meaning of their arrival in the United States based on three interview questions: Why did they come to the U.S.? How did they come? What did they find once they arrived? Among the immigrants interviewed are recent arrivals from Cuba, Taiwan, Vietnam, and the USSR. Nonfiction.

Naisbitt, John. **Megatrends: Ten New Directions Transforming Our Lives.** Warner Books, 1984.

Here is an updated look at the way in which our society has restructured itself from an industrial-based to an information-centered culture. Divided into ten chapters, this easy-to-read compilation focuses on the megatrends that are shaping our lives and our society today. Nonfiction.

Rau, Margaret. **Holding Up the Sky: Young People in China.** Photographs by Diane Lewis. Lodestar Books, 1983.

In any country, the economic and social future depends on its youth. This interesting and well-researched series of case studies brings you into the everyday lives of Chinese young people. You'll experience almost firsthand the work habits, traditions, laws, family life-styles, history, and religions of the people of this fascinating, mysterious, and impressive country. Nonfiction.

Sculatti, Gene, editor. **The Catalog of Cool.** Warner Books, 1982.

A compendium of articles, essays, lists, and pictures chronicling such "cool" aspects of our culture as jazz, sci-fi movies, old TV shows, "hip" musicians (Bob Dylan and Motown singers and songwriters, to name a few), Lord Buckley (mentor to most comedians from 1906–1960), clothing fads (pegged pants, sunglasses, mini and maxi dresses), hairstyles, automobiles, and food. Photographs spice up this collection of "cool." Nonfiction.

Shipler, David K. **Russia: Broken Idols, Solemn Dreams.** Penguin Books, 1984.

The daily life of the inhabitants of the Soviet Union is examined by a *New York Times* correspondent who spent 1975–79 in Moscow with his wife and children. Shipler reports on the people and their education, society, and adaptation to the Marxist-Leninist government as seen through the eyes of an American living on the outskirts of a private and hard-to-crack community. His observations on his travels throughout the country provide a glimpse into the complexities and the difficulty of life in the USSR. Nonfiction.

Terkel, Studs. **Hard Times: An Oral History of the Great Depression.** Washington Square Press, 1978.

To know what people experienced and how they felt about the Great Depression, Terkel has tape-recorded their memories. These oral histories, divided into five chapters, recreate a historical era that is slowly being forgotten. Nonfiction.

Space and Space Exploration

Branley, Franklyn M. **Halley: Comet 1986.** Illus. Sally J. Bensusen. Lodestar Books, 1983.

Branley explores the intriguing history as well as the present composition and movement of the famous Halley's comet. The author discusses the important return of the comet in 1986 and the missions of space probes which will be sent to meet it. Nonfiction.

Branley, Franklyn M. **Space Colony: Frontier of the Twenty-First Century.** Illus. Leonard D. Dank. Elsevier/Nelson Books, 1982.

Speculating about how future colonies might be built in space, Branley examines problems such as obtaining air, water, food, and heat, as well as the control of day/night cycles and gravity. Nonfiction.

Chapman, Clark R. **Planets of Rock and Ice: From Mercury to the Moons of Saturn.** Rev. ed. Charles Scribner's Sons, 1982.

This is a technical and speculative look at the discoveries resulting from the *Voyager* missions to the outer solar system. Seen through the eyes of scientists, the planets play a central role in our understanding of our own world and the circumstances which have made intelligent life possible. Originally published as *The Inner Planets.* Nonfiction.

Cooper, Henry S. F., Jr. **Imaging Saturn.** Holt, Rinehart and Winston, 1982.

The *Voyager I* and *II* expeditions provided information about the planet Saturn. Color photographs of Saturn and its moons add beauty to the data collected on this strangely ringed planet. Nonfiction.

Ferris, Timothy. **Space Shots: The Beauty of Nature beyond Earth.** Pantheon Books, 1984.

An awesome selection of space photographs from the Johnson Space Center and the Jet Propulsion Laboratory is presented here in an artistic format accompanied by informative narratives or captions. Each photograph captures the brilliant computer-enhanced colors of nature outside our own planet. Nonfiction.

Gallant, Roy A. **The Planets: Exploring the Solar System.** Four Winds Press, 1982.

Information in this guidebook to the planets in our solar system was gathered from recent U.S. and Soviet space probes and from radio and optical telescopes. Photographs of the planets with their moons, comets, asteriods, and meteoroids highlight these explo-rations. Nonfiction.

Herbst, Judith. **Sky Above, Worlds Beyond.** Atheneum, 1983.

An introduction to astronomy, this book includes a tour of the moon, the solar system, stellar motion, and explanations of comets, meteors, and auroras. Easy-to-understand accounts of ancient astronomical ideas as well as today's theories of the universe are nicely illustrated. Nonfiction.

Jastrow, Robert. **Red Giants and White Dwarfs.** Warner Books, 1984.

Delve into the extraordinary life story of the stars from the moment of their creation to the appearance of humans on the planet Earth. Expanding upon the CBS television series, this book explains clearly, without jargon, new ideas regarding the origin of humans. Photographs from the *Viking* and *Voyager* spacecraft reveal fasci-nating sights never before witnessed by humans. Nonfiction.

Jastrow, Robert. **Until the Sun Dies.** Warner Books, 1984.

Human nature dictates that as we evolve intellectually, we will choose to leap beyond the boundaries of the solar system. Our search will take us to other galaxies, possibly inhabited by new and different life forms, some less and others more advanced than we are. Jastrow calls this a new Darwinism—a quest that will continue "until the sun dies." Nonfiction.

McAleer, Neil. **The Cosmic Mind-Boggling Book.** Warner Books, 1982.

Recent dramatic discoveries about the universe have raised cosmic consciousness to a new level. Explorations of the planets, stars, and galactic outskirts will dazzle the reader. Did you know, for example, that a square mile of sunlight in your hand would weigh three pounds? Did you know that if you dropped a kernel of popcorn on a neutron star, it would produce as much energy as an atomic bomb? These and other fascinating facts will enhance your understanding of our universe. Nonfiction.

Moché, Dinah L. **Astronomy Today.** Illus. Harry McNaught. Random House, 1982.

If the heavens fascinate you, you'll enjoy this illustrated introduction to the planets, stars, and space exploration, which includes information about space satellites, planetary probes, and space stations of the future. Basic astronomy is presented, complete with maps for stargazers. Nonfiction.

Oberg, James Edward. **Mission to Mars: Plans and Concepts for the First Manned Landing.** Meridian Books, 1983.

James Oberg, former mission flight controller at the Johnson Space Center, maintains that we now have the technology to land humans on Mars and can do so "by the end of this century with an equivalent expenditure of about half of what it took in the 1960s to send Apollo astronauts to the moon." In this illustrated text, he describes how it can be done, including propulsion, site selection, and future colonization. Nonfiction.

Oberg, James Edward. **New Earths: Restructuring Earth and Other Planets.** Meridian Books, 1983.

A former mission flight controller for NASA explores the scientific concepts of terraforming and environmental engineering of other planets in order to make them livable for human beings in the future. Oberg explains such possibilities as how a "greenhouse effect" might be used to release frozen waters on Mars, and how hydrogen might be transported from Saturn in order to create water on Venus. Nonfiction.

Olesky, Walter. **UFO: Teen Sightings.** Illus. Dave Sullivan. JEM Books, 1984.

Have you ever seen a UFO? Many teenagers claim to have witnessed unidentified flying objects and even strange creatures. The stories in this book were reported to UFO researcher Dr. J. Allen Hynek by teenagers in different parts of the world. Nonfiction.

Ritchie, David. **Spacewar.** Plume Books, 1983.

The possibility of war in space may no longer be just another science fiction story. Today's space technology and weapons systems have advanced to the point where computerized laser cannons and high orbital satellites may soon come close to resembling Darth Vader's Death Star. Nonfiction.

Sagan, Carl. **Cosmos.** Random House, 1983.

Cosmos, based on Sagan's PBS television series, is about science in its broadest sense. The author explores space missions, the human brain, ancient civilizations, the origin of life, and the evolution of galaxies, suns, and worlds. Nonfiction.

Weiss, Malcolm E. **Far Out Factories: Manufacturing in Space.** Lodestar Books, 1984.

Experiments in space manufacturing show that there may soon be working factories in outer space. Already, perfect silicon crystals have been grown, lifesaving enzymes have been made, and new alloy metals have been produced. Who will own and run these space factories of the future? This is just one of the questions raised by this concept that is made possible by the success of the space shuttle. Nonfiction.

Sports

Aaseng, Nate. **Baseball: You Are the Manager.** Laurel-Leaf Library, 1984.

There's a runner on third, two outs, and an excellent hitter at bat. What would you do if you were the manager? This book gives you ten situations which actually happened and allows you the opportunity to sharpen your skills as a manager. You can compare your moves with those the major league managers actually made. Nonfiction.

Aaseng, Nate. **Basketball: You Are the Coach.** Laurel-Leaf Library, 1983.

Your star center, Dave Cowens of the Boston Celtics, just got his fifth foul at the beginning of the fourth quarter in the NBA championship game. What would you do if you were the coach? This book allows you to match wits with the top professional coaches in this and nine other critical game situations to develop your understanding of basketball and increase your appreciation of the unsung heroes—the coaches. Nonfiction.

Aaseng, Nate. **Football: You Are the Coach.** Laurel-Leaf Library, 1983.

You are the coach pacing the sidelines with fifty-six seconds remaining in the 1972 playoff. Your 49ers are on defense against the Dallas Cowboys, who trail 29-23 but have the ball on your ten-yard line. What defense should you call? This book allows you to match wits with the top professional coaches in this situation and nine others. You will develop an understanding of some of the critical decisions made by coaches. Nonfiction.

Aaseng, Nate. **Hockey: You Are the Coach.** Laurel-Leaf Library, 1984.

The hockey game is tied, thirty seconds left in the game. What would you do as the coach? This book describes ten situations from the National Hockey League to help you sharpen your skills. You can compare your decisions with the ones the coaches actually made. Nonfiction.

Aaseng, Nathan. **Baseball's Hottest Hitters.** Lerner, 1983.

Despite the high quality of baseball pitchers, there have been batters who consistently hit above .300 year after year. This book describes eight of baseball's hottest hitters: George Brett, Rod Carew, Steve Garvey, Keith Hernandez, Fred Lynn, Al Oliver, Dave Parker, and Pete Rose. A volume in the Sports Heroes Library. Nonfiction.

Aaseng, Nathan. **Basketball's Sharpshooters.** Lerner, 1983.

Name eight of the greatest "shots" in professional basketball. When you have your list ready, read *Basketball's Sharpshooters* and compare your choices with those selected by Nathan Aaseng. A few hints may be helpful: one of the greatest sharpshooters was born in French Lick, Indiana, dropped out of Indiana University, collected garbage, and then returned to college at Indiana State where he became an all-American. This book provides a behind-the-scenes look at some of the greatest basketball talent ever produced in America. A volume in the Sports Heroes Library. Nonfiction.

Aaseng, Nathan. **Comeback Stars of Pro Sports.** Lerner, 1983.

This is the story of eight professional athletes who encountered setbacks but managed to make it to the top again. The comeback stars described are football's Jim Plunkett and Woody Peoples, baseball's Steve Stone and Matt Keough, basketball's James Silas, hockey's Reggie Leach, racing's Niki Lauda, and tennis champ Virginia Wade. A volume in the Sports Heroes Library. Nonfiction.

Aaseng, Nathan. **Football's Super Bowl Champions I–VIII.** Lerner, 1982.

The Orange Bowl in Miami was the scene of the greatest upset in Super Bowl history. The New York Jets, representing the new American Football League, were led by a quarterback who loudly announced that his Jets would win easily over the champion Baltimore Colts. What happened that January afternoon in 1969 made football history and created a new legend in its hero, Joe Namath. Readers can share the drama, excitement, joys, and disappointments in this and seven other action-packed Super Bowls described here. A volume in the Sports Heroes Library. Nonfiction.

Aaseng, Nathan. **Football's Super Bowl Champions IX–XVI.** Lerner, 1982.

Super Bowl Sunday is a media event which draws the attention of sports fans from around the world. In this second book on Super Bowl champions, fans can read about the great performances of the Pittsburgh Steelers, Oakland Raiders, Dallas Cowboys, and San Francisco 49ers in their Super Bowl victories from 1975 through 1982. A volume in the Sports Heroes Library. Nonfiction.

Aaseng, Nathan. **Memorable World Series Moments.** Lerner, 1982.

Boston's Fenway Park was the scene of game six of the World Series between the Boston Red Sox and the Cincinnati Reds in 1975. Tony Perez, Luis Tiant, Johnny Bench, Carl Yastremzki, and Carlton Fisk are a few of the names that still echo when fans remember this exciting game, one of eight World Series games described and pictured in this book which covers the period from 1912 to 1975. A volume in the Sports Heroes Library. Nonfiction.

Alfano, Pete. **Super Bowl Superstars: The Most Valuable Players in the NFL's Championship Game.** Zander Hollander Sports Books, 1982.

Fifteen stars voted Most Valuable Players of their Super Bowls are described here. You will read about the feats of Joe Montana, Jim Plunkett, Joe Namath, and many others. It will be Super Bowl Sunday every time you open this book. Nonfiction.

Anderson, Dave, editor. **The Red Smith Reader.** Random House, 1982.

In the first autobiographical piece included here, Smith admits that he had a lot of writing heroes and learned from all of them, mostly through a process of shameless imitation. Now Smith himself, who died in 1982, has become a model for anyone who cares about capturing the frantic and poignant moments of sports through carefully honed reporting. The reader of this collection will be able to go from season to season and from the Olympics to solitary fishing because Red Smith felt that sports were an important part of being human and that they deserved to be described in carefully crafted prose. Nonfiction.

Angell, Roger. **Five Seasons: A Baseball Companion.** Warner Books, 1983.

What happened to baseball between 1972 and 1979? Why does baseball represent the consciousness of America? The author is willing and able to tell us in this book which presents a well-written, new view of the great American game. Nonfiction.

Axthelm, Pete. **The City Game: Basketball from the Garden to the Playgrounds.** Penguin Books, 1982.

The City Game describes the stars, bit players, and fallen idols of basketball. What happens to the players who never make it in the big time? is one of the questions that this book answers. A volume in the Penguin Sports Library. Nonfiction.

Boswell, Thomas. **How Life Imitates the World Series.** Penguin Books, 1983.

Americans frequently have a lifelong passion for the game of baseball. Boswell describes the development of the sport by analyzing the spirit and tempo of each month in the season from March's spring training to October's World Series tension. The author feels that the most important reason for our fascination with baseball is that we can get so close to the game's skin that we can hear it breathing. A volume in the Penguin Sports Library. Nonfiction.

Breslin, Jimmy. **Can't Anybody Here Play This Game?** Penguin Books, 1982.

Breslin's book is a hilarious attempt to capture all the antics of the desolate New York Mets in 1962, their first season. Under manager Casey Stengel, the "Hitless Wonders" captured the attention and love of the fans as they labored to become the team with the worst record in baseball history. This enjoyable book will bring you many laughs and a few tears. A volume in the Penguin Sports Library. Nonfiction.

Cebulash, Mel. **Ruth Marini, Dodger Ace.** Lerner, 1983.

In this novel, Ruth Marini breaks the sex barrier in professional baseball! Many people felt that she would never make it through spring training, but there she is on opening day in a Dodger uniform. How will she handle the pressures of the major leagues? Can she successfully compete with the other pitchers? As the all-star game approaches, Ruth faces a decision that could end her short major league career. One of the Ruth Marini on the Mound series. Fiction.

Cebulash, Mel. **Ruth Marini of the Dodgers.** Lerner, 1983.

In this novel about the first woman to play major league baseball, eighteen-year-old Ruth Marini, the star of her high school baseball team, gets a tryout at the L.A. Dodgers' training camp. But will she last through spring training? Can she make it in the major leagues? One of the Ruth Marini on the Mound series. Fiction.

Crutcher, Chris. **Running Loose.** Greenwillow Books, 1983.

For senior Louie Banks, living by what is right is much more important than being popular. When his football coach instructs the team to "play dirty" against an outstanding player on a rival team, Louie walks off the field. That turns out to be the most important decision of his life, because he then has to face the ridicule of his former teammates, the disappointment of his parents, the insinuations from his classmates, and his own self-image. Fiction.

Davis, Terry. **Vision Quest.** Bantam Books, 1985.

Anyone who has ever puffed and sweated and strained to get into shape will understand part of what drives eighteen-year-old Louden Swain in his quest to reach 147 pounds so he can be a champion high school wrestler. But there is more to Louden's life than workouts: there are the antics of his half-Indian friend and teammate Kuch, the excitement of his sexually active live-in girlfriend Carla, and the pleasures of taking quiet hikes in the wilderness or pondering the issues in great books. As Louden grows stronger, wiser, more sensitive, and more mature, he begins to feel invincible. Fiction.

Dean, Anabel. **Wind Sports.** Westminster Press, 1982.

The wind was the first force harnessed by humans. In recent years, we have renewed our interest in the wind's energy for generating electricity and for play. Many people now use wind sports for recreation: for gliding, hang gliding, parachuting, sailboarding, and ice boating. *Wind Sports* recounts the history of these sports as well as their uses today. Nonfiction.

Due, Linnea A. **High and Outside.** Bantam Books, 1982.

Seventeen-year-old Nikki is a fantastic student and the star of her high school softball team. She's such a "good" kid that no one questions her integrity or actions. Even her parents excuse away her "light, social drinking" as normal for a modern teenager. But Nikki soon progresses from innocent tasting to drinking fifths of gin, which causes blackouts and serious impairment to her physical and intellectual abilities. The book explores Nikki's losses, depression, hysteria, and ultimate decision to help herself. Fiction.

Dygard, Thomas J. **Quarterback Walk-On.** William Morrow, 1982.

Many dream of becoming a quarterback on a nationally ranked college football team. Denny Westbrook had that dream, but he was content to play as the fourth-string quarterback until a series of injuries to the team changed his dream into reality. Will Denny be ready? What will happen to the team during its final two crucial games? *Quarterback Walk-On* depicts college football with humor and sensitivity. Fiction.

Dygard, Thomas J. **Rebound Caper.** William Morrow, 1983.

Coach Orville Flynn has a problem: Gary Whipple, the clown of the basketball team, is disrupting team practices. So Gary is benched until he can be more serious about his sport. But sitting out the season isn't what Gary had in mind, so he joins another team—the girls' team! What follows is an amusing, lively uproar with the school board arguing, the principal upset, and Kimberly, Gary's girlfriend, refusing to speak to him. Fiction.

Fleming, G. H. **The Unforgettable Season.** Penguin Books, 1982.

What was baseball like at the turn of the century? The 1908 season is said by some to have been the most exciting pennant race of all time. *The Unforgettable Season* provides a rare opportunity to be close to the stars of that season through the eyes of the author. A volume in the Penguin Sports Library. Nonfiction.

French, Michael. **The Throwing Season.** Laurel-Leaf Library, 1983.

The shot-put circle offers Henry "Indian" Chevrolet a chance to prove himself and to escape his unhappy years in high school. Then during his junior year, he faces stiff competition for the first time from a recent transfer to his school, and a local businessman offers him a bribe to throw the track meet. Will Indian accept the money, or will he try for a possible athletic scholarship? Fiction.

Gordon-Watson, Mary. **The Handbook of Riding.** Alfred A. Knopf, 1982.

Experienced riders will appreciate this heavily illustrated manual of horsemanship that covers learning to ride and advanced riding, as well as training and keeping a horse. This carefully compiled reference, written by an Olympic gold medalist, is accompanied by numbered instructions and diagrams to aid the equestrian. Nonfiction.

Guy, David. **Football Dreams.** Signet Vista Books, 1982.

With humor and realism, the author takes us into the locker room, onto the practice fields, into the football games, and through the mind and feelings of Dan Keith, a not-so-special freshman trying to pass his courses and make the team at Arnold Academy. By his fourth season, Dan wonders if he has the talent and the courage to be the kind of middle linebacker he has always dreamed of being. Fiction.

Haskins, James. **Sugar Ray Leonard.** Lothrop, Lee and Shepard Books, 1982.

Sugar Ray Leonard began his boxing career at age fourteen when he went to the Palmer Park Recreation Center and met Dave Jacobs, a volunteer coach there. Biographer James Haskins follows the personal and professional life of Ray Charles Leonard from his beginnings in Wilmington, South Carolina, to his introduction to boxing, to the 1976 Montreal Olympics, and to his turning pro. Coverage of two world championship bouts and a look at the ringside action add to the story of this champion fighter. Nonfiction.

Herrin, Lamar. **The Rio Loja Ringmaster.** Bard Books, 1981.

Dick Dixon had pitched in the major leagues, been a hero of the World Series, and then lost his touch. Now he is pitching for a team in the Mexican cactus league. He is still looking for the perfect no-hitter—and still looking for himself. Was the price he paid for success too high? Dixon is a man eager for competition, but apparently destined to lose. Fiction.

Hollander, Phyllis, and Zander Hollander, editors. **Dan Fouts, Ken Anderson, Joe Theismann and Other All-Time Great Quarterbacks.** Zander Hollander Sports Books, 1983.

The Hollanders present portraits of Theismann, Staubach, Namath, Bradshaw, and six other famous American quarterbacks. They include highlights from the career accomplishments of these great athletes, as well as stories of their childhood experiences and college days. Nonfiction.

Hollander, Phyllis, and Zander Hollander, editors. **Touchdown! Football's Most Dramatic Scoring Feats.** Zander Hollander Sports Books, 1982.

Sonny Jurgensen stood deep in his own end zone and fired a pass complete to Jerry Allen on the thirty-one-yard line, and Allen ran the remaining distance for the longest pass-and-run play in National Football League history. This story and the fifty others included here capture the excitement of football's most dramatic scoring feats. Nonfiction.

Hollander, Zander, editor. **Strange But True Football Stories.** Random House, 1983.

Colonel Blaik, the West Point football coach in 1958, organized a new strategy to surprise most of his opponents. Bill Carpenter would be the "lonely end" and would not join the huddles that year, yet somehow would know each play. The new offense worked. The reader of *Strange But True Football Stories* will discover twenty-three unusual football stories like this one. Nonfiction.

Honig, Donald. **The American League: An Illustrated History.** Crown, 1983.

In 1903, a new professional baseball league came into existence. Since that time, the American League has been known as the "star league" with the names of Cobb, Speaker, Ruth, Fox, Williams, DiMaggio, and Jackson playing dominant roles. Honig's pictorial history has more than 550 pictures of the past and present greats of baseball. Each of the eight chapters is introduced with a brief history of the era under discussion. The reader will see how the game has changed in some respects yet remained unchanged in spirit and excitement. Nonfiction.

Honig, Donald. **The National League: An Illustrated History.** Crown, 1983.

From its beginning in 1876, the National League has seemed to emphasize team play and balance; the St. Louis Cardinals' "Gas House Gang," the Brooklyn Dodgers, and the Cincinnati Reds are typical examples. Honig's pictorial history contains over 550 pictures, many of which have never been published before. Each chapter is introduced with a brief history of a particular era from John McGraw to Koufax and Seaver. The changes in baseball over the past one hundred years are clearly illustrated. Nonfiction.

Jackson, Reggie (with Mike Lupica). **Reggie: The Autobiography.** Villard Books, 1984.

Reggie Jackson shares his private life and gives us an insider's view of professional baseball. We meet such sports personalities as Charles O. Finley, George Steinbrenner, and Billy Martin as they struggle with the often controversial Jackson. But the most revealing part of the autobiography comes in the early chapters when Jackson tells of his growing-up years in Philadelphia. Nonfiction.

Johnson, Earvin "Magic," and Richard Levin. **Magic.** Viking Press, 1983.

Capturing the excitement of professional basketball without neglecting the personal story of Johnson's rise to stardom, the authors present alternating chapters of past and present. Here we watch "Magic" develop from a schoolboy athlete in Lansing, Michigan, into a multimillionaire superstar with the Los Angeles Lakers. Nonfiction.

Kinsella, W. P. **Shoeless Joe.** Houghton Mifflin, 1982.

What do cornfields, J. D. Salinger, insurance agents, and Shoeless Joe Jackson have in common? The answer is baseball and dreams. Ray, the main character and narrator of this novel, is an insurance agent who loves baseball and hears voices. First a voice tells Ray to build a stadium in his cornfield; then it tells him to kidnap J. D. Salinger. From these elements, the author weaves an intriguing and spellbinding adventure against a baseball background. Fiction.

Knudson, R. R. **Just Another Love Story.** Farrar, Straus and Giroux, 1983.

When Mariana Fleming tells Dusty Glaisdale their romance is over, Dusty tries to kill himself by driving his car into the ocean at Muscle Beach, Long Island. Rescued from drowning by Rush, a champion body builder, and aided by Frank Boyar, who coaches and trains him, Dusty sets out to pump iron. In the process, his attitude about himself and his life is dramatically changed. Fiction.

Knudson, R. R. **Speed.** Photographs by Linda Eber. Skinny Books, 1983.

Winning the Los Angeles City Track and Field Championship is important for the students of Watts High. Can a woman coach help? Ron, Luther, Hollywood, and Tyrone, members of the track team, are not sure. Coach Huey has proven that she can run, but can she teach them speed? And can running help Tyrone get over the pain of breaking up with his girlfriend? Coach Huey believes in the team; they only need to believe in themselves. Fiction.

Knudson, R. R. **Zan Hagen's Marathon.** Farrar, Straus and Giroux, 1984.

Zan has just won the cross-country championship, so her coach suggests that she train for the marathon. Is he crazy to suggest this to her? Or is he developing her hidden talents? This book carries the reader along with Zan on training runs and through the excitement of competition. Fiction.

Lieberman, Nancy (with Myrna Frommer and Harvey Frommer). **Basketball My Way.** Photographs by Kimberly Butler. Charles Scribner's Sons, 1982.

In addition to describing and illustrating both offensive and defensive basketball skills, the nation's top female player explains the philosophy of playing that earned her an Olympic silver medal and enabled her to become the first woman to play in the previously all-male New York Professional Summer League. Also included are tips on nutrition and conditioning and a section on official basketball rules for both men and women. Nonfiction.

Lipsyte, Robert. **Assignment: Sports.** Rev. ed. Harper and Row, 1984.

Robert Lipsyte's collection of sports vignettes includes stories from his fourteen years as a *New York Times* sportswriter and his television assignments for CBS's *Sunday Morning* program with Charles Kuralt. Some of his most famous articles are here—the story of Muhammad Ali and the tragedy of Nigerian boxer Dick Tiger are only two examples. Lipsyte introduces many sports figures, such as Tracee Talavera, an Olympic gymnast torn between her family and her sport, and Mickey Mantle, a baseball great who regrets he didn't concentrate on physical fitness during his career. Nonfiction.

Liss, Howard. **The Giant Book of More Strange But True Sports Stories.** Illus. Joe Mathieu. Random House, 1983.

"Win one for the Gipper" is one of the most familiar lines from sports history, but do you know the full story? Knute Rockne, Notre Dame's football coach, used the line during a half-time pep

talk in 1928; in the second half, Notre Dame rallied to beat unde-
feated Army 12-7. This is one of 150 strange but true stories
presented by Liss from baseball, football, boxing, golf, and auto
racing. Nonfiction.

Liss, Howard. **Strange But True Basketball Stories.** Random House,
1983.

Spencer Haywood leads a flock of "second best" basketball players
to the 1968 Olympic championship game. Through determination
and drive, the American team unexpectedly wins the gold medal,
thus demonstrating their talents to the world. This story and seventeen others provide a behind-the-scenes view of basketball stars
and teams. Nonfiction.

Lyttle, Richard B. **The Games They Played: Sports in History.** Illus.
by author. Atheneum, 1982.

Have you ever wondered what the original Olympic games were
like? What individual and team events took place at that time?
The Games They Played describes the development of the Olympics
in the context of Greek history. The author also traces other individual and team sports back to their beginnings, utilizing archaeological evidence of sports such as lacrosse and polo. Nonfiction.

Madden, John (with Dave Anderson). **Hey, Wait a Minute, I Wrote a
Book!** Villard Books, 1984.

Perhaps best known as a coach of the Oakland Raiders, John
Madden is familiar to television viewers today for his work as a
sports commentator and a celebrity in beer commercials. Always
quick with a quip, Madden transfers that same wit to his book as
he takes us behind the scenes of college and professional football.
More a collection of anecdotes than an autobiography, Madden's
book parades one football personality after another in front of us.
Nonfiction.

Meyer, Gladys C. **Softball for Girls and Women.** Charles Scribner's
Sons, 1982.

The fastest growing sport for women and girls during recent years
has been softball, but this is the first book devoted exclusively to
the subject. From her playing and coaching experience, Gladys
Meyer explains the fundamentals of throwing, catching, fielding,
batting, running, training, and organizing practice sessions. As

informative for the novice player as it is for coaches and parents, this book also includes an extensive section on official softball rules. Nonfiction.

Moore, Kenny. **Best Efforts: World Class Runners and Races.** Doubleday, 1982.

The running mania in America during the 1970s produced a national obsession with physical fitness and sports. Frank Shorter and Kenny Moore were two personalities who became associated with "running fever." Moore's well-written book begins with the Munich Olympics of 1972 in which Shorter emerged as the impressive winner in the marathon. Each chapter provides a glimpse of some of the great names in track: Bill Rogers, Grete Waitz, John Akii-Bua, Ron Clark, Mary Decker, Eamonn Coghlan, and Lasse Viren. Moore's style makes the reading of *Best Efforts* second in pleasure only to running itself. Nonfiction.

Murphy, Jim. **Baseball's All-Time All-Stars.** Clarion Books, 1984.

Americans love to argue about who were the greatest baseball players of all times. Over thirteen thousand men have played organized baseball since 1876, which makes the task of agreeing on the selections of all-stars extremely difficult. Who would you select for the all-time, all-star teams from the American and National Leagues? Compare your selections to the individuals chosen by Jim Murphy. A brief summary of the career of each of the twenty-six players selected is included. Nonfiction.

Myers, Walter Dean. **Hoops.** Laurel-Leaf Library, 1983.

At seventeen, Lonnie Jackson is at a key point in his life. If he and his team do well in the city-wide basketball tournament, he will be assured of a college position that could lead to a professional basketball career and a way out of Harlem. Lonnie feels the pressure to succeed, but some heavy bettors are also putting pressure on Lonnie's coach. For both of them, integrity becomes as important as talent. Fiction.

Myers, Walter Dean. **The Outside Shot.** Delacorte Press, 1984.

When Lonnie Jackson realizes that he has only one outside shot at college, he is not just thinking about his jump shot. Lonnie knows that his future depends on how he does in college; he has only one year to demonstrate that he has what it takes to be a college man. Studies, basketball pressures, and bribes all tempt him. Fiction.

Navratilova, Martina (with Mary Carillo). **Tennis My Way.** Photographs by Kimberly Butler. Penguin Books, 1984.

Would you like to have a private tennis lesson from Martina Navratilova? *Tennis My Way* puts you in contact with her through words and pictures. Improve your game with the help of one of the greatest tennis players around today. Nonfiction.

Perry, Dave. **Winning in One-Designs.** Illus. Brad Dellenbaugh. Dodd, Mead, 1984.

An Olympic contender known for his teaching as well as his sailing, Dave Perry clearly imparts his knowledge of all aspects of sailing competition. He describes approaches already tried in his racing seminars that have proved to be understandable and helpful. Anecdotes that clarify various tactics and rules also make this book valuable reading for both the racing enthusiast and the novice sailor. Nonfiction.

Plimpton, George. **The Bogey Man.** Penguin Books, 1983.

George Plimpton's name has become synonymous with courage—the courage to compete in any sport against the best. Here, Plimpton describes how he, as an eighteen-handicap amateur golfer, challenged the touring professional golfers. What is it like to feel the pressures of professional golf where one shot means the difference between one thousand dollars and sixty thousand dollars in prize money? George describes the feeling in *The Bogey Man,* which was first published in 1968. A volume in the Penguin Sports Library. Nonfiction.

Plimpton, George. **Out of My League.** Penguin Books, 1983.

At some time in their lives, most people have had a fantasy about how it would feel to dance with the New York Ballet or act in an epic movie or play football with the Dallas Cowboys. Few have the courage to try to make their dreams a reality, however. In this classic sports book (originally published in 1961), George Plimpton describes how he made his dream of playing baseball with the New York Yankees a reality. His experiences will entertain and amuse you. Nonfiction.

Prugh, Jeff. **Herschel Walker: From the Georgia Backwoods and the Heisman Trophy to the Pros.** Zander Hollander Sports Books, 1983.

Herschel Junior Walker was the fifth child born to Willis and

Christine Walker, tenant farmers in rural Georgia. It was here in the rural South that Herschel grew up, went to school, ran foot races with his sister Veronica, and started to play football for the Johnson County Trojans. This book traces Walker's success in football and concludes with his controversial decision to leave college for a career in the newly formed United States Football League. Nonfiction.

Salassi, Otto R. **On the Ropes.** Bantam Books, 1982.

When Constance Gains dies, she leaves behind her seventeen-year-old daughter Julie and her eleven-year-old son Squint, along with a foreclosure notice on the family farm effective in two weeks' time. The children's home and future are salvaged through the efforts of a bizarre cast of characters headed by their father, Claudius—a pool shark, con artist, and wrestling manager of such characters as the Baron, Panzer Kaufman, the Masked Marvel, the Steel Claw, Seymour the Bear, and the Angel of Sorrow. Fiction.

Schaap, Dick. **Steinbrenner!** G. P. Putnam's Sons, 1982.

We all know George Steinbrenner as the controversial owner of the New York Yankees. Here, through the author's personal observations as well as interviews with Steinbrenner's friends and foes, we get a balanced view of both the public and private life of one of the most famous men in sports. In his analysis of Steinbrenner's childhood and early family relationships, the author examines forces that may have motivated and shaped George Steinbrenner. Nonfiction.

Schrier, Eric W., and William F. Allman, editors. **Newton at the Bat: The Science in Sports.** Charles Scribner's Sons, 1984.

When you line up a golf shot, should it have topspin, backspin, or no spin? Which wax should you use on your cross-country skis? Nearly half the running backs in the National Football League will suffer knee injuries; how can they protect themselves against such injuries? *Newton at the Bat* catalogs the answers to these and hundreds of other questions that deal with the physical and physiological aspects of sports such as golf, sailing, wrestling, and frisbee. Nonfiction.

Siner, Howard, editor. **Sports Classics: American Writers Choose Their Best.** Coward-McCann, 1983.

In this splendid collection of sports writing, Siner has brought together some of the best examples of how journalism enhances victory and defeat in covering athletic competition. Included are pieces from the *New York Post, The Saturday Evening Post, Sports Illustrated, Esquire,* and *The New Yorker.* Nonfiction.

Smith, Red. **To Absent Friends.** Plume Books, 1983.

There are 182 tributes in this collection, and every one of them immortalizes both its subject and its creator. Among the great sports figures described here are the well-known Vince Lombardi, Jim Thorpe, Babe Ruth, and Joe Louis, as well as lesser-known figures such as Clark Daniel Shaughnessy, Chalky Wright, and Joe Liebling. Smith's compassion and humor grace every page. Nonfiction.

Smith, Roger. **The Penguin Book of Orienteering.** Illus. Raymond Turvey. Penguin Books, 1982.

Orienteering is a competitive sport which combines cross-country running and navigational skills. Intended for the beginner, this volume is a complete guide to orienteering and includes information on techniques, physical conditioning, clothing and equipment, orienteering maps, and compass reading. Nonfiction.

Solomon, Diane S. **Teaching Riding: Step-by-Step Schooling for Horse and Rider.** Illus. William R. Culbertson and Ann Williams. Photographs by Robert G. Harvey and Kris Illenberger. University of Oklahoma Press, 1982.

If riding horses is your strong interest, this book will show you a step-by-step approach to handling, training, equipment, and exercises. The descriptions of these topics are highlighted with numerous pictures and charts. Nonfiction.

Sperling, Dan. **A Spectator's Guide to Football: The Action, Rules, and Beauty of the Game.** Avon Books, 1983.

Even those who know and enjoy the game of football are not always sure of what is meant by terms like *encroachment, false start, fair-catch interference,* or *wide-side receiver.* This guide clearly and briefly describes the various offensive and defensive formations and what football is all about. For some readers it will serve as a review; for others, it will provide a quick and enjoyable introduction to the game of football. Nonfiction.

Strasser, Todd. **Friends till the End.** Laurel-Leaf Library, 1982.

Senior David Gilbert has it all: he's a star soccer player, he's a member of the "in" crowd, and he's headed for college. But his life is changed when he befriends newcomer Howie Jamison, a victim of leukemia. In trying to deal with the ups and downs of Howie's illness, David must also handle his family's and girlfriend's questioning of his new goals and the new direction he sets for himself. Fiction.

Stretton, Barbara. **You Never Lose.** Alfred A. Knopf, 1982.

As Jim Halpert begins his senior year in high school, he learns that his father, who is also his football coach and hero, is dying of cancer. Jim's adjustments to his friends, who idolize his father, and to his girlfriend Mimi begin to confuse his life and his feelings for his father. Then along comes new student, Agnes "Gus" Palmer, who helps Jim understand that "You never lose. But sometimes the clock runs out on you." Fiction.

Sullivan, George. **Better Cross-Country Running for Boys and Girls.** Dodd, Mead, 1983.

With the recent interest in cross-country running, the valuable information in this book will be helpful to both the novice and the varsity athlete. Through pictures and narrative, the author deals with strategy, training, form, and equipment. Nonfiction.

Uecker, Bob, and Mickey Herskowitz. **Catcher in the Wry.** G. P. Putnam's Sons, 1982.

Bob Uecker is one of those individuals who manages to develop average abilities and skills into superior performances. Uecker spent six years in the minors before playing baseball for the Milwaukee Braves and the St. Louis Cardinals. Following his playing career, he remained associated with sports as an announcer. *Catcher in the Wry* provides humorous insights into baseball's way of life with its frustrations and its moments of glory. Nonfiction.

Voigt, Cynthia. **Tell Me If the Lovers Are Losers.** Fawcett Juniper Books, 1983.

When three women enter Stanton College and become roommates, the differences in their personalities quickly surface. Can the three become friends, sharing things in common? Even when playing volleyball together, the three view the game differently. Ann, Niki, and Hildy may not be able to survive . . . without each other. Fiction.

Television, Movies, and Entertainment

American Film Institute (edited by Joseph McBride). **Filmmakers on Filmmaking.** 2 vols. J. P. Tarcher, 1983.

Serious students of filmmaking will enjoy the comments from twenty-six filmmakers found in this two-volume set. The comments are excerpted from more than two decades of discussion between Fellows of the American Film Institute and the filmmakers. Among the filmmakers included are Richard Zanuck, Ingmar Bergman, and Joseph E. Levine. Nonfiction.

Clemens, Virginia Phelps. **Behind the Filmmaking Scene.** Westminster Press, 1982.

The author of this book went to the people who work behind the scenes in filmmaking and asked them to describe their jobs. This guide is the result. It covers familiar behind-the-scenes jobs such as director and stunt person, as well as some not-so-familiar ones such as sound mixer, editor, and cinematographer. In each case, the education, experience, and personality needed are described. Nonfiction.

Cohen, Daniel. **Masters of Horror.** Clarion Books, 1984.

Horror-film fans will delight in this close-up account of the classic actors and actresses featured in many frightening movies. Writers and stars like Stephen King, Boris Karloff, Steven Spielberg, Bela Lugosi, and many others are profiled to help you better understand the horror of it all. Nonfiction.

Drucker, Malka, and Elizabeth James. **Series TV: How a Television Show Is Made.** Clarion Books, 1983.

This book follows the making of a series TV show, from the story idea through the script development, right up to the final taping. Television viewers will recognize photographs of scenes from popular TV shows; there are numerous photographs of what goes on behind the scenes as well. The book also covers the working life of a series actor or actress—which is not as glamorous as many of us think. Nonfiction.

Johnston, Norma. **Timewarp Summer.** Atheneum, 1983.

Scott, Bettina, and Laura form a love triangle in this unusual story about people living—or reliving—their seventeenth summer. Bettina, the girl next door, and Laura, a scientist at the lab where all three work, help Scott to fulfill his dream of making a film during summer vacation. While they are caught up in this project, all three become involved in relationships that are as intense as they are dangerous. Fiction.

Kael, Pauline. **Taking It All In.** William Abrahams Books, 1984.

Film critic for *The New Yorker,* Pauline Kael has been an authoritative voice for movie fans for many years. In this, her seventeenth collection of film reviews, Kael displays her insightful and witty opinions on dozens of recent films, including *Chariots of Fire, The Blues Brothers, Tex, The Road Warrior, Ordinary People, E.T., Fanny and Alexander, Sophie's Choice,* and *Fast Times at Ridgemont High.* Nonfiction.

LeBaron, John, and Philip Miller. **Portable Video: A Production Guide for Young People.** Illus. Mary Aufmuth. Prentice-Hall, 1982.

Those who find the manuals provided by manufacturers of video equipment confusing and hard to follow will find a clearly presented alternative here. The book gives a short history of video and offers descriptions of the various parts of a video system. It concentrates on Beta and VHS systems, the two that are most widely used today. The guide also provides hints on how to write successful video programs, and describes games and activities that make learning about video enjoyable. Nonfiction.

Maltin, Leonard, editor. **The Whole Film Sourcebook.** Plume Books, 1983.

Interested in filmmaking? Among the topics covered here is a report on colleges and universities offering programs in film study. The clearly referenced text does not contain reviews or listings of popular films, but it does list addresses of film festivals, sources of funding, and an annotated bibliography of film books. Nonfiction.

Minton, Lynn. **Movie Guide for Puzzled Parents.** Delacorte Press, 1984.

Minton provides a guide for parents and others who are concerned about the movies children watch on television, cable television, and videocassettes. The guide provides additional information for those who are not satisfied with the traditional G, PG, R, and X ratings, and specific references are made to violence, vulgarity, nudity, and "adult situations." For each movie that is reviewed, a specific recommendation for appropriate viewing ages is offered. Nonfiction.

Nicholls, Peter. **The World of Fantastic Films: An Illustrated Survey.** Dodd, Mead, 1984.

This guide traces the history of the fantastic film from its beginning to *E.T.* and covers both science fiction and horror films. The book includes hundreds of photographs taken directly from the films, many in color. Nonfiction.

Robinson, Richard. **The Video Primer: Equipment, Production, and Concepts.** 3d ed. Perigee Books, 1983.

Beginners as well as more expert video enthusiasts will find a great deal of useful information in this volume. Each chapter covers a specific topic, such as editing or lighting, and is well illustrated with drawings of video systems and photographs of state-of-the-art equipment. The book also contains a complete glossary of video terms and step-by-step instructions on the use of equipment. Nonfiction.

War

Cunningham, Ann Marie, and Mariana Fitzpatrick. **Future Fire: Weapons for the Apocalypse.** Warner Books, 1983.

Cunningham and Fitzpatrick provide us with a look at the new megaweapons, the history of the U.S. and Soviet nuclear buildup, and the future world of possible unrestrained nuclear proliferation. Nonfiction.

Ferry, Charles. **Raspberry One.** Houghton Mifflin, 1983.

In 1944, Nick and Phil, members of Torpedo Squadron 43, prepare to leave Franny and Diane as they ship out for the Pacific. Nick's bewilderment over war only strengthens his determination as he and Phil see firsthand the horrors of war and the mental and physical devastation it causes. Fiction.

Ground Zero. **Nuclear War: What's in It for You?** Pocket Books, 1982.

This antinuclear group presents basic, factual information on nuclear weapons and nuclear war. Detailed and informative answers to technical questions are outlined with varied arguments. Nonfiction.

Hartman, Evert (translated by Patricia Crampton). **War without Friends.** Crown Publishers, 1982.

In Holland during World War II, fourteen-year-old Arnold Westervoort must come to grips with his own feelings about the war and with his father's fervent support of the German National Socialist Party (the Nazis). Arnold becomes a member of the Hitler youth group, only to be taunted and beaten by his classmates. In the end, he must resolve his own feelings and answer the demands of his growing conscience. Fiction.

Hough, Richard. **Razor Eyes.** Lodestar Books, 1983.

Forty years after World War II, Mich "Razor Eyes" Boyd relates his experiences flying for the Royal Air Force of England. Sent on a dangerous and top-secret mission, Mick encounters the horrors of war and the ultimate test of his courage. Fiction.

Lawson, Don. **The French Resistance.** Julian Messner, 1984.

These true espionage stories illustrate the courage of the French Resistance freedom fighters during the 1940 Nazi occupation. Numerous undetected acts of sabotage and intelligence gathering are detailed with long-kept information. A prediction of the Pearl Harbor invasion by Dusko Popov, the British double agent who served as the model for James Bond, reads like an Ian Fleming novel. A volume in the Spy Shelf series. Nonfiction.

Leekley, John. **The Blue and the Gray.** Dell Books, 1982.

The fury of the Civil War forces two families, the Geysers and the Hales, to break the bond between them. Famous Civil War battles are seen through the eyes of John Geyser, an artist for the *Gettysburg Compiler,* in this companion to the television miniseries of the same title. Fiction.

Marrin, Albert. **Victory in the Pacific.** Atheneum, 1983.

The devastation of Pearl Harbor on December 7, 1941 was the beginning of World War II in the Pacific. *Victory in the Pacific* analyzes the naval and land campaigns that led to the Allied victory over Japan in 1945. But the book is not just about battles—it also explains the operation of the submarines, battleships, aircraft carriers, torpedoes, and guns that were used by the U.S. Navy and Marine Corps. Illustrated with photographs. Nonfiction.

Mazer, Harry. **The Last Mission.** Laurel-Leaf Library, 1982.

Joining the Air Force before his sixteenth birthday, Jack Raab, a Jewish kid from New York City, is determined to do his part to fight Hitler's madness in Europe. But his exciting fantasies turn to boredom when, as a waist gunner in a B-17, he never even sees an enemy plane. Then suddenly his plane is shot down over Czechoslovakia. The only survivor among his crew, Jack spends the remaining days of the war in a POW camp, contemplating the effects of war. Fiction.

McCombs, Don, and Fred L. Worth. **World War II Super Facts.** Warner Books, 1983.

For trivia buffs, here is an alphabetical collection of facts that are not generally covered by the standard historical approaches to

World War II. Do you know, for example, how a dead poet managed to pass on news of D-Day? Nonfiction.

McKee, Alexander. **Dresden 1945: The Devil's Tinderbox.** E. P. Dutton, 1984.

The controversial 1945 bombing raid by the Royal Air Force and the American flying fortresses on the city of Dresden is described here by eyewitnesses. Dresden survivors tell what it was like to be in the city when thirty-five thousand people were slaughtered during this massive air attack. Firsthand accounts by pilots who flew this mission substantiate the horror on the streets of Dresden. Nonfiction.

Page, Tim. **Tim Page's Nam.** Alfred A. Knopf, 1983.

A vivid report on the Vietnam War is provided through the camera and words of war correspondent Tim Page. The photographs provide images of the primitive and sometimes appalling conditions that civilians and soldiers had to endure. Nonfiction.

Prager, Arthur, and Emily Prager. **World War II Resistance Stories.** Illus. Steven Assel. Laurel-Leaf Library, 1980.

These true stories of six brave patriots (both men and women) who fought in secret during World War II show the importance of undercover work. These resistance fighters' greatest desire was to help their country, but they were successful only because of the many everyday people who worked to help them accomplish their goals. Nonfiction.

Ritchie, David. **Spacewar.** Plume Books, 1983.

The possibility of war in space may no longer be just another science fiction story. Today's space technology and weapons systems have advanced to the point where computerized laser cannons and high orbital satellites may soon come close to resembling Darth Vader's Death Star. Nonfiction.

Rosenblatt, Roger. **Children of War.** Anchor Press, 1983.

First published in *Time* magazine in 1982, this is the story of Roger Rosenblatt's forty-thousand-mile journey to the war zones of Northern Ireland, Israel, Lebanon, Cambodia, and Vietnam. He spoke to the children in these places, who have grown up knowing nothing but war, and asked them what they think of the world, of politics, of their parents, of friendship, and of God. This book contains their unforgettable answers. Nonfiction.

Sullivan, Mary Ann. **Child of War.** Holiday House, 1984.

Life in Northern Ireland changes for Maeve after her little brother Brendan is killed. Caught up in her feelings of guilt and horror about his death, Maeve becomes despondent. She tries to join the other neighborhood children in their fight against the IRA, but only falls deeper and deeper into an unreal world. Fiction.

Taylor, Theodore. **Battle in the English Channel.** Illus. Andrew Glass. Flare Books, 1983.

Third in a series about the great sea battles of World War II, this volume describes the events of the 1942 battle between the British Navy and German battleships over control of the English Channel. It details the escape route of three major German ships as they tried to run up the English Channel and were pursued by the British Navy and the Royal Air Force. Nonfiction.

Terry, Wallace. **Bloods: An Oral History of the Vietnam War by Black Veterans.** Random House, 1984.

In the years immediately after the Vietnam War, very little was written about the soldiers' experiences. Now, in the outpouring of stories about that confusing war comes *Bloods,* an account from twenty black veterans. In their own sensitive yet brutal, honest, and insightful words, we can see and feel the uncertainty, the fear, the pride, the horror, and the heroism of their experiences along with the racial battles that plagued them in and out of the military. Nonfiction.

Tregaskis, Richard. **Guadalcanal Diary.** Random House, 1984.

What is it like to be in the midst of an actual battle? Can the American army be successful when they are outnumbered and unfamiliar with the territory? These inquiries plagued journalist Richard Tregaskis during the battle of Guadalcanal. As an eye-witness to one of the most crucial battles of World War II, Tregaskis presents the drama of the operation with immediate excitement. First published in 1943. Nonfiction.

The West

Bergon, Frank, editor. **The Western Writings of Stephen Crane.** Signet Classics, 1979.

Stephen Crane spent only a few months in the West in 1895; yet, in this collection of stories, reports, and sketches, he conveys the reality of the Old West through his depiction of such people as gunslingers, cowboys, and gamblers, and of such places as Texas, Mexico, and Nebraska. Fiction and nonfiction.

Brand, Max. **The Making of a Gunman.** Warner Books, 1984.

Tommy Mayo is a lazy do-nothing around his dad's ranch until he kills a gunman with a single shot. Then Henry Grant, gambler and gunslinger, takes Tommy on as a student, and Tommy acquires an unbeatable black stallion, a pair of matched revolvers, and an urge to kill. Fiction.

Brand, Max. **Thunder Moon Strikes.** Warner Books, 1984.

In this sequel to *Thunder Moon's Challenge,* white-born Cheyenne warrior Thunder Moon rejoins his white family. His divided loyalties are tested when his Cheyenne father, Big Hard Face, is arrested. Thunder Moon goes to the rescue but, after the jailbreak, is accused of murder and must run. Fiction.

Erdoes, Richard, and Alfonso Ortiz, editors. **American Indian Myths and Legends.** Pantheon Books, 1984.

The vibrant folklore tradition of the North American Indian is magnificently depicted in this collaboration between an anthropologist and a storyteller who have gathered together 166 myths and legends from tribal societies stretching from the Northeast to the Far West. While some of the familiar legends have been retold in a contemporary style, many others have never before been recorded. Imagination, humor, courage, and spiritual beliefs pervade these tales about creation, grisly monsters, heroes, warriors, tricksters, and the spirit world.

Foreman, Paul. **Quanah: The Serpent Eagle.** Northland Press, 1983.

Quanah Parker, son of a white captive and a Comanche chief, challenges Captain Ronald MacKenzie, U.S. Army, by leading his band of Indian warriors on innumerable raids on white settlers and army units. An intelligent and fearless chief, Quanah combines his Comanche expertise, his skill with horses, and his use of peyote to frustrate the army's effort to resettle the Indians in accordance with the Medicine Lodge Treaty of 1867. Fiction.

Gard, Wayne. **The Chisholm Trail.** Illus. Nick Eggenhofer. University of Oklahoma Press, 1984.

Cowboys herding cattle from Texas to railroads in Kansas between 1867 and 1884 often used the Chisholm Trail. The trip was always exciting and filled with danger from rattlesnakes, Indians, snowstorms, lightning, river crossings, rustlers, and the longhorns themselves. But the end of the trail always promised riches and places in which to spend them—saloons, gambling parlors, and dance halls. This book looks at the truth behind the legends of the famous trail. Nonfiction.

Haruf, Kent. **The Tie That Binds.** Holt, Rinehart and Winston, 1984.

The unyielding landscape of the Colorado high plains is reflected in the bleakness of the life Edith Goodnough lived after the early death of her mother in 1914. Hemmed in by the meanness of her father, Edith devotes herself to nurturing and sheltering her brother Lyman. Lyman escapes the farm in 1941, only to return twenty years later after the death of his crippled father. Covering a period of eighty years, this novel shows Edith to be a dauntless woman devoted to family and duty with ultimately tragic results. Fiction.

Haycox, Ernest. *Alder Gulch* **and** *A Rider of the High Mesa.* Signet Books, 1983.

This is a dual selection of titles by a classic Western author. In *Alder Gulch* (first published in 1941), Jeff Pierce and Diane Castle run from trouble by heading for the Montana gold country. Alder Gulch is a town riddled with crime until the stalwart Pierce confronts the crooks and a team of vigilantes weed out the bad guys. *A Rider of the High Mesa* (originally published in 1927) is about Lin Ballou, who is suspected of rustling, but who, in truth, is tracking down the real villains. Fiction.

Hogan, Ray. **The Law and Lynchburg.** Signet Books, 1983.

Reno Magatagan, in finally avenging his father's death, thinks he has killed his last man. But that's before he stops at Lynchburg, where he is handed the marshall's badge and has to face a corrupt army colonel who feels he owns the town and the best-looking woman in it. Fiction.

Jones, Douglas C. **Gone the Dreams and Dancing.** Holt, Rinehart and Winston, 1984.

Civil War veteran Liverpool Morgan, working as an army contract driver and Indian interpreter at Fort Sill in 1875, watches the surrender of Comanche chief Kwahadi and his people. Mutual respect between these two warriors leads to Liver's search for Kwahadi's white mother, Chosen, who was retaken by the Texas Rangers in 1854. While learning and adapting to the white world, Kwahadi instills in Liver an appreciation of the Indian way of life. Liver marries into the tribe and remains a friend and brother to The People as Oklahoma emerges into statehood. Fiction.

Jones, Douglas C. **Season of Yellow Leaf.** Holt, Rinehart and Winston, 1983.

Morfydd Parry, a white ten-year-old girl, is taken captive by a group of Comanches under the leadership of Sanchess in the 1830s. Given the new name of Chosen and raised by the Comanches, she grows to accept herself as one of The People and slowly comes to realize their dignity, courage, and compassion—along with their fearsomeness—as the encroaching white world slowly destroys their way of life. Fiction.

L'Amour, Louis. **Son of a Wanted Man.** Bantam Books, 1984.

Ben Curry, leader of the most successful and best-organized gang of criminals pulling jobs from Canada to Mexico, is depending on his foster son, Mike Bastian, to succeed him. Trained but untested, Mike must decide whether to follow his father's outlaw career or to stay straight as Tyrel Sackett and Borden Chantry team up to pursue the Curry gang. Fiction.

Martin, Russell, and Marc Barasch, editors. **Writers of the Purple Sage: An Anthology of Recent Western Writing.** Penguin Books, 1984.

This collection of nineteen fiction and nonfiction pieces includes selections written by Native American authors, other native-born Westerners, and authors who have immigrated to the area. In stories ranging from the tale of a Montana logger seeking revenge against a killer grizzly bear to an article about the outlaw who killed two game wardens in 1981, the writing captures the variety and vitality of the contemporary West. Authors represented include N. Scott Momaday, Leslie Marmon Silko, Ivan Doig, John Nichols, Norman MacLean, Elizabeth Tallent, Edward Abbey, and Thomas McGuane. Fiction and nonfiction.

Rosa, Joseph G. **The Gunfighter: Man or Myth?** University of Oklahoma Press, 1982.

Settlement of the land west of the Mississippi in the last half of the nineteenth century created the legend of the coolheaded, pistol-packing, straight-shooting gunfighter, and Western literature and movies have contributed to the myth. In this well-documented study, the author distinguishes fact from fiction as he pits the myths about gunfighters against the authentic recorded accounts of their exploits. Nonfiction.

Shirley, Glenn. **Belle Starr and Her Times: The Literature, the Facts, and the Legends.** University of Oklahoma Press, 1982.

Just about everybody has heard of Belle Starr, famous outlaw of the Old West. This biography traces Starr from her birth in Missouri in 1848 to her travels throughout the West after the Civil War. Belle lived among renegade Indians, married, had children, and, although never convicted of a major crime, spent most of her life outside of the law. The author presents both myth and reality, fact and fiction in this portrait of an Old West figure. Nonfiction.

Stewart, Elinore Pruitt. **Letters of a Woman Homesteader.** Illus. N. C. Wyeth. Houghton Mifflin, 1982.

An intrepid young widow with a two-year-old daughter, Elinore Stewart is determined to win her livelihood by homesteading in Wyoming. She narrates her joys and sorrows in a series of letters to her former employer. A natural gift for storytelling and a sense of humor enliven this true tale of pioneer life. Originally published in 1913. Nonfiction.

Tuska, Jon, editor. **The American West in Fiction.** Mentor Books, 1982.

The romance, myth, and reality of the American West from the early frontier period to the present day are captured in this anthology of short stories which includes authors ranging from Mark Twain and Willa Cather to Luke Short and Louis L'Amour. Fiction.

Young, Herbert V. **Water by the Inch: Adventures of a Pioneer Family on an Arizona Desert Homestead.** Northland Press, 1983.

The author, with the aid of his family, recounts the experiences of his pioneer father's existence over two decades on a hot dusty ranch in Arizona. Nonfiction.

Women

Abbott, Shirley. **Womenfolks: Growing Up Down South.** Ticknor and Fields, 1983.

Abbott examines her own life as a woman growing up in Arkansas in the 1940s, as well as the lives of her mother, aunts, grandmothers, and other female relatives. Interwoven with her personal recollections are historical, religious, and mythological fragments which fill out this quest for the ingredients that go into the makeup of Southern females. Nonfiction.

Anderson, Jessica. **Tirra Lirra by the River.** Penguin Books, 1984.

Nora Porteous arrives at "The House" where many of the experiences that make up her personality have taken place. For the adult Nora, life has been a series of escapes, and Anderson's vignettes bring the reader an impression of how Nora's seventy-year roundabout journey has led her to discover who she is. Fiction.

Bradley, Marion Zimmer. **City of Sorcery.** DAW Books, 1984.

This Darkover novel traces the quest of Magdalen Loone, who builds, through her life and journeying, a series of bridges that span experiences, cultures, and planets. *City of Sorcery* stresses the several and particular gifts of women acting alone and in community. Fiction.

Franklin, Miles. **My Brilliant Career.** Washington Square Press, 1981.

Written in 1901 when Franklin was sixteen, *My Brilliant Career* is a classic with a contemporary theme. Sybylla Melvyn, a talented but plain young woman, faces the social and personal problems of many teenagers. The fears, conflicts, and mysteries of life presented to her as a settler in the Australian bush country help the contemporary reader relate to the situations, even if separated by geography and time. Fiction.

Harragan, Betty Lehan. **Knowing the Score: Play-by-Play Directions for Women on the Job.** Signet Books, 1984.

Knowing the Score is derived from Betty Lehan Harragan's columns in *Savvy* and *Working Woman.* Designed to give women information on how to analyze a job situation, the book presents specific strategies for dealing with career advancement. In the section on the basic rules of the working game, for example, Harragan explains how to understand the madness that often prevails on the job and the unwritten rules implied in the system. Nonfiction.

Hill, Rebecca. **Blue Rise.** Penguin Books, 1984.

Jeannine Lewis's return to Blue Rise, Mississippi, brings back memories of typical deep Southern roots, family tradition, and religious fervor. In her return and her seeking, Jeannine comes to terms with who she was and who she is. Fiction.

LaBastille, Anne. **Women and Wilderness.** Sierra Club Books, 1984.

Excitement, adventure, and commitment mark the lives and careers of the fifteen women naturalists profiled in this book. From white-water rafting to Olympic monitoring and Alaskan homesteading, the lives of these vital modern women embracing the outdoors are vastly different from the roles women have historically played in the wilderness. These former roles are detailed in brief case studies of pioneer women on the American frontier, and, as a contrast, the book also explores the opening of new and varied career options for women interested in outdoor occupations. Nonfiction.

Magill, Kathleen. **Megan.** Dodd, Mead, 1983.

An independent, courageous, and uncompromising woman struggling for freedom and self-realization, Megan flees from her father's farm to a boomtown in Idaho, where she discovers the truth about herself and her passions. A marvelous cast of realistic characters helps to capture the period and to show Megan's perseverance in a rough and tough town. Fiction.

McKinley, Robin. **The Blue Sword.** Greenwillow Books, 1982.

Harry, bored with her sheltered life in the remote orange-growing colony of Darta, discovers magic in herself when she is kidnapped by a native king with mysterious powers. Fiction.

Morrison, Toni. **Sula.** Plume Books, 1982.

With poetic lines, Toni Morrison traces the lives of two small-town black girls, Sula Peace and Nel Wright, as they confront their feelings, view the sometimes strange actions of their families, seek their places in the world, and examine their relationship with each other as they become adults and grow old. One stays in the place of her birth and raises a family; the other, more rebellious, leaves for college and to see the world before returning home. From the harshness of their realistically portrayed lives come two mature women with very different strengths. Fiction.

Munro, Alice. **Lives of Girls and Women.** Plume Books, 1983.

In this novel about growing up in Canada during World War II, we meet Del, an innocent ten-year-old, and watch her progress through the years into a curious and original young woman. The novel traces her dreams, the changes in her life, and her search for sexual experiences and love. Fiction.

Peavy, Linda, and Ursula Smith. **Women Who Changed Things.** Charles Scribner's Sons, 1983.

Described as "nine lives that made a difference," this collection of biographies researches the lives of nine women who made an impact on our social history. They lived in turn-of-the-century America, and together they made significant changes in the fields of medicine, religion, politics, business, the arts, education, athletics, and social action. They opened doors to new opportunities for generations of women to come. Nonfiction.

Selden, Bernice. **The Mill Girls: Lucy Larcom, Harriet Hanson Robinson, Sarah G. Bagley.** Atheneum, 1983.

As the first planned industrial community, the textile mills of Lowell, Massachusetts, set the scene for subsequent American industrial development. Unique in its efforts to assist its employees, the mill system in turn educated, emancipated, and appalled working women. Focusing on the lives of Lucy Larcom, Harriet Hanson Robinson, and Sarah G. Bagley, who shared the Lowell experience as weavers and dressers during different periods of the nineteenth century, this book cites their contributions as educators and labor reformers to raising the consciousness of the American working woman. Nonfiction.

Solomon, Barbara H., and Paula S. Berggren, editors. **A Mary Woll-stonecraft Reader.** Mentor Books, 1983.

Mary Wollstonecraft can truly be described as a pioneer in the feminist movement. From the beginning, she courageously raged against the denigration of women in the male-dominated eighteenth century. This carefully researched collection illustrates her development and showcases her spirit as she braved censure for both her political views and her private life. Nonfiction.

Steinem, Gloria. **Outrageous Acts and Everyday Rebellions.** Plume Books, 1983.

In this collection, Steinem unites many of her classic pieces into a continuum which traces the growth of consciousness—hers and ours. Some of the pieces are funny, all are moving, and in total they become authentic social history which carries a mandate for change and justice. Nonfiction.

Walker, Alice. **The Color Purple.** Washington Square Press, 1983.

In a series of letters to God and her sister Nettie, Celie tells the story of her checkered life—from the horrifying details of childhood sexual abuse to glorious material success as an adult. Sparing no details, Walker's Pulitzer Prize-winning novel vividly etches into the reader's experience what it means to be poor, to be abused, to be challenged, and to find self-worth. Fiction.

Directory of Publishers

Abingdon Press, 1015 Visco Dr., Nashville, TN 37210

William Abrahams Books. Imprint of E. P. Dutton, Two Park Ave., New York, NY 10016

Ace Tempo Books. Imprint of Berkley Publishing Group, 200 Madison Ave., New York, NY 10016

Anchor Press. Imprint of Doubleday Publishing Co. Orders to: 501 Franklin Ave., Garden City, NY 11530

Archway Paperbacks, c/o Pocket Books, 1230 Avenue of the Americas, New York, NY 10020

Arco Publishing. Division of Prentice-Hall, 215 Park Ave. S., New York, NY 10003

Argo Books. Imprint of Atheneum Publishers. Distributed by Riverside Distribution Center, Front and Brown Sts., Riverside, NJ 08075

Atheneum Publishers. Distributed by Riverside Distribution Center, Front and Brown Sts., Riverside, NJ 08075

Avon Books, 1790 Broadway, New York, NY 10019

Ballantine Books. Division of Random House. Orders to: 400 Hahn Rd., Westminster, MD 21157

Bantam Books. Orders to: 414 E. Golf Rd., Des Plaines, IL 60016

Bard Books. Imprint of Avon Books, 1790 Broadway, New York, NY 10019

Berkley Books. Imprint of Berkley Publishing Group, 200 Madison Ave., New York, NY 10016

Bradbury Press. Distributed by Macmillan Publishing Co., Riverside, NJ 08370

Brady Communications Co., Rtes. 197 and 450, Bowie, MD 20715

Robert J. Brady Co. Distributed by Brady Communications Co., Rtes. 197 and 450, Bowie, MD 20715

Broadside Press Publications, 74 Glendale Ave., Highland Park, MI 48203

Clarion Books. Imprint of Houghton Mifflin Co., One Beacon St., Boston, MA 02108

CompuSoft Publishing, 535 Broadway, El Cajon, CA 92021

Coward-McCann. Distributed by the Putnam Publishing Group. Orders to: 200 Madison Ave., New York, NY 10016

Coward, McCann and Geoghegan. Distributed by the Putnam Publishing Group. Orders to: 200 Madison Ave., New York, NY 10016

Crown Publishers, One Park Ave., New York, NY 10016

DAW Books, c/o New American Library, 1633 Broadway, New York, NY 10019

Delacorte Press, One Dag Hammarskjold Plaza, 245 E. 47th St., New York, NY 10017

Dell Books. One Dag Hammarskjold Plaza, 245 E. 47th St., New York, NY 10017

Del Rey Books. Imprint of Ballantine Books. Orders to: 400 Hahn Rd., Westminster, MD 21157 `

Dial Books. Imprint of E. P. Dutton, Two Park Ave., New York, NY 10016

Dial Books for Young Readers. Imprint of E. P. Dutton, Two Park Ave., New York, NY 10016

Dial Press. Distributed by Doubleday and Co. Orders to: 501 Franklin Ave., Garden City, NY 11530

Dodd, Mead and Co., 79 Madison Ave., New York, NY 10016

Doubleday and Co. Orders to: 501 Franklin Ave., Garden City, NY 11530

E. P. Dutton, Two Park Ave., New York, NY 10016

Editorial Justa Publications. Orders to: P.O. Box 2131-C, Berkeley, CA 94702

Elsevier/Nelson Books. Imprint of Elsevier-Dutton, Two Park Ave., New York, NY 10016

Enslow Publishers, Bloy St. and Ramsey Ave., Box 777, Hillside, NJ 07205

Esquire Press, Two Park Ave., New York, NY 10016

Everest House Publishers. Orders to: P.O. Box 141000, Nashville, TN 37214

Fairfax Press. Distributed by Crown Publishers, One Park Ave., New York, NY 10016

Farrar, Straus and Giroux, 19 Union Square W., New York, NY 10003

Fawcett Crest Books. Imprint of Fawcett Book Group, 201 E. 50th St., New York, NY 10022

Fawcett Juniper Books. Imprint of Fawcett Book Group, 201 E. 50th St., New York, NY 10022

Flare Books. Imprint of Avon Books, 1790 Broadway, New York, NY 10019

Four Winds Press. Imprint of Scholastic. Orders to: P.O. Box 7502, 2931 E. McCarty St., Jefferson City, MO 65102

Gold Medal Books. Imprint of Fawcett Book Group, 201 E. 50th St., New York, NY 10022

Greenwillow Books. Orders to: William Morrow and Co., Wilmor Warehouse, Six Henderson Dr., West Caldwell, NJ 07006

Grosset and Dunlap. Division of the Putnam Publishing Group, 200 Madison Ave., New York, NY 10016

Guinness Superlatives Ltd. Distributed by Sterling Publishing Co., Two Park Ave., New York, NY 10016

Harper and Row, Publishers. Orders to: Keystone Industrial Park, Scranton, PA 18512

Hastings House, Publishers, 10 E. 40th St., New York, NY 10016

Herald Press. Division of Mennonite Publishing House, 616 Walnut Ave., Scottsdale, PA 15683

Lawrence Hill and Co., 520 Riverside Ave., Westport, CT 06880

Hill and Wang. Division of Farrar, Straus and Giroux, 19 Union Square W., New York, NY 10003

Hillside Books. Imprint of E. P. Dutton, Two Park Ave., New York, NY 10016

Hiway Books. Imprint of Westminster Press. Orders to: P.O. Box 718, William Penn Annex, Philadelphia, PA 19105

Holiday House, 18 E. 53rd St., New York, NY 10022

Zander Hollander Sports Books. Imprint of Associated Features, Box 1762, Murray Hill Station, New York, NY 10156

Holt, Rinehart and Winston, 383 Madison Ave., New York, NY 10017

Houghton Mifflin Co., One Beacon St., Boston, MA 02108

JEM Books. Imprint of Julian Messner, 1230 Avenue of the Americas, New York, NY 10020

Alfred A. Knopf. Orders to: 400 Hahn Rd., Westminster, MD 21157

Laurel Editions. Imprint of Dell Publishing Co., One Dag Hammarskjold Plaza, 245 E. 47th St., New York, NY 10017

Laurel-Leaf Library. Imprint of Dell Publishing Co., One Dag Hammarskjold Plaza, 245 E. 47th St., New York, NY 10017

Merloyd Lawrence Books, 102 Chestnut St., Boston, MA 02108

Lerner Publications. Orders to: 241 First Ave. N., Minneapolis, MN 55401

Lodestar Books. Imprint of E. P. Dutton, Two Park Ave., New York, NY 10016

Lothrop, Lee and Shepard Books. Orders to: William Morrow and Co., Wilmor Warehouse, Six Henderson Dr., West Caldwell, NJ 07006

Margaret K. McElderry Books. Imprint of Atheneum Publishers. Distributed by Riverside Distribution Center, Front and Brown Sts., Riverside, NJ 08075

Mentor Books. Imprint of New American Library. Orders to: 120 Woodbine St., Bergenfield, NJ 07621

Meridian Books. Imprint of New American Library. Orders to: 120 Woodbine St., Bergenfield, NJ 07621

Julian Messner, 1230 Avenue of the Americas, New York, NY 10020

William Morrow and Co. Orders to: Wilmor Warehouse, Six Henderson Dr., West Caldwell, NJ 07006

New Trend Books. Distributed by Dodd, Mead and Co., 79 Madison Ave., New York, NY 10016

Nilgiri Press, P.O. Box 477, Petaluma, CA 94953

Northland Press, P.O. Box N, Flagstaff, AZ 86002

W. W. Norton and Co., 500 Fifth Ave., New York, NY 10110

Owl Books. Imprint of Holt, Rinehart and Winston, 383 Madison Ave., New York, NY 10017

Pacer Books. Imprint of the Putnam Publishing Group, 51 Madison Ave., New York, NY 10010

Pantheon Books. Orders to: Random House, 400 Hahn Rd., Westminster, MD 21157

Patient Care Publications, 16 Thorndal Circle, Darien, CT 06820

Penguin Books, 40 W. 23rd St., New York, NY 10010

Perigee Books. Imprint of the Putnam Publishing Group, 200 Madison Ave., New York, NY 10016

Persea Books, 225 Lafayette St., New York, NY 10012

Philomel Books. Distributed by the Putnam Publishing Group. Orders to: 200 Madison Ave., New York, NY 10016

Pinnacle Books, 1430 Broadway, New York, NY 10018

Plays, Inc., Eight Arlington St., Boston, MA 02116

Plume Books. Imprint of New American Library, 1633 Broadway, New York, NY 10019

Pocket Books. Division of Simon and Schuster, 1230 Avenue of the Americas, New York, NY 10020

Prentice-Hall. Orders to: P.O. Box 500, Englewood Cliffs, NJ 07632

G. P. Putnam's Sons. Distributed by the Putnam Publishing Group. Orders to: 200 Madison Ave., New York, NY 10016

Random House. Orders to: 400 Hahn Rd., Westminster, MD 21157

Random House Library of Knowledge. Orders to: 400 Hahn Rd., Westminster, MD 21157

Reader's Digest Association. Orders to: Customer Service, Pleasantville, NY 10570

Scarborough Books. Imprint of Stein and Day, Scarborough House, Briarcliff Manor, NY 10510

Scholastic. Orders to: P.O. Box 7502, 2931 E. McCarty St., Jefferson City, MO 65102

Scholastic Book Services. Division of Scholastic. Orders to: P.O. Box 7502, 2931 E. McCarty St., Jefferson City, MO 65102

Charles Scribner's Sons. Orders to: Front and Brown Sts., Riverside, NJ 08075

Sierra Club Books. Distributed by Random House Distribution Center, 400 Hahn Rd., Westminster, MD 21157

Signet Books. Imprint of New American Library. Orders to: 120 Woodbine St., Bergenfield, NJ 07621

Signet Classics. Imprint of New American Library. Orders to: 120 Woodbine St., Bergenfield, NJ 07621

Signet Modern Classics. Imprint of New American Library. Orders to: 120 Woodbine St., Bergenfield, NJ 07621

Signet Vista Books. Imprint of New American Library. Orders to: 120 Woodbine St., Bergenfield, NJ 07621

Skinny Books, Box A 94, New York, NY 10272

South-Western Publishing Co., 5101 Madison Rd., Cincinnati, OH 45227

St. Martin's Press, 175 Fifth Ave., New York, NY 10010

Sterling Publishing Co., Two Park Ave., New York, NY 10016

J. P. Tarcher. Distributed by Houghton Mifflin Co., Wayside Rd., Burlington, MA 01803

Tempo Books. Imprint of Berkley Publishing Group. Distributed by ICD, 250 W. 55th St., New York, NY 10019

Ten Speed Press, P.O. Box 7123, Berkeley, CA 94707

Ticknor and Fields. Distributed by Houghton Mifflin Co., Two Park St., Boston, MA 02108

Timescape Books. Imprint of Pocket Books, 1230 Avenue of the Americas, New York, NY 10020

Unicorn Books. Imprint of E. P. Dutton, Two Park Ave., New York, NY 10016

University of Oklahoma Press. Orders to: P.O. Box 1657, Hagerstown, MD 21741

Vanguard Press, 424 Madison Ave., New York, NY 10017

Viking Press. Orders to: Viking/Penguin, 299 Murray Hill Pkwy., East Rutherford, NJ 07073

Villard Books. Distributed by Random House, 201 E. 50th St., New York, NY 10022

Wadsworth Publishing Co., 10 Davis Dr., Belmont, CA 94002

Wallaby Books. Imprint of Pocket Books, 1230 Avenue of the Americas, New York, NY 10020

Warner Books, 666 Fifth Ave., New York, NY 10103

Washington Square Press, 1230 Avenue of the Americas, New York, NY 10020

West Publishing Co., 50 W. Kellogg Blvd., P.O. Box 43526, St. Paul, MN 55164

Westminster Press. Orders to: P.O. Box 718, William Penn Annex, Philadelphia, PA 19105

Wideview/Perigee Books. Imprint of the Putnam Publishing Group, 200 Madison Ave., New York, NY 10016

Author Index

Aaseng, Nate, 303
Aaseng, Nathan, 304, 305
Abbott, Edwin A., 252
Abbott, Shirley, 296, 331
Abrahams, Roger D., 205
Adams, Douglas, 179
Adler, C. S., 100, 189, 227
Adoff, Arnold, 213
Aiken, Joan, 145, 167, 271
Akers, Keith, 140
Aks, Patricia, 227
Alcott, Louisa May, 53
Aldrich, Bess Streeter, 145, 227
Alexander, Lloyd, 121
Alfano, Pete, 305
Alkema, Chester, J., 161
Allen, T. D., 21
Allman, William F., 316
Alsop, Joseph, 27
American Film Institute, 319
Ames, Mildred, 133
Anaya, Rudolfo A., 95, 133, 281
Andersen, Hans Christian, 205
Anderson, Dave, 90, 305
Anderson, Jessica, 331
Anderson, Madelyn Klein, 240
Anderson, Mary, 71, 281
Anderson, Scott, 43
Angell, Judie, 100, 179
Angell, Roger, 305
Angelou, Maya, 95, 213
Appel, Willa, 225
Arnold, Caroline, 140
Arnold, Peter, 140
Arnosky, Jim, 24
Arrick, Fran, 100, 173, 225, 281
Asbjørnsen, Peter Christen, 205
Ashabranner, Brent, 173
Ashe, Arthur, 27
Asher, Sandy, 65, 95, 100, 173, 268, 282
Asheri, Michael, 225
Asimov, Isaac, 121, 240, 252, 253, 254, 271, 272, 273
Audubon Society, 240
Augsburger, David, 182

Austen, Jane, 53
Axthelm, Pete, 306

Babbie, Earl, 60
Bach, Alice, 65, 133
Baker, Russell, 27
Baldwin, Neil, 27
Barasch, Marc, 328
Barrett, William E., 182
Bartholomew, Barbara, 101
Barzini, Luigi, 153
Bauer, Marion Dane, 133
Bavier, Robert N., Jr., 221
Bayrd, Ned, 140
Beagle, Peter S., 121
Bear, John, 83
Beattie, Ann, 273
Beckman, Delores, 228, 282
Bell, Clare, 122
Bellow, Saul, 53
Benchley, Peter, 1
Bennett, Hal Z., 223
Bennett, Jack, 1
Bennett, Jay, 189, 228
Bentley, Toni, 185
Berger, Fredericka, 101
Berger, Phil, 60
Berggren, Paula S., 334
Bergon, Frank, 326
Berry, Liz, 228
Bernstein, Carl, 217
Bethancourt, T. Ernesto, 122, 185, 189
Biebel, David B., 65
Bierhorst, John, 95, 205, 213
Binchy, Maeve, 1
Birnbach, Lisa, 83
Bishop, Elizabeth, 213
Bloch, Robert, 167
Blume, Judy, 65, 268
Blumenthal, Shirley, 153
Bober, Natalie S., 28
Bodecker, N. M., 213
Bograd, Larry, 190
Boissard, Janine, 101
Bolles, Richard N., 43

Bond, Nancy, 66
Bonham, Frank, 190, 228
Bontemps, Arna, 208
Booher, Dianna Daniels, 83
Bornstein, Jerry, 240
Bornstein, Sandy, 240
Bosse, Malcom J., 1
Boswell, Thomas, 306
Bradford, Richard, 282
Bradley, Marion Zimmer, 122, 123, 273, 274, 331
Bradshaw, Gillian, 123
Brancato, Robin F., 66, 282
Brand, Max, 326
Branfield, John, 66
Branley, Franklyn M., 299
Braymer, Marjorie, 21, 206
Brenner, Barbara, 12
Brenner, Martha, 241
Breslin, Jimmy, 306
Bridges, Sue Ellen, 101
Briggs, Carole S., 221
Brontë, Charlotte, 53
Brontë, Emily, 54
Brown, Dee, 145
Brown, John A., 157
Brown, John Russell, 71
Brown, Michael H., 241
Bruce, Preston, 28, 153
Brunn, Robert, 167
Brunner, John, 255
Brunvand, Jan Harold, 206
Bruun, Bertel, 241
Bruun, Ruth Dowling, 241
Buchwald, Art, 90, 179
Bunn, Scott, 101, 228
Bunting, Eve, 2, 255
Burchard, Peter, 102
Burness, Tad, 51
Burton, Philip, 12
Busnar, Gene, 185
Busoni, Rafaello, 28
Butterfield, John, 221
Byrd, Elizabeth, 102, 229
Byrne, James, 43
Byrne, Josefa Heifetz, 83

Caesar, Sid, 28
Calder, Nigel, 90
Califano, Joseph A., Jr., 75
Callan, Jamie, 282
Calvert, Patricia, 2, 12, 66, 102
Calvino, Italo, 206
Capote, Truman, 29
Capra, Fritjof, 217
Carlson, Dale, 78, 84, 255

Carr, Nicole, 229
Carr, Philippa, 229
Carroll, James, 190
Carter, Alden R., 102
Carter, Forrest, 145
Carter, Lin, 123
Cassell, Dana K., 60
Catalyst Editors, 43
Cavallaro, Ann, 134
Cavanna, Betty, 13, 102, 190
Cebulash, Mel, 306
Chambers, Kate, 191
Chancellor, John, 43
Chapman, Clark R., 299
Cherryh, C. J., 124, 255
Chester, William L., 2
Childress, Alice, 103
Ching, Lucy, 29, 182
Christopher, John, 255
Clarke, Arthur C., 256
Clavell, James, 146
Claypool, Jane, 229
Cleaver, Bill, 2, 103
Cleaver, Vera, 2, 103
Clemens, Virginia Phelps, 44, 319
Clements, Bruce, 3, 283
Cody, Liza, 191
Cohen, Barbara, 103
Cohen, Daniel, 78, 167, 206, 319
Cohen, Jamey, 191
Coker, Carolyn, 191
Collins, Wilkie, 54, 192
Colman, Hila, 103, 229, 283
Cone, Molly, 78
Conford, Ellen, 3, 283
Conner, Patrick, 24
Consumer Guide Editors, 60
Cook, Don, 29
Cook, T. S., 109
Coolidge, Grace, 296
Coombs, Charles, 51, 221, 222
Cooney, Caroline B., 230
Cooper, Henry S. F., Jr., 299
Cooper, James Fenimore, 54
Corbett, W. J., 13
Corcoran, Barbara, 174, 283
Cormier, Robert, 66, 274
Correy, Lee, 256
Corsaro, Maria, 268
Crane, Stephen, 55
Craven, Linda, 103
Crichton, Michael, 61
Crispin, A. C., 256
Croall, Stephen, 241
Cross, Amanda, 192
Cross, Gillian, 192

Crutcher, Chris, 284, 307
Culin, Charlotte, 75, 104
Cumming, Robert, 24
Cunningham, Ann Marie, 322
Curnow, Ray, 61
Curran, Susan, 61
Curry, Jane Louise, 124
Curtis, Patricia, 13, 44

Dana, Richard Henry, Jr., 55
Dank, Gloria Rand, 124
Danziger, Paula, 104, 284
Darwin, Charles, 55, 242
Davidson, Robyn, 3
Davis, Burke, 154
Davis, Daniel S., 154
Davis, Ossie, 71
Davis, Terry, 284, 307
Dawidowicz, Lucy S., 154
de France, Marie, 207
de Mille, Agnes, 30
De Santo, Charles P., 183, 225
Dean, Anabel, 307
Debo, Angie, 29
Defoe, Daniel, 55
Deford, Frank, 182
Degens, T., 164
Deighton, Len, 192
del Rey, Lester, 256
Dempsey, Michael W., 242
Denyer, Ralph, 185
Devereux, Stephen E., 143
Diagram Group, 141, 242
Dick, Philip K., 256
Dickens, Charles, 55, 56
D'Ignazio, Fred, 61
Dock, V. Thomas, 61
Dodson, Susan, 192
Doig, Ivan, 3
Dolan, Edward F., Jr., 217, 296
Dominguez, Richard H., 141
Douglas, Martha C., 44
Downs, Robert B., 90, 154
Doyle, Sir Arthur Conan, 56, 193, 274
Dragonwagon, Crescent, 120
Drucker, Malka, 319
Duane, Diane, 257
Due, Linnea, A., 75, 307
Duffy, Kevin, 21
Duncan, David James, 210
Duncan, Lois, 3
Duprey, Richard, 257
Durrell, Gerald, 210, 242
Dvorkin, David, 257
Dygard, Thomas J., 308

Easwaran, Eknath, 30
Eberhart, Mignon G., 193
Ecker, B. A., 268
Elfman, Blossom, 104, 230, 284
Ende, Michael, 124
Engel, Beth Bland, 174
Erdoes, Richard, 207, 326
Esquire Press, 30
Evslin, Bernard, 207
Ewers, John C., 22, 155
Eyerly, Jeannette, 104, 230

Faber, Doris, 30
Farber, Norma, 146
Farmer, Philip José, 257
Feiffer, Jules, 179, 218
Ferman, Edward L., 258
Ferris, Jean, 230
Ferris, Timothy, 299
Ferry, Charles, 322
Fields, Mike, 84
Finney, Shan, 296
First, Julia, 105
Fitzgibbon, Dan, 84
Fitzpatrick, Mariana, 322
Fixx, James F., 84, 85, 161
Fleming, Alice, 85
Fleming, G. H., 308
Fletcher, Colin, 210
Foley, June, 231
Ford, Barbara, 22, 155
Ford, Daniel F., 242
Foreman, Paul, 146, 327
Forrest, Anthony, 146
Fortune, J. J., 4, 79
Fossey, Dian, 14
Foster, Alan Dean, 125
Fox, Paula, 105
Francis, Dick, 193
Francis, Dorothy B., 296
Franklin, Miles, 331
Freedman, Russell, 14, 243
Freilich, Morris, 22, 91
French, Michael, 4, 231, 308
Fretz, Sada, 141
Friends of Darkover, The, 123, 274
Froman, Katherine, 44, 134, 183
Frost, Robert, 214
Fugard, Athol, 71, 174
Fuller, Elizabeth, 4

Gadd, Laurence D., 243
Gadney, Reg, 30
Gaeddert, LouAnn, 225
Gaines, Ernest J., 96

Gajda, Robert S., 141
Gallant, Roy A., 300
Gallo, Donald R., 274
Gard, Wayne, 155, 327
Gardam, Jane, 275
Garden, Nancy, 4, 207, 269
Gardner, John, 85, 194
Gardner, Robert, 14, 243
Garver, Susan, 96, 218
Gauch, Patricia Lee, 5
Gedge, Pauline, 125
Geiogamah, Hanay, 72
George, Jean Craighead, 5
Geras, Adèle, 147
Gerber, Merrill Joan, 105
Giff, Patricia Reilly, 79, 194
Gilbert, Harry M., 61
Gilbert, Martin, 31
Gilbert, Sara, 85
Gilbert, Sara D., 105
Gill, Derek, 40
Gillers, Stephen, 45
Gillespie, Oscar, 141
Gillespie, Paul F., 226
Giovanni, Nikki, 96, 214
Girion, Barbara, 66, 134, 231, 275
Gittelman, Philip, 46
Glenn, Mel, 214
Gold, Robert S., 275
Golden, Frederic, 243
Goldman, William, 126
Goldreich, Gloria, 226
Goldstein, Larry Joel, 62
Goldstein, Lisa, 126
Goldstein, Martin, 62
Goldstein, Patti, 16, 47
Goldstein, Sue, 86
Goldstein, Thomas, 244
Goodall, Jane, 14
Goodchild, Peter, 31
Goode, Stephen, 297
Gordon, John, 126
Gordon, Karen Elizabeth, 86
Gordon, Suzanne, 45, 186
Gordon-Watson, Mary, 222, 308
Gosner, Kenneth L., 244
Goudge, Eileen, 231
Goulart, Ron, 194, 275
Gowlett, John, 22
Grace, Fran, 284
Graham, Lawrence, 86
Grant, Cynthia D., 285
Graves, Robert, 207
Greenberg, Jan, 68, 285
Greenberg, Jan W., 72, 134

Greenberg, Martin H., 121, 240, 253, 254, 271, 272, 273
Greenberg, Martin Harry, 263, 278
Greene, Bette, 186, 285
Greene, Bob, 91
Greenwald, Sheila, 232, 285
Griesbach, Ellen Norma, 251
Griffiths, Helen, 14
Grinnell, George Bird, 208
Grizzard, Lewis, 91, 179
Ground Zero, 322
Guernsey, JoAnn Bren, 286
Guest, Judith, 105
Gunn, James, 258, 275
Gunning, Thomas G., 79
Guthrie, A. B., Jr., 147
Guthrie, Woody, 31
Guy, David, 309
Guy, Rosa, 194

Haas, Jessie, 15
Haines, Gail Kay, 244
Haldeman, Joe, 258, 276
Hall, Lynn, 106
Hallman, Ruth, 134
Hallstead, William F., 45
Hamill, Dorothy, 31
Hamilton, Virginia, 5, 106
Hammer, Charles, 5
Hanby, Jeannette, 15
Hansen, Joyce, 96, 286
Hansen, Skylar, 15
Haralson, Carol, 25
Hardy, Thomas, 56
Hargrove, Jim, 222
Harragan, Betty Lehan, 46, 332
Harrington, S. W., 86
Harris, Geraldine, 126, 127
Harris, Marilyn, 96, 174, 286
Hart, John, 210
Hartman, Evert, 322
Haruf, Kent, 327
Haskins, James, 32, 97, 174, 186, 309
Hautzig, Deborah, 134
Hawes, Gene R., 46
Hay, Henry, 161
Haycox, Ernest, 327
Hayes, Billy, 5
Healey, Larry, 6
Heaven, Constance, 147, 232
Heidenstam, Oscar, 141
Heidish, Marcy, 147
Heinlein, Robert A., 258, 259
Helprin, Mark, 127
Hendrich, Paula, 244

Henry, Fran Worden, 46
Hentoff, Nat, 175, 186
Herbert, Frank, 62
Herbert, Kathleen, 147
Herbert, Marie, 6
Herbst, Judith, 300
Herrin, Lamar, 309
Herskowitz, Mickey, 318
Heyerdahl, Thor, 6
Heyman, Anita, 106
Hickler, Holly, 34, 67
Hijuelos, Oscar, 97
Hill, Douglas, 127, 259
Hill, Rebecca, 106, 332
Hindle, Lee J., 127
Hirshon, Sheryl L., 86, 297
Hitchcock, Alfred, 194, 195, 276
Hitching, Francis, 244
Hoban, Russell, 127
Hodgell, P. C., 127
Hodges, Margaret, 148
Hoffman, Jeffrey, 51
Hogan, Ray, 328
Hoke, Helen, 168, 276
Holiday, Billie, 32
Hollander, Phyllis, 32, 309, 310
Hollander, Zander, 32, 309, 310
Holmes, Marjorie, 232
Honig, Donald, 310
Honigmann, David, 221
Hoover, H. M., 260
Hopkins, Jerry, 33
Hopper, Nancy J., 232
Hough, Richard, 322
Houston, James, 6
Houston, Jean, 87
Howe, Fanny, 107, 232
Howe, Imogen, 168
Huddy, Delia, 260
Hughes, Langston, 208
Hughes, Monica, 6, 67, 260
Hughey, Roberta, 107
Hugo, Victor, 56
Hull, Eleanor, 135
Hurmence, Belinda, 148, 175
Hyde, Lawrence E., 245
Hyde, Margaret O., 245

Irwin, Hadley, 107
Irwin, Walter, 260

Jackson, Reggie, 33, 311
Jackson, Shirley, 195
Jackson, Steve, 260
Jacobs, Anita, 286

Jaffe, Rona, 195
James, Elizabeth, 319
James, Henry, 57
James, P. D., 195, 196
Janeczko, Paul B., 214
Jastrow, Robert, 245, 300
Jenkinson, Denis, 51
Jeppson, J. O., 254
Johnson, Earvin "Magic," 33, 311
Johnson, S. A., 222
Johnston, Norma, 208, 233, 320
Johnston, Velda, 196
Jones, Diana Wynne, 168
Jones, Douglas C., 148, 328
Jordan, Lee, 168
Josephs, Rebecca, 135
Josephy, Alvin M., Jr., 155
Judy, Stephen, 72
Judy, Susan, 72

Kael, Pauline, 91, 320
Kamerman, Sylvia E., 72, 261
Kaplan, Janice, 233
Karl, Jean E., 261
Karmel-Wolfe, Henia, 164
Kata, Elizabeth, 135
Kaufman, Barry Neil, 183
Kelley, Leo P., 79, 169, 261
Kellogg, Marjorie, 135, 286
Keneally, Thomas, 164
Kennedy, William, 7
Kent, Alexander, 148
Kerr, M. E., 33, 107, 135, 226, 287
Kidd, Ronald, 107
Kiefer, Irene, 245
Kiesel, Stanley, 180
King, Stephen, 52, 169, 277
Kingstone, Brett, 46
Kinsella, W. P., 311
Klagsbrun, Francine, 67
Klass, Sheila Solomon, 108
Klein, Norma, 108, 269
Knight, David C., 62
Knudsen, James, 233
Knudson, R. R., 80, 311, 312
Koebner, Linda, 15, 245
Kohl, Herbert, 16
Kohl, Judith, 16
Koontz, Dean R., 169
Korn, Ellen, 162
Korzeniowsky, Carole, 268
Kotzwinkle, William, 7
Krasnoff, Barbara, 63
Krefetz, Gerald, 46
Krementz, Jill, 108

Kresh, Paul, 33
Kritsick, Stephen, 16, 47

L'Amour, Louis, 328
LaBastille, Anne, 47, 211, 332
Lampton, Christopher, 246
Landau, Elaine, 142
Landis, J. D., 109
Larky, Arthur I., 61
Laski, Harold J., 218
Laurance, Alice, 254, 273
Lawrence, R. D., 16
Lawson, Don, 323
Leavitt, Caroline, 109
LeBaron, John, 320
Lee, Harper, 57, 175
Lee, Joanna, 109
Lee, Mildred, 233
Lee, Tanith, 128
Leekley, John, 149, 323
L'Engle, Madeleine, 196, 234
Leokum, Arkady, 87
Leon, George de Lucenay, 246
Leonard, Constance, 197
Lerner, Elaine, 47
Leslie, Robert Franklin, 16
Lester, Julius, 97, 277
Leuthner, Stuart, 156
Levenkron, Steven, 136, 142
Levin, Richard, 33, 311
Levitin, Sonia, 234
Levoy, Myron, 287
Levy, Elizabeth, 197, 234
Levy, Marilyn, 136
Lewis, Norman, 87
Lieberman, Nancy, 312
Lien, David A., 63
Lightner, A. M., 261
Likhanov, Albert, 136, 234
Lindsey, Robert, 34, 197
Lingard, Joan, 109
Lipsyte, Robert, 287, 312
Liss, Howard, 312, 313
List, Julie Autumn, 109
Livingston, Myra Cohn, 170, 215
Livingstone, Ian, 222
Llewellyn, Edward, 261, 262
Llywelyn, Morgan, 149
Lockhart, Robin Bruce, 34, 197
Lofts, Norah, 149
London, Jack, 57
Love, G. B., 260
Ludlum, David M., 246
Luger, Harriett, 110
Lyall, Gavin, 198

Lyle, Katie Letcher, 235
Lyttle, Richard B., 156, 313

Macaulay, David, 25
MacAvoy, R. A., 128
MacCracken, Mary, 136
Mace, Nancy L., 142
Mack, John E., 34, 67
MacKellar, William, 198
MacLeod, Charlotte, 110, 198
Madden, John, 34, 313
Magill, Kathleen, 7, 332
Magubane, Peter, 175
Major, Kevin, 75, 110, 269, 287
Malamud, Bernard, 128
Maltin, Leonard, 320
Manes, Stephen, 67
Marino, John, 223
Marrin, Albert, 323
Marriott, Alice, 22
Marshall, Evan, 87
Marston, Elsa, 198
Martin, Russell, 328
Martin, Toni, 47
Marzollo, Jean, 176
Math, Irwin, 63
Matthee, Dalene, 7
Matthews, Greg, 7
Maurer, Alan, 246
Maxwell, Ann, 129
Maxwell, William, 110
May, Julian, 262
May, Lawrence, 223
Mayhar, Ardath, 129
Mays, Lucinda, 110, 176
Mazer, Harry, 8, 269, 323
Mazer, Norma Fox, 111, 235, 269, 270,
  277
McAleer, Neil, 300
McCallum, Andrew, 73
McClanahan, Ed, 288
McCombs, Don, 323
McCoy, J. J., 16
McCoy, Kathy, 142
McCullough, David Willis, 198
McCunn, Ruthanne Lum, 149
McDonald, Gregory, 199
McDonnell, Margot B., 288
McGinniss, Joe, 211
McGregor, Rob Roy, 143
McGuire, Paula, 96, 218, 270
McHargue, Georgess, 80, 170
McKee, Alexander, 324
McKinley, Robin, 129, 332
McNamara, John, 288

McPhee, John, 247
McTaggart, Lynne, 35
Mears, Walter R., 43
Mebane, Mary E., 35
Mellow, James R., 35
Meluch, R. M., 262
Merriam, Eve, 215
Meyer, Carolyn, 288
Meyer, Gladys C., 313
Michael, Jeannine Masterson, 144
Michener, James A., 150
Miklowitz, Gloria, 226
Miklowitz, Gloria D., 67, 111, 112, 235
Miller, Arthur R., 218
Miller, Frances A., 288
Miller, Jason, 73
Miller, Jonathan, 36, 247
Miller, Peter M., 143
Miller, Philip, 320
Milne, Lorus, 17, 247
Milne, Lorus J., 247
Milne, Margery, 17, 247
Mims, Forrest M., III, 60
Miner, Jane Claypool, 76
Minton, Lynn, 320
Mitchell, Joyce Slayton, 48
Moché, Dinah L., 301
Moe, Jørgen, 205
Moeri, Louise, 112
Molloy, John T., 87
Moon, William Least Heat (William Trog-
    don), 211
Moore, Kenny, 314
Moore, Ruth Nulton, 150
Morpurgo, Michael, 17
Morrison, Joan, 297
Morrison, Toni, 97, 289, 333
Mowat, Farley, 8, 17
Mulford, Philippa Greene, 270
Muller, Peter, 48, 63
Mulligan, Kevin, 112
Munro, Alice, 270, 333
Murphy, Barbara Beasley, 235, 289
Murphy, Jim, 52, 199, 314
Murray, John, 73
Myers, Arthur, 143
Myers, Irma, 143
Myers, Walter Dean, 8, 112, 199, 314

Naisbitt, John, 297
Nash, Jay Robert, 199, 200
Navratilova, Martina, 315
Naylor, Phyllis Reynolds, 112
Neff, Pauline, 76
Neimark, Anne E., 36
Nemiroff, Robert, 73

Neufeld, John, 136, 176
Newton, Suzanne, 113, 186
Nicholls, Peter, 247, 321
Nilsson, Lennart, 248
Nixon, Joan Lowery, 80, 200
Nixon, Richard, 36, 218
Nolan, Paul T., 73, 208
Nolane, Richard D., 262, 277
Norby, Lisa, 235
Norton, Andre, 129
Norton, Peter, 63
Norwick, Kenneth P., 176

Oates, Stephen B., 36, 150
Oberg, James Edward, 301
Oberski, Jona, 164
Okimoto, Jean Davies, 200
O'Leary, Brian, 257
Olesky, Walter, 23, 301
Olney, Patricia J., 219
Olney, Ross R., 52, 219
O'Neal, Regina, 74
Oneal, Zibby, 68, 136
Oppenheimer, Joan, 289
Orczy, Baroness, 57
Orgel, Doris, 113
Ortiz, Alfonso, 207, 326
Orwell, George, 57
Osborn, John Jay, Jr., 219
Osborne, Mary Pope, 113, 236
Otfinoski, Steven, 80
Ozer, Jerome S., 153

Page, Tim, 324
Palmer, David R., 262
Parker, Philip, 221
Parmet, Herbert S., 37
Paterson, Katherine, 150
Patient Care Publications, 17
Paulsen, Gary, 8
Peavy, Linda, 37, 333
Peck, Richard, 68, 200, 236, 289
Pelletier, Louis, 117, 139, 293
Penman, Sharon Kay, 151
Perlberg, Deborah, 290
Perrin, Linda, 156
Perry, Dave, 223, 315
Perske, Robert, 137
Petersen, P. J., 9, 180, 290
Peterson, Lee Allen, 211, 248
Pevsner, Stella, 113, 236, 291
Pfeffer, Susan Beth, 68, 113, 176, 291
Phillips, Carolyn E., 183
Phipson, Joan, 170
Piercy, Marge, 215
Pinkwater, Daniel, 180, 263

Pinkwater, Jill, 17
Pizer, Vernon, 92
Platt, Kin, 81, 137
Plimpton, George, 315
Plotz, Helen, 25, 215
Poe, Edgar Allan, 58, 170, 277
Pohl, Frederik, 263
Polikoff, Judy, 137, 183
Porter, Jane, 58, 208
Porter, Kent, 64
Powell, Padgett, 114, 291
Powers, John R., 181
Powers, Thomas, 92
Powledge, Fred, 114
Prabhu, Barbara Williams, 17
Prager, Arthur, 81, 324
Prager, Emily, 81, 324
Pringle, Laurence, 248
Prinz, Lucie, 160
Prugh, Jeff, 37, 315
Purcell, John, 248

Quilter, Chris, 140

Rabins, Peter V., 142
Rabkin, Jacob, 18
Rabkin, Richard, 18
Radley, Gail, 114, 137
Ransom, Candice F., 236
Rashke, Richard, 165
Rau, Margaret, 297
Reader's Digest Editors, 23, 226
Ready, Kirk L., 52
Reed, Kit, 114
Restak, Richard M., 249
Reuben, Liz, 81
Rhue, Morton, 165, 177
Riland, George, 171
Riley, Jocelyn, 114, 137
Rinaldi, Ann, 68
Rips, Gladys Nadler, 157
Ritchie, David, 249, 301, 324
Robbins, Albert, 157
Roberts, David, 9
Roberts, Rachel Sherwood, 9
Robinson, Frank M., 10
Robinson, Phyllis C., 37
Robinson, Richard, 321
Robson, Bonnie, 115
Rodriguez, Richard, 38, 92
Roessler, Carl, 162
Rofes, Eric E., 115
Rogers, Betty, 38
Rollin, Betty, 38
Rooney, Andrew A., 92, 181
Roosevelt, Elliott, 39

Rosa, Joseph G., 39, 209, 329
Rosen, Winifred, 77
Rosenbaum, Alvin, 88
Rosenberg, Joel, 130
Rosenblatt, Roger, 324
Roth, Arthur, 9, 76, 115
Roth, Geneen, 143
Rothchild, Sylvia, 165
Rowland-Entwistle, Theodore, 18
Roy, Ron, 81, 200
Royko, Mike, 92
Rubins, Harriett, 18
Ruby, Lois, 97, 278
Ruby, Robert H., 157
Ryan, Jeanette Mines, 76
Rydjord, John, 88

Sachs, Marilyn, 81, 138, 291
Sagan, Carl, 302
Saha, Arthur W., 130, 278
Salassi, Otto R., 10, 316
Salisbury, Harrison E., 157
Sallis, Susan, 138
Sams, Ferrol, 115
Samuels, Gertrude, 115, 177
Samuels, Harold, 39
Samuels, Peggy, 39
Santiago, Danny, 98, 291
Saperstein, Alan, 10
Sattler, Helen Roney, 18, 249
Saunders, Rubie, 48
Savitz, Harriet May, 138, 237, 292
Saxton, Mark, 130
Schaap, Dick, 39, 316
Schneider, Meg, 88, 237
Schreiber, Flora Rheta, 40
Schrier, Eric W., 316
Scoppettone, Sandra, 237, 292
Scortia, Thomas N., 10
Sculatti, Gene, 298
Sebestyen, Ouida, 116
Seide, Diane, 49
Seidler, Tor, 292
Selden, Bernice, 158, 333
Settle, Mary Lee, 249
Seuling, Barbara, 49
Shaffer, Peter, 74
Shakespeare, William, 58, 74
Shanahan, William F., 49
Shane, June Grant, 64
Shanks, Ann Zane, 93
Shapiro, James E., 93, 223
Sharmat, Marjorie, 237, 238, 292
Shaw, Bob, 263
Shaw, Richard, 116
Shea, Michael, 130

Sheldon, Sidney, 201
Shelley, Mary, 58, 171
Shepard, Jim, 116
Sheridan, Jeff, 162
Shipler, David K., 298
Shippey, T. A., 130
Shirley, Glenn, 40, 329
Shook, Robert L., 49
Shreve, Susan, 116
Shwartz, Susan, 263, 278
Siegal, Aranka, 40, 165
Silsbee, Peter, 116, 138
Silverberg, Robert, 263, 278
Silverstein, Alvin, 249
Silverstein, Virginia B., 249
Simak, Clifford D., 264
Simon, Seymour, 82
Simpson, George Gaylord, 250
Siner, Howard, 93, 316
Singer, Isaac Bashevis, 278
Sleator, William, 201
Slepian, Jan, 293
Smith, David, 219
Smith, Lee, 139
Smith, Ray, 162
Smith, Red, 93, 317
Smith, Robert Kimmel, 68, 117
Smith, Roger, 317
Smith, Steven Phillip, 77
Smith, Ursula, 37, 333
Smith, William Jay, 215
Snodgrass, Melinda, 264
Snyder, Anne, 77, 117, 139, 293
Snyder, Zilpha Keatley, 117
Solomon, Barbara H., 334
Solomon, Diane S., 317
Southhall, Ivan, 10
Spark, Muriel, 59
Sperling, Dan, 317
Spretnak, Charlene, 217
Springstubb, Tricia, 238
Squire, Susan, 143
St. George, Judith, 201
Stabile, Toni, 144
Stambler, Irwin, 52
Stanek, Lou Willett, 293
Stedman, Raymond William, 177
Stefansson, Evelyn, 158
Steinem, Gloria, 93, 334
Stephensen, A. M., 270
Sterling Editors, 18
Sternberg, Patricia, 88
Stevenson, Robert Louis, 58, 59, 171
Stewart, Elinore Pruitt, 329
Stewart, Marjabelle Young, 88
Stine, G. Harry, 162

Stoker, Bram, 58, 171
Stolzenberg, Mark, 74, 163
Stone, Irving, 151
Strasser, Todd, 68, 187, 293, 317
Stretton, Barbara, 69, 294, 318
Strickland, Rennard, 25
Stucky, Solomon, 98, 177
Sucharitkul, Somtow, 130
Sugerman, Danny, 33
Sullivan, George, 158, 250, 318
Sullivan, Mary Ann, 10, 325
Sullivan, Mary W., 264
Sullivan, Tom, 40
Sunshine, Tina, 238
Sutcliff, Rosemary, 151
Sweeney, Joyce, 117
Switzer, David C., 22, 155
Switzer, Ellen, 49, 187

Tamar, Erika, 117
Tateishi, John, 158
Taylor, Jerry Duncan, 251
Taylor, Louise Todd, 251
Taylor, Theodore, 325
Tchudi, Stephen, 294
Tenny, Dixie, 171, 201
Terhune, Albert Payson, 18
Terkel, Studs, 298
Terris, Susan, 117, 139
Terry, Wallace, 98, 325
Thomas, Joyce Carol, 98, 118
Thomas, Lewis, 41, 94, 250
Thompson, Hunter S., 94, 219
Thompson, Ida, 250
Thompson, Julian F., 11, 118
Thoreau, Henry David, 59, 94
Thum, Gladys, 212
Thum, Marcella, 212
Tolkien, J. R. R., 131
Towne, Mary, 171
Townsend, Peter, 11
Trebor, Robert, 264
Tregaskis, Richard, 82, 325
True, Dan, 19
Truman, Margaret, 201, 202
Turner, Ann, 11, 151
Tuska, Jon, 279, 329
Twelveponies, Mary, 19, 223
Tyler, Anne, 118, 187, 294

Uecker, Bob, 318
Ullyot, Joan L., 89, 144
Underhill, Ruth M., 159

Valens, E. G., 139
Van Dyk, Jere, 159

Van Vogt, A. E., 265
Van Wormer, Joe, 163
Varner, Jeannette Johnson, 19
Varner, John Grier, 19
Vedral, Joyce L., 89
Ventura, Piero, 25
Vine, Louis L., 19, 20
Vinge, Joan D., 264, 265, 279
Voigt, Cynthia, 69, 118, 119, 318
Vosper, Alice, 151

Wade, Edwin, 25
Wagner, Karl Edward, 172, 279
Waldron, Ann, 26
Walker, Alice, 98, 334
Walker, Irma, 265
Wallace, Terry, 159
Wallach, Janet, 89
Wallin, Luke, 99, 152
Walter, Mildred Pitts, 177
Warner, William W., 212
Wartski, Maureen Crane, 99, 294
Waterfield, Giles, 26
Watson, James, 11
Waugh, Charles G., 121, 253, 254, 263, 272, 273, 278
Wayne, Kyra Petrovskaya, 20
Webb, Sharon, 265, 266
Webster, Joanne, 172
Weil, Andrew, 77
Weinberg, Larry, 82, 202
Weisman, John, 202
Weiss, Malcolm E., 302
Weitzman, David, 26
Wells, Rosemary, 202
West, Beverly Henderson, 251
Westall, Robert, 172, 280
Wheaton, Philip D., 238
Wheeler, Robert W., 41
White, Ellen Emerson, 202, 220
White, Rick, 224

White, Theodore H., 159, 220
Whitney, Phyllis A., 203
Whitt, Anne Hall, 119
Wibbelsman, Charles, 142
Wideman, John Edgar, 41
Wiener, Jon, 41
Wilder, Cherry, 131
Wilkins, Roy, 42, 178
Williamson, Amy, 238
Wilroy, Mary Edith, 160
Wisler, G. Clifton, 152
Witt, Reni L., 144
Wolfe, Gene, 131
Wolitzer, Hilma, 119
Wolkoff, Judie, 289
Wollheim, Donald A., 266, 280
Wonger, B., 99
Wood, Gerald L., 20
Woodward, Bob, 217
Woolrich, Cornell, 203
World Almanac Editors, 243, 251
Worth, Fred L., 323
Wright, Betty Ren, 172, 203
Wright, L. R., 69, 120
Wulforst, Harry, 64, 160
Wylie, Philip, 267

Yahn, Linda C., 158
Yep, Laurence, 203, 204
Yolen, Jane, 70, 131, 132, 204
York, Carol Beach, 239
Young, Herbert V., 11, 330
Young, John Richard, 20
Young, Louise B., 94, 251

Zabusky, Charlotte Fox, 297
Zalben, Jane Breskin, 239
Zebrowski, George, 240, 254
Zenoff, Victoria B., 43
Zindel, Paul, 120, 239, 295
Zyskind, Sara, 166

Title Index

About David, 68
Ace Hits the Big Time, 289
Adventures of the Speckled Band, The, and Other Stories of Sherlock Holmes, 56, 193, 274
African Folktales: Traditional Tales of the Black World, 205
Aground, 197
Alcohol and Teens, 76
Alder Gulch and *A Rider of the High Mesa*, 327
Alex: The Life of a Child, 182
Alfred Hitchcock's Daring Detectives, 194, 276
Alfred Hitchcock's Sinister Spies, 195, 276
Alice with Golden Hair, 135
Alien Citadel, 258
Alien Gold, 79, 261
Alive and Starting Over, 108
All about Your Money, 84
All the Colors of the Race, 213
All the President's Men, 217
Am I Getting Paid for This?, 38
Amanda, 236
Amateur Magician's Handbook, The, 161
Amateur Naturalist, The, 210, 242
Amazing Escapes, 79
Amen, Moses Gardenia, 230
America in Search of Itself: The Making of the President, 1956–1980, 159, 220
American Beat, 91
American Indian Myths and Legends, 207, 326
American League, The: An Illustrated History, 310
American Mosaic: The Immigrant Experience in the Words of Those Who Lived It, 297
American Weather Book, The, 246
American West in Fiction, The, 279, 329
Anackire, 128
And Also Teach Them to Read, 86, 297
And Both Were Young, 234
And Justice for All: An Oral History of the Japanese American Detention Camps, 158

And More by Andy Rooney, 92, 181
And Nobody Knew They Were There, 10
. . . And Still in the Running: A Horse Called Port Conway Lane, 17
And Then the Harvest: Three Television Plays, 74
Angry Mountain, 6
Animal Partners: Training Animals to Help People, 13, 44
Animal Shelter, The, 13
Anne and Jay, 101
Annie on My Mind, 269
Another Man's Murder, 193
Ape inside Me, The, 81, 137
Apple Logo for Teachers, 60
Aren't You the One Who . . . ?, 288
Art of Fiction, The: Notes on Craft for Young Writers, 85
As in a Vision: Masterworks of American Indian Art, 25
Ascent to Civilization: The Archaeology of Early Man, 22
Assignment: Sports, 312
Astronomy Today, 301
Atlantis: The Biography of a Legend, 21, 206
Atlas of the Bible: An Illustrated Guide to the Holy Land, 23, 226
Attack from Atlantis, 256
Audubon Society Field Guide to North American Fishes, Whales, and Dolphins, The, 240
Audubon Society Field Guide to North American Fossils, The, 250
Auto Album, The, 51
Avenger, The, 148

Baby-Sitting for Fun and Profit, 48
Bad Apple, 190
Bad Company, 191
Ballad of T. Rantula, The, 114
Barracuda Gang, The, 1
Baseball: You Are the Manager, 303
Baseball's All-Time All-Stars, 314
Baseball's Hottest Hitters, 304
Basketball: You are the Coach, 303

Basketball My Way, 312
Basketball's Sharpshooters, 304
Battle in the English Channel, 325
Be a Winner in Windsurfing, 221
Beach Towels, 81, 291
Beggar Queen, The, 121
Beginners' Love, 269
Beginning Quick Job-Hunting Map, The:
   A Fast Way to Help, 43
Behind Barbed Wire: The Imprisonment
   of Japanese Americans during World
   War II, 154
Behind the Filmmaking Scene, 44, 319
Bell Tree, The, 260
Belle Starr and Her Times: The
   Literature, the Facts, and the Legends,
   40, 329
Berlin Game, 192
Best Efforts: World Class Runners and
   Races, 314
Best from Fantasy and Science Fiction,
   The, 24th Series, 258
Best Is Yet to Be, The, 238
Best Little Girl in the World, The, 136
Best of *Trek* No. 6, The: From the
   Magazine for *Star Trek* Fans, 260
Best Wishes, Joe Brady, 236
Better Cross-Country Running for Boys
   and Girls, 318
Big Way Out, The, 116, 138
Big Words, 174
Birds of Summer, 117
Bits and Pieces: Understanding and
   Building Computing Devices, 63
Black Alibi, 203
Black Child, 175
Black Diamonds: A Search for Arctic
   Treasure, 6
Black Feeling, Black Talk, 96, 214
Black Mountain Breakdown, 139
Black Tower, The, 195
Blackfeet, The: Raiders on the
   Northwestern Plains, 22, 155
Blimp, 134
Blissful Joy and the SATs: A Multiple-
   Choice Romance, 232
Bloodletters and Bad Men, Book 1:
   Captain Lightfoot to Jesse James, 199
Bloodletters and Bad Men, Book 2: Butch
   Cassidy to Al Capone, 199
Bloodletters and Bad Men, Book 3:
   Lucky Luciano to Charles Manson,
   200
Bloods: An Oral History of the Vietnam
   War by Black Veterans, 98, 159, 325
Blue and the Gray, The, 149, 323

Blue Highways: A Journey into America,
   211
Blue Planet, The, 94, 251
Blue Rise, 106, 332
Blue Sword, The, 129, 332
Blues for Silk Garcia, 117
BMX: A Guide to Bicycle Motocross, 51,
   222
Bogey Man, The, 315
Boll Weevil Express, The, 9, 290
Bonnie Dundee, 151
Book of Darwin, The, 250
Book of Incomes, The, 46
Book of Negro Folklore, The, 208
Books That Changed the World, 90,
   154
Born of the Sun, 192
Bound for Glory, 31
Brain, The: A User's Manual, 242
Brain, The: The Last Frontier, 249
Break of Dark, 172, 280
Breakaway, 134
Breaking Tradition: The Story of Louise
   Nevelson, 28
Breakthrough to the Computer Age, 64,
   160
Bright Shadow, 118
Broadcasting Careers for You, 45
Brothers and Keepers, 41
Bumblebee Flies Anyway, The, 66
Burg-O-Rama Man, The, 294
Busted Lives: Dialogues with Kids in Jail,
   93
But We Are Not of Earth, 261

Cages of Glass, Flowers of Time, 75, 104
Call of the Wild, The, and Selected
   Stories, 57
Call the Darkness Down, 171, 201
Camilla, 234
Camp, 10
Can Bears Predict Earthquakes? Unsolved
   Mysteries of Animal Behavior, 14, 243
Candle and the Mirror, The, 110, 176
Can't Anybody Here Play This Game?,
   306
Careers in Health Services, 49
Caretaker, The, 76
Caring Enough to Hear and Be Heard,
   182
Castaway, The, 9
Catalog of Cool, The, 298
Catamaran Racing: Solutions, Secrets,
   Speed, 224
Catcher in the Wry, 318
Cat's Eyes, 168

Caught in the Organ Draft: Biology in
    Science Fiction, 253, 272
Center Line, 117
Ceres Solution, The, 263
Chance to Grow, The, 44, 134, 183
Charles de Gaulle: A Biography, 29
Chernowitz!, 173
Child of War, 10, 325
Childhood, 164
Children of the Forest, 21
Children of the Wind, The, 126
Children of War, 324
China: One Hundred Years of Revolution,
    157
Chisholm Trail, The, 155, 327
Chocolate to Morphine: Understanding
    Mind-Active Drugs, 77
Christine, 52, 169
Cirak's Daughter, 198
Circles in a Forest, 7
Circles on the Water, 215
Citadel of the Autarch, The, 131
Citizen of the Galaxy, 258
City Game, The: Basketball from the
    Garden to the Playgrounds, 306
City Kid, 136
City of Sorcery, 122, 331
Civil War, The: Strange and Fascinating
    Facts, 154
Class Dismissed! High School Poems, 214
Cliffs of Cairo, The, 198
Cloning and the New Genetics, 245
Close Enough to Touch, 68, 236
Close to Nature: An Exploration of
    Nature's Microcosm, 248
Close to the Edge, 67, 111
Cloud Horse, 17
Clown for Circus and Stage, 163
Collected Stories of Isaac Bashevis Singer,
    The, 278
College—Yes or No, 49
Color out of Time, The, 130
Color Purple, The, 98, 334
Come Back, Mr. Magic, 138
Come Together: John Lennon in His
    Time, 41
Comeback Stars of Pro Sports, 304
Coming About, 283
Coming to America: Immigrants from
    Northern Europe, 157
Coming to America: Immigrants from
    Southern Europe, 157
Coming to America: Immigrants from the
    British Isles, 153
Coming to America: Immigrants from the
    Far East, 156

Coming to North America: From Mexico,
    Cuba, and Puerto Rico, 96, 218
Common Sense Book of Complete Cat
    Care, 19
Complete Book of Cat Health and Care,
    The, 16
Complete Poems, The: 1927–1979, 213
Complete Walker III, The: The Joys
    and Techniques of Hiking and
    Backpacking, 210
Computerworld, 265
Conduct of Major Maxim, The, 198
Conquering College Life: How to Be a
    Winner at College, 86
Corvette: America's Supercar, 51
Cosmic Mind-Boggling Book, The, 300
Cosmos, 302
Creations: The Quest for Origins in Story
    and Science, 240, 254
Creature Comforts: The Adventures of a
    City Vet, 16, 47
Crisis at Pemberton Dike, 9
Cujo, 169
Cults in America: Programmed for
    Paradise, 225
Curious Book, The, 87
Custom Cars, 52
Cyrion, 128

Daddy's Girl, 109
Daffodils in the Snow, 225
Dan Fouts, Ken Anderson, Joe
    Theismann and Other All-Time Great
    Quarterbacks, 32, 309
Dancers! Horizons in American Dance,
    49, 187
Dancer's Illusion, 129
Danger in the Old Fort, 191
Dani Trap, The, 197
Dark But Full of Diamonds, 235
Darwin for Beginners, 36, 247
Daughters of the Law, 95, 100
Dawn of Modern Science, 244
Day of the Dissonance, The, 125
Day the Loving Stopped, The, 109
Day the Senior Class Got Married, The,
    112, 235
Day They Came to Arrest the Book, The,
    175
Days of Fear, 80
Days of the Dragon's Seed, The, 208
Deaf Child Listened, A: Thomas
    Gallaudet, Pioneer in American
    Education, 36
Dear Lola; or, How to Build Your Own
    Family, 100

Dear Tim, 183, 225
Death Run, 199
Deerslayer, The; or, The First Warpath, 54
Demon in the Skull, 263
Demonic, Dangerous and Deadly, 168, 276
Denison's Daughter, 106
Dicey's Song, 118
Dicing with Dragons, 222
Different Seasons, 169, 277
Dinner at the Homesick Restaurant, 118
Distant Water: The Fate of the North Atlantic Fisherman, 212
Distortions, 273
Divorce Express, The, 104
DNA and the Creation of New Life, 246
Do You Love Me, Harvey Burns?, 176
Do You See What I See?, 201
Does This School Have Capital Punishment?, 175
Dog at the Window, The, 14
Dog Who Wouldn't Be, The, 17
Dogs of the Conquest, 19
Dollhouse Murders, The, 172, 203
Don't Tell Me That You Love Me, 229
Doris Fein: Legacy of Terror, 189
Dorothy Hamill: On and off the Ice, 31
Double Standard, 234
Down to a Sunless Sea, 123
Downtown, 111
Dr. Jekyll and Mr. Hyde, 58, 171
Dracula, 58, 171
Dragon Fall, 127
Dragon's Blood, 131
Dragons in the Waters, 196
Drawing from Nature, 24
Dreamboy for Katie, A, 227
Dreamstone, The, 124
Dresden 1945: The Devil's Tinderbox, 324
Dress for Success, 87
Dupe, 191

Early Disorder, 135
Earth Song, 266
Earthchild, 265
Earthquake 2099, 264
Easy Connections, 228
Easy-to-Understand Guide to Home Computers, 60
Eat the Grapes Downward: An Uninhibited Romp through the Surprising World of Food, 92
Edge of the World, The, 126
Edisto, 114, 291

EEVeTeC: The McGregor Solution for Managing the Pains of Fitness, 143
Eight Plus One, 274
Eighty Fairy Tales, 205
Eleanor Roosevelt, with Love: A Centenary Remembrance, 39
Electronic Life: How to Think about Computers, 61
Emerald, 203
Emergence, 262
Emergency Handbook: A First Aid Manual for Home and Travel, 140
Encyclopedia of Ghosts, The, 167
Encyclopedia of Monsters, The, 206
End of the Dream, The, 267
Energy Forever: Power for Today and Tomorrow, 246
Equus, 74
Escape from Sobibor, 165
Europeans, The, 153
Every Loving Gift: How a Family's Courage Saved a Special Child, 137, 183
Everything You Want to Know about Cosmetics; or, What Your Friendly Clerk Didn't Tell You, 144
Evidence That Wasn't There, The, 189
Evil in Paradise, 4
Executioner, The, 189
Exploring Military America, 212
Exploring Mime, 74, 163
Eye Language: Understanding the Eloquent Eye, 87
Eye's Delight: Poems of Art and Architecture, 25, 215
Eyes of Amber and Other Stories, 264, 279

Faces, 26
Facing Up, 66, 282
Fair Land, Fair Land, 147
Falcon and the Snowman, The, 34, 197
Fall of the House of Usher, The, and Other Tales, 58, 170, 277
Family Trade, 190
Family Trap, The, 103
Famous All Over Town, 98, 291
Far from Home, 116
Far from Shore, 75, 110
Far Out Factories: Manufacturing in Space, 302
Fast Track to the Top Jobs in Computer Careers, The, 48, 63
Fast Track to the Top Jobs in Engineering Careers, The, 48
Fat Girl, The, 138

Favorite, The, 69, 120
Favorite Tales from Grimm, 207
FDR: A Centenary Remembrance, 1882–1945, 27
Feeding the Hungry Heart: The Experience of Compulsive Eating, 143
Few Minutes with Andy Rooney, A, 92, 181
Field Guide to Edible Wild Plants of Eastern and Central North America, A, 211, 248
Field Guide to the Atlantic Seashore, A: Invertebrates and Seaweeds of the Atlantic Coast from the Bay of Fundy to Cape Hatteras, 244
Fifty Who Made the Difference, 30
Filmmakers on Filmmaking, 319
Final Grades, 106
Fingers, 201
Fires of Jubilee, The: Nat Turner's Fierce Rebellion, 150
Fireworks Tonight!, 241
First Step, 77
First the Egg, 112
Firstborn, 77
Fish Facts and Bird Brains: Animal Intelligence, 18, 249
Five Seasons: A Baseball Companion, 305
Five Summers, 286
Flatland: A Romance of Many Dimensions, 252
Fletch and the Man Who, 199
Flights, 116
Flying Free, 19
Folk Tale Plays round the World, 73, 208
Food for Champions: How to Eat to Win, 140
Football: You Are the Coach, 303
Football Dreams, 309
Football's Super Bowl Champions I–VIII, 304
Football's Super Bowl Champions IX–XVI, 304
For Conscience' Sake, 98, 177
Forest of App, The, 124
Forever . . ., 268
Forgotten Animals: The Rehabilitation of Laboratory Primates, 15, 245
Formal Feeling, A, 68
Forty Thousand in Gehenna, 255
Four Great Comedies, 58, 74
Four Great Tragedies: *Hamlet, Othello, King Lear, Macbeth,* 58, 74
Fox in Winter, The, 66
Foxfire 7, 226
Frankenstein, 58, 171

Frederic Remington: A Biography, 39
French Resistance, The, 323
Friends for Life, 202
Friends Till the End, 68, 317
Frog People, The, 78, 255
From Hand Ax to Laser: Man's Growing Mastery of Energy, 248
From the Door of the White House, 28, 153
Fun with Stagecraft, 73
Further Adventures of Huckleberry Finn, The, 7
Future Fire: Weapons for the Apocalypse, 322
Futurelife: The Biotechnology Revolution, 249

Games for the Superintelligent, 84, 161
Games They Played, The: Sports in History, 156, 313
Gandhi the Man, 30
Gathering of Old Men, A, 96
Geronimo: The Man, His Time, His Place, 29
Getting It Together: The Black Man's Guide to Good Grooming and Fashion, 84
Ghost Walker, The, 16
Ghosts, 82
Giant Book of More Strange But True Sports Stories, The, 312
Girl Called Boy, A, 175
Girl from Paris, The, 145
Girl in the Plastic Cage, The, 136
Girl in the White Ship, The, 11
Girl of the Sea of Cortez, The, 1
Girl on the Outside, The, 177
Girl Who Wanted a Boy, The, 239, 295
Go for It! How to Get Your First Good Job: A Career-Planning Guide for Young Adults, 44
God and the Astronomers, 245
God Stalk, 127
God's Grace, 128
Gods of Riverworld, 257
God's Radar, 225, 281
Going to Extremes, 211
Going Vegetarian: A Guide for Teenagers, 141
Gold Crew, The, 10
Golden Path, The: The Lure of Gold through History, 156
Golden Torc, The, 262
Gone the Dreams and Dancing, 148, 328
Goodbye, Paper Doll, 139
Gorilla Signs Love, The, 12

Gorillas in the Mist, 14
Great British Detective, The, 194, 275
Great Detectives: A Century of the Best
    Mysteries from England and America,
    198
Great Exploration Hoaxes, 9
Great Painters, 25
Great Shark Hunt, The: Strange Tales
    from a Strange Time, 94, 219
Greek Myths, 207
Green Place, A: Modern Poems, 215
Green Politics: The Global Promise, 217
Greyhaven: An Anthology of Fantasy,
    122, 273
Grounding of Group Six, The, 11, 118
Growing Season, 102
Growing Up, 27
Guadalcanal Diary, 82, 325
Guardian Angels, The, 97, 174
Guinea Pigs: An Owner's Guide to
    Choosing, Raising, Breeding, and
    Showing, 18
Guinness Book of Animal Facts and
    Feats, The, 20
Guitar Handbook, The, 285
Gunfighter, The: Man or Myth?, 209, 329
Gypsy Gift, 172

Habitats, 263, 278
Halley: Comet 1986, 299
Hallucination Orbit: Psychology in Science
    Fiction, 254, 273
Handbook of Model Rocketry, 162
Handbook of Riding, The, 222, 308
Handful of Stars, A, 134
Hard Love, 285
Hard Times: An Oral History of the
    Great Depression, 298
Hard Way Home, The, 116
Harold J. Laski on *The Communist
    Manifesto,* 218
Hatter Fox, 96, 174, 286
Havoc in Islandia, 130
Hawes on Getting into College, 46
Hawkmistress!, 123
He Noticed I'm Alive . . . and Other
    Hopeful Signs, 237, 292
Headless Roommate, The, and Other
    Tales of Terror, 78
Healthy Body, The: A Maintenance
    Manual, 141
Heart of Aztlan, 95, 281
Heartaches, 290
Heart's Blood, 132
Help! We're Moving, 83
Henderson the Rain King, 53

Hercules, 207
Here Is Alaska, 158
Here's Looking at You, Kid, 239
Here's to the Sophomores, 180, 290
Hero and the Crown, The, 129
Herpes: What to Do When You Have It,
    141
Herschel Walker: From the Georgia
    Backwoods and the Heisman Trophy
    to the Pros, 37, 315
He's My Baby, Now, 104
Hey, Wait a Minute, I Wrote a Book!, 34,
    313
High and Outside, 75, 307
Hilton Head Metabolism Diet, The, 143
Hitchhiker's Guide to the Galaxy, The,
    179
Hockey: You Are the Coach, 303
Holding Up the Sky: Young People in
    China, 297
Hollow Land, The, 275
Home Boy, 96, 286
Homecoming, 119
Hooded Avengers, The, 82, 202
Hoops, 314
Horse Goddess, The, 149
Horse Identifier, 18
Hour of the Gate, The, 125
Hour of the Wolf, The, 2, 102
How It Feels to Be Adopted, 108
How It Feels When Parents Divorce,
    108
How Life Imitates the World Series, 306
How to Be a Wildlife Photographer, 163
How to Draw and Paint What You See,
    162
How to Get the Degree You Want: Bear's
    Guide to Non-Traditional College
    Degrees, 83
How to Get Your Parents to Give You
    Everything You've Ever Wanted, 86
How to Live with a Single Parent, 105
How to Meet a Gorgeous Guy, 238, 292
How to Survive Medical School, 47
How to Take Tests, 85
How to Test Your ESP, 78
How to Write a Children's Book and Get
    It Published, 49
Human Body, The: Your Body and How
    It Works, 241
Humboldt Effect, The, 260
Hunchback of Notre Dame, The, 56
Hunger of Memory: The Education of
    Richard Rodriguez, 38, 92
Hungry Woman, The: Myths and Legends
    of the Aztecs, 205

Hunter in the Dark, 6, 67
Huntsman, The, 127

I Am a Thief, 81, 200
I Dare You: How to Use Psychology to
    Get What You Want Out of Life, 89
I Love You, Stupid!, 269
I Never Said I Loved You, 228
I Tell a Lie Every So Often, 3
I Will Call It Georgie's Blues, 113, 186
IBM PC: An Introduction to the
    Operating System, BASIC
    Programming and Applications, 62
IBM PCjr: Introduction, BASIC
    Programming and Applications, 62
Icebreaker, 194
If It's Not Funny, Why Am I Laughing?,
    270
If Only I Could Tell You: Poems for
    Young Lovers and Dreamers, 215
If You Believe in Me, 233
If You Can't Be the Sun, Be a Star, 292
If You Could See What I Hear, 40
I'll Always Remember You . . . Maybe,
    236
I'll Get By, 102
I'll Live, 67
Illustrated Fact Book of Science, 242
Illustrated Facts and Records Book of
    Animals, 18
I'm Gonna Make You Love Me: The
    Story of Diana Ross, 32, 186
I'm Not Your Other Half, 230
Imaging Saturn, 299
In a Lonely Place, 172, 279
In Afghanistan: An American Odyssey,
    159
In Our House Scott Is My Brother, 100
In Search of Liberty, 150
In Suspect Terrain, 247
In the Middle of a Rainbow, 231
In the Shadow of Man, 14
In the Shadow of the Wind, 99, 152
In Winter's Shadow, 123
Independence Day, 268
Indian Place-Names: Their Origin,
    Evolution, and Meanings, Collected in
    Kansas from the Siouan, Algonquian,
    Shoshonean, Caddoan, Iroquoian, and
    Other Tongues, 88
Indians of the Pacific Northwest: A
    History, 157
Indy 500, The, 52
Initiation, The, 167
Innocent Blood, 195
Inside Blair House, 160

Inside Nuclear Submarines, 250
Inside the IBM PC: Access to Advanced
    Features and Programming, 63
Instant Word Power, 87
Intergalactic Empires, 253, 272
Ironweed, 7
Isaac Asimov Presents the Great Science
    Fiction Stories, Vol. 7, 1945, 252, 271
Isaac Asimov Presents the Great Science
    Fiction Stories, Vol. 9, 1947, 252, 271
Isaac Asimov Presents the Great Science
    Fiction Stories, Vol. 10, 1948, 252, 271
Isaac Asimov Presents the Great Science
    Fiction Stories, Vol. 11, 1949, 253, 272
Isaac Bashevis Singer: The Story of a
    Storyteller, 33
Island Keeper, The, 8
It All Began with Jane Eyre, 285
It Had to Be You, 229
It Won't Happen to Me: Teenagers Talk
    about Pregnancy, 270
It's No Crush, I'm in Love!, 231
Italian Folktales, 206

J. Robert Oppenheimer: Shatterer of
    Worlds, 31
Jack: The Struggles of John F. Kennedy,
    37
James Joyce Murder, The, 192
Jane Eyre, 53
Jane's House, 68, 117
Jasmine Finds Love, 229
Jazz Country, 186
Jim Thorpe: World's Greatest Athlete, 41
John Marino's Bicycling Book, 223
Jonathan: You Left Too Soon, 65
Jules Feiffer's America: From Eisenhower
    to Reagan, 179, 218
Just Another Love Story, 311
Just Friends, 233
Just Hold On, 101, 228
Just Imagine: Ideas in Painting, 24
Just the Way You Are, 235

Kathleen Kennedy: Her Life and Times,
    35
Kathy Sue Loudermilk, I Love You, 91,
    179
Keeper of the Isis Light, The, 260
Kennedy, 30
Kestrel, The, 121
Keys to Racing Success, 221
Kid Brother, 112
Kidnapped, 59
Kids' Book of Divorce, The: By, for and
    about Kids, 115

Killdeer Mountain, 145
Kingdom of Summer, 123
Kioga of the Wilderness, 2
Knave of Hearts, 229
Knowing the Score: Play-by-Play
    Directions for Women on the Job, 46,
    332
Kolokol Papers, The, 190

Lad of Sunnybank, 18
Lady Sings the Blues, 32
Langston: A Play, 71
Language of Goldfish, The, 136
Lantern in Her Hand, A, 145
Lasers: Light Wave of the Future, 246
Last Catholic in America, The, 181
Last Mission, The, 323
Last of the Mohicans, The: A Narrative
    of 1757, 54
Last Unicorn, The, 121
Late Night Thoughts on Listening to
    Mahler's Ninth Symphony, 94
Laughing Space, 254
Law and Lynchburg, The, 328
Laying Waste: The Poisoning of America
    by Toxic Chemicals, 241
Leaders, 36, 218
Learning IBM BASIC, 63
Let the Trumpet Sound: The Life of
    Martin Luther King, Jr., 36
Letters of a Woman Homesteader, 329
Liar, Liar, 203
Lies, 232
Life and Adventures of Nicholas Nickleby,
    The, 55
Lifeguards Only beyond This Point, 231
Light a Penny Candle, 1
Lilies of the Field, The, 182
Lindsay, Lindsay, Fly Away Home, 113,
    291
Lions Share: The Story of a Serengeti
    Pride, 15
Lisa Birnbach's College Book, 83
Lisa, Bright and Dark, 136
Little Destiny, A, 2
Little Little, 135, 287
Little Love, A, 5, 106
Little Women, 53
Lives of Girls and Women, 270, 333
Living Jewish: The Lore and Law of
    Being a Practicing Jew, 225
Lobbying for Freedom in the 1980s: A
    Grass-Roots Guide to Protecting Your
    Rights, 176
Long Night Watch, The, 10
Long Time between Kisses, 237, 292

Long Way from Home, A, 99, 294
Look Who's Beautiful!, 105
Looking at Law School: A Student Guide
    from the Society of American Law
    Teachers, 45
Lords of the Triple Moons, 129
Lorraine Hansberry: The Collected Last
    Plays, 73
Lost in the Barrens, 8
Love Always, Blue, 113
Love and Rivalry: Three Exceptional
    Pairs of Sisters, 30
Love Bombers, The, 226

Madselin, 149
Magic, 33, 311
Maid of Honor, 110
Making Money with Your Home
    Computer, 60
Making of a Gunman, The, 325
Man in the Woods, The, 202
Man Who Was Don Quixote, The: The
    Story of Miguel de Cervantes, 28
Manna, 256
Manners That Matter: For People under
    Twenty-One, 84
Marek and Lisa, 164
Mark Twain Murders, The, 203
Marked by Fire, 98, 118
Marx's *Kapital* for Beginners, 219
Mary, 35
Mary Jane Harper Cried Last Night, 109
Mary, Wayfarer, 35
Mary Wollstonecraft Reader, A, 334.
Mask Making, 161
"Master Harold" . . . and the Boys, 71,
    174
Mastering Underwater Photography,
    162
Masters of Horror, 167, 319
Matter of Feeling, A, 101
Matter of Principle, A, 176, 291
Max, the Dog That Refused to Die, 20
Mazes and Monsters, 195
Me Me Me Me Me: Not a Novel, 33
Me, the Beef, and the Bum, 5
Medieval Fables, 207
Meditations from the Breakdown Lane:
    Running across America, 93, 223
Meet the Vampire, 80, 170
Meet the Werewolf, 80, 170
Meeting Rozzy Halfway, 109
Mega Tips: How to Get and Keep Any
    Restaurant Job, 43
Megan, 7, 332
Megan's Beat, 293

Megatrends: Ten New Directions
    Transforming Our Lives, 297
Memorable World Series Moments, 305
Mercy Short: A Winter Journal, North
    Boston, 1692–93, 146
Michelle, 183
Midnight Express, 5
Mill Girls, The: Lucy Larcom, Harriet
    Hanson Robinson, Sarah G. Bagley,
    158, 333
Miller's Court, 218
Mind to Murder, A, 196
Missing Pieces, 65
Mission to Mars: Plans and Concepts for
    the First Manned Landing, 301
Modern Monologues for Young People, 73
Mom, I'm Pregnant, 144
Money Creek Mare, The, 12
Moon on a String, The, 238
Moonstone, The, 54, 192
More Games for the Superintelligent, 84,
    161
More Than a Summer Love, 230
Morelli's Game, 5
Morning Star, Black Sun: The Northern
    Cheyenne Indians and America's
    Energy Crisis, 173
Mountain Climbing, 222
Movie Guide for Puzzled Parents, 320
Mr. Sammler's Planet, 53
Mrs. Byrne's Dictionary of Unusual,
    Obscure, and Preposterous Words,
    Gathered from Numerous and Diverse
    Authoritative Sources, 83
Murder in the White House, 201
Murder on Capital Hill, 202
My Brilliant Career, 331
My Enemy, My Ally, 257
My Name Is Davy—I'm an Alcoholic, 77
My Own Worst Enemy, 288
My Parents Are Divorced, Too: Teenagers
    Talk about Their Experiences and
    How They Cope, 115

Naked Face, The, 201
Nathaniel Hawthorne in His Times, 35
National League, The: An Illustrated
    History, 310
Natural Man, The, 288
Nature in the West: A Handbook of
    Habitats, 18
Nature's Great Carbon Cycle, 247
Navahos Have Five Fingers, 21
Navajos, The, 159
Nebula Award Stories Seventeen, 258, 276
Neck of the Giraffe, The: Darwin,
    Evolution, and the New Biology, 244

Neverending Story, The, 124
New American Computer Dictionary, The,
    64
New Earths: Restructuring Earth and
    Other Planets, 301
New Found Land, 255
New Frontiers in Genetics, 240
New Guys around the Block, 194
New Kind of Love, A, 227
New Muscle Building for Beginners, The,
    141
New Native American Drama: Three
    Plays, 72
New Steinerbooks Dictionary of the
    Paranormal, The, 171
News Business, The, 43
Newton at the Bat: The Science in Sports,
    316
Nice Girl from Good Home, 100
Nicholas Factor, The, 8
Night Chasers, The, 191
Night of Fire and Blood, 79, 169
Night of the Bozos, The, 293
Nima: A Sherpa in Connecticut, 4
1982 Report on Drug Abuse and
    Alcoholism, The, 75
1983 Annual World's Best SF, The, 266,
    280
1984, 57
1984 and Beyond, 90
1984 Annual World's Best SF, The, 266,
    280
No Dragons to Slay, 134
No One Here Gets Out Alive, 33
No Scarlet Ribbons, 117
Noble House: A Novel of Contemporary
    Hong Kong, 146
Nobody Else Can Walk It for You, 9
Nobody's Brother, 117, 139
North of Boston: Poems, 214
Norwegian Folk Tales, 205
Not for Love, 283
Notes for Another Life, 101
Nothing's Impossible! Stunts to Entertain
    and Amaze, 162
Now That the Buffalo's Gone: A Study of
    Today's American Indians, 155
Nuclear Energy at the Crossroads, 245
Nuclear Power for Beginners, 241
Nuclear War: What's in It for You?, 322
Nuisance, 101
Number of the Beast, The, 259

Off Balance: The Real World of Ballet,
    45, 186
Off-Roading: Racing and Riding, 52
Off the Court, 27

Oil in Troubled Waters, 240
On Equal Terms: Jews in America, 1881–
    1981, 154
On the Ropes, 316
One Another, 235
One Christmas, 29
One of the Lucky Ones, 29, 182
Only Love, 138
Only My Mouth Is Smiling, 114, 137
Origin, The: A Biographical Novel of
    Charles Darwin, 151
Origin of Species, The, 55, 242
Other David, The, 191
Other Karen, The, 196
Other Side of the Mountain, The, 139
Our Children's Children, 264
Our House in the Last World, 97
Out of Love, 119
Out of My League, 315
Outcasts of Heaven Belt, The, 265
Outrageous Acts and Everyday
    Rebellions, 93, 334
Outside Shot, The, 314
Over the Hill at Fourteen, 282
Overcoming Computer Illiteracy: A
    Friendly Introduction to Computers, 61

Pack, Band, and Colony: The World of
    Social Animals, 16
Pandora Secret, The, 146
Paper Chase, The, 219
Patch of Blue, A, 135
Paul David Silverman Is a Father, 78
Paul's Game, 171
Penguin Book of Orienteering, The, 317
People at Home, 24
People at Work, 24
People Therein, The, 233
Pet Sematary, 169
Phantoms, 169
Pig-Out Blues, The, 285
Pigeon Cubes and Other Verse, 213
Pigman's Legacy, The, 295
Place Apart, A, 105
Place to Come Back To, A, 66
Planet of the Warlord, 259
Planets, The: Exploring the Solar System,
    300
Planets of Rock and Ice: From Mercury to
    the Moons of Saturn, 299
Please Don't Kiss Me Now, 105
Pleasures of Anthropology, The, 22, 91
Poetspeak: In Their Work, about Their
    Work, 214
Poland, 150
Popcorn Days and Buttermilk Nights, 8
Porsche Past and Present, 51

Portable Video: A Production Guide for
    Young People, 320
Portal to E'ewere, 265
Possible Human, The: A Course in
    Extending Your Physical, Mental, and
    Creative Abilities, 87
Postmark Murder, 193
Practical Pascal, 61
Prelude to Chaos, 261
Premonitions, 190, 228
Prentice-Hall Encyclopedia of
    Mathematics, The, 251
President's Daughter, The, 220
Pride and Prejudice, 53
Prime of Miss Jean Brodie, The, 59
Prince of the Godborn, 127
Princess Bride, The: S. Morgenstern's
    Classic Tale of True Love and High
    Adventure, 126
Princess of the Chameln, A, 131
Programming for Microcomputers: Apple
    II BASIC, 64
Protect Your Legal Rights: A Handbook
    for Teenagers, 217
Psion, 265
Pursuit, 4
Putting on a Play: A Guide to Writing
    and Producing Neighborhood Drama,
    72
Pyramid, 25

Quanah: The Serpent Eagle, 146, 327
Quarterback Walk-On, 308
Queen of the Lightning, 147
Queen of the What Ifs, The, 108
Question Box, The, 107

Radiation: Waves and Particles/Benefits
    and Risks, 248
Radio City, 107
Rags to Riches, 151
Railroaders, The, 156
Rainbow Jordan, 103
Ransom, 3
Raspberry One, 322
Ratha's Creature, 122
Razor Eyes, 322
Rebels of the Heavenly Kingdom, 150
Rebound Caper, 308
Reckless, 76
Red Badge of Courage, The: An Episode
    of the American Civil War, 55
Red Giants and White Dwarfs, 300
Red Magician, The, 126
Red Sky at Morning, 282
Red Smith Reader, The, 90, 305
Reggie: The Autobiography, 33, 311

Reilly: Ace of Spies, 34, 197
Representing Super Doll, 289
Reprieve: A Memoir, 30
Return of the Battleship, 158
Return of the Whistler, The, 104, 230, 284
Revenge in the Silent Tomb, 4, 79
Revenge of the Nerd, 288
Revolution of Mary Leary, The, 116
Riddley Walker, 127
Ring of Fire, The, 249
Ringo, the Robber Raccoon: The True
    Story of a Northwoods Rogue, 16
Rio Loja Ringmaster, The, 309
Risking Love, 113
River Why, The, 210
Road to Middle-Earth, The, 130
Road to Science Fiction No. 4, The: From
    Here to Forever, 258, 275
Roadside Valentine, 227
Roaming Free: Wild Horses of the
    American West, 15
Robinson Crusoe, 55
Robotics: Past, Present, and Future, 62
Robots: Reel to Real, 63
Rock 'n' Roll Nights, 187
Romance! Can You Survive It? A Guide
    to Sticky Dating Situations, 88, 237
Roses, 103
Run, Don't Walk, 138
Run, Shelley, Run!, 115, 177
Run with the Horsemen, 115
Runes of the Lyre, 129
Running Free: A Guide for Women
    Runners and Their Friends, 89, 144
Running Loose, 284, 307
Russia: Broken Idols, Solemn Dreams,
    298
Ruth Marini, Dodger Ace, 306
Ruth Marini of the Dodgers, 306

Sacred Path, The: Spells, Prayers, and
    Power Songs of the American Indians,
    95, 213
Salvage and Destroy, 262
Saturday Night, 232
Saturday's Children: Poems of Work, 215
Saving America's Birds, 244
Scarlet Pimpernel, The, 57
Schindler's List, 164
Schooling of the Horse, The, 20
Science Fiction A to Z: A Dictionary of
    the Great S.F. Themes, 253, 272
Science Fictional Dinosaur, The, 263, 278
Science in Science Fiction, The, 247
Scottish Chiefs, The, 58, 208
Sea Change, 102
Sea Runners, The, 3

Season of Yellow Leaf, 328
Second Heaven, 105
Second Star to the Right, 134
Secret Annie Oakley, The, 147
Secret Lover of Elmtree, The, 115
Secrets on Beacon Hill, The, 191
Series TV: How a Television Show Is
    Made, 319
Sez Who? Sez Me, 92
Shadow Dancers, 124
Shadow Like a Leopard, A, 287
Shadowkeep, 125
Shadows across the Sand, 192
Shadows across the Sun, 136, 234
Shadows of the Indian: Stereotypes in
    American Culture, 177
Shadows on Little Reef Bay, 189
Shaker, Why Don't You Sing?, 95, 213
Shakespeare and His Theatre, 71
Shoeless Joe, 311
Show Me No Mercy: A Compelling Story
    of Remarkable Courage, 137
Silver Link, the Silken Tie, The, 133
Sixteen: Short Stories by Outstanding
    Writers for Young Adults, 274
Skull beneath the Skin, The, 196
Sky Above, Worlds Beyond, 300
Slaves of Spiegel, 180, 263
Sleeping Dragon, The, 130
Slender Balance, The: Causes and Cures
    for Bulimia, Anorexia and the Weight-
    Loss/Weight-Gain Seesaw, 143
Slipping-Down Life, A, 187, 294
Slowly, Slowly I Raise the Gun, 189
Small Civil War, A, 176
Snarkout Boys and the Avocado of Death,
    The, 180
Snowbird, The, 2, 12
So Long, See You Tomorrow, 110
So You're Adopted, 114
Softball for Girls and Women, 313
Solitary Blue, A, 119
Solve It!, 85, 161
Someone Is Hiding on Alcatraz Island, 2
Someone to Love, 269
Son of a Wanted Man, 328
Son of Someone Famous, The, 107
Son Rise, 183
Song of Pentecost, The, 13
Space, 150
Space and Science Fiction Plays for Young
    People, 72, 261
Space Colony: Frontier of the Twenty-First
    Century, 299
Space Shots: The Beauty of Nature
    beyond Earth, 299
Spaceship Titanic, 257

Spacewar, 301, 324
Speak to Me: How to Put Confidence in
Your Conversation, 88
Spectator's Guide to Football, A: The
Action, Rules, and Beauty of the
Game, 317
Specter, The, 200
Speculations, 254, 273
Speed, 80, 311
Spellsinger, 125
Sport Diving, 221
Sports Classics: American Writers Choose
Their Best, 93, 316
Stamp Twice for Murder, 190
Standing Fast: The Autobiography of Roy
Wilkins, 42, 178
Star Dog, 261
Star Light, Star Bright, 238
Stargate, 125
Starship Traveller, 260
Starting with Melodie, 113
State-of-the-Art Robot Catalog, The, 60
STD: A Commonsense Guide to Sexually
Transmitted Diseases, 268
Steinbrenner!, 39, 316
Stepfamilies: New Patterns in Harmony,
103
Stepping Stones, 275
Stolen Years, 166
Stone Pony, The, 66
Stone Silenus, The, 70, 204
Storm in Her Heart, 102
Stowaway, 197
Strange But True Basketball Stories, 313
Strange But True Football Stories, 310
Strange Things Happen in the Woods, 255
Strangers in the House, 109
Strike!, 174, 283
String of Chances, A, 112
Strings: A Gathering of Family Poems,
214
Structured COBOL: American National
Standards, 61
Student Entrepreneur's Guide, The: How
to Start and Run Your Own Part Time
Small Business, 46
Success to the Brave, 148
Suds, 179
Sugar Ray Leonard, 32, 309
Suitcases, The, 119
Sula, 289, 333
Summer Begins, 173, 282
Summer Girls, Love Boys and Other
Short Stories, 277
Summer I Learned about Life, The, 288
Summer Rules, 287
Summer's End, 237

Sunday Morning, 232
Sung in Shadow, 128
Sunne in Splendour, The, 151
Super Bowl Superstars: The Most
Valuable Players in the NFL's
Championship Game, 305
Super Champions of Auto Racing, 52
Superman III, 7
Supermen, 253, 272
Superstars of Country Music, 185
Suspect, 79, 194
Sweet Whispers, Brother Rush, 106
Sword and Sorceress: An Anthology of
Heroic Fantasy, 123, 274
Sword of Chaos and Other Stories, 123,
274
Sybil, 40

Taking It All In, 91, 320
Taking Terri Mueller, 111
Tale of Two Cities, A, 56
Tales of a Dead King, 199
Talking Earth, The, 5
Talking in Whispers, 11
Tancy, 148
Tangle of Roots, A, 66
Tangled Butterfly, 133
Tapestry Warriors, The, 131
Tar Baby, 97
Tea with the Black Dragon, 128
Teach Yourself Calligraphy: For Beginners
from Eight to Eighty, 162
Teaching Riding: Step-by-Step Schooling
for Horse and Rider, 317
Tears of the Singers, The, 264
Teen Girls' Guide to Social Success, The,
88
Teenage Body Book, The, 142
Teepee Neighbors, 296
Tell Me If the Lovers are Losers, 69, 318
Tell Me That You Love Me, Junie Moon,
135, 286
Ten Grandmothers, The, 22
Tennis My Way, 315
Term Paper, 68
Terpin, 292
Terra SF II: The Year's Best European SF,
262, 277
Terror Run, 198
Tess of the D'Urbervilles: A Pure
Woman, 56
Test-Tube Mysteries, 244
That Championship Season, 73
That's Not My Style, 281
Theater Careers: A Comprehensive Guide
to Non-Acting Careers in the Theater,
45, 72

Them That Glitter and Them That Don't, 186, 285

There Are No Problem Horses—Only Problem Riders, 19, 223

There's a Bat in Bunk Five, 284

They Called Him Wild Bill: The Life and Adventures of James Butler Hickok, 39

Things Are Seldom What They Seem, 268

Thinking about the Next War, 92

Thirty-Six Exposures, 269, 287

Thirty-Six Hour Day, The: A Family Guide to Caring for Persons with Alzheimer's Disease, Related Dementing Illnesses, and Memory Loss in Later Life, 142

This Strange New Feeling, 97, 277

Thousand Pieces of Gold, 149

Three Mile Island: Thirty Minutes to Meltdown, 242

Through a Brief Darkness, 200

Throwing Season, The, 308

T.H.U.M.B.B., 185

Thunder Moon Strikes, 326

Thunder on the Tennessee, 152

Tie That Binds, The, 327

Tiger Eyes, 65

Tigris Expedition, The: In Search of Our Beginnings, 6

Tim Page's Nam, 324

Time to Be Born, A: An Almanac of Animal Courtship and Parenting, 17, 247

Timewarp Summer, 233, 320

Tirra Lirra by the River, 331

To Absent Friends, 93, 317

To All Gentleness: William Carlos Williams, the Doctor-Poet, 27

To All My Fans, with Love, from Sylvie, 3, 283

To Kill a Mockingbird, 57, 175

To See My Mother Dance, 108

To Take a Dare, 120

Tom Sawyer Fires, The, 204

Tomorrow Connection, The, 122

Too Fat? Too Thin? Do You Have a Choice?, 140

Too Much Too Soon, 231

Too Young to Die: Youth and Suicide, 67

Tortuga, 133

Total Body Training, 141

Total Dog Book, The, 20

Total Eclipse, 255

Touchdown! Football's Most Dramatic Scoring Feats, 310

Tough Love: How Parents Can Deal with Drug Abuse, 76

Toughing It Out at Harvard: The Making of a Woman MBA, 46

Tracks, 3

Trading Secrets, 81

Treasure Island, 59

Treasures of the Deep: Adventures of Undersea Exploration, 23

Treasury of Jewish Literature from Biblical Times to Today, A, 226

Treating and Overcoming Anorexia Nervosa, 142

Tree of Swords and Jewels, The, 124

Trellisane Confrontation, The, 257

Trembling Earth, The: Probing and Predicting Quakes, 243

True or False? Amazing Art Forgeries, 26

Truth of the Matter, The, 294

Turn It Up!, 187

Turn of the Screw, The, and Other Short Novels, 57

Twice Shy, 193

Twilight Zone: The Movie, 167

Two Point Zero, 293

2010: Odyssey 2, 256

Two Truths in My Pocket, 97, 278

Two Years before the Mast: A Personal Narrative, 55

UBIK, 256

UFO: Teen Sightings, 301

Ultralights: The Flying Featherweights, 222

Unbirthday, 270

Uncanny Tales of Unearthly and Unexpected Horrors, 168, 276

Underground, 25

Underground Shopper's Guide to Off-Price Shopping, The, 86

Underwater Dig: The Excavation of a Revolutionary War Privateer, 22, 155

Un-Dudding of Roger Judd, The, 110

Unfinished Tales of Númenor and Middle-Earth, 131

Unforgettable Season, The, 308

Unidentified Woman, 193

Until the Sun Dies, 245, 300

Up against the Law: Your Legal Rights as a Minor, 219

Up in Seth's Room, 270

Upon the Head of the Goat: A Childhood in Hungary, 1939–1944, 40, 165

Upward Mobility, 43

Utopia Hunters: Chronicles of the High Inquest, 130

V, 256

Vandalism: The Crime of Immaturity, 296

Vanishing Eagles, 12
Vanishing Hitchhiker, The: American Urban Legends and Their Meanings, 206
Vegetarian Sourcebook, A, 140
Very Brief Season, A, 275
Very Private Performance, A, 284
Vicious Circle, 168
Victory in the Pacific, 323
Video Primer, The: Equipment, Production, and Concepts, 321
Village of Vampires, 80
Violence in America, 297
Vision Quest, 284, 307
Visit, The, 164
Vivienne: The Life and Suicide of an Adolescent Girl, 34, 67
Voice in the Night, 196
Voices from the Holocaust, 165
Voyage, 147
Voyage of the Lucky Dragon, The, 1

Waiting for Johnny Miracle, 65, 133
Walden; or, Life in the Woods and *On the Duty of Civil Disobedience,* 59, 94
Walg: A Novel of Australia, 99
Walking Softly in the Wilderness: The Sierra Club Guide to Backpacking, 210
Wanted: A Girl for the Horses, 13
War between the Pitiful Teachers and the Splendid Kids, The, 180
War Horse, 17
War without Friends, 322
'Ware Hawk, 129
Warriors of the Wasteland, 259
Watch for Me on the Mountain, 145
Watchdogs, 202
Watcher in the Garden, The, 170
Water by the Inch: Adventures of a Pioneer Family on an Arizona Desert Homestead, 11, 330
Water World, 249
Watersmeet, 4
Wave, The, 165, 177
Way Home, The, 11, 151
Way to Go, The: A Woman's Guide to Careers in Travel, 47
We Have Always Lived in the Castle, 195
Well-Tempered Sentence, The: A Punctuation Handbook for the Innocent, the Eager, and the Doomed, 86
Western Writings of Stephen Crane, The, 326
Whale Watchers' Guide, The, 14, 243
What about Grandma?, 107
What Happens in Therapy, 85

What I Really Think of You, 226, 287
What Is Dungeons and Dragons?, 221
What to Say When You Don't Know What to Say, 85
What's Best for You, 100
When We First Met, 111, 235
Where Has Deedie Wooster Been All These Years?, 286
Where Have I Been?, 28
Where Love Begins, 239
Where the Lilies Bloom, 103
While Reagan Slept, 90, 179
Whisper in the Night, A: Tales of Terror and Suspense, 167, 271
Whistling Skeleton, The: American Indian Tales of the Supernatural, 208
White Bird Flying, A, 227
Who Did It, Jenny Lake?, 200
Who Is Felix the Great?, 107
Who Loves Sam Grant?, 228, 282
Whole Film Sourcebook, The, 320
Why Am I Grown So Cold? Poems of the Unknowable, 170, 215
Why Are They Starving Themselves? Understanding Anorexia Nervosa and Bulimia, 142
Why Didn't I Think of That!, 49
Why You Feel Down—and What You Can Do about It, 143
Wildcliffe Bird, The, 147, 232
Will Rogers: His Wife's Story, 38
Willa: The Life of Willa Cather, 37
Wind Child, 262
Wind Sports, 307
Windmills, Bridges, and Old Machines: Discovering Our Industrial Past, 26
Wings and Roots, 139
Winning in One-Designs, 223, 315
Winston Churchill: The Wilderness Years, 31
Winter of the White Seal, 6
Winter Season: A Dancer's Journal, 185
Winter's Tale, 127
Wish You Were Here, 119
Witch Week, 168
Without Me You're Nothing: The Essential Guide to Home Computers, 62
Witness at Large, 193
Wizards, 121, 273
Wollheim's World's Best SF, Series 7, 266, 280
Women and Wilderness, 47, 211, 332
Women Who Changed Things, 37, 333
Womenfolks: Growing Up Down South, 296, 331
Won't Know Till I Get There, 112

Workin' for Peanuts, 293
Working on It, 289
Working Robots, 61
Working Trot, 15
Working Wardrobe: Affordable Clothes
    that Work for You, 89
World Almanac Book of the Strange,
    The, 251
World Almanac Book of the Strange No.
    2, The, 243
World of Fantastic Films, The: An
    Illustrated Survey, 321
World Turned Inside Out, The, 114, 137
World War II Resistance Stories, 81, 324
World War II Super Facts, 323
Worthy Opponents, 229
Would You Settle for Improbable?, 290
Writers of the Purple Sage: An Anthology
    of Recent Western Writing, 328
Wuthering Heights, 54

X-Rated Romance, An, 238
XT Called Stanley, An, 264

Yeah, But, 232
Year of Sweet Senior Insanity, The, 234
Year's Best Fantasy Stories, The: 10, 130,
    278
Year's Best Horror Stories, The, Series X,
    172, 279
Year's Best Horror Stories, The, Series
    XII, 172, 279
You Can't Get There from Here, 71, 281
You Never Lose, 69, 318
Young Legionary, 259
Young People's Yellow Pages, The: A
    National Sourcebook for Youth, 88
Youngest Science, The: Notes of a
    Medicine-Watcher, 41, 250
Your Dog: An Owner's Manual, 17
Your Job in the Computer Age: The
    Complete Guide to the Computer
    Skills You Need to Get the Job You
    Want, 48
Youth Gangs, 296

Zan Hagen's Marathon, 312

90680